JOHANNES KIP §§§ THE GLOUCESTERSHIRE ENGRAVINGS

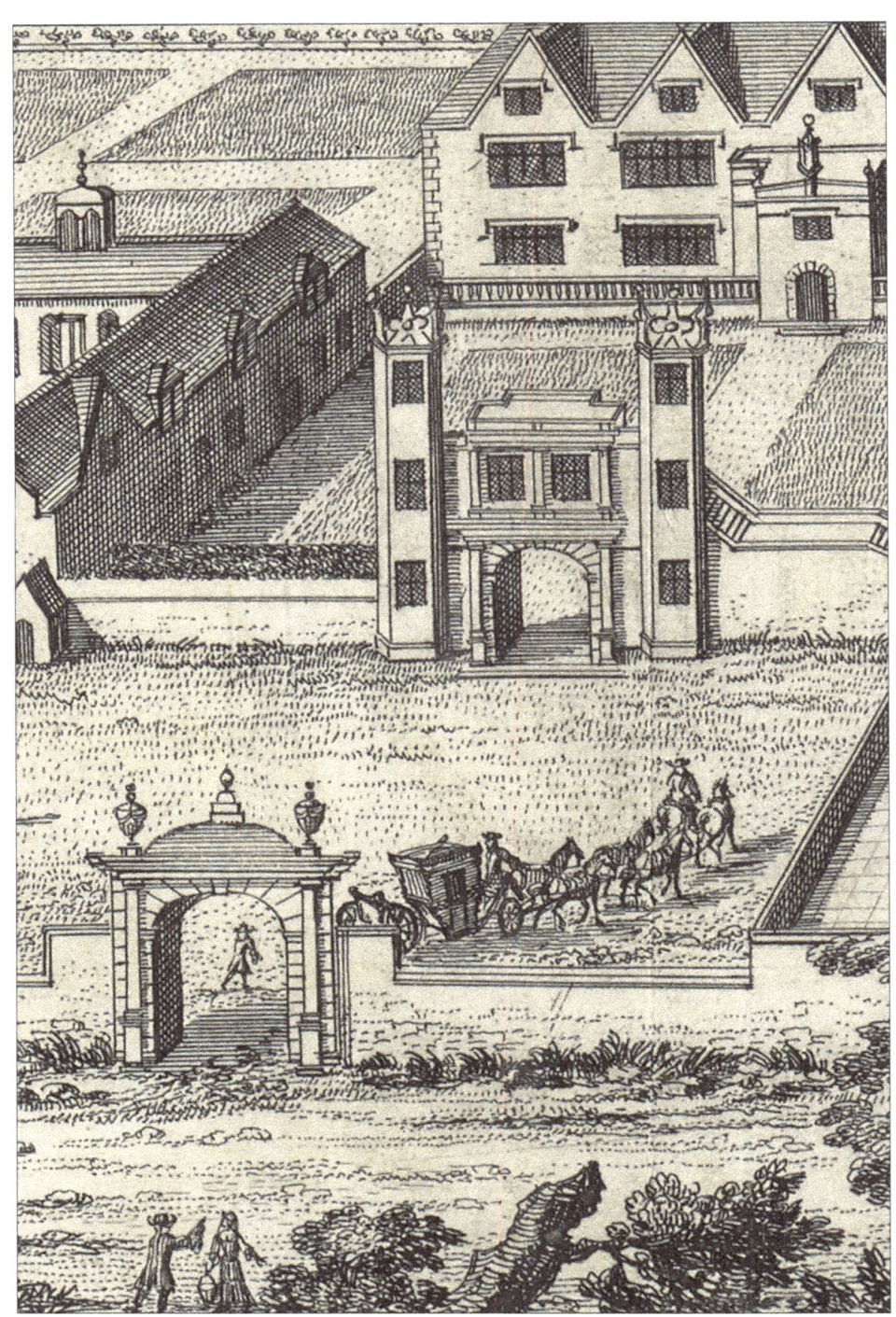

'A very handsome gatehouse' at Walter Estcourt's manor house

JOHANNES KIP

THE GLOUCESTERSHIRE ENGRAVINGS

edited by

ANTHEA JONES

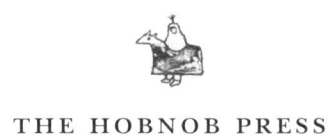

THE HOBNOB PRESS

First published in the United Kingdom in 2021

by The Hobnob Press,
8 Lock Warehouse,
Severn Road,
Gloucester GL1 2GA
www.hobnobpress.co.uk

in association with
Gloucestershire Gardens and Landscape Trust
Hamfield Cottage,
Ham Road
Charlton Kings
Cheltenham GL52 6NG

British Library Cataloguing in Publication Data
A catalogue record for this book is available from the British Library

ISBN 978-1-906978-99-0 casebound
ISBN 978-1-914407-17-8 paperback

Typeset in ITC New Baskerville 10/12 pt.
Typesetting and origination by John Chandler

CONTENTS

The Gloucestershire Gardens and Landscape Trust   6

Foreword, by Nicholas Kingsley   7

Map   8

Introduction   9

Editorial Conventions   18

THE ENGRAVINGS

2	Gloster City	20		23	Didmarton	68
3	The West Prospect of			24	Upper Dowdeswell	70
	Gloucester City	25		25	Sandywell	72
4	Gloster Cathedral	28		26	Dumbleton	74
5	Wyck	28		27	Dyrham	76
6	Alderly	30		28	Eastington	80
7	Knole	32		29	Wotton	82
8	Over	34		30	Fairford	84
9	Alveston	37		31	Flaxley	86
10	Amney Crucis	40		32	Hampton	88
11	Shurdington	42		33	Hardwick Park Court	90
12	Badminton	44		34	Hatherop	92
13	Barrington	44		35	Hales Abbey	94
14	Battsford	46		36	Henbury (Harcourt)	96
15	Berkley	48		37	Henbury (Sampson)	98
16	Broadwell	52		38	Kingsweston	101
17	Cirencester	54		39	Hull als Hill	104
18	Cirencester Abbey	57		40	Kempsford	106
19	Southam	60		41	Leckhampton	108
20	Williamstrip	62		42	Cleeve Hill	110
21	Little Compton	64		43	Miserden	112
22	Coberly	66		44	Clower-Wall (Clearwell)	114

45	Nibley	116
46	Rendcomb	118
47	Saperton	120
48	Sherborn	122
49	Shipton Moyne (Hodges)	126
50	Shipton Moyne (Estcourt)	128
51	Syston	130
52	Stanway	132
53	Stoke Gifford	136
54	Maugersbury	138
55	Lupiatt	140
56	Swell	142
57	Chepstow Castle	144
58	Toddington	146
59	Tortworth	148
60	Westbury Court	150
61	Stoke Bishop	153
62	Sneed Park	156
63	Witcombe Park	158
64	Bradley Court	160
65	Sevenhampton	164

Select Bibliography	167
Acknowledgements	169
Picture Credits	170
Index	171

THE GLOUCESTERSHIRE GARDENS AND LANDSCAPE TRUST

MANY READING THIS BOOK will be familiar, I am sure, with the engravings by Johannes Kip which he produced for Sir Robert Atkyns's *The Ancient and Present State of Glostershire*, published in 1712. Kip made a speciality of engraved views of English country houses, represented in detail from the bird's-eye view, a pictorial convention for topography. Maybe you have already used them in your own research. However, never before has there been such an opportunity to study and delight in all the known Kip drawings for the old county of Gloucestershire; in fact, sixty-four of them.

This idea to research and collate all the known information into one publication was the brainchild of Anthea Jones. By bringing together this record into a single volume, she has revealed and brought to life a highly significant proportion of Gloucestershire's major estates of the early eighteenth century. The author is a long-standing member of The Gloucestershire Gardens and Landscape Trust, founded in 1991 as a charity to raise awareness of the immense value of the historic landscapes, parks and gardens in our county for the benefit of present and future generations. This volume provides a very significant contribution to this body of knowledge.

The Trust seeks to protect and conserve the many known, and as yet unknown, designed landscapes through research and close cooperation with owners, as well as local and national bodies concerned with the conservation of historic gardens and designed landscape. The historical research which is being undertaken by Trust members is now appearing in our Newsletters and Journal; it is of great help in our response to planning applications which impinge on known sites. None of this could have happened without the unstinting support of the head of our research group, Gay Chamberlayne.

It is both a delight and a privilege to contribute a Foreword to this important book, of which the Trust is an important sponsor.

Anna Ball
Chairman,
Gloucestershire Gardens and Landscape Trust

FOREWORD

FORTY YEARS AGO, I produced a small exhibition about *The Gloucestershire Country House* at what was then the County Record Office. Putting the exhibition together led me to study, for the first time, the sixty-four wonderful early 18th century prints by John Kip which are the subject of this book. They were commissioned by Sir Robert Atkyns junior for his county history, *The Ancient and Present State of Glostershire*, which was published posthumously in 1712. What makes the group unique is their being such a large number of views by a professional artist for a single county at such an early date. This achievement, which as Dr. Jones shows was accomplished in just five short years between 1706 and 1711, must have been facilitated by Atkyns, who as a Gloucestershire gentleman himself could persuade his peers not only to allow their houses to be depicted but to pay for the privilege. A later county historian, Samuel Rudder, who did not have the advantage of approaching landowners as a social equal, tried to use the same model, but secured only a handful of commissions, and those mostly from aspirants to the gentry.

The Ancient and Present State of Glostershire was republished in 1768, with the original plates, but both the 1712 and 1768 editions have always been scarce, perhaps because part of the print run was destroyed by fire in each case. As a result, an 18th century copy of the book with all its plates will now cost at least £3,000. A facsimile edition was published in 1974, but with the plates bound separately, and even this now fetches £300 second-hand. Dr. Jones therefore does Gloucestershire historians a considerable service by making the Kip prints available at a modest price on a scale large enough for the details to be studied. Even better, she provides a commentary on the drawings which demonstrates her eagle eye and brings out points of interest about both individual views and the series as a whole which even the informed observer could easily miss.

As Dr. Jones notes in her introduction, most previous commentators on Kip – myself included – have concentrated on his depiction of country houses and their gardens. These features were the primary subject of the drawings and they were what helped to make a county history an appealing acquisition for the intended market among the county gentry and clergy of Gloucestershire and their friends. But Dr. Jones demonstrates how much can also be gleaned from the incidental details in the prints: the depictions of churches, cottages, stables, outbuildings, roads, lanes and the surrounding countryside. And for the first time, I think, she gives proper attention to those places where the views overlap, especially at Henbury, Cirencester and Dowdeswell, where one house can be seen in the background of another. Her analysis makes clear just how much information the individual prints can yield, and I hope it will act as both a guide and a stimulus to future research in this unique resource.

Nicholas Kingsley
Formerly County & Diocesan Archivist for Gloucestershire
and Secretary of the Historical Manuscripts Commission.

Anthea Jones MA, PhD, was Head of History and Director of Studies at Cheltenham Ladies' College before retirement. She is the author of A Thousand Years of the English Parish and several books on Gloucestershire local history, and edited the Record Series volume for Bristol and Gloucestershire Archaeological Society on *Dissenters' Meeting House Certificates and Registrations for Bristol and Gloucestershire, 1672–1852*. She enjoys walking and gardening.

1 Glostershire A. D. 1712

The map of the county at the beginning of Sir Robert Atkyns's *Ancient and Present state of Glostershire* was unsigned, and it is suggested it closely resembles Robert Morden's map published in Camden's *Britannia* (1695). In its place a map shows the sites of Johannes Kip's engravings of 60 gentlemen's 'seats', together with three of Gloucester also by Kip, and one of Badminton which was not. The following list is arranged alphabetically by parish. Parish names are as they are presented today, and house names, where different, are cross referenced.

Abson & Wick (Wick & Abson) 5
Alderley 6
Almondsbury (Knole & Over) 7 & 8
Alveston 9
Ampney Crucis 10
Badgeworth (Shurdington) 11
Badminton, Great 12
Barrington, Great 13
Batsford 14
Berkeley 15
Bishop's Cleeve (Southam) 19
(Bradley Court) Wotton-under-Edge 64
Broadwell 16

(Brockhampton) Sevenhampton 65
(Chepstow) Tiddenham 57
Cirencester (Bathurst & Master) 17 & 18
(Clearwell) Newland 44
(Cleve Hill) Mangotsfield 42
Coberley 22
Coln St Aldwyns (Williamstrip) 20
Compton Abdale (Little Compton) 21
Didmarton 23
Dowdeswell (Sandywell & Upper Dowdeswell) 24 & 25
Dumbleton 26

Dyrham 27
Eastington (Easington) 28
Fairford 30
Flaxley 31
Gloucester aerial view, prospect and cathedral 2 3 & 4
Gloucester, North Hamlets (Wotton) 29
Hailes 35
(Hampton) Minchinhampton 32
Hardwick 33
Hatherop 34
Henbury (Harcourt & Sampson) (& Kings Weston) 36 37 & 38

INTRODUCTION

THREE HUNDRED YEARS AGO, in early August 1721, Johannes Kip suddenly 'dropt down dead' at his home in St John's Street, Westminster; he was buried in St Margaret's Church, Westminster, on 12 August 1721. Kip was sufficiently well-known for his death to be reported in the *Daily Journal* on 15 August. His precise birth date is not known, but was before 1653, so he was about 68 years old. He had been living in England since 1688, but his early life had been spent in Amsterdam. He was 'the Dutch engraver' recorded in the accounts of Berkeley Castle in 1708.[1]

The tercentenary of Kip's death is an appropriate time to record and celebrate the sixty-three plates which he both drew and engraved, itself a remarkable achievement, and which were bound in with *The Ancient and Present State of Glostershire* published in 1712 by the executors of Sir Robert Atkyns, who had died on 29 November 1711. The production of such a large number of engravings, all close in date, and all of one county, was unique. Atkyns also included a map of Gloucestershire, unsigned and possibly based on the map by Robert Morden and a drawing of Badminton by Leonard Knyff, which was engraved by Kip and had already been published in 1707.

Not all the engravings were of gentlemen's houses, although these have been the focus of much discussion about Kip's work. Atkyns devoted a long initial section to general county facts and figures, and a detailed account of the county town and cathedral, and clearly looked for illustrations for this section. For the many pages on Gloucester itself Kip produced two interesting drawings. The first is a picture map of the city containing an astonishing amount of detail, and, to illustrate this, four sections of the map have been extracted and a commentary written on each.[2] The text points to the buildings for which Kip's drawings are the only known indication of their appearance. The second illustration is the West Prospect of the city; in this plate, too, there are interesting details. Kip also both drew and engraved a large-scale illustration of Gloucester cathedral.

After the substantial initial sections, Atkyns continues on page 198 with an account of 'The parishes in the county of Gloster'. The remaining sixty-one plates are spread fairly regularly through this larger section of the book and each was bound in close to the parish it relates to. The engravings showing the houses are often reproduced, as in the two volumes in the series the *Buildings of England: Gloucestershire*, but much less interest has been shown in the scenes within which the houses are embedded. Yet they are full of detail and demonstrate that Kip took in a wide variety of information about each location, tailoring it to the particular situation of each house and possibly the particular demands of each owner.

Johannes Kip: the Gloucestershire Engravings presents all the illustrations in *The Ancient and Present State of Glostershire*, with the exception of the county map. A different map is provided here showing where each site engraved by Kip was located. A brief commentary places each plate in the context of the owner and of the area depicted. It shows that Kip's work can reveal many aspects of a scene, and deserves this tercentenary celebration.

'The Dutch engraver'

Kip used the word 'engraving' to describe his work, although in practice he used two techniques, engraving

Hill (Hull) 39
Kempsford 40
(Kings Weston) Henbury 38
(Knole) Almondsbury 8
Leckhampton 41
(Little Compton) Compton Abdale 21
Lypiatt 55
Mangotsfield (Cleve Hill) 42
(Maugersbury) Stow-on-the-Wold 54
Minchinhampton (Hampton) 32
Miserden 43
Newland (Clearwell) 44
North Nibley 45

(Over) Almondsbury 7
Rendcomb 46
(Sandywell) Dowdeswell 25
Sapperton 47
Sevenhampton (Brockhampton) 65
Sherborne 48
Shipton Moyne (Hodges & Estcourt) 49 & 50
(Shurdington) Badgeworth 11
Siston 51
(Southam) Bishop's Cleeve 19
Stanway 52
Stoke Gifford 53

Stow-on-the-Wold (Maugersbury) 54
Swell, Lower 56
Tiddenham (Chepstow) 57
Toddington 58
Tortworth 59
Westbury-on-Severn 60
Westbury-on-Trym (Stoke Bishop & Sneed Park) 61 & 62
Wick (& Abson) 5
(Williamstrip) Coln St Aldwyns 20
Witcombe, Great 63
(Wotton) Gloucester, North Hamlets 29
Wotton-under-Edge (Bradley Court) 64

and etching. Both produced copper plates carrying a design which could be used to print many copies, perhaps as many as 2,000, though the quality deteriorated with use, sooner with etchings than engravings. Both techniques could be used in one print and 'engraving' is the name commonly used of prints made by either method.

Engraving involved cutting out lines from a copper plate with a tool called a burin. It was a skill learnt over several years of apprenticeship in the workshop of a master engraver. Etching was the method by which Kip made the majority of the Gloucestershire plates. A design was cut through a coating or 'ground' of wax, gum or resin laid on a copper plate, using an etching needle, which enabled more freedom in drawing than the burin directly gouging out the copper. The plate was then placed in an acid bath which ate into it where the ground had been removed. This also was a skill learnt over a period of apprenticeship. The freedom it gave encouraged painters to use it, most notably Rembrandt, particularly for landscapes which were a particular interest in the Netherlands. Rembrandt had moved to Amsterdam in 1631-32, and had experimented widely with the medium, producing more than 300 etchings, the last in 1659. He died in Amsterdam in 1669. It is likely that Kip was familiar with Rembrandt's etchings.[3]

Johannes Kip was born in Amsterdam before 1653, and trained there as an engraver and etcher for two years from 1668 under Bastiaen Stopendael. Kip's first engraving is from 1672. By 1686 his reputation was clearly established; that year he made six plates of *William of Orange, his wife and attendants near The Hague.* Dutch artists in the seventeenth century dominated topographical painting and print-making, and after the restoration of Charles II in 1660, 'a stream of Dutch oil painters' came to England, followed by engravers.[4] Two brothers, Jacob and Leendert Knyff, Kip's compatriots, came to England some years before him. Jacob died in 1681 at his brother's house in St Martin-in-the-Fields. Leendert, generally known as Leonard Knyff, continued to work in England for several decades; he was both a painter and picture dealer, and is known for still-life pictures as well as for bird's-eye drawings of great houses. Johannes Kip, when he came to England, engraved many of Knyff's drawings.

Kip in England

Kip came to England in 1688. His arrival appears to have preceded William and Mary's because his first known English print was an engraving made while James II and Queen Mary were still on the throne. The interior of the Queen's Chapel, St James's Palace, is lettered 'Prospectus interior Sacelli Serenissima Mariae Magnae Britanniae Reginae' and 'J. Kip delin. Sculp. et excudit. Londini.', after which, inscribed in pen and ink, 'To Be sold at The Dutch Glasiers hous in Standehopestreet [Stanhope Street to the east

of Drury Lane]'. 'Serenissima' was changed in ink to 'serenissimae' in the title. The British Museum catalogue entry notes that the print must have been produced after the installation of the organ gallery in the summer of 1688, but before Queen Mary's final departure from London for exile on 10 December. At the end of the month *The London Mercury* reported that French Protestants had already used the chapel.[5]

Notably Kip had drawn as well as engraved this plate, and he planned to produce further prints with the patronage of William III. A *History of Learning*, published in London in 1691, carried an advertisement for 'A Prospect of Chelsey Colledge, curiously drawn, and engraved in a large Copper-plate, with a prospect also of the Country contiguous; by J. Kip, who designs to Publish the Draughts of all the King's Houses.'[6] A number of bird's-eye views of the King's and Queen's houses was certainly made. Kip's mention of 'a prospect also of the country contiguous', a strong feature of the Gloucestershire engravings, was significant. In this respect his drawings were more impressionistic than Knyff's, although the house at the centre of the estate was rendered in a precise and architectural way, as were other buildings in each view.

This proposal may have led to a notable collaboration with Leonard Knyff, with whom a joint venture was started about 1697. Knyff may have been the entrepreneur. The proposal was to publish a volume of a hundred engravings of the houses of 'Noblemen and Gentlemen', to be drawn by Knyff and engraved by Kip. Subscriptions were invited of £10 for which each would receive two prints of their house and grounds, together with their coat of arms incorporated in the design; one would be supplied printed on a double folio page. In 1701 an advertisement in the *Post Man* noted that sixty engravings which had been subscribed for were completed, and further subscribers were invited to come, or send, to Knyff's house in Old Palace-Yard. But 'For want of Subscriptions, and on account of his Health, (the time first proposed being long since expir'd) [he] is oblig'd to desist', Knyff declared in the *Daily Courant* in 1707. He auctioned off his stock, paintings, prints and possibly the engravings, although these may have been partly Kip's property or even the printers', and left England.[7] He did return, however, dying in London one year after Kip, and left a modestly prosperous estate.[8] Kip, on the other hand, in 1707 had possibly started on the Gloucestershire commission.

Eighty views, though not the hundred planned, were published in 1707 by the Dutch printer David Mortier ('Book-Seller at ye Sign of Erasmus's head near Bedford house, all sorts of French and Latin Books'), who also came from Amsterdam and had set up as a book seller in The Strand in 1698. The volume was titled '*Britannia Illustra or views of several of the Queen's Palaces as also of the principal Seats of the Nobility and Gentry of Great Britain, curiously engraven on 80 copper plates.* (L.

Knyff delin. I. Kip sculp)'. This volume, of outstanding houses, has completely overshadowed Kip's subsequent independent career. It was republished by Mortier the following year with a French title, *Nouveau theatre de la Grande Bretagne: ou Description exacte des palais de la reine, et des maisons les plus considerables des seigneurs & des gentilhommes de la Grande Bretagne,* maybe hoping to capture a foreign market. A second volume with this title was published in 1713 containing churches and cathedrals, amongst other subjects, and by 1717 there were four volumes in the series.

Over the next twenty-two years many more engravings were added to the original eighty, and a considerable number of different selections was published, some under the title of *Britannia Illustrata* and some as *Nouveau Theatre.*[9] David Mortier or Joseph Smith were the publishers of repeat volumes. As each plate was separately printed, it was easy to assemble different selections; volume 1 containing the original eighty was the most stable collection. Nearly all Kip's Gloucestershire engravings, published in *The Ancient and Present State of Glostershire,* were republished as a set by Joseph Smith under the title *Britannia Illustrata* in 1715, in volume 2 of a two-volume set, with the 1707 collection comprising volume 1. The most comprehensive collection of prints was a four-volume edition published in 1724 by Joseph Smith, 'Marchand Libraire proche D'Exeter Exchange, a L'Enseigne D'Inigo Jones, dans le Strand'. One copy of volume 2, containing all but three of the plates in *The Ancient and Present State of Glostershire* in 1712, is in Gloucestershire Archives, and is the source of the majority of the engravings reprinted in this book.[10] The three omissions: the cathedral, Badminton and Chepstow Castle, show the rationale of the volume; Badminton was omitted presumably because it was not Kip's work, though he did slightly amend the engraving for Atkyns, the cathedral because it is not a gentleman's seat, and Chepstow because the castle is in Monmouthshire; as half of Chepstow bridge was Gloucestershire's responsibility, it was closely linked with the parish of Tidenham, and the landscape is relevant to the county, it is included in the gazetteer which follows.[11]

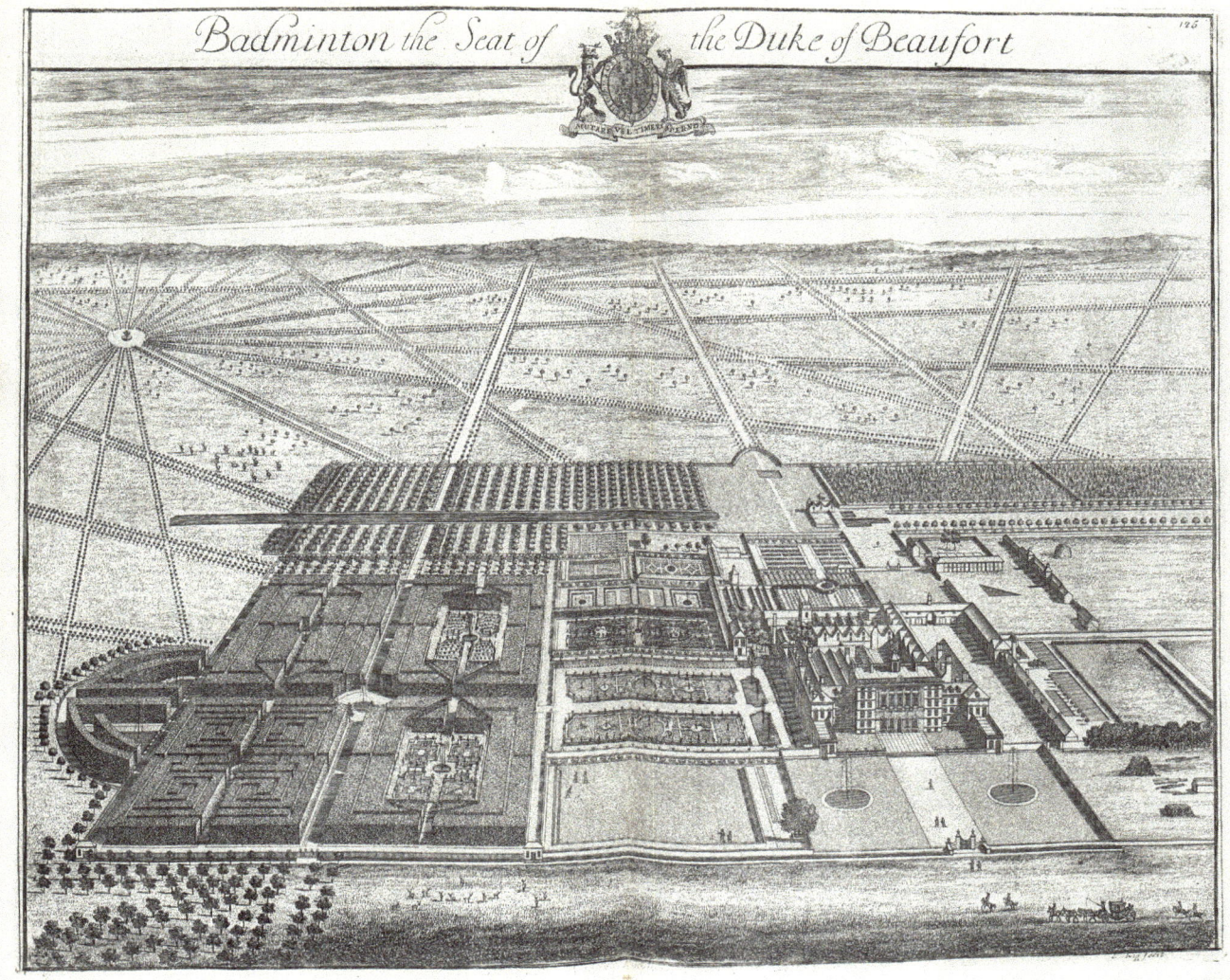

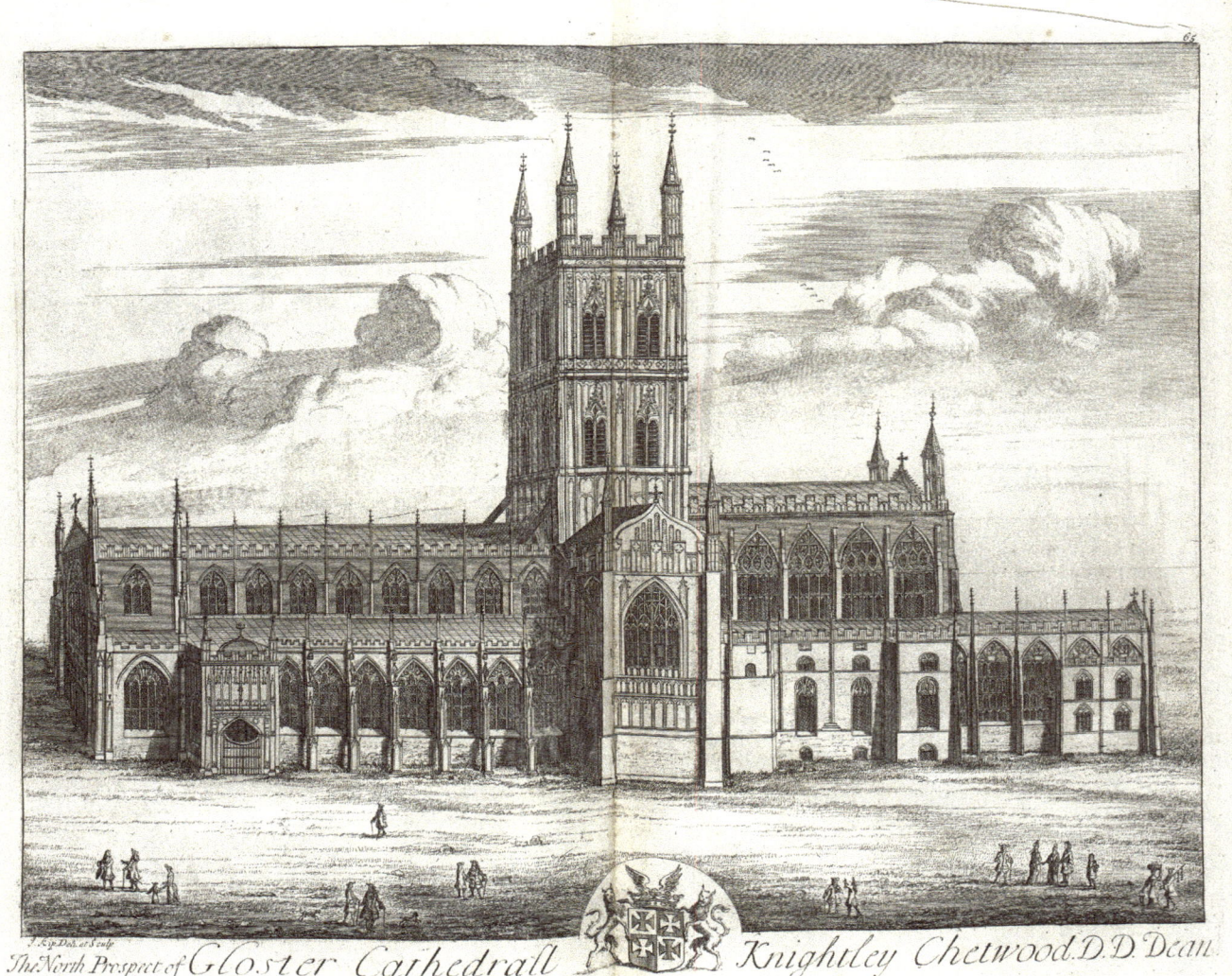

The North Prospect of *Gloster Cathedrall*   *Knightley Chetwood.D.D.Dean.*

The style of the Badminton engraving is rather more formal and less impressionistic than Kip's drawings. The very powerful sets of radiating avenues, although not strongly engraved, nonetheless dominate the picture and there is no room for features in the Gloucestershire landscape. The mansion house is quite small. The 1st Duke died in 1700 and the Duchess had the engraving printed and circulated to friends to show the beauty of the grounds created by the Duke.[12] It was one of the eighty prints in *Britannia Illustrata* in 1707.

Gloucester cathedral is in the style of an architectural drawing, and though with Kip's characteristic human interest, or 'staffage', there is no wider view. Knightley Chetwood became dean of Gloucester in 1707, so the cathedral was probably drawn in the same two or three years that Kip was travelling round Gloucestershire. It was possibly done with the projected volume on cathedrals and collegiate churches in *Nouveau Theatre* in mind; one of a two-volume set was published in 1713 by Mortier and again in 1714 or 1715 in a three-volume set, and was volume 3 of the four

volumes of 1724. There is an unfortunate mistake in the print bound into the second edition of Atkyns's book of 1768; written underneath is 'The North Prospect of Gloster cathedral'. Some copies have had the erroneous description removed. Kip drew the south prospect.

After his collaboration with Atkyns had come to an end, Kip continued to live in London, and to make topographical drawings and prints.[13] He engraved nineteen out of the thirty-six drawings by Thomas Badeslade in John Harris's *The History of Kent*, published in 1719, including a townscape of Tunbridge Wells; a few prints do not have the artist's name on them but they were all by Badeslade.[14] The 'superb engravings of country houses' are today considered the main value of Harris's book.[15] Like Atkyns, Harris died shortly before his book was published and before completing the projected second volume, for which Badeslade had drawn and Kip had engraved Howland Great Dock near Deptford. There are other parallels between Atkyns and Harris. Both may have been inspired by *Britannia Illustrata*, in which there was the Badminton print and two of Kentish houses.[16] Harris may also have been inspired by Atkyns - he issued a prospectus for his *History of Kent* in 1713, and as well as the country houses, it included two townscapes as did *The Ancient and Present State of Glostershire*.

Atkyns and Harris might have been followed very shortly by an illustrated history of Yorkshire. In October 1719, just as Harris's *History* was published, Ralph Thoresby, John Warburton and Samuel Buck met to discuss illustrations for the history on which Warburton was working. Buck made some preliminary sketches, but Warburton abandoned the project. Buck, however, was launched on a career of topographical drawings and town 'prospects' to which he added antiquities. After a couple of years, he and his brother Nathaniel toured and worked together, producing with some assistants 344 English views, 84 Welsh views, and 73 town perspective views which developed further the prospects of London which Kip had drawn and engraved.[17] Their work became more widely known than Kip's, partly through their grasp of methods of publicity.

Kip did not branch out into estate surveying and mapping as Badeslade did after Harris's death,[18] but continued to work as an artist and engraver. He 'was the key figure in English topographical printmaking for twenty years',[19] providing a whole miscellany of book illustrations, frontispieces, portraits, travel and architectural images. He sold prints from his home at 4, St John's Street in Westminster; if his practice was similar to Badeslade's, he would have had a large number of spare prints in his possession. While much of his work may have been done in London, he travelled as far as Carlisle sometime before 1716 in order to make a much more accurate engraving of the cathedral from personal observation than the one used in *Nouveau Theatre*; it was dedicated to the dean Thomas Gibbon, who died in 1716, and in 1724 it replaced the earlier one.[20]

Kip lived long enough to see the fifth edition of Stow's survey of London (dated 1598) published in 1720. John Strype had updated the text from the last printing eighty years before. The project had been advertised in 1708, to be illustrated with about 'one hundred large Copper Cutts ... this work has been long preparing, the Cutts requiring much time and great expences, but they are now all finished'.[21] It took another twelve years to complete the project. Kip may have been the principal engraver supplying the 'fine draughts and the more eminent and publick edifices and monuments'. His name appears on half of the twenty-eight engraved views, and the rest are in a similar style and were probably his work. Typically some plates were re-used from *Britannia Illustrata*.

In 1720 also, as he announced in the *Daily Courant*, Kip finished the 'large prospect of St James's Park, the cities of London and Westminster, and the river Thames, from the farthest part of Westminster to Limehouse, drawn in a perfect (tho' uncommon) manner, giving a splendid view of those magnificent cities.' Each plate was 7 foot by 5 foot [2m x 1.5m] and the detail on these large plates was remarkable. They had taken five years to complete, as he had advertised in the *Daily Courant* for subscriptions in 1715. He must have had tremendous perseverance and patience, as well as energy, to bring this project to completion.[22] The final panorama was dedicated to Caroline Princess of Wales, a fitting conclusion to his career. The plates appear to have been reprinted a number of times, one example being in the Royal Collection. Kip died the year after their completion; he did not apparently leave a will. In a distinguished though not very well-known career, the sixty-three Gloucestershire engravings stand out as a major achievement.

Sir Robert Atkyns, *The Ancient and Present State of Glostershire*

The relationship between Atkyns and Kip can only be inferred from the few known facts surrounding their co-operation. Atkyns was not the first historian of a county to include engravings in his book, though their number and coherence was exceptional. Robert Plot's *Natural History of Staffordshire*, published in 1686, included engravings by the Dutchman Michael Burghers, but not all were of houses; one was an interesting picture of a pottery. Sir Henry Chauncey commissioned three artists to provide illustrations for his *Historical Antiquities of Hertfordshire*, published in 1700, and again not all were of houses, though a few included a wider scene as the background to a house.[23] These would almost certainly have been known to Atkyns. He was likely also to have known of the publication of *Britannia Illustrata*. At least one of Kip's engravings from a painting of Badminton by Knyff was probably in Atkyns's possession, as the Duchess of Beaufort circulated copies amongst friends. Atkyns's conception, however, was on a large scale, and commissioning Knyff and Kip to produce upwards of sixty plates may have been an expense he could not contemplate. Moreover, Knyff left England in 1707. Kip, however, remained, and was established as 'the foremost topographical illustrator' in the country;[24] he himself may have suggested to Atkyns that he could provide the initial artwork as well as engrave the Gloucestershire illustrations.

What prompted Atkyns to include sixty birds-eye views of the county's larger country houses in his *Ancient and Present State of Glostershire*? Was it his loyalty to the county, or to encourage his fellow gentry to feel pride in their county, that determined him to commission Kip? His Preface talks of his 'true and hearty love for his country', by which he was referring to his county rather than the meaning of country today, and that 'with a pious affection' he submitted his book to 'his Neighbours and Countrymen'. Was it also his intention to show the delightful characteristics of the Gloucestershire countryside with the bird's-eye views, as a modern author uses photographs? The houses portrayed by Kip are not always very close to the viewer, but are set amongst hills, woods and fields, like Leckhampton, Rendcomb, Miserden, Bradley, Hatherop, Lypiatt, Sneed and Witcombe.

Personal factors no doubt influenced the list of properties chosen for illustration. There were not many major houses like Badminton in the county, but there was a good number of more modest 'gentlemen's seats', like Sir Robert Atkyns senior's properties in Sapperton and Lower Swell, both of which Kip drew, which may suggest Sir Robert was helping with the project despite his considerable political disagreement with his son. The universities, Inns of Court and Parliament were where Atkyns would have met many of the owners who might have become his friends. One small indication is the meeting in November 1710 with Sir John Dutton in a coffee house in London; afterwards the pair went to Atkyns's house - it is tempting to think that they discussed the Kip project. Evidence from Dyrham suggests Atkyns worked closely with owners.[25]

A list of the seats in the county would certainly have included a number owned by members of parliament for the county and for Gloucester city, Cirencester and Tewkesbury, and twelve whose owners were elected to parliament at some time between 1690 and 1710 were the subjects of engravings: Great Barrington, Berkeley, Cirencester, Dumbleton, Hardwicke, Lypiatt, Rendcomb, Sherborne, Stoke Gifford, Tortworth, Westbury Court and Williamstrip.[26] These men would have spent time in London, creating opportunities for discussion of the project and for canvassing support. Atkyns had himself been a member of parliament while the Stuarts were on the throne but did not support William III; however his Tory principles did not determine his choice of subjects, or he would not have included Williamstrip. Henry Powle was a supporter of William III, and his son-in-law Henry Ireton, who succeeded him as owner, was the son of one of Cromwell's generals and the grandson of Cromwell himself.

There are surprising omissions, as Kingsley noted. The seat of John Grobham Howe of Stowell, for example, was not the subject of an engraving, despite Atkyns's mention of the 'handsome large house' and 'pleasant seat and park'. Howe was an exceptionally active parliamentarian, and may not have spent much time in the county; the house may have been shut up when Kip was in the county. Atkyn's description of Highnam, (in Churcham parish), the seat of William Cooke, was unusually enthusiastic; he commented on the 'large beautiful Seat, and great Gardens and Plantations and large Ponds', also the large prospect of the city of Gloucester, and the large park. It is a matter of regret that Kip did not produce an engraving of Highnam. William Cooke I, and his grandson William Cooke II were both briefly members of parliament, their memberships terminated by death, the grand-father in 1703, the grandson in 1709, pre-deceasing his father.

The family's misfortunes may have led Atkyns not to intrude. Charles Coxe, a long-standing member, was in process of building a 'neat' house at Lower Lypiatt and although Atkyns suggested it was new built, a rainwater head has the date 1717, so it may not have been sufficiently far advanced for Kip to draw it. These are examples of circumstances which may have led Atkyns to omit a particular house from his list, considerations which it is now hard to know.

Payments to Kip for drawings of Berkeley Castle and Dyrham, in the latter case mentioning drawing and engraving, indicate that Atkyns negotiated with owners their direct financing of Kip's work. Some owners may have declined to assist Atkyns. The payments, of £5-7s-6d in 1708 and £6-9-0 in 1710 respectively might equate to approximately £850 in the early twenty-first century;[27] the payments were less than the £10 subscription Knyff proposed about 1700 for two copies of a print (over £1,000 today), which also included the cost of making the engraving. The price of an individual print once the engraving was made was quite modest. Badeslade estimated the value of the five hundred sets of the thirty-six Kentish prints which he owned when he died in 1745 at 7s6d a set, equivalent to about £62 in 2019 or £1.72 each.[28] The arrangement John Harris had with owners is described in the Preface to *The History of Kent*, and appears likely to have been similar to the one Atkyns had. 'And whoever pleases to consider the Price of Paper, and Rolling-Presses for the Copper Plates, will easily see, that notwithstanding the Lords and Gentlemen have been at the Expence of having their several Seats Designed and Engraved, yet the Paper, and the working them off, hath been at my Charge'.[29] As a result of the arrangement, Kip, like Badeslade, may unfortunately have been left with bad debts. Nonetheless his engravings in *The Ancient and Present State of Glostershire* 'have made the book a collectors' item …. They form a gallery of the mansions and manor houses of a prosperous county, and were not matched later in quality'.[30]

Dating Kip's engravings

The dating of Kip's engravings is of interest because they are often used to establish when alterations were made to the houses or when the gardens were laid out. Kip's travels round Gloucestershire were likely to have extended over at least two and probably more than two years; he had to travel the length and breadth of a large county when weather conditions were favourable. The engravings show he reached the east, south and western boundaries of the county, though not the extreme north-east or north-west. The map of the distribution of the houses (*qv*) shows the clustering of sites, suggesting he had a base in several parts of the county from which he covered houses in the neighbourhood. There is a cluster round Cheltenham, another round Gloucester, and possibly Berkeley and Cirencester provided bases, while near Bristol there is the largest concentration, no fewer than twelve in the vicinity.

Britannia Illustrata took at least from 1701 to 1707 for the eighty engravings to be completed. Kip had to survey and sketch the town of Gloucester and probably the cathedral, and sixty 'seats' of the county's gentry; Badminton was already engraved (and with the map of Gloucestershire made the total illustrations to sixty-five). Sixty-three engravings was a substantial number for Kip to cover on his own. Did Atkyns determine precisely how many engravings he would use? In the text he described warmly more houses than were illustrated, as with Highnam and Stowell. However, as he died before the book was published, his executors may have been responsible for the selection of plates bound in with the book.

There are clues to the period Kip was at work in the engravings themselves, in the names of the owners entered on the top of each. The earliest date identified in this way is 20 June 1706 when Matthew Hale died, leaving his widow in possession of Alderley. Samuel Barker, the owner named at Fairford, died on 1 May 1708, so it is possible that Kip drew Fairford in the spring of 1708, but it is also possible that he had been to Fairford in 1707. One of the two houses in Shipton Moyne was also engraved after Thomas Hodges died in 1708, leaving 'Mrs Hodges Relict of Tho: Hodges' in possession. Kip had probably finished work on Sapperton and Swell by 1710, when Sir Robert Atkyns senior died; Sir Michael Hickes at Witcombe and Richard Freeman at Batsford also died in 1710, though the latter was succeeded by his son also named Richard. Henry Ireton at Williamstrip died in 1711, the same year as Atkyns himself.

Other hints of the dates Kip was at work are in the buildings. Wotton House near Gloucester has a date stone '1707' over the entrance, and Atkyns's comment in the text is 'Mr Horton of Comb-End has a very handsome new-built house in this place'. Sandywell Park in Dowdeswell was new-built between 1704-08. Sir Ralph Dutton transferred Sherborne to his son in 1709, but he is named as the owner both by Kip and Atkyns. Kip captured the appearance of Kings Weston before the new house had started building about 1710, as indicated by a beam dated 1711.

The evidence of entries in the accounts of Berkeley Castle and Dyrham Park support a similar period of activity in Gloucestershire. John Kip was paid on 3 July 1708 for a drawing of Berkeley Castle, and William Blathwayt's accounts record the payment to Kip in September 1710 'for Drawing and Engraving the House and Gardens etc for Sr Robert Atkins's survey of the County'. Drawings of the houses close to Bristol – quite a collection of them – were probably made at the same period as Dyrham. While payment could lag well behind completion of the work, the Blathwayt entry gives the latest date for Kip's journeys to Gloucestershire. Kingsley's suggestion of 1708-09 as the date of Kip's Gloucestershire engravings certainly covers the main period but it might possibly have extended to 1707-10.

Each engraving tells a story

It is not known whether Kip had been trained in surveying techniques, which were being developed and standardised in the sixteenth century; in the Netherlands Jan Pietersz Dou and Johan Sems published *Practijck des Lantmetens* in 1600,[31] and in England John Norden's *Surveyor's Dialogue* was published in 1607, marking a clear step forward in technical knowledge and skill a century before Kip's Gloucestershire tours. The bird's-eye views of country houses and estates drawn by Knyff and Kip required some familiarity with surveying techniques, so that buildings, and features at a distance from the house, were drawn and positioned with some accuracy. The bird's-eye view was being used in the century before they were at work. It is not like a modern map; in order to compress the scene onto a single plate, the scale could not be the same throughout.[32] Nonetheless modern maps do indicate that Kip placed features correctly in relation to the house, albeit the distances involved are often foreshortened and the orientation sometimes adjusted; thus at Berkeley, house and church were drawn to present a full façade of each, and the angle of Gloucester cathedral in the background of Wotton House has been adjusted to show the whole north side. Discussion of accuracy in Kip's engravings, although not explicitly stated, is inevitably influenced by Ordnance Survey maps and modern photography. Kip achieved an approximation to the accuracy of a map and the atmosphere of a sketch.

It is possible that Atkyns envisaged the engravings as a form of survey of the county, offering a compact format where the greater comprehensiveness of estate maps was not practicable. Kip was clearly an observant and intelligent observer. Chepstow Castle, for example, places the important (if rather rickety-looking) bridge over the river Wye in the foreground and the river was the county boundary. Several engravings of houses in the neighbourhood of Bristol likewise feature the rivers Avon and Severn, with plentiful shipping drawing attention to the commerce and the port; although small vignettes, Kip included the watch towers overlooking the waterways. Houses in this area tended to be bought by Bristol merchants, but the growth of Bristol and its economy has meant that twentieth century housing has steadily encroached on them. The port of Gloucester, also, has many ships at the quayside and Kip drew some industrial buildings there.

The variety and individuality of characterisation of each engraving is striking. Kip captured the rather grim Stoke Gifford and the airiness of Sneed Park. Avenues march boldly across the countryside, as at Cleve Hill House, where there is little else to take the attention, and are a common feature in many engravings. Upper Dowdeswell, like Stoke Gifford, is dominated by the steep slope of the hill. At Southam, the exposed Cotswold stone of Cleeve Hill edge draws the eye. The house dominates some engravings, like Sir Robert Atkyns senior's house at Sapperton or Berkeley Castle. At Hatherop it is the walled kitchen garden which commands attention. The church in close proximity to the house is the focus at Broadwell and Minchinhampton. In two engravings the 'bury' at Henbury is very prominent.

Gardens are important everywhere. The formal layouts and parterres are almost universal, some showing the influence of the recent fashion for canals associated with Dutch influence. A set of standard marks on the engravings indicated the different features. The grass of pasture was distinguished by scattered upright dashes, lawns by close-together dots, and bowling greens, which were popular at that period, by men playing bowls. Parks were shown with a herd of antlered deer. Parallel lines across a stream or canal indicated water, also ducks or swans on a moat or pond. Gravel was indicated by spaced-out dots. Roads were distinguished from gaps in the vegetation by puddles and ruts, and also by riders on horseback, carriages and wagons; the surface at the best would have been stones. The development of turnpike trusts had only just started. Did Kip travel by coach, with his drawing equipment, or did he travel on horseback? He would certainly have known the roads which led to the houses he visited.

Kip must have discussed with owners, however briefly, what was wanted before he spent time walking and riding round the area. Owners must have pointed out notable trees on their estates, like the ancient Tortworth chestnut, the ancient yew in St Helen's churchyard in Alveston, and the yew walk at Hatherop. At Williamstrip the elaboration of the garden points to Henry Ireton's enthusiasm to make a mark on a property he had just gained possession of by right of his wife. Kip was probably subject sometimes to pressure from owners to represent a garden as favourably as possible, and perhaps to exaggerate its extent if not its layout. The canal at Flaxley was made to seem longer than it was in reality. At Fairford Kip did not show wide sweeps of countryside nor much of the town or the notable church, but was apparently required to concentrate on the immediate and formal layout of the large garden and grounds.

Owners in other cases wanted the engraving to demonstrate their extensive estates. The principle was exemplified by the Duke of Newcastle, who made clear to Knyff in 1697 that for his picture of Haughton 'the prospects to be regularly taken a mile about ye house'.[33] The wide panorama around the rather small drawing of Miserden manor house seems designed to show the large extent of William Sandys' land-holding, including parks in neighbouring parishes, and the same is the case with Witcombe. The picture of a park, with its deer, was an important indication of status and is found in twelve of the engravings, while nearly every house drawn by Kip had a park, if not in his view.

The overall composition and the detail included in each engraving, therefore, had particular relevance. Atkyns' own comments on each house do not suggest that he would have been able to give such detailed instructions, like showing the urns commemorating the marriages of the Fust family at Hill Court. The chancel of the church in the engraving of Leckhampton Court seems to have been devised to reflect the Revd Norwood's clerical status; he was both patron and rector of the church. There is a strange anomaly at Henbury, where the same church features in two engravings, but with a different top to the tower; it is possible that the owner of one house had plans for the tower to be altered. The decision to draw Cirencester town with a rather inconspicuous house belonging to Allen Bathurst may reflect the fact that he was the member of parliament for Cirencester, so it was his 'seat' in more than one sense. At Hailes, it is clear that Kip was instructed to omit the monastic ruins. These engravings were meant for show, not for exact topography. When it is considered how many details Kip included, the standard of all sixty-two prints described in the gazetteer is amazing.

Sixty prints, including Badminton, each related to a particular house, and sixteen of these have completely gone. In some cases the site has been taken over by housing, as at Cleve Hill and Sneed, and in a few cases the site is open ground, like one of the Shipton Moyne sites, Cirencester Abbey or Hailes, though here monastic ruins have been preserved, even though invisible in Kip's engraving. Six houses have been demolished and a successor large house has been built on a new site, like Batsford, Tortworth or Toddington, and six completely different houses to those Kip drew occupy the same site, as at Alderley, Clearwell or Rendcomb. Twenty-seven houses drawn by Kip survive and eleven others may preserve some parts dating from Atkyns's time though largely rebuilt.

It is interesting to note that thirteen of the Kip engravings show properties released to laymen by the dissolution of the monasteries, colleges and chantries, but the Reformation explains only part of the rebuilding which took place in Gloucestershire in the sixteenth and seventeenth centuries. The amount of alteration, adaptation and addition which had naturally occurred over the years before Kip visited make it difficult to summarise what Kip's engravings suggest as to the age of the houses. It is clear that only small parts of the six oldest houses were medieval, though these are a distinguished group, including Berkeley Castle and Leckhampton Court which are both still standing. Twenty-four houses appear to have been to some extent sixteenth century, of which Siston and Southam are good surviving examples. The largest group, twenty-seven, were in part at least seventeenth century, some reflecting the turn-over of property due to the civil war and its effect on royalist landowners. It includes the least altered of all the Kip houses, Wick Court. Over half, thirty-three, are traditional manor houses with the parish church close by, and one, Lypiatt, has the family chapel still standing.

It is always possible to say more about each individual engraving, but the purpose of this book is to suggest how much can be seen and learnt from the engravings and so stimulate further investigation, particularly on the ground. Archaeology may contribute to the discussion, as with Cirencester Abbey Grounds. Layouts and boundaries can be explored, which are long-lasting features of many of the sites, and footpaths can be walked round parks, opening up new views of the countryside, as they have for the researchers working on this book; the footpath at Sandywell, for example, showed the extensive and beautiful scenery with hills on three sides of the house, lying in a secluded bowl with its fish ponds. The owners of these houses appreciated their views, and they built viewing platforms on their houses, or towers strategically placed in the grounds. Kip's Gloucestershire engravings are valued as historical evidence of the architecture of the houses he drew, of the layout of the gardens and of the status and aspirations of their owners, but it is hoped they will also be appreciated for their stimulating and perceptive pictures of the countryside.

1 Nicholas Grindle, 'Kip, Johannes', *Oxford On-line Dictionary of National Biography* (*ODNB*) (2018). It is usually said that Kip was born in 1653, but this recent review of his life states that he was born before 1653. Similarly his date of death is usually given as 1722. https//:doi.org/10.1093/ref:odnb/1564. Berkeley Account Books GBB 113, 140.

2 Two sections of Kip's picture map, Figs 5 & 7, are reproduced in Peter Clark, 'Early modern Gloucester 1547-1720', *Victoria History of the County of Gloucester: Volume 4, the City of Gloucester*, ed. N M Herbert (London, 1988), 101-123.

3 Anthony Griffiths, *Prints and Printmaking. An introduction to the history and techniques* (The British Museum, reprinted with revisions 2016), 39-48.

4 David Jacques, 'Who knows what a Dutch garden is?', *Garden History*, Vol. 30, No. 2 (2002), 115.

5 British Museum (BM) catalogue entry 1853,0813.108.

6 BM G,2.165.

7 Chethams Library blog. https://library.chethams.com/blog/seventeenth-century-crowdfunding-with-knyff-and-kip/.

8 Paul Taylor, 'Knijff, Leendert [known as Leonard Knyff]', *ODNB* (2008).

9 Bernard Adams, *London Illustrated 1604-1851* (The Library Association 1983), 36-45. The book sets out the general content and dates of the principal volumes of *Britannia Illustrata* and *Nouveau Theatre*.

10 Gloucestershire Archives (GA) SR8/48982GS. This volume is called the 'second book' in a set of four. A copy in Chetham's Library also stating it was the second book contains different engravings. The Gloucester volume is not tightly bound and so Andrew Parry, senior archives assistant, Gloucestershire Archives, was able to secure good scans of the prints for Gloucestershire Gardens and Landscape Trust. These images have been made available to the publisher of this book.

11 These three images have been scanned by Andrew Parry from the second edition of Atkyns (GA SR8-48980GS).

12 Nicholas Kingsley, 'Kip's conundrum', *Country Life* (November 15, 1990), 60-61.

13 Gardens Trust blog. https://thegardenstrust.blog/2017/04/08/kip-and-knyff-part-2-kip.

14 They were republished by H Chapelle as *Thirty-six different views of noblemen and gentlemen's seats in the county of Kent, all designed upon the spot by the late T. Badeslade, esq., surveyor, and engraved by the best hands* (London, n.d. [c.1750]).

15 N Yates, 'Kent', C R J Currie & C P Lewis eds, *English County Histories* (1994),- 210.

16 Colin Flight, http://www.durobrivis.net/library/1719-badeslade.pdf.

17 Ralph Hyde, 'Buck, Samuel', *ODNB* (2004) and 'Introduction' to *A Prospect of Britain* (Pavilion Books (1994).

18 Bob Sylvester, 'Thomas Badeslade: his life and career from eastern England to north Wales', Steven Ashley & Adrian Marsden eds, *Landscapes and Artefacts: Studies in East Anglian Archaeology* presented to Andrew Rogerson (Archaeopress Archaeology 2014), 217-229.

19 Jacques, 'Who knows what a Dutch garden is?', 115.

20 British Library, Grant Lewis, Topography 'being in no respect like it': illustrations of Carlisle Cathedral.

21 Adams, *London Illustrated, 51-55*.

22 Gardens Trust blog 'kip-and-knyff'.

23 John Harris, *The artist and the country house* (Sotheby Parke Burnet, 1979), 91.

24 Adams, *London Illustrated, 52*.

25 Brian Smith, 'Introduction' to Sir Robert Atkyns, *The Ancient and Present State of Glostershire* (reprint EP Publishing Ltd 1974), xii.

26 https://www.historyofparliamentonline.org/research/members.

27 See entries for each engraving in gazetteer. Estimation of values in this paragraph: https://www.measuringworth.com/calculators/ukcompare/relativevalue.php

28 Sylvester, 'Thomas Badeslade: his life and career, 227. Badeslade owned copper plates at his death, estimated to be worth £150 each, which appears an extraordinary sum, £25,000 in the twenty-first century; £15 would equate to £2,500.

29 John Harris, *The History of Kent* vol 1 (1719): 'The Preface', i.

30 N Herbert, 'Gloucestershire and Bristol', C R J Currie & C P Lewis eds, *English County Histories* (1994), 154-55.

31 Alette Fleischer, 'The garden behind the dyke: land reclamation and dutch culture in the 17th century', *Icon*, vol. 11, 2005, pp. 16–32. JSTOR, www.jstor.org/stable/23787020. Accessed 30 Jan. 2021.

32 Some pointers to the ways in which maps of this period can be understood have been drawn from the 'Introduction' by Mary R Ravenhill & Margery M Rowe eds, *Devon maps and map-makers: manuscript maps before 1840* (Devon and Cornwall Record Society New Series, 43, Exeter, 2002).

33 Harris, *The artist and the country house*, 92.

EDITORIAL CONVENTIONS

The use of capital letters and the punctuation in quotations from Atkyns have generally been modernised.

Numbered prints. The prints bound into the 1st editions of Sir Robert Atkyns, *The Ancient and Present State of Glostershire*, were not numbered. Prints in the 1724 edition of Nouveau theatre de la Grande Bretagne, which are reproduced here, were numbered very discreetly in the top right-hand corner, but had been marked up for different sequences; although the numbers suggest ordering by alphabetical name of the house, this is not invariable. The index numbers used here follow the order in the 1st edition, as used in the volume reproducing the plates published by E P Publishing Ltd in collaboration with Gloucestershire County Library in 1974.

Orientation. As noted above, the orientation of a Kip engraving may not be completely precise, but an arrow indicating 'north' is inserted on the right-hand edge of the page to guide the reader.

Parishes. The engravings were arranged by the relevant parish, but not all parish names were as written today. Kip headed his engravings with a statement of the owner's name and the name of the house. His spelling was decidedly idiosyncratic. If Atkyns had lived to see the book through the press, would he have asked Kip to alter any of the headings? To identify where a comment by Atkyns on the subject of the engraving may be found, the parish is indicated in square brackets together with the page(s) relating to it.

Postcodes. As a convenient method of finding a site, the post town and postcode have been given for each.

(qv) [*quod vide* – 'which see']. The relevance of maps, drawings and photographs to the text is indicated by (*qv*).

Abbreviations

NGR National Grid Reference

VCH. The Victoria History for the County of Gloucester. Volumes published to date are an invaluable source and the relevant volume number and pages are given in the heading to an engraving wherever available.

THE ENGRAVINGS

2 **Gloster City Tho: Brown Esq. Alderman [Atkyns** 82-83]

'Gloster is an handsom neat City, and yeilds a pleasant Prospect, especially from the west side. It is adorned with many beautif

The western prospect referred to by Atkyns is the subject of the third engraving. This plate, a picture map of the city, is dedicated to Thomas Brown(e) who was appointed an alderman in 1687, and served as mayor of the city in 1691. The heading includes the Browne family shield with 'three lions passant'.

A small, simplified aerial view of Gloucester was produced by John Speed within his map of Gloucestershire published in 1610. Just over a century later Johannes Kip drew his highly detailed version. He has presented a view with north at the top, but has slightly adjusted the orientation so that Westgate street is parallel with the paper. He must have spent many hours walking the streets of the city to produce so many drawings of buildings. A number of those he drew are shown with great accuracy, and although some of these are well-known historically, Kip's views remain the only known record of their appearance. The numbers identifying these in the following four sections are marked with an asterisk. A number of the inn signs projecting out over the road are there, but he must have found too many for his patience in engraving; there were over a hundred known licensed inns in Gloucester in the early part of the eighteenth century.

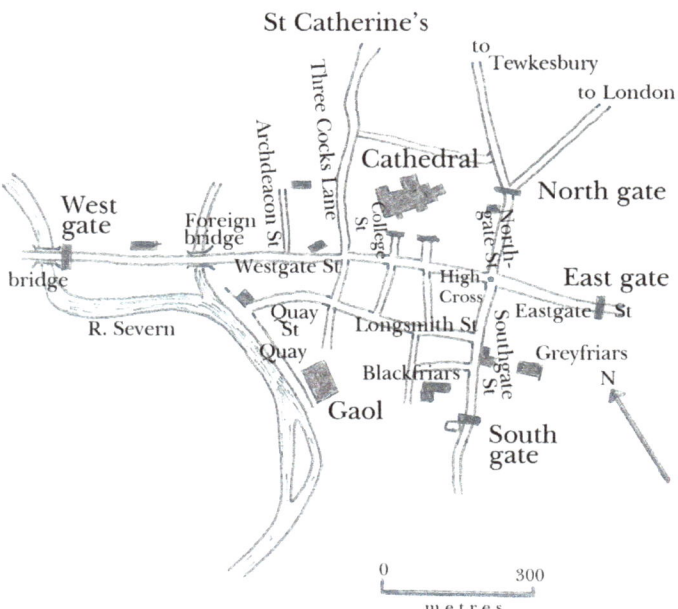

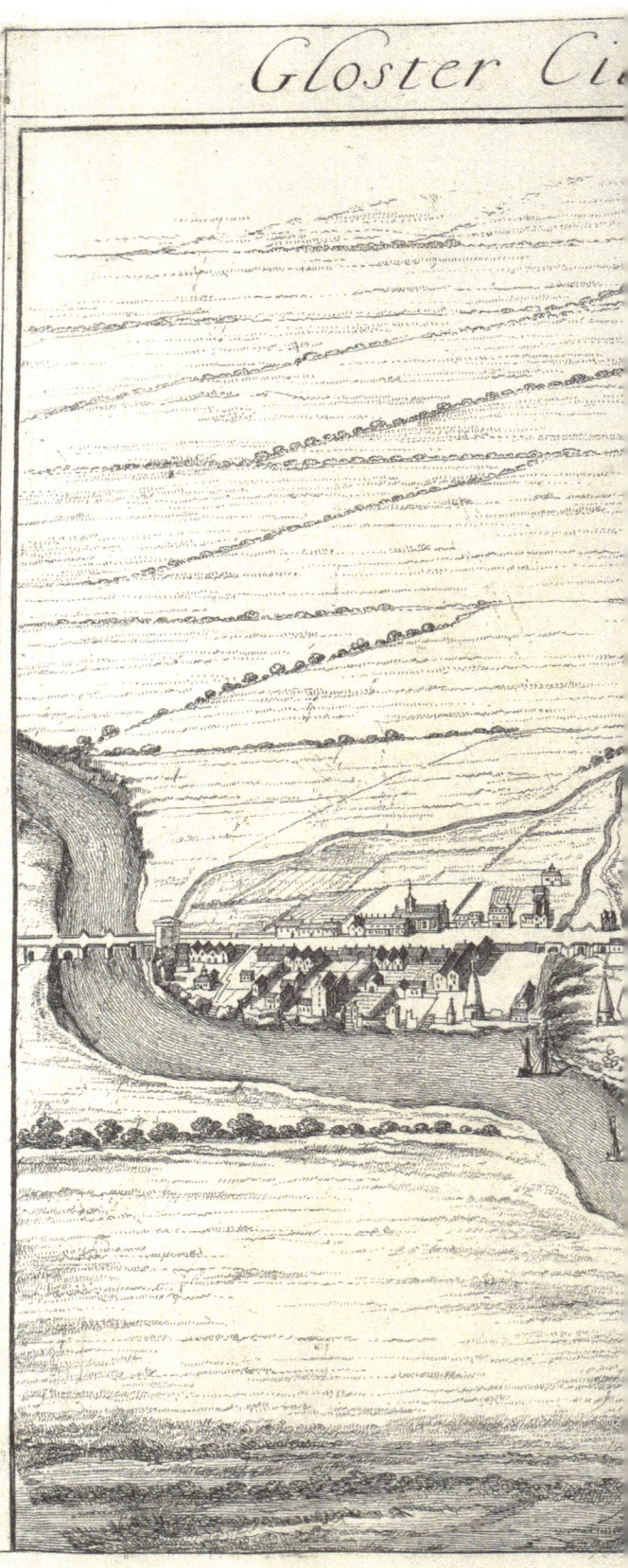

A walk along Kip's streets follows.

VCH IV

wers and spires, and more remarkably with the stately tower of the Cathedral church.'

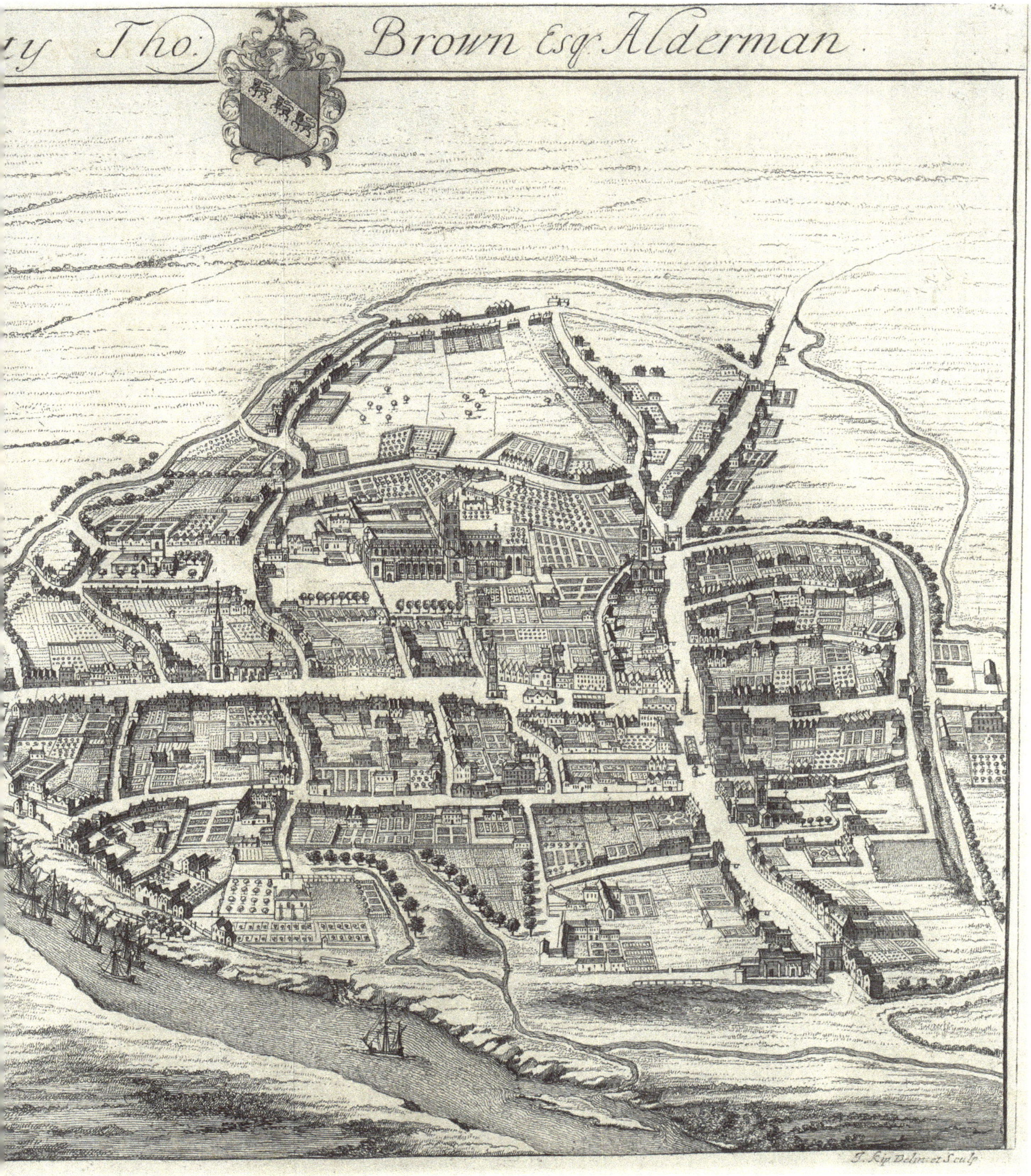

ty Tho: Brown Esq. Alderman

T. Kip Delineet Sculp

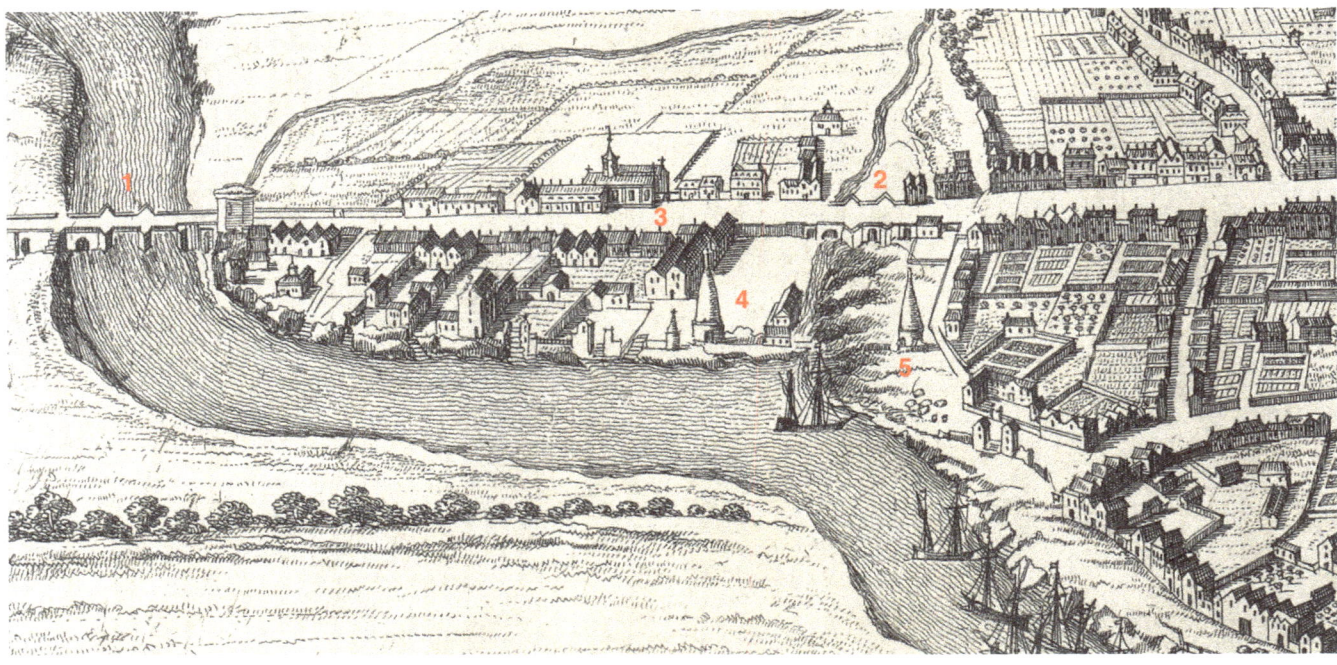

I Gloucester South-West

1 The highway from the west crosses the Severn by way of Westgate bridge and passes through the West gate.

2 A little further on is the medieval Foreign bridge with arches and cutwaters spanning the Old Severn that was once the main east channel of the river. The area between the two bridges is known as The Island as it is surrounded on all sides by water courses.

3 The large building with the small steeple or lantern on its roof is St. Bartholomew's, an almshouse providing accommodation for 59 people. Westgate Street is lined with tenements, shops and inns, but there are more on the south than on the north side.

4 The large conical kiln on the riverside produces lime

for building and agricultural use (later converted for the manufacture of glass vessels). To the west of it, the southern part of The Island contains a variety of trades and industries such as tanneries, felt making and dye works that utilise the river water.

5 The second conical kiln, south of Foreign bridge, was built in 1694 by a partnership that included Thomas Browne, producing glassware for the bottling of the cider commercially produced in Gloucestershire and Herefordshire. To the south of the kiln, the quayside is lined with warehouses and inns providing storage for goods to be transported up river to the Midlands and downstream to Bristol. The little Custom House building stands in the enclosure to the north of the junction with Quay Street.

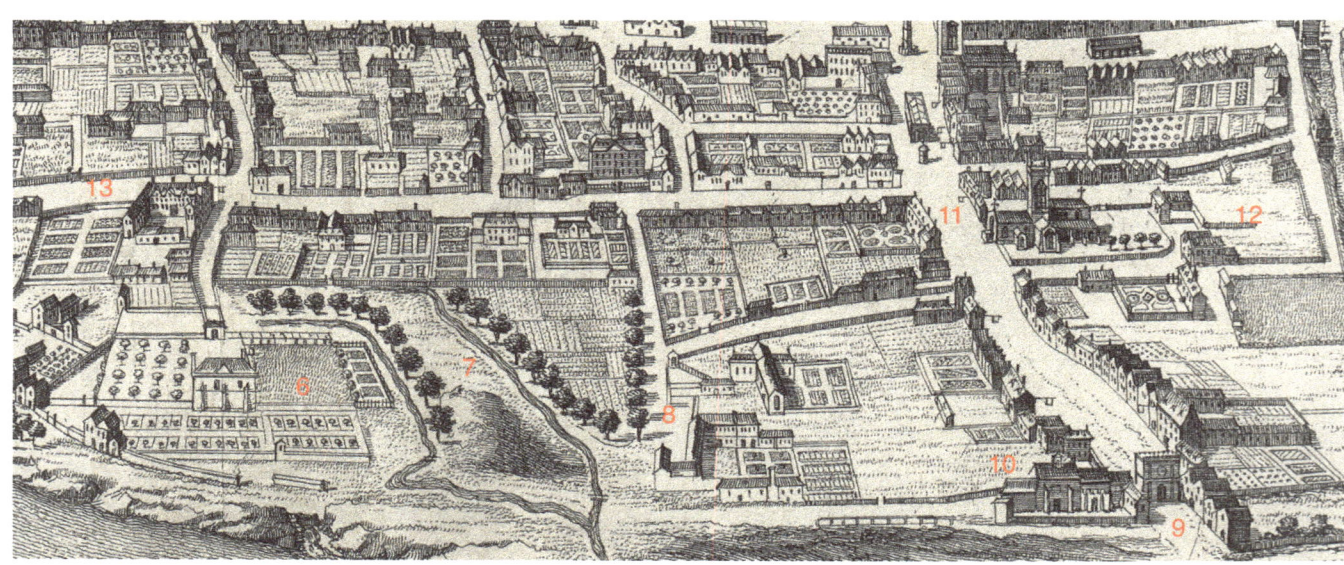

II Gloucester South-East

6 Set back from the quay at its southern end is a large building with a pedimented roof, set within its own grounds. This is Gloucester Gaol, housed within the remains of the medieval castle keep.

7 To the east are two tree-lined watercourses that once formed part of ditch system that surrounded the castle. Between the two streams is a mound known as The Barbican, a remnant of the Norman castle motte.

8 The collection of buildings immediately east of the mound once housed the medieval priory of the Dominicans or Blackfriars. Just prior to 1712 the entire property was purchased by Samuel Cockerell J.P., a particularly unsavoury character, who sold off parts of the priory estate.

9 South-east of Blackfriars is the South gate, rebuilt in 1644 following extensive damage during the siege of the city in the previous year.

10* Close to the gate to the north-east is the Talbot Inn and on its western side stands the ancient chapel of St. Kyneburgh built in the twelfth century to house the relics of this local saint. By the early 1700s it housed the cordwainers hall, with other parts altered in the sixteenth century to an almshouse for six people.

11 The road from the South gate runs northwards, past the ancient parish church of St. Mary de Crypt, to the High Cross which stood at the junction of the four main streets.

12. To the east of the four trees behind the church are the buildings that once housed the priory of the Franciscans or Greyfriars. The grassed area immediately to the south is a newly created bowling green that stretches eastward to the city ditch.

13* The large building with a courtyard on the southwest corner of Castle Lane and Longsmith Street is the New Bear Inn that opened in 1647.

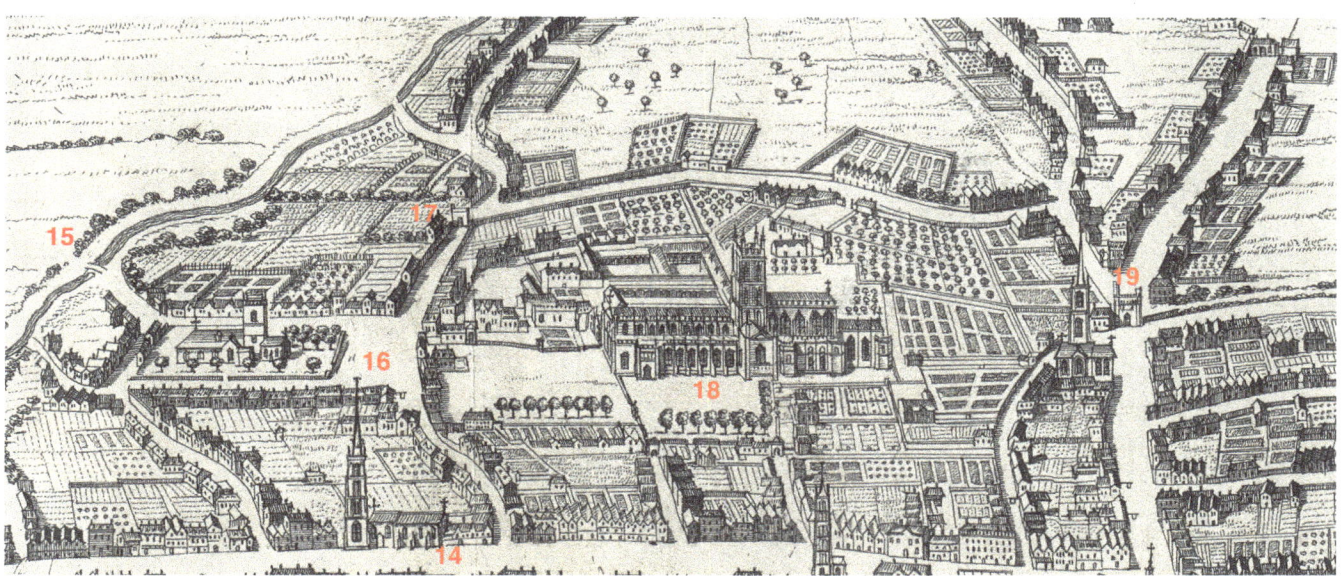

III Gloucester North

14 St. Nicholas church is in the lower part of Westgate Street which stretches from the Foreign bridge to the High Cross in the commercial centre of the city.

15 Just to the west of St. Nicholas's tower and steeple is Archdeacon Street which continues to a small bridge over the Old Severn to give access to grazing pasture in the meadows beyond.

16 To the east of St. Nicholas church is Portcullis Lane, known today as Three Cocks Lane; both names derive from an alehouse. The lane runs northwards past St Mary de Lode.

17* Further north the lane comes to the Blind gate that formed part of the northern defences of the city. Beyond it lie the outer suburbs of St. Catherine Street.

18 The precincts of Gloucester cathedral occupy an area that is virtually identical to that of today, although a number of buildings were added during the eighteenth and nineteenth centuries. The two gates giving access to the cathedral from Westgate Street are clearly shown at the northern ends of College Street and College Court.

19* Just beyond the church of St. John the Baptist is the inner North gate. Outside the gate the road forks; the left hand route is the main road to Tewkesbury and the Midlands, the right hand passes through the Outer north gate to Cirencester and London.

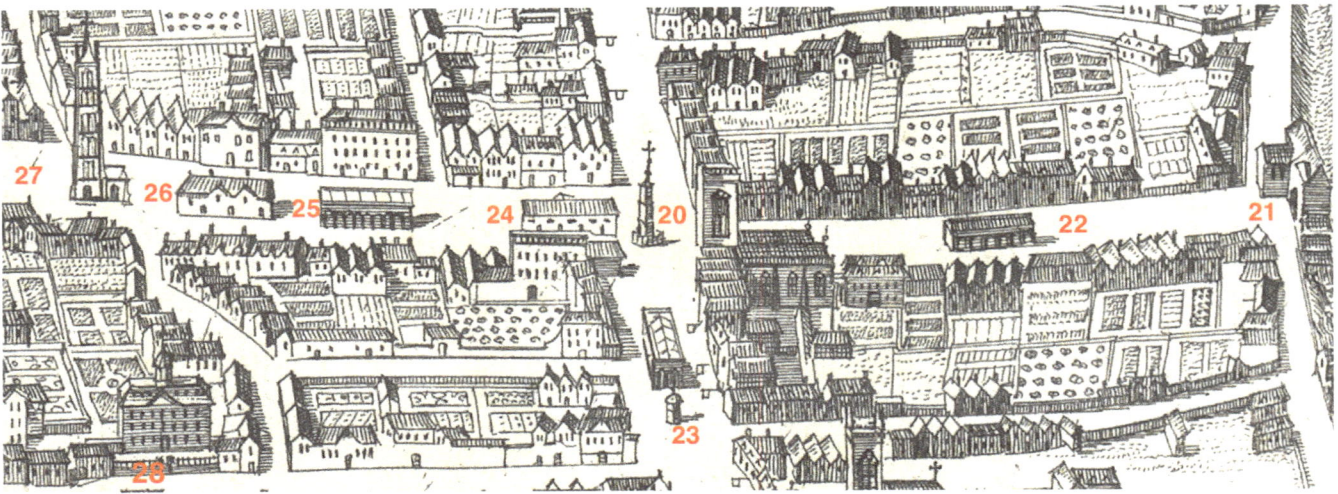

IV The High Cross

20. The High Cross stands at the meeting point of the four main streets. It has been a focal point since the thirteenth century and provides a source of fresh water piped in from Robins Wood Hill.

21* To the east the road leads down to the East Gate of the city, past the church of St. Michael.

22* The building in the centre of the roadway is the Barley market, constructed in 1636 to replace an earlier market that stood nearer to the gate.

23 In the centre of the roadway to the south of the cross is the Wheat market, with a little conduit structure close by. The conduit was built by Alderman John Scriven in 1636 to provide an additional supply of fresh water. This little building still survives in Hillfield Gardens in London Road. Inn signs to the right of the conduit project like flags; one opposite the Conduit belongs to the White Lion, and the one above is the famous Bell Inn, immortalised by Henry Fielding in his book *Tom Jones*.

24 To the west of the cross are four buildings in the middle of the roadway. The first is a row of shops and tenements built in 1495.

25* The second building, with a series of arches in the south wall, is the fourteenth-century King's Board that housed the cheese and butter market. Part of this building survives today in the form of an eighteenth-century summerhouse in Hillfield Gardens.

26 Moving westward, the next building with two gables contains shops and tenements. Directly north of this is a house with a single gable, built in the late sixteenth century by John Browne, a mercer, who was a forebear of Alderman Thomas Browne. The building is better known today as 26 Westgate Street, one of the finest examples of its type and age in Britain.

27 Finally there is the tower of Holy Trinity church. The nave and chancel were taken down in 1699 leaving the tower as a prominent landmark in Westgate Street. A clock and chimes were installed in the upper part in 1702 and the ground floor was storage for the city fire engine.

28 In the bottom left hand corner of the view is the grand Ladybellegate House built c.1704 by Henry Wagstaffe. This drawing is the only known depiction of its original appearance showing a pediment above the façade and a cupola on the roof. These features have been removed, probably in the nineteenth century. The interior contains the largest quantity of richly moulded plasterwork in the rococo style to be seen in Gloucester today.

3 The West Prospect of Gloucester City   To the Mayor and Aldermen VCH IV
Sold by Jos. Smith in London

West Prospect of Gloster Sr John Powell Judge of the Queens Bench

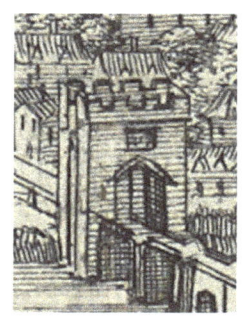

This was the heading on the original 1712 print. The West Prospect was both drawn and engraved by Kip, as were all the illustrations in Atkyns except Badminton, but this plate, in volume 2 of *Nouveau Theatre* published in 1724 containing Kip's Gloucestershire engravings, is an example of how a plate could be altered to suit commercial interests. The updated plate has the modern spelling of Gloucester and a dedication to the Mayor and Aldermen, considerably widening its appeal. No other detail appears to have been changed.

Sir John Powell was the town clerk of Gloucester in 1674-85 and 1687-92; his office was at the Cross, and his house was Greyfriars (*qv 12 in plate 2*). Knighted in 1691, he became a judge of the Queens Bench in 1702. He died in 1713 and a large monument in the Lady Chapel in the cathedral was erected in his memory by his heir, John Snell.

The viewpoint chosen for the Prospect is the high ground at Over, looking generally eastwards. The building in the centre foreground is an inn known as The Talbot, which in more recent times was known as The Dog. The important trade route from South Wales and Hereford crosses the western arm of the River Severn by way of the medieval Over bridge, which leads to the causeway across Alney Island, to the bridge that spans the eastern channel of the river, and to the West gate. Beneath the causeway are a series of arched tunnels that allow the passage of flood water across the island. The restricted width of the carriageway permits single file wheeled traffic only at busy times. Kip has drawn a small carriage, riders and pedestrians. There are two boats above the bridge (*qv*).

A by-pass trackway runs down from the eastern end of Over bridge and runs parallel to the causeway, re-joining it close to Westgate bridge. A little way along this route another trackway branches off to the left along the line of the modern Maisemore Road. The goal post structure between it and the river is the gallows (*qv*), where convicted felons and murderers were hanged following their incarceration in Gloucester Gaol.

This engraving contains a more elaborate view of the crenellated West gate (*qv*) than the map picture, where it was seen from a different angle, emphasising the round towers on the corners. In both, the gate is much larger than the houses. It suggests a little caution in interpreting Kip's pictures. Nonetheless many of the details in the two Gloucester engravings are closely matched. The riverside and Quay have been described. From this angle, the west end and tower of the cathedral dominate the view. To the right is the spire of St. John the Baptist church. The other three churches to the right are St. Nicholas, Holy Trinity and St. Michael respectively. Kip has used a little artistic licence in the siting of these, as from his chosen viewpoint they were directly in line with each other, with the first obscuring the latter two. Further to the right is the tower of St. Mary de Crypt parish church and to its left can be seen the cupola of Ladybellegate House. In the background are prominent hills, Churchdown to the north-east and Robins Wood to the south, and in the centre Crickley Hill, more distant.

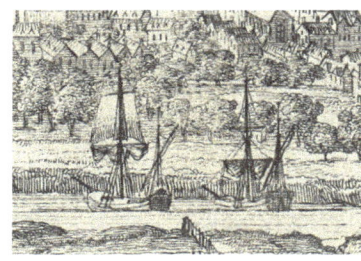

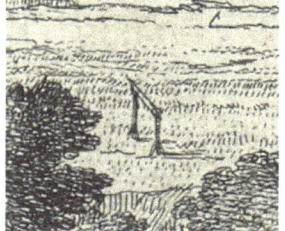

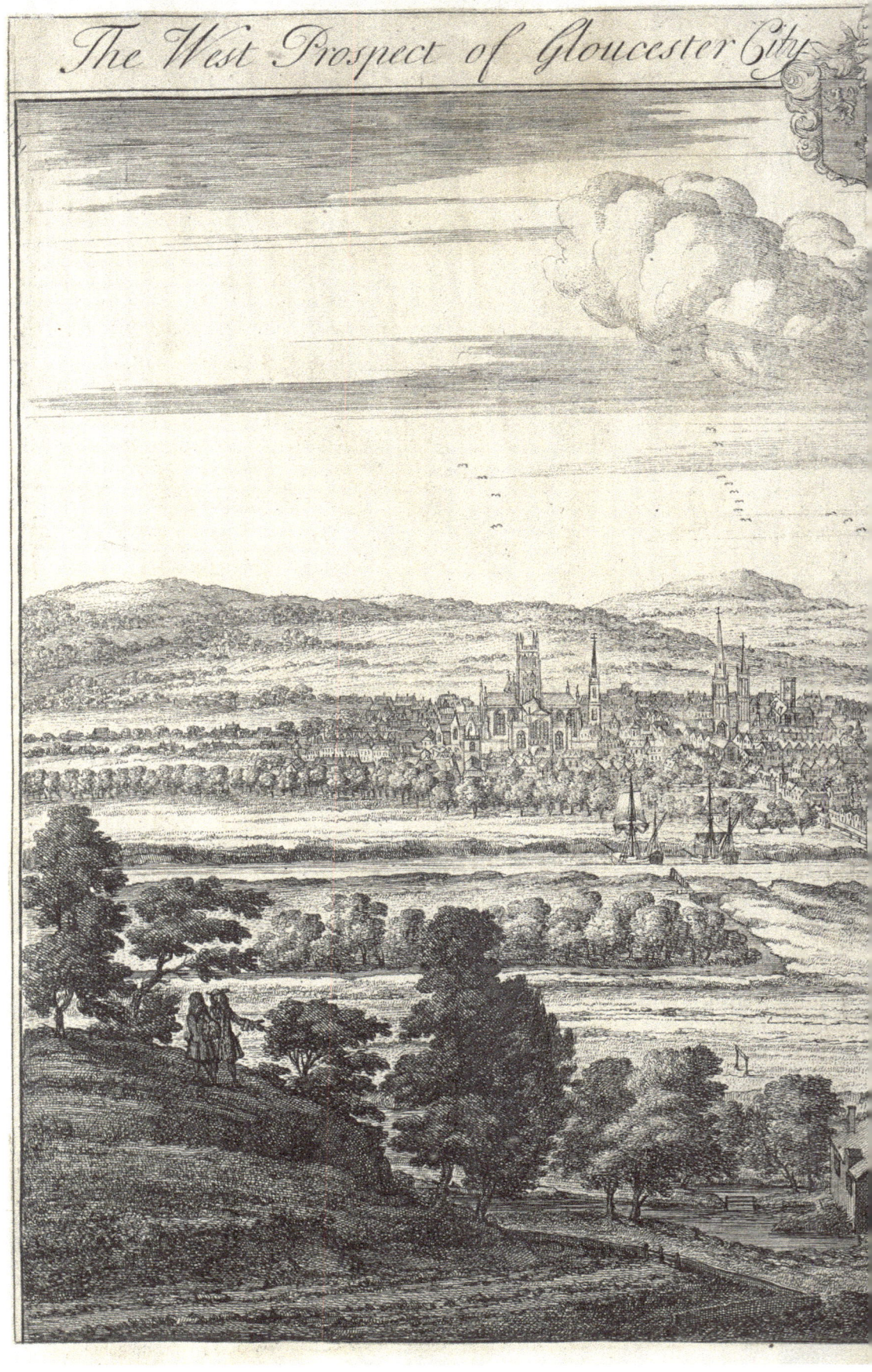

The West Prospect of Gloucester City

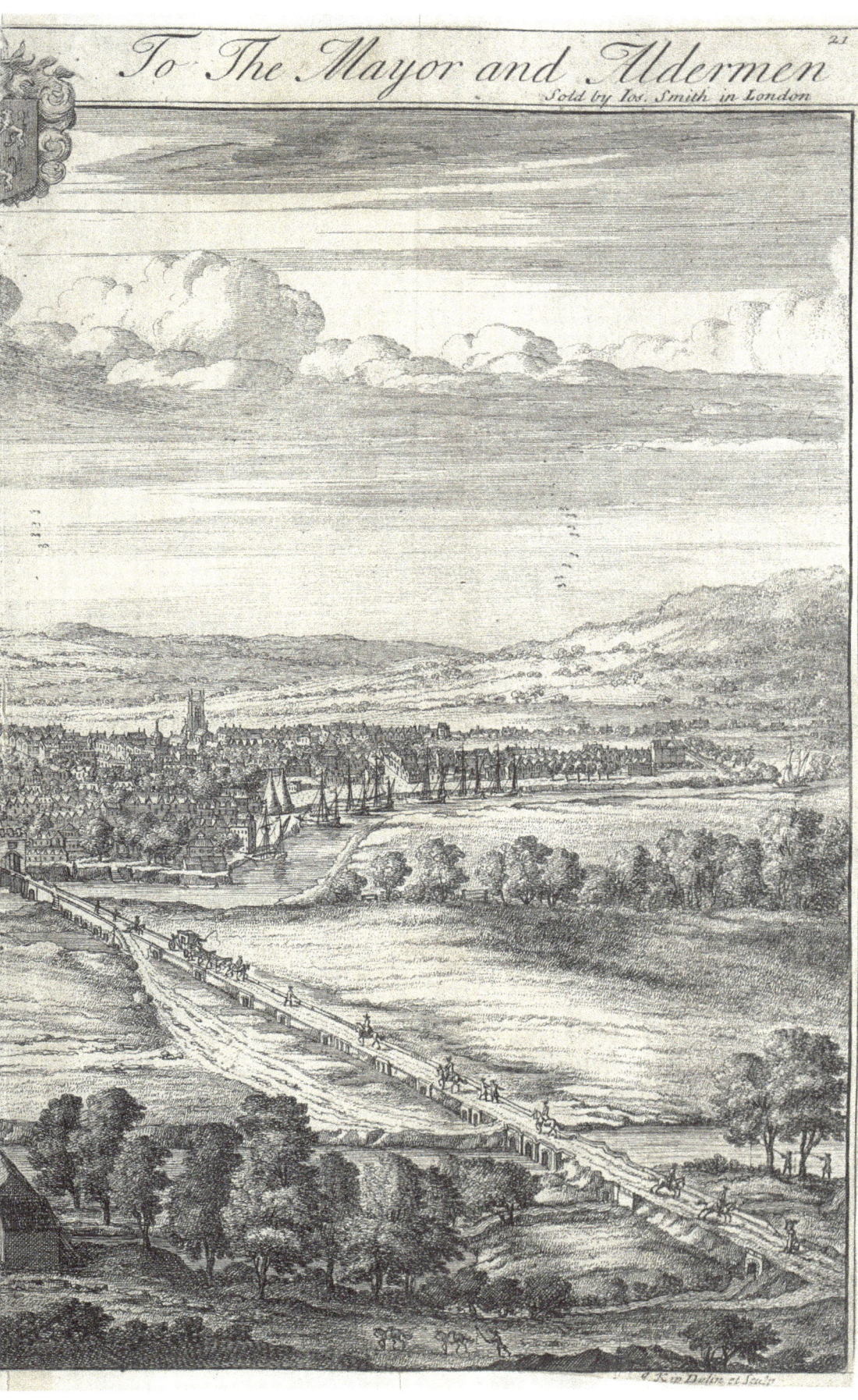

To The Mayor and Aldermen
Sold by Ios. Smith in London

4 **Gloster Cathedral**   *See Introduction*

5 **Wyck the seat of Richard Haines Esq** [Atkyns: Abson & Wyck, 200-201]

' [Richard Haines] has an handsom Seat at Wyke, and a large estate here and in other places of this county. This family hath

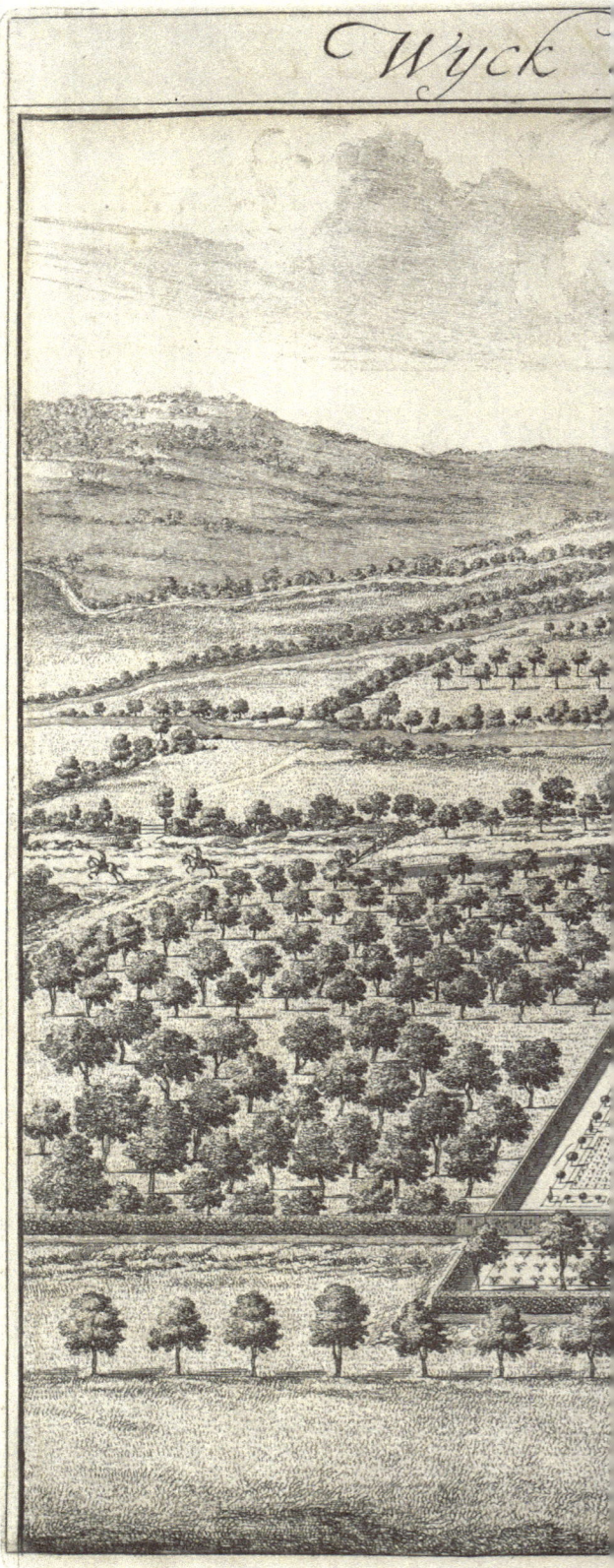

Wick Court and its surroundings have hardly changed in three hundred years; the house is listed grade I. Sir Edward Wynter, lord of the manor in 1608, may have been the builder; an early seventeenth-century doorway is set into a wall, and Wick Court was originally plastered with yellow ochre from his nearby mines. The colour is still evident. His son, John, the Royalist Lydney ironmaster, sold the estate in 1665 to Thomas Haines, a wealthy Westbury-on-Trym grocer, who might alternatively have been the builder. His son was the owner in 1712 and the family remained at Wick Court until 1816.

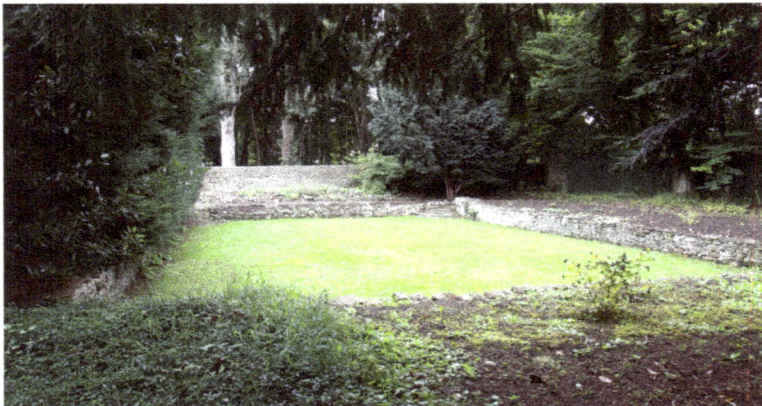

Kip's view is of the south-east garden front; the only change is the roof of the projecting porch and the Ipswich window.

Walls mark nearly all the divisions of the garden, including round a sunken garden (*qv*), though Kip drew some fences; four large yew trees may survive from the formal planting. A gateway with columns topped by balls was a modest sign of pretension, but today simply leads into fields. Beyond it there was an avenue, and some fine trees survive from that period.

The three-storey wings of the entrance front are hinted at beyond the roof-line where a lane leads to the house. There are traces of the small house on the laneside, possibly where servants lived, and wood was stacked for seasoning. The secluded site is close to the river. The four arches of Boyd Bridge carry the highway to Bristol, with a single laden cart coming down the hill, and the back road to Pucklechurch; it crosses the head-race of the estate's corn mill to the west. There was formerly an inn on the far side (*qv*). In the background are Homeapple, Abstone, and Naishcombe Hills.

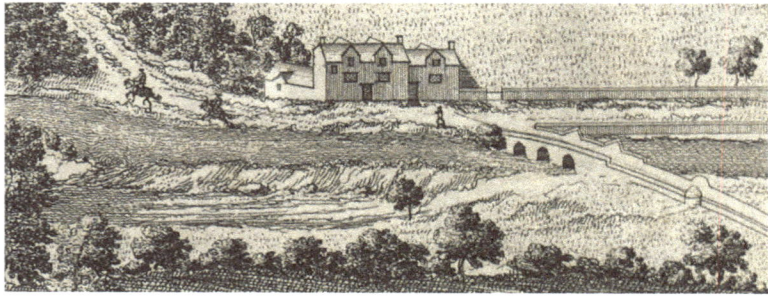

Postcode: Wick BS30 5**RB. NGR: ST** 70056 72665**.**

ong resided in Glostershire'.

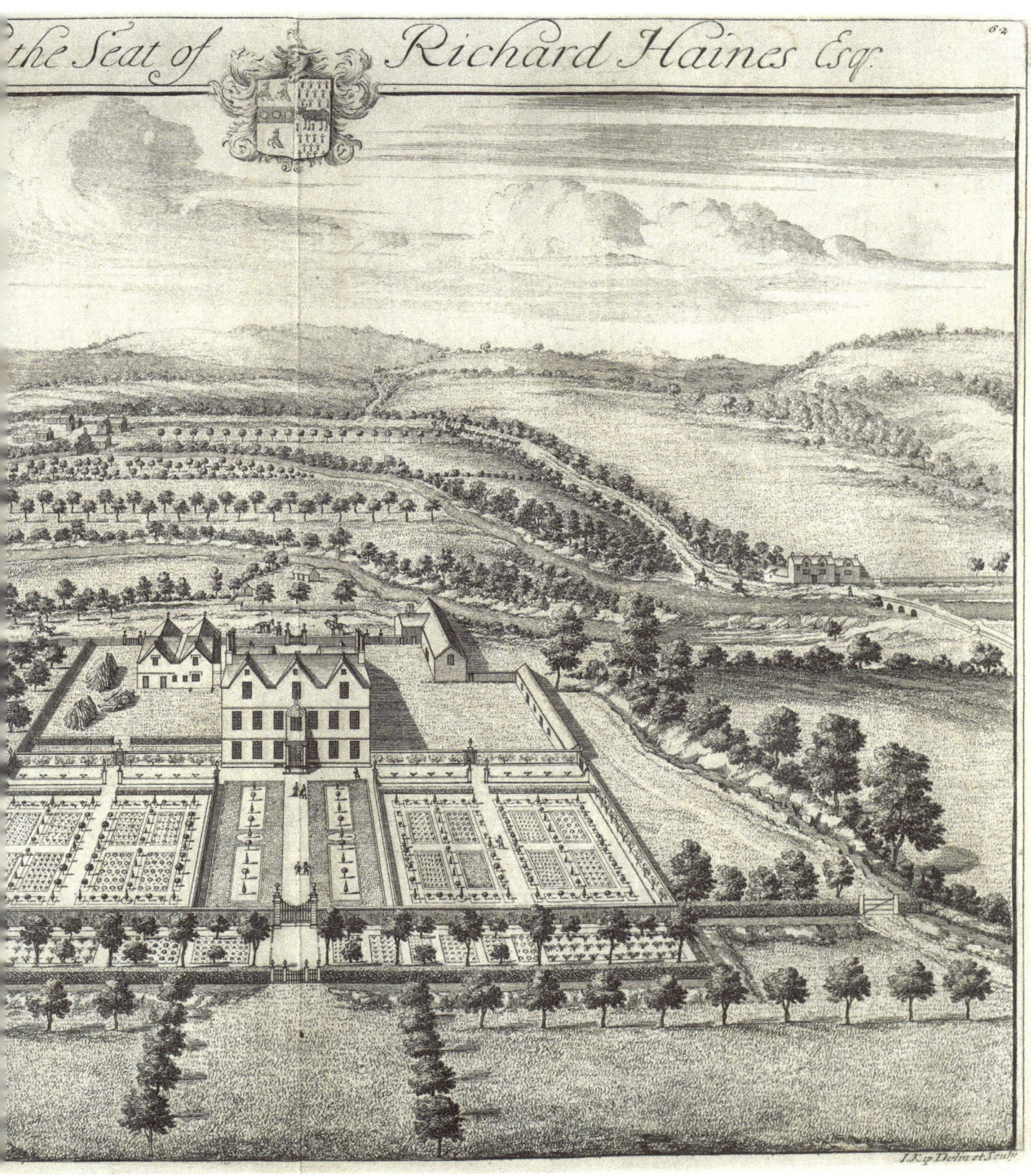

the Seat of   Richard Haines Esq.

6 **Alderly the Seat of Mrs Hale Widdow of Matthew Hale Esq** [Atkyns: Alderley, 208-20~~~

'[Mrs Hale] hath a good house and a large estate in this place. The family of the Hales has been of ancient standing in this

While the house and church occupy the foreground, at Alderley Kip drew houses scattered through the village, as can be illustrated from the tithe map of 1838 (*qv*). Alderley House was built in mid-seventeenth century by a new owner, Sir Matthew Hale, later Lord Chief Justice. Kip's view is of the south front. The gardens are terraced on sharply sloping ground; their style was formal, with beds of flowers and vegetables, and to the west possibly an orchard or grove. All are now much simplified though traces of the layout exist, as in the triangle

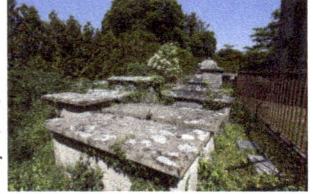

of garden next to the road (*qv* 278 *on map*). The house was rebuilt in the nineteenth century; the garden door became a garden ornament. The church was also rebuilt apart from the tower. Atkyns observed 'a tower at the west end with pinnacles', which Kip drew, including the central one. He also drew the Hale family's chest tombs on the edge of the churchyard nearest the house (*qv*); one is for Matthew Hale, died 1706, leaving his widow in possession when Kip visited Alderley.

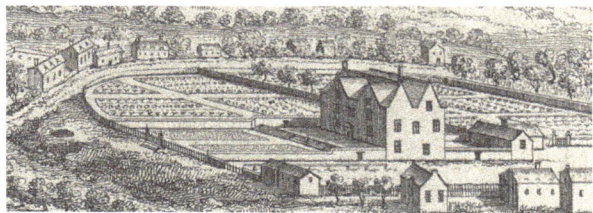

The Hale's Upper House is distinguished by a large garden laid out on a simple cross. Its appearance has been unknown, only its position, but Kip gives us a picture. It was later rebuilt (*qv* 380a *on map*).

Across the road to the east of Alderley manor is The Mount, where Marianne North designed a garden; Kip drew a mount to the south with one tree on top. Immediately north of the church was an apparently medieval house, probably the Rectory. The Grange, where Sir Matthew Hale was born, appears as quite a small house; in 1838 a park adjoined it to the north (*qv* 263a & 264 *on map*).

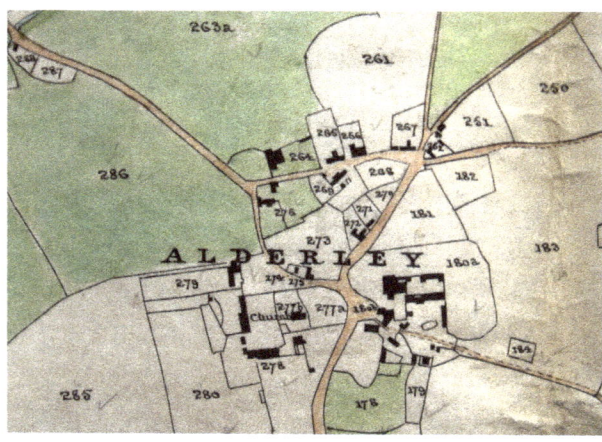

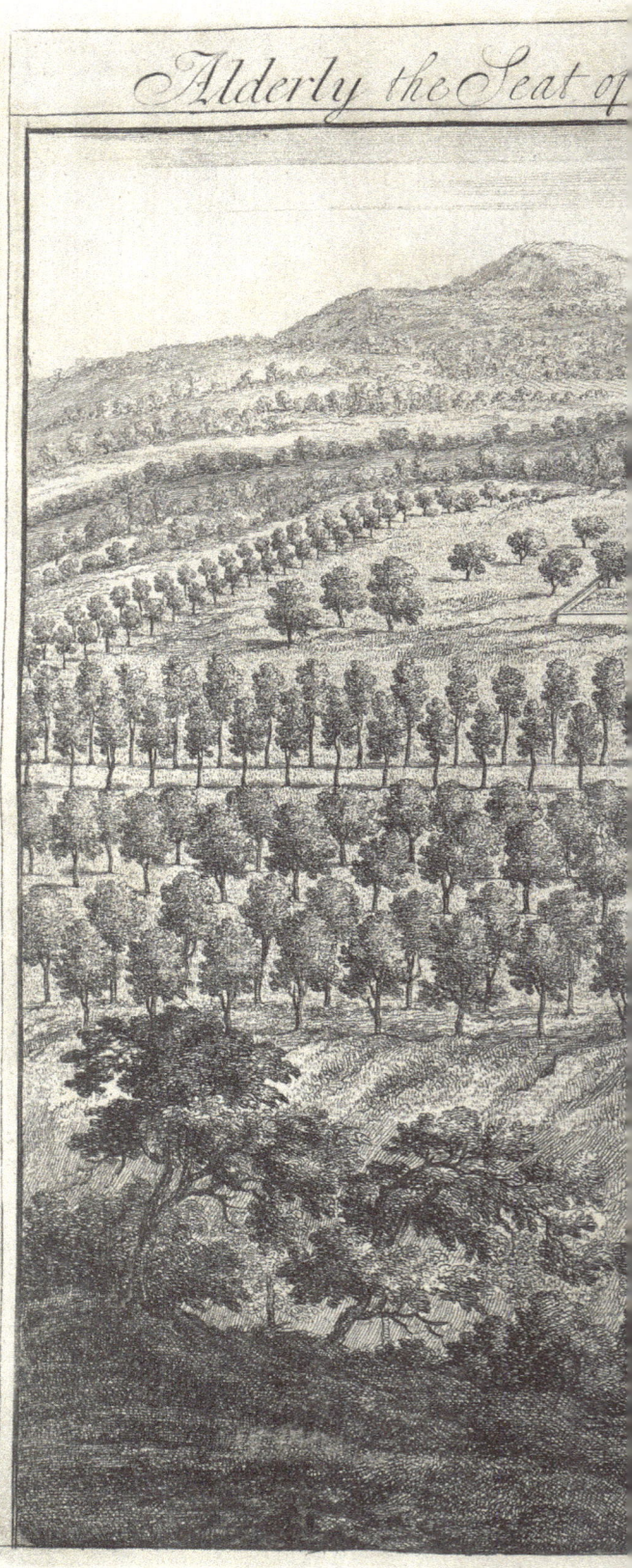

Alderly the Seat of

Postcode: Wotton-under-Edge GL12 7QT. NGR: ST 76812 90765.

county, and always esteemed for their probity and charity.'

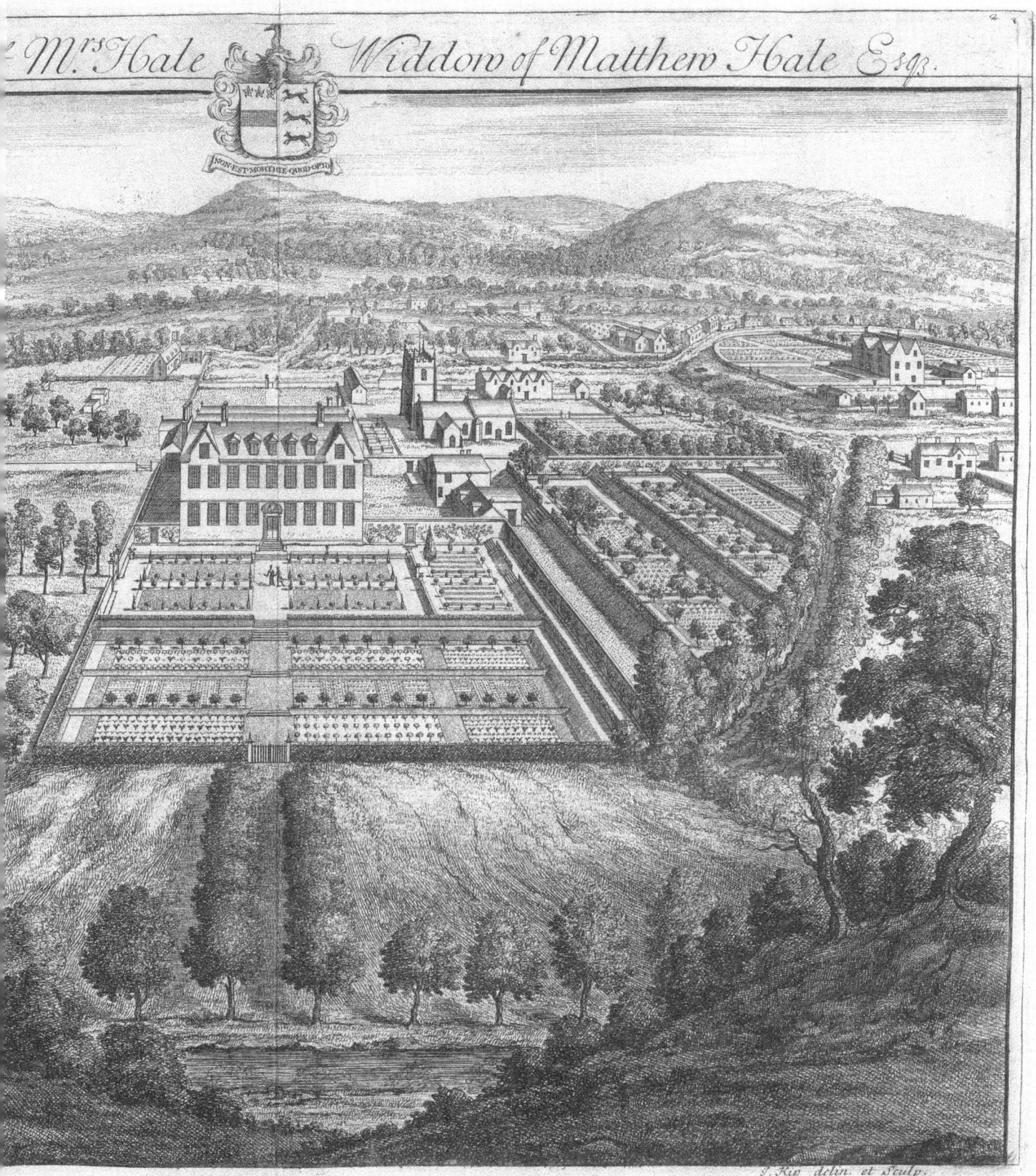

Mrs Hale Widdow of Matthew Hale Esqr.

NON EST MORTALE QUOD OPTO

J. Kip delin. et Sculp.

7 Knole The Seat of Thos: Chester Esq [Atkyns: Almondsbury, 212-213].

'Thomas Chester ... born in the year 1696 ... is the present lord of the mannor, and keeps a court-leet. He hath a large house whence is a pleasant prospect over the Severn into Wales.'

Almondsbury

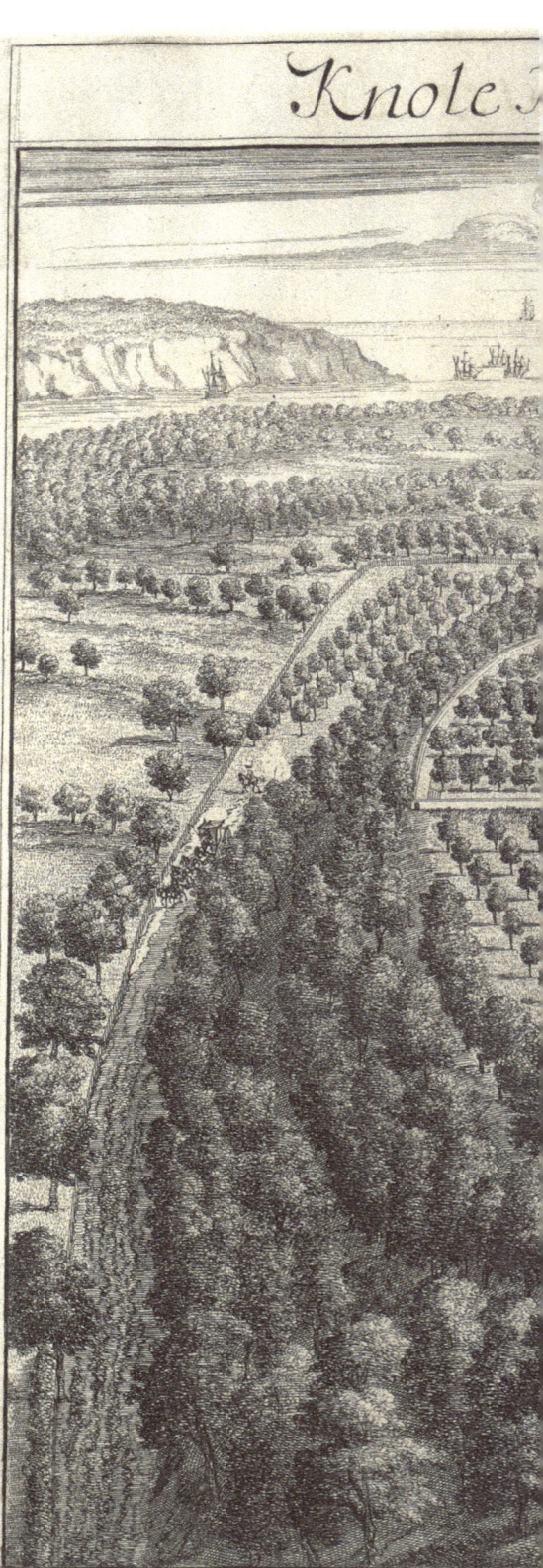

Almondsbury before the Dissolution was one of a string of properties between Bristol and Berkeley controlled by Bristol Abbey. Proximity to a busy water route and major port helped the area prosper. In modern times, situated on a major motorway crossroads, this prosperity continues. The abbey surrendered to the King in December 1539. After some changes of ownership, Thomas Chester bought the manor in 1569, and built a new manor house at Knole, though preserving the former manor house which still stands near the church. Over was a freeholding in Almondsbury manor in the hands of the Berkeley family, who had originally endowed Bristol abbey with the manor. These two houses were able to exercise an influence over affairs similar to that of the abbey, and their histories ran the same course: purchased by wealthy families; their manor houses rebuilt; a period of stability followed by irreversible decline; and eventual demolition.

Knole Park

The horse-shoe-shaped site of Knole Park was originally a multivallate Iron Age hillfort on one of several natural spurs of the north-east to south-west escarpment in this border area overlooking the Severn and its junction with the Avon (*qv map*).

By the fifteenth century an octagonal lookout tower had been built, later made part of the Elizabethan manor house. (Kip has drawn angled sides but later drawings suggest the tower was round.) The Severn some miles away forms the background to Kip's engraving.

Thomas Chester, a merchant, then mayor of Bristol, bought the site, a short distance from Almondsbury, in 1569, and he or his son William built the new manor house portrayed by Kip. Later additions and refenestrations left irregular elevations, and Kip shows a splendid site

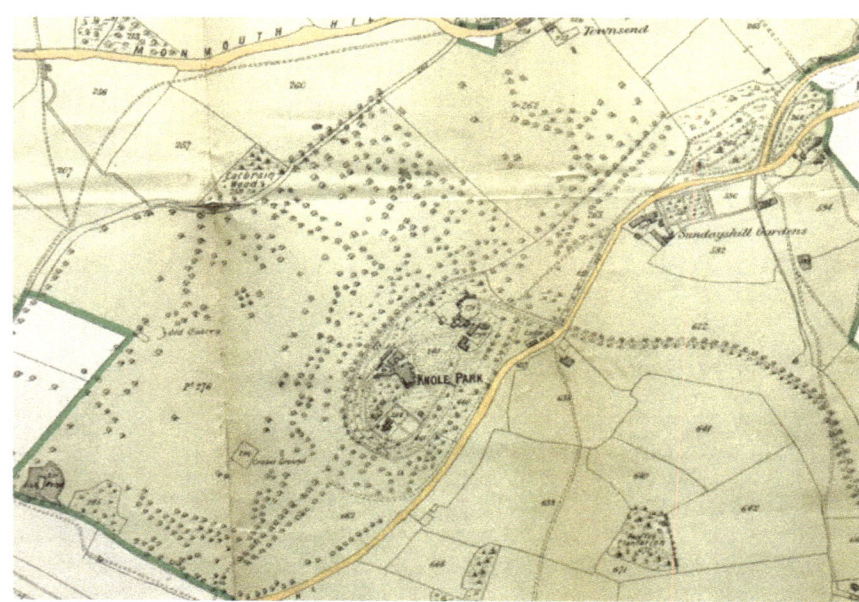

Postcode: Almondsbury BS32 4**BS. NGR: ST** 596834.

called 'Knowl', situated in the middle of a park, upon a high hill, surrounded with a double ditch and rampire, from

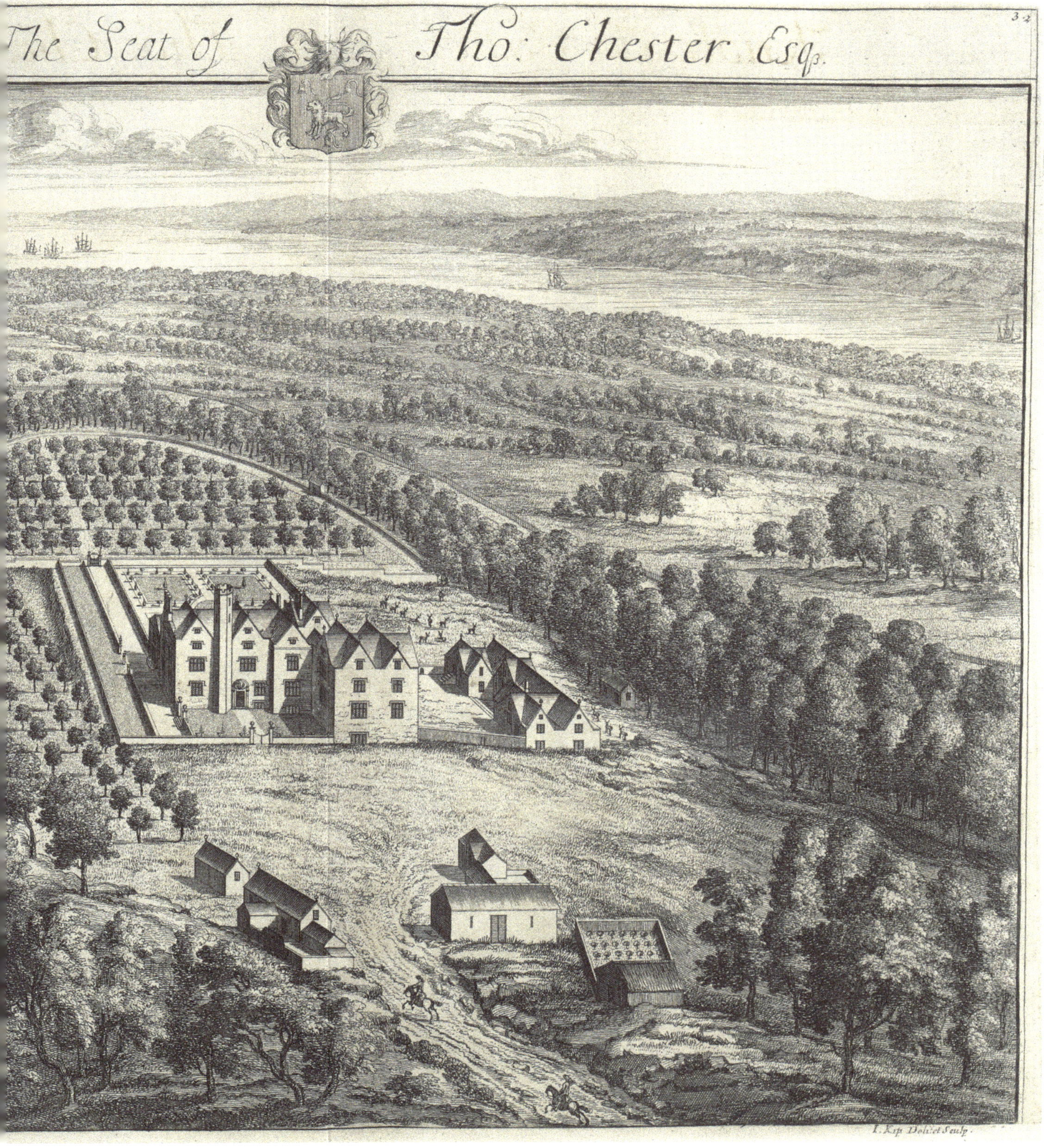

The Seat of   Tho: Chester Esq.

occupied by a disappointing jumble of buildings. A
park amid the trees was stocked with deer, pictured
close to the house, and Kip drew the park pale
running on the low-lying land below the hillfort.

The house faced north-east. It consisted of
a three bay, three storey block plus attics, with the
tall tower by the entrance (*qv*); a two bay, three
storey square block was added to make an L-shaped
entrance front, behind which is a smaller square
block. All faces are copiously gabled. The rear
looks on to a meagre walled garden and the rising
headland beyond. Except for the service range east
of the house, the estate buildings, barn, stables, and
storehouses are scattered some distance from the
entrance.

An engraving of the house which
accompanied sales particulars of 1892 shows that
in two hundred years there had been little change

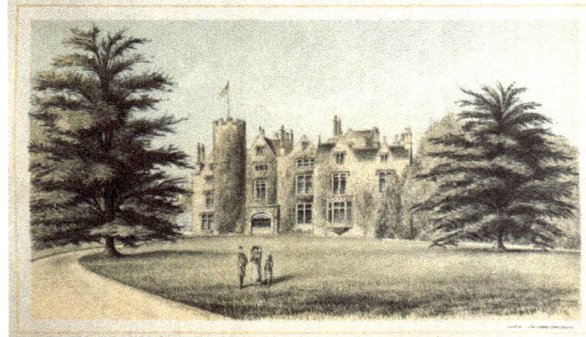

(*qv*). The house was demolished in 1970 except
for the tower, which was reduced in size and
incorporated into a modern house where it appears
completely out of proportion. Also surviving is the
Grade II listed lodge (dated 1731) at the entrance
on Over Lane. Much of the rest of the site has been
given over to modern housing.

8 Over the Seat of John Dowell Esq [Atkyns: Almondsbury, 214-215]. Postcode: Almondsbury BS32 4DG. NGR: ST 58691 82309.

*'John Dowel … is the present lord of the mannor,
and keeps a court-leet, and hath a large estate, and
a pleasant seat in the middle of a park, in which the
tracts of a large round camp are still visible'.*

The manor house of the Berkeleys, built
about 1347 in the small village of Over, was
demolished in 1590 and replaced with a late
Elizabethan building for John Dowell, Bristol
merchant and customs official, whose descendants
lived there for two centuries. Kip's view shows a
house of two storeys plus gabled attics, the south-

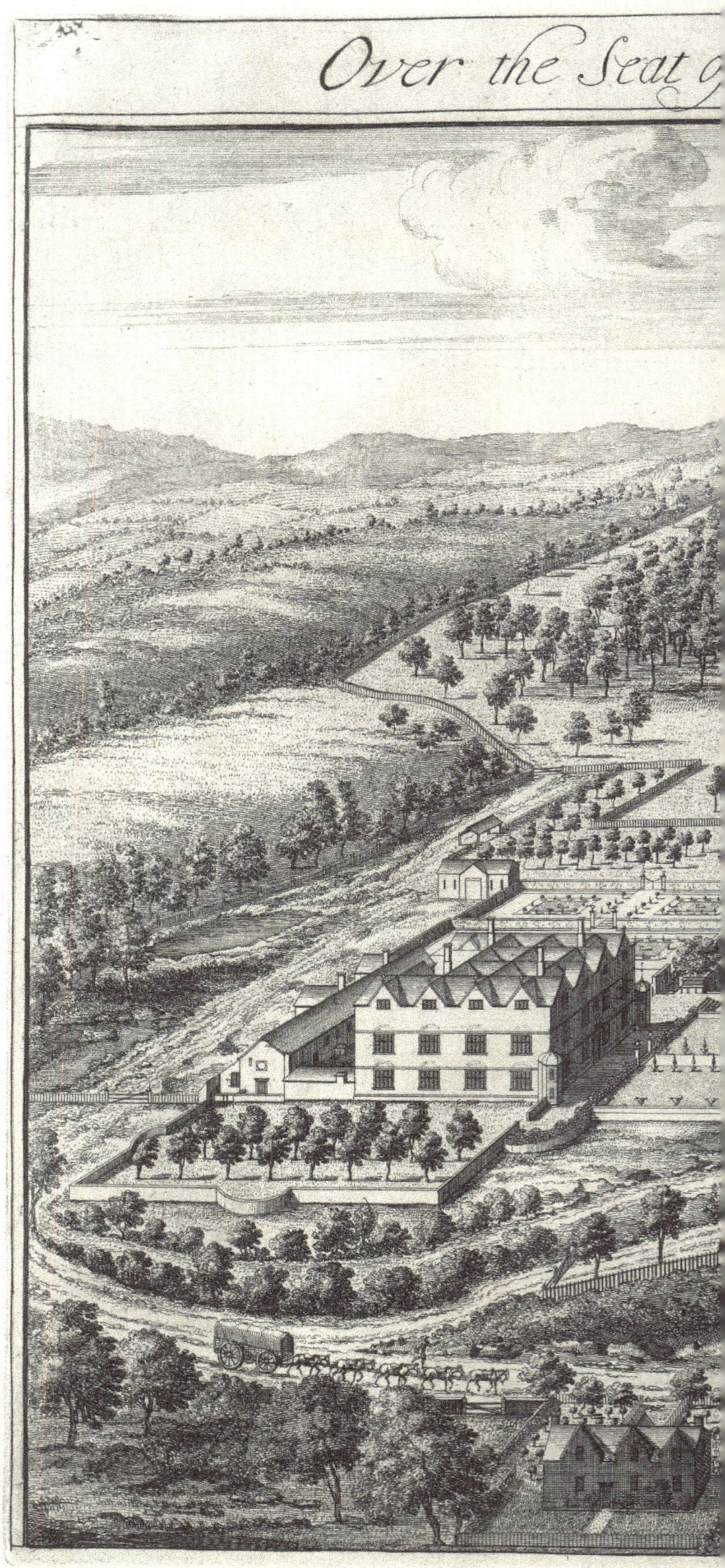

Over the Seat o

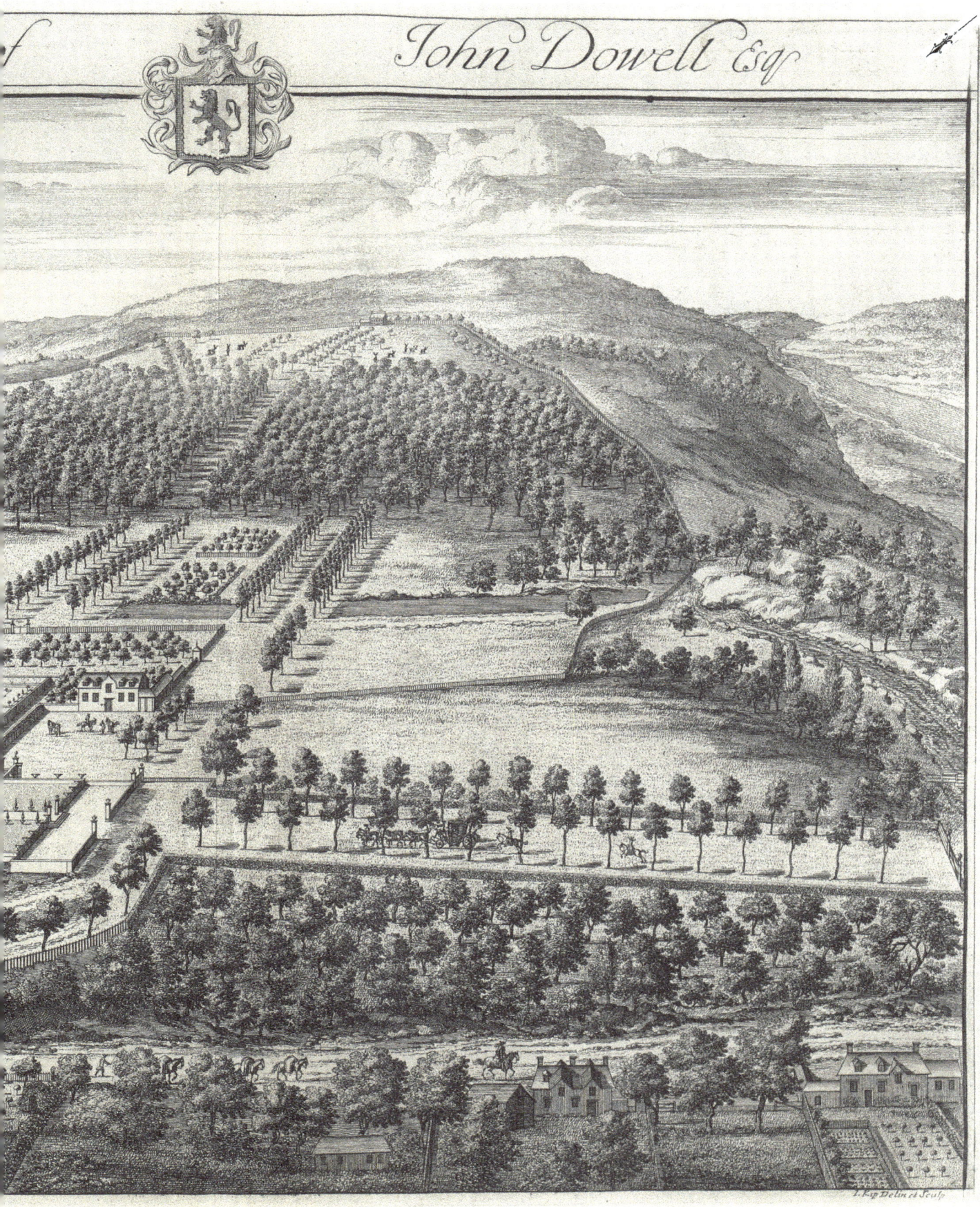

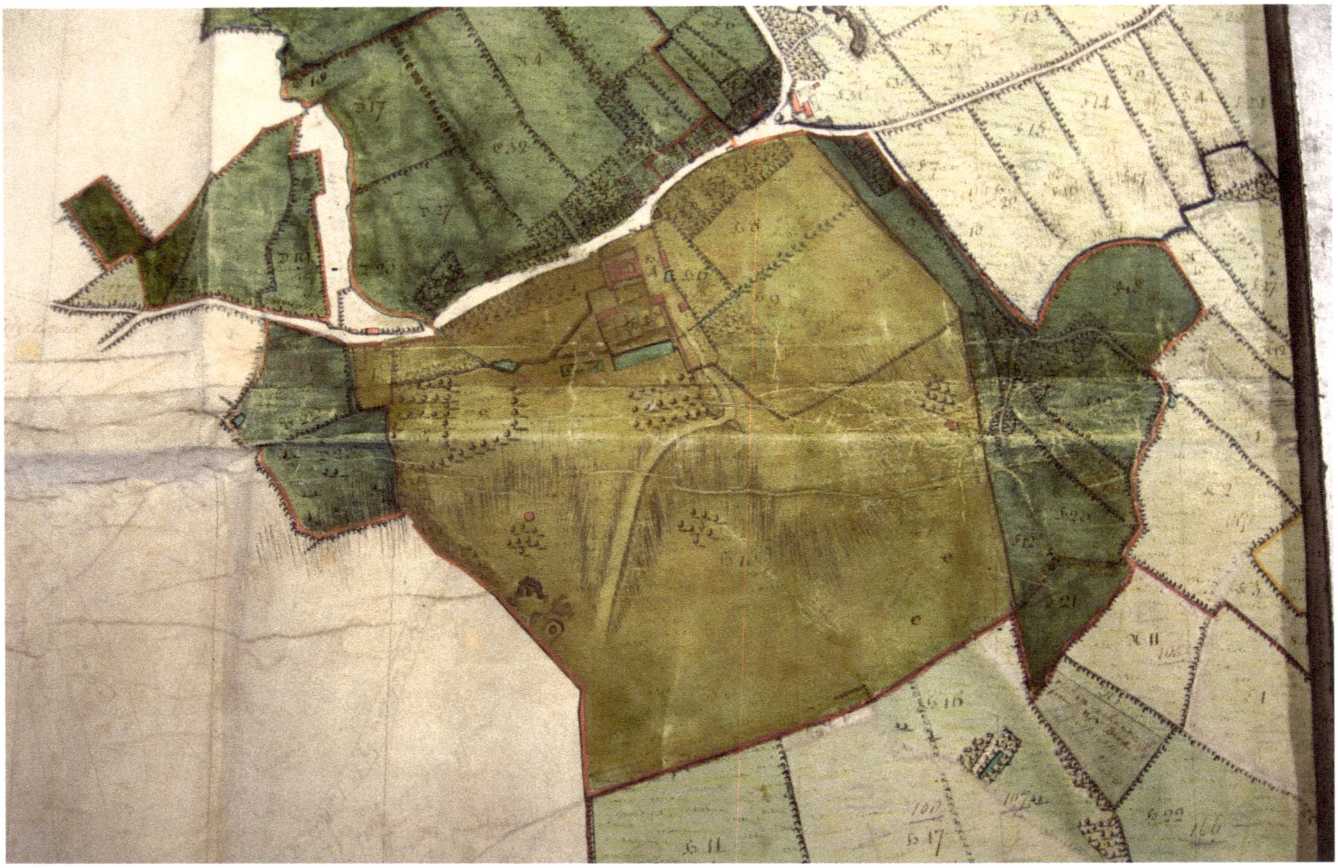

west facing entrance front looking over a lawned square to a wide tree-lined carriage approach. Service ranges at the rear have fishponds beyond. A small house with a court may have been for the estate steward. Despite the rectilinear layout of the immediate surroundings, formal gardens were not a major feature.

Over Lane, which is the village street with well-spaced crofts, is at the bottom of Kip's drawing, and is to the north-west of Over Court. Ferdinando Stratford mapped Over Court estate in 1756 (*qv*), and while he did not draw a picture of the house, the layout of buildings, water, and the avenue forming the entrance gradually converging on Over Lane, confirm Kip's engraving.

At the top of a wide central avenue through the wooded slopes of the park there is a keeper's lodge with a herd of deer pictured close by. The lighter green on Ferdinando Stratford's map marks the area of the park, which Atkyns observed surrounded the house. Kip shows the park pale very clearly. A deer park had been created in the thirteenth century but appears to have been extended and become less extensively wooded later in the eighteenth century. The owner in 1901 said it had been enclosed for 'several centuries' and that the herd of fallow deer had been maintained ever since.

A detached rusticated archway, listed Grade II*, a very elaborate and decorative structure, was built about 1750 after the stables and coach-house had been relocated and a new entrance drive created, and these are all that remain after a major fire in 1977. The site was cleared and built over after 1980.

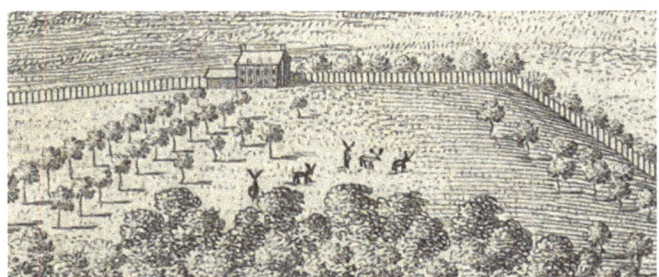

9 Alveston the Seat of Edward Hill Esq [Atkyns: Alveston, 216-217].
Postcode: Rudgeway BS35 3SQ. NGR: ST 63191 86497.

'Edward Hill esq … is the present lord of the mannor; he hath a large handsome house by the church, and a great estate in this and other places of this county.'

Assuming that Johannes Kip did not exaggerate the architectural grandeur of Alveston manor house, it was almost certainly at its zenith when he made his engraving, with a new south-facing wing (demolished in the late eighteenth century) and a balustrade in front of the roof of the older portion. Behind the new wing Kip drew a ladder laid on the tiles, leading to a viewing platform above the roof, also surrounded by a balustrade, though no one is standing there as they are at Henbury (*qv*). To the north-east the view was of ships sailing up the River Severn and on the far side the hills of the Forest of Dean, both visible in Kip's engraving. Today the river is obscured by trees (*qv*).

Edward Hill, whose seat it was, probably acquired the house a few years before Kip's visit. Nicholas Veel was the previous owner, possibly the builder of the fashionable south wing; he died in 1703 and was buried in the church. Nicholas Veel, his grandfather, built an entrance on the west front which has the Veel coat of arms and the date 1588 over the doorway, reflecting almost certainly the year he had acquired the house. Parts of the building are older than this, but the elaborate ceiling with its Tudor roses in one room would likely be his work.

As Sir Robert Atkyns explained, Edward Hill had 'other places in this county' and Alveston clearly did not receive long-term attention. An estate map by Ferdinando Stratford of 1756 suggests that the house, its garden and its avenue had remained static except more areas were planted with trees, perhaps fruit trees (*qv*). A map of 1809 shows the boundaries of the garden intact,

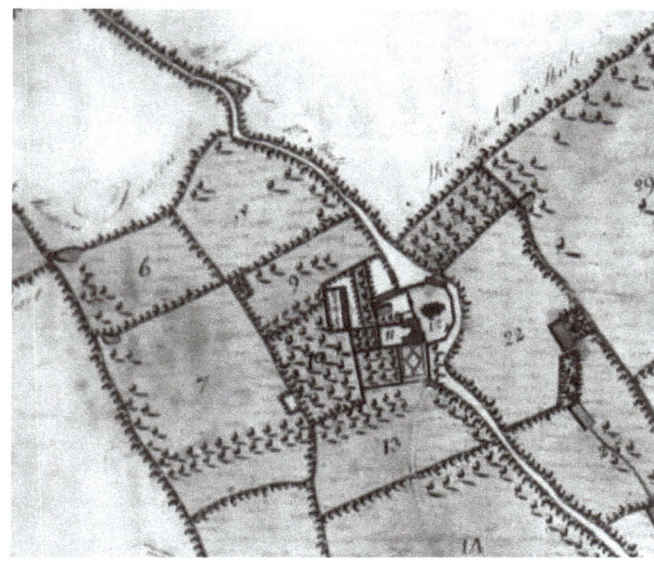

but the south wing with its twin sundials (*qv*), vanished.

No longer called Alveston Manor, it is now Old Church Farm. In 1885 a wealthy resident built a new church near his home. The ancient St Helen's, a dedication indicative of early origins, was abandoned (*qv*). The church and a small part of Alveston had belonged to St Peter's Bath in the early tenth century, and the house as well as the church site may be very ancient. It is interesting that Bath Abbey's manor was squeezed between Tockington park to the west and the King's much larger Domesday manor and park of Alveston to the east; the boundaries appear in Kip's engraving,

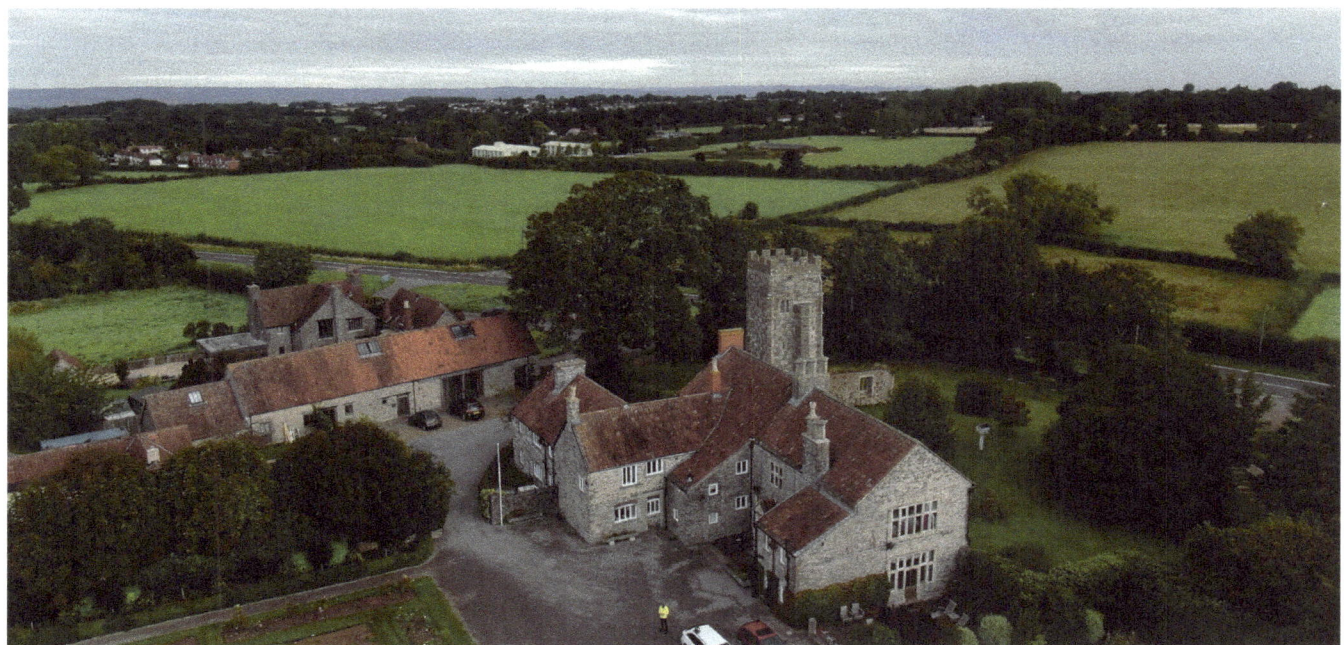

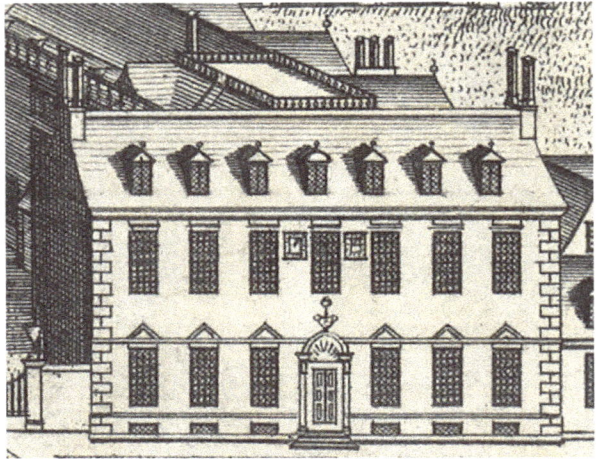

that of the King's manor very close to the curving churchyard wall. In the 1960s the church was shamefully demolished as a Civil Defence exercise, save its tower. The curving road, suggesting a round churchyard, was brutally straightened.

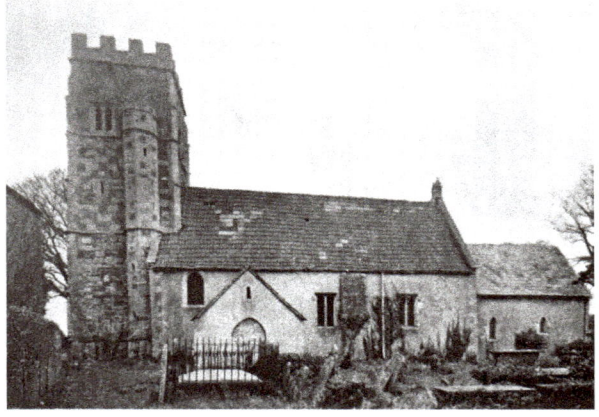

All that said, Kip's manor house and the footprint of the gardens surrounded by walls as Kip drew them, survives. Two buildings of the stable yard still stand. The great yew tree in the churchyard remains, in the position where Kip placed it. The house, though reduced in height and re-arranged internally is a truly magical place, retaining much that Edward Hill would recognise.

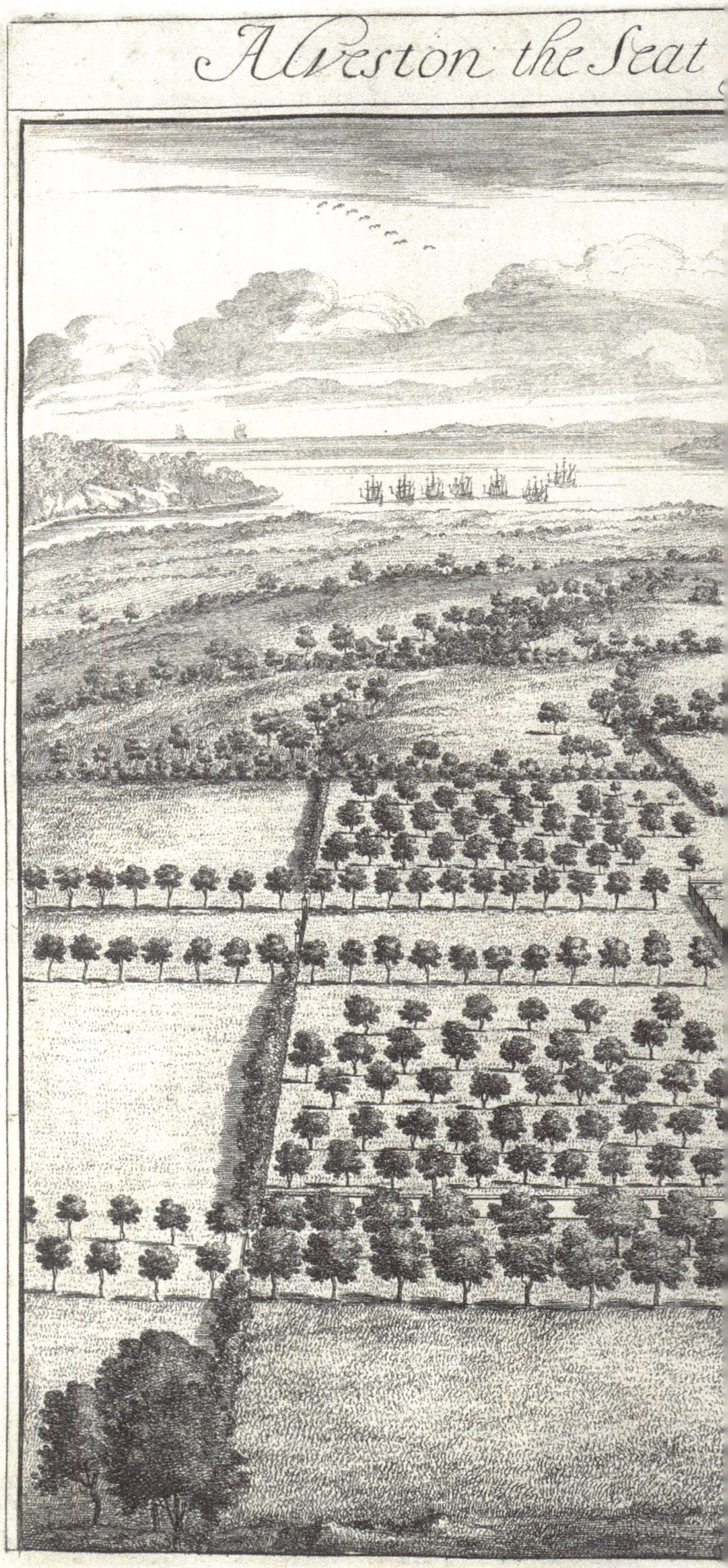

Alveston the Seat

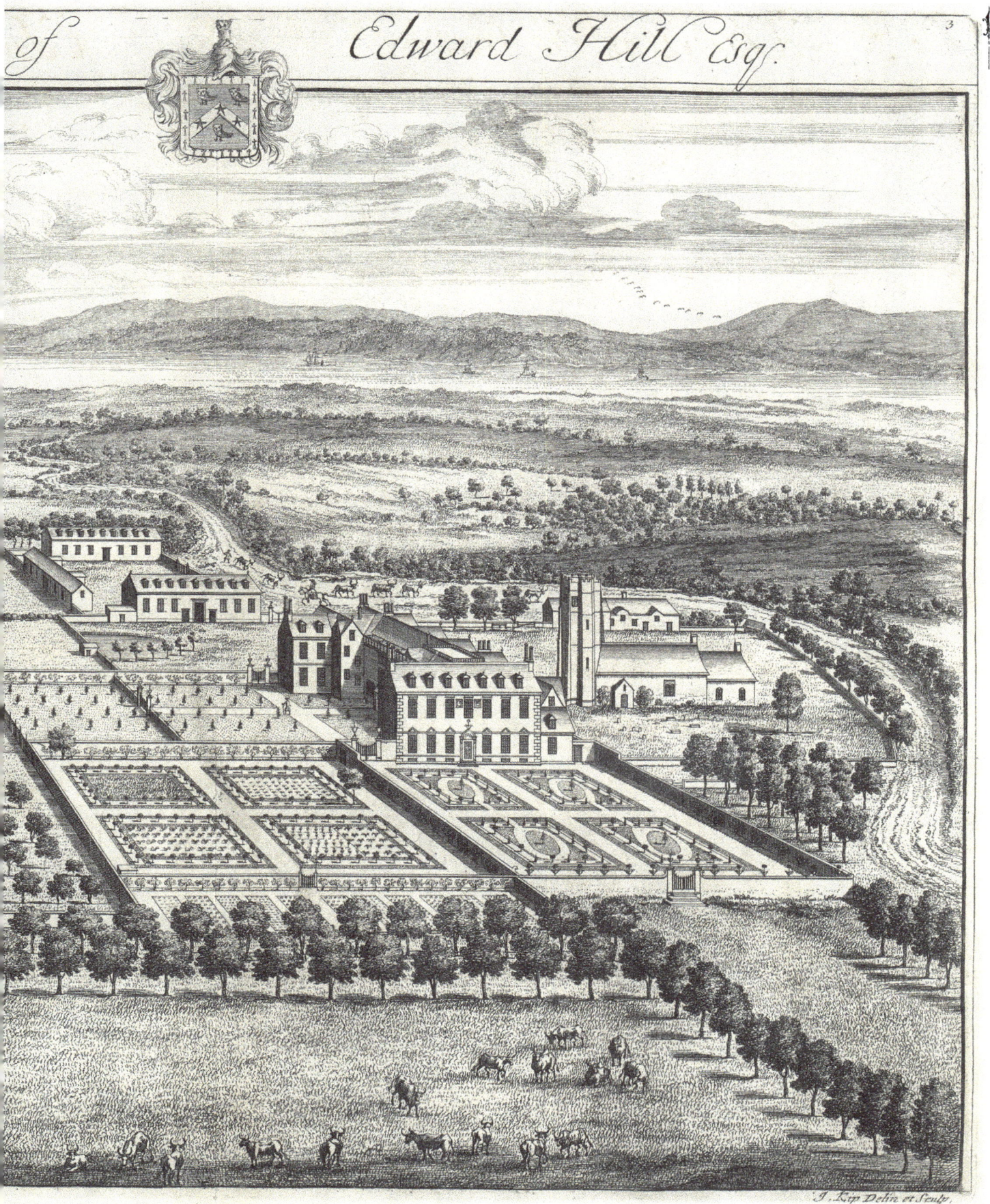

of *Edward Hill Esq.*

J. Kip Delin et Sculp.

10 Amney Crucis the Seat of Robert Pleydell Esq [Atkyns, Amney Crucis, 218-219].

'Robert Pleydel was High Sheriff of the County in 1682 and is the present lord of the mannor of Holy-Rood Amney, and has a

The spelling 'Amney' reflects the pronunciation, but the intrusive 'p' appears to have been introduced by the church in mid-sixteenth century. The church is dedicated to the Holy Rood. Kip drew the base of the late-fourteenth century cross in the churchyard, but it was without the head which was found in 1860. The church, however, with the dominating tower, is not much altered since his engraving.

Ampney Crucis manor was granted to John Pleydell in 1562 and the house (listed grade II) is late sixteenth century with a large eighteenth century extension to the north and nineteenth century additions. Alterations had begun before Kip's visit as he shows a door with classical doorcase in the wall of the parlour, leading to a long flight of steps. At the south side of the house the terracing is still extant, where Kip drew fashionable urns and fastigiate yews. The walled deer park, where he drew a herd of deer, is separated from the formal gardens by a haha and iron railings. Avenues, no longer in evidence, led through the park; but in the distance, leading out of the park, the curved wall and gate remain.

The Ampney brook runs to the west and south of the park and the road still runs close to the brook for a short distance, but now is within the walled area. It once fed a corn mill, and the two streams join close to the bridge over which a carriage from the big house had probably just passed (*qv*).

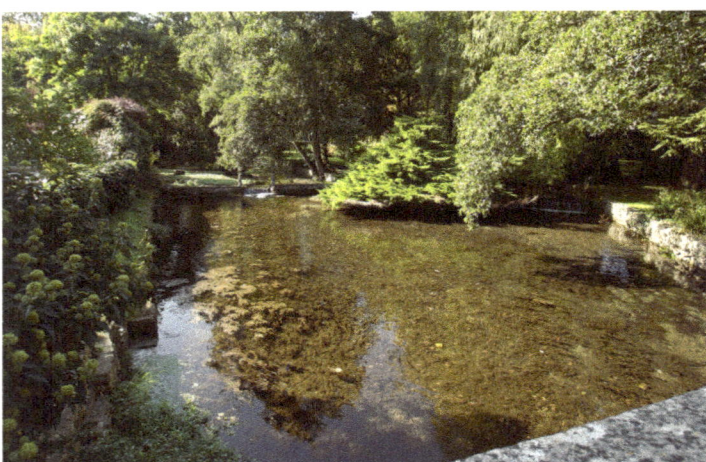

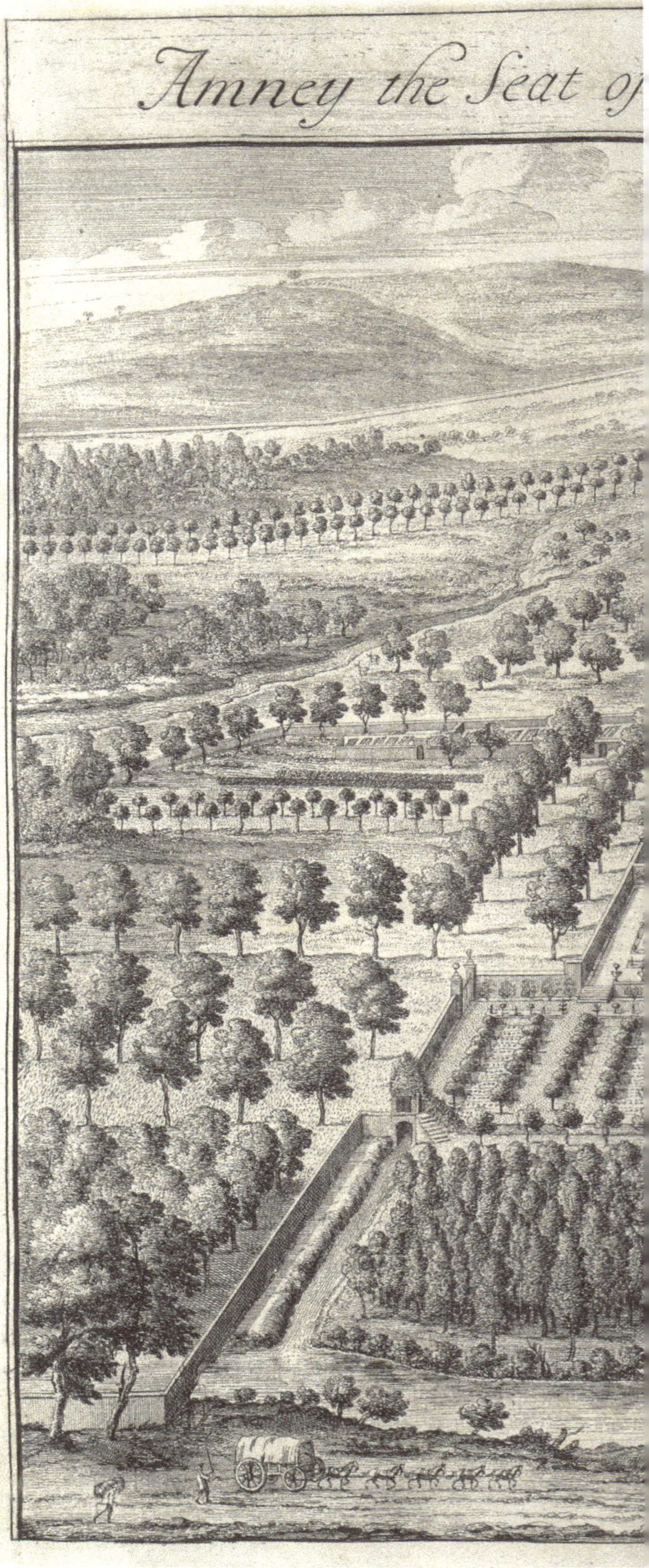

The house passed out of Pleydell family ownership in 1765 and continued as a private residence until 1982; a hotel for a short period, it has returned to private ownership. The water gardens and pleasure gardens adjoining the house are being maintained.

Amney the Seat of

Postcode: Cirencester **GL**7 5**RY. NGR: SP** 06455 01902.

arge house near the church, with pleasant gardens and a delightful park adjoining, with a clear river running thro' it.'

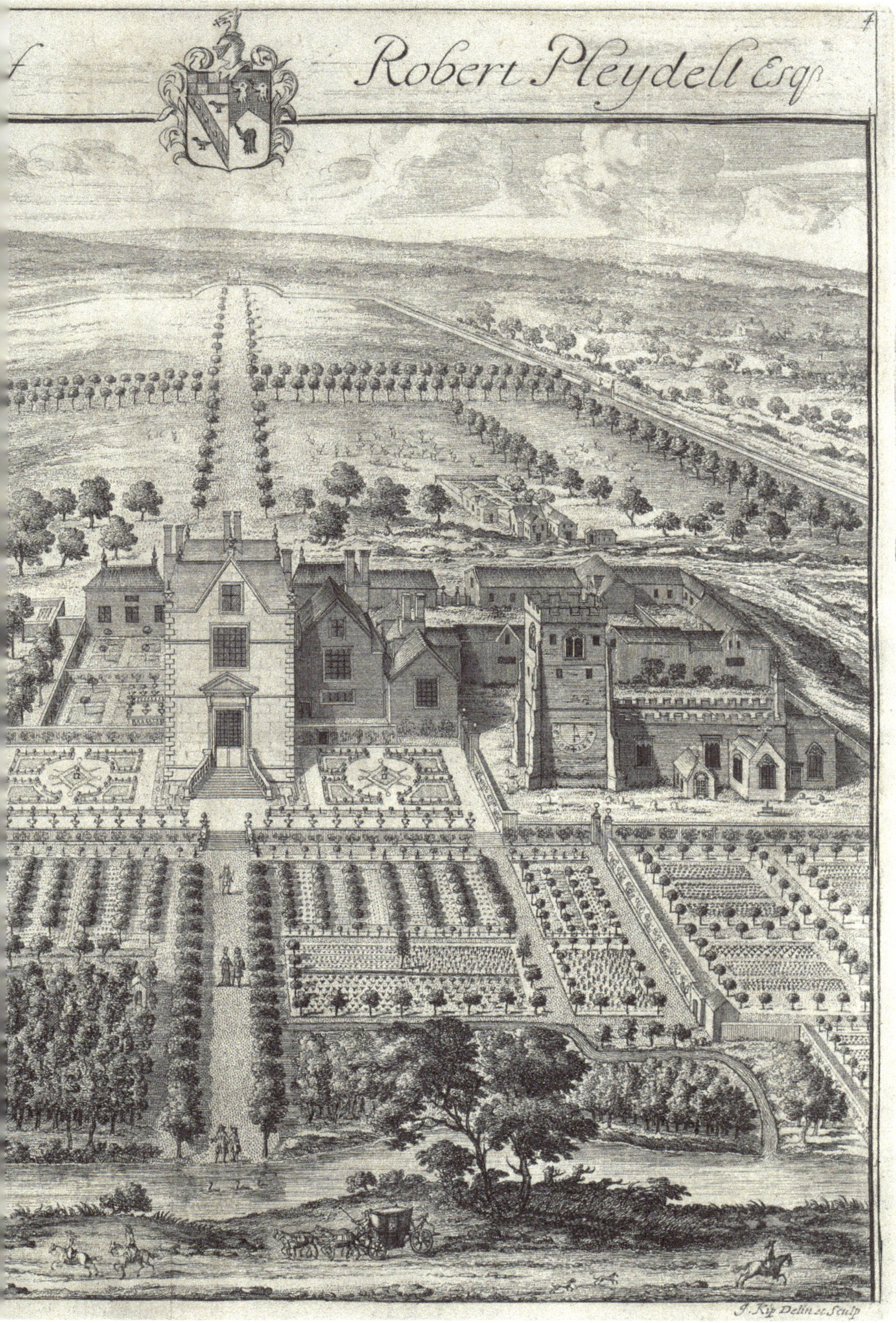

Robert Pleydell Esq

J. Kip Delin et Sculp

11 Shurdington the Seat of Dulcibella Laurence Relict of Wm Laurence [Atkyns, Badge

'Mr Lawrence has an handsome Seat, and a large estate, at the Green Way ... which is now in dower to his widow ... at little

Little Shurdington, which Atkyns referred to, is in Badgeworth parish, and the Greenway was drawn by Kip running up Shurdington hill towards the Crippets; it may have been the droveway used by Gloucester Abbey in the eighth century. The Lawrence's house is now a country house hotel called The Greenway.

William Lawrence's great-grandfather bought the estate in 1561 and his grandfather inherited it in 1582 and built the house; the estate was some 700 acres (283 ha). The front of the house, facing north-west, is stepped as indicated by Kip, with narrow projections almost like towers on each side of the entrance. William Lawrence inherited the estate in 1682, but enjoyed it for just ten years as his wife and only son both died in early 1692. He was overwhelmed with grief, which he expressed by reworking the formal garden, introducing urns on pillars shaped like pyramids, commemorating his family with Latin inscriptions and dates, planting cypress trees, and entering each area through gates representing the stages of life. An unusual description of his 'garden of mourning' survives in two letters Lawrence wrote to a friend.

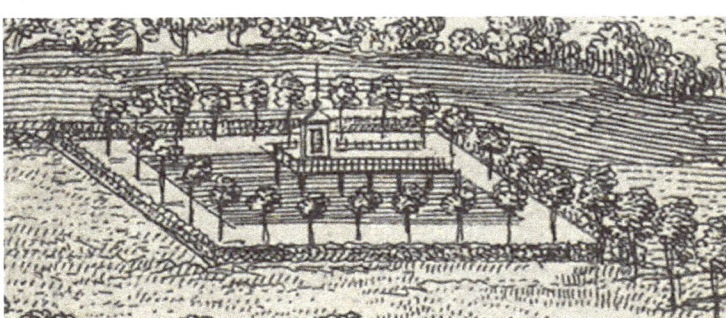

Lawrence died in 1697, leaving instructions to his second wife, Dulcibella, to finish his designs. Kip's drawing might partly show what was planned, like the walled square fishpond with a shelter on a platform over the water (*qv*); the pond exists and there is some evidence of the walls.

The Lawrence family owned The Greenway until 1854. The octagonal room above the roof, designed as a study for his son, was removed in 1970, and ground fronting the Shurdington road is a garden centre. But many impressive trees in the gardens survive including the 'room' on the south side of the house, now surrounded by yew hedges (*qv*).

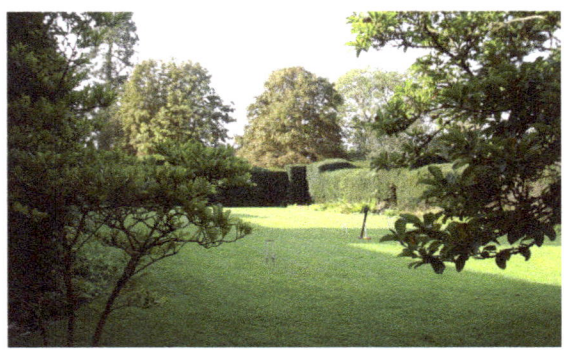

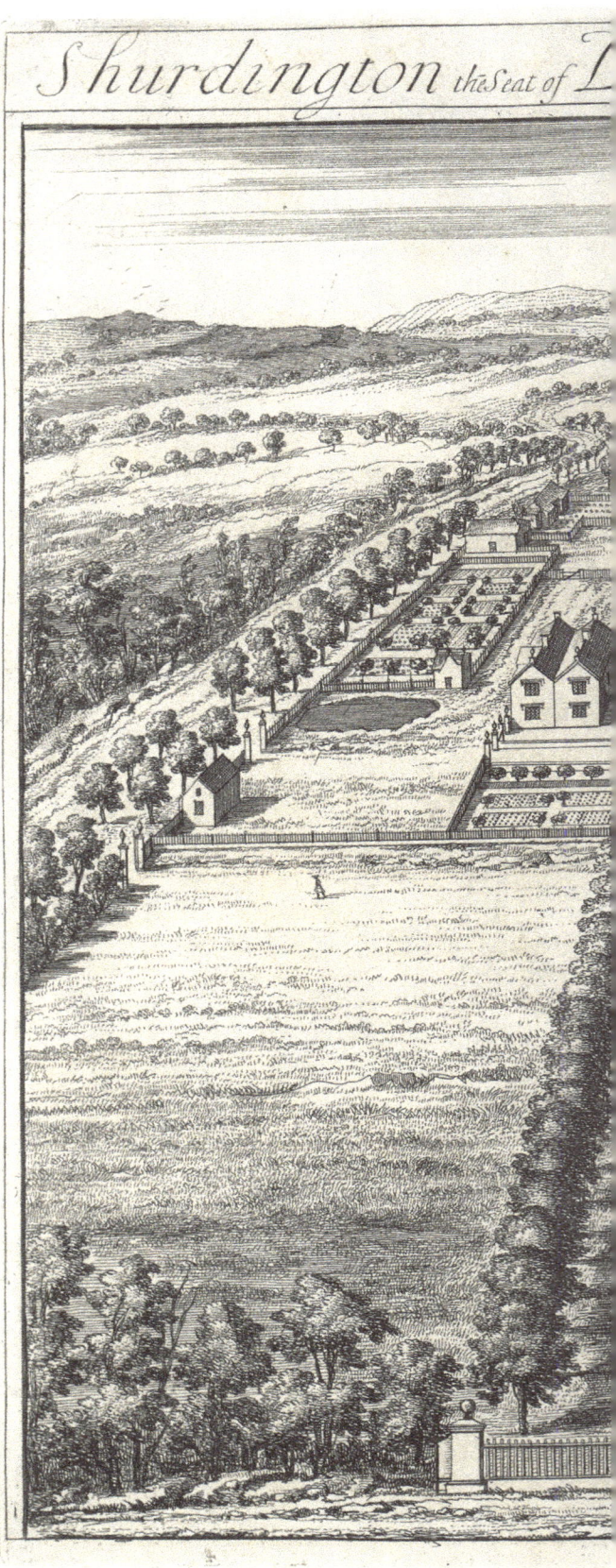

Shurdington the Seat of L

worth, 240-241]. Postcode: Cheltenham GL51 4UG. NGR: SO 91985 17822 '

Shurdington.'

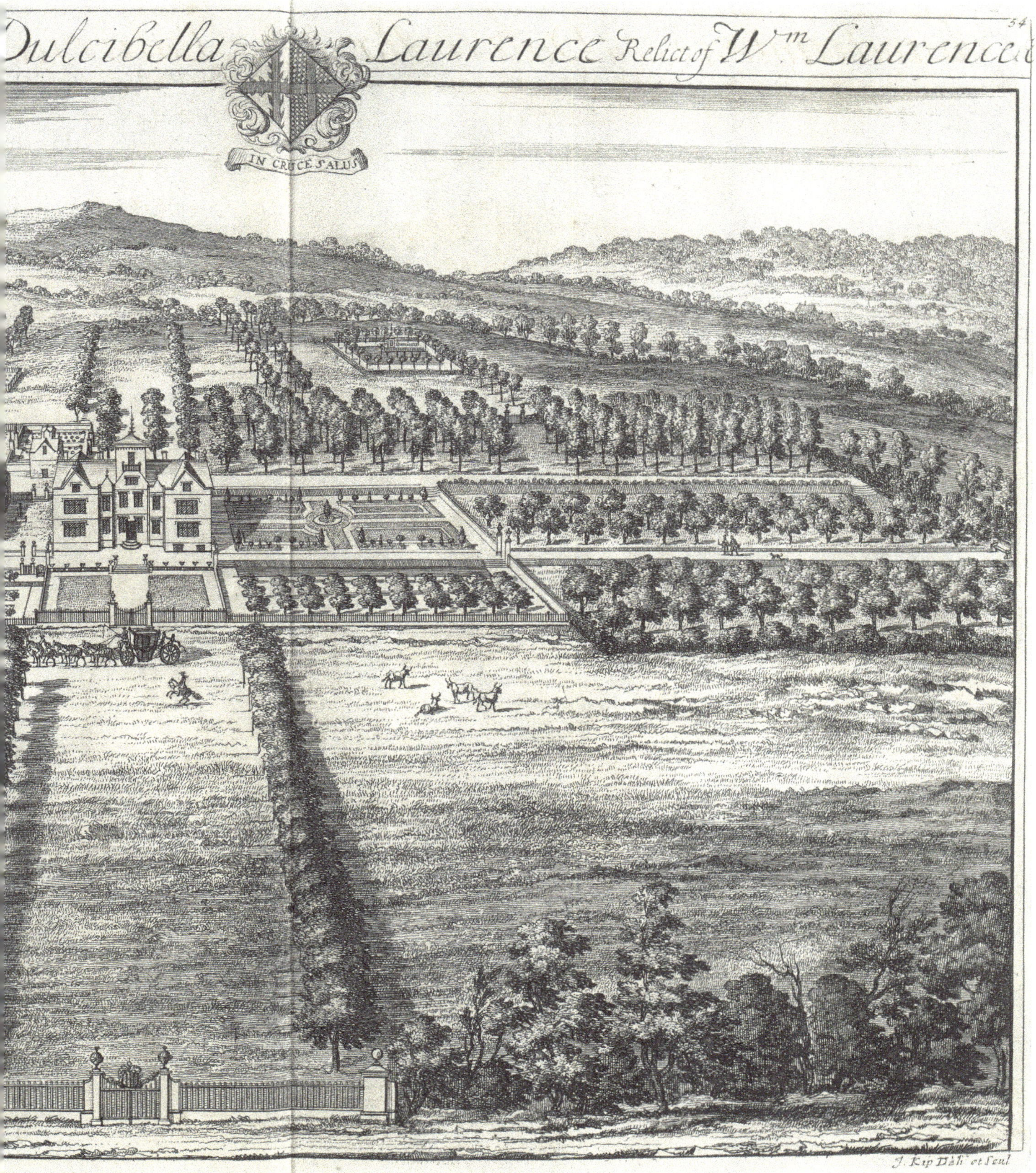

Dulcibella Laurence Relict of Wm Laurence

IN CRUCE SALUS

J. Kip Delin et Sculp

12 Badminton *See Introduction*

13 Barrington the Seat of Edmond Bray [Atkyns: Barrington Great, 250-251]

'Edmond Bray Esq ... hath a large house and park in this place, and a very great estate in this and other counties. His house

Edmund Bray's ancestors bought Barrington manor in 1555; his son sold it in 1735. The following year the house was damaged by fire and a more fashionable 'Palladian villa' was built a little further west, while part of the old house close to the church was preserved as stables and offices (*qv*).

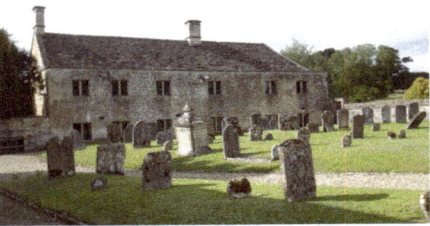

The site is a gravel terrace above a canalised mill leat and the Windrush. Near a river crossing, now bridged, the church may be on the site occupied by the Domesday priest. To the east, the road leads to the village and continues to the county boundary and Taynton in Oxfordshire, while northwards it winds uphill to the Rissingtons.

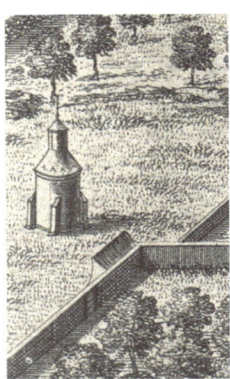

Kip drew a complex of buildings which largely existed when Llanthony Priory owned Barrington; the prior stayed there, the bailiff and later the lessee live there. The partly-embattled south front of the large house appears to be early seventeenth century, facing a bowling green, with a lawn and parterre to the side. Two adjoining courts appear a century older. A smaller house stood to the west, also stables and several barns; none survives. Notably the avenues in the park led away from this smaller house. A park probably existed as early as 1327; Kip shows it had been extended and walled, and drew the fallow deer, which are still maintained. Two round buildings, perhaps dovecotes, existed before any eighteenth-century modernising (*qv*).

The road is no longer close to the church; it has been moved eastwards to include the vegetable garden within the walled curtilege, and the farmhouse in the corner of the park has been removed. The approach to the church is now along a walled drive. Ralph Bigland's engraving of about 1780 shows there had been few changes to the church since Kip's engraving (*qv*), and it remains largely the same today.

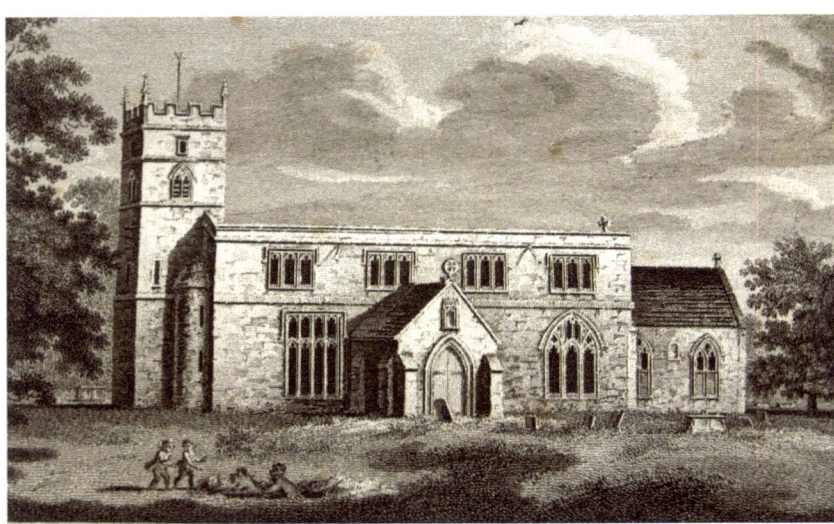

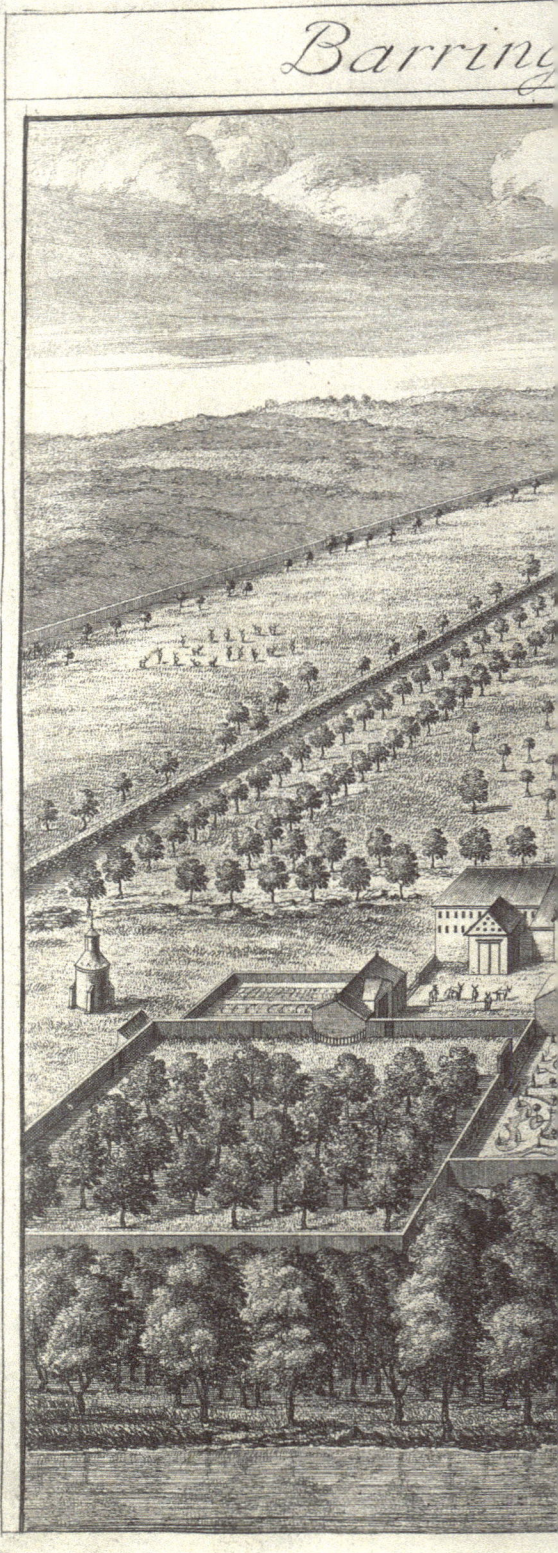

Barring

Postcode: Burford OX18 4**UR. NGR: SP** 19965 12275**. VCH VI** 16-27

standeth part in Glosterhire, and part in Oxfordshire; he is descended of a very ancient and eminent family.

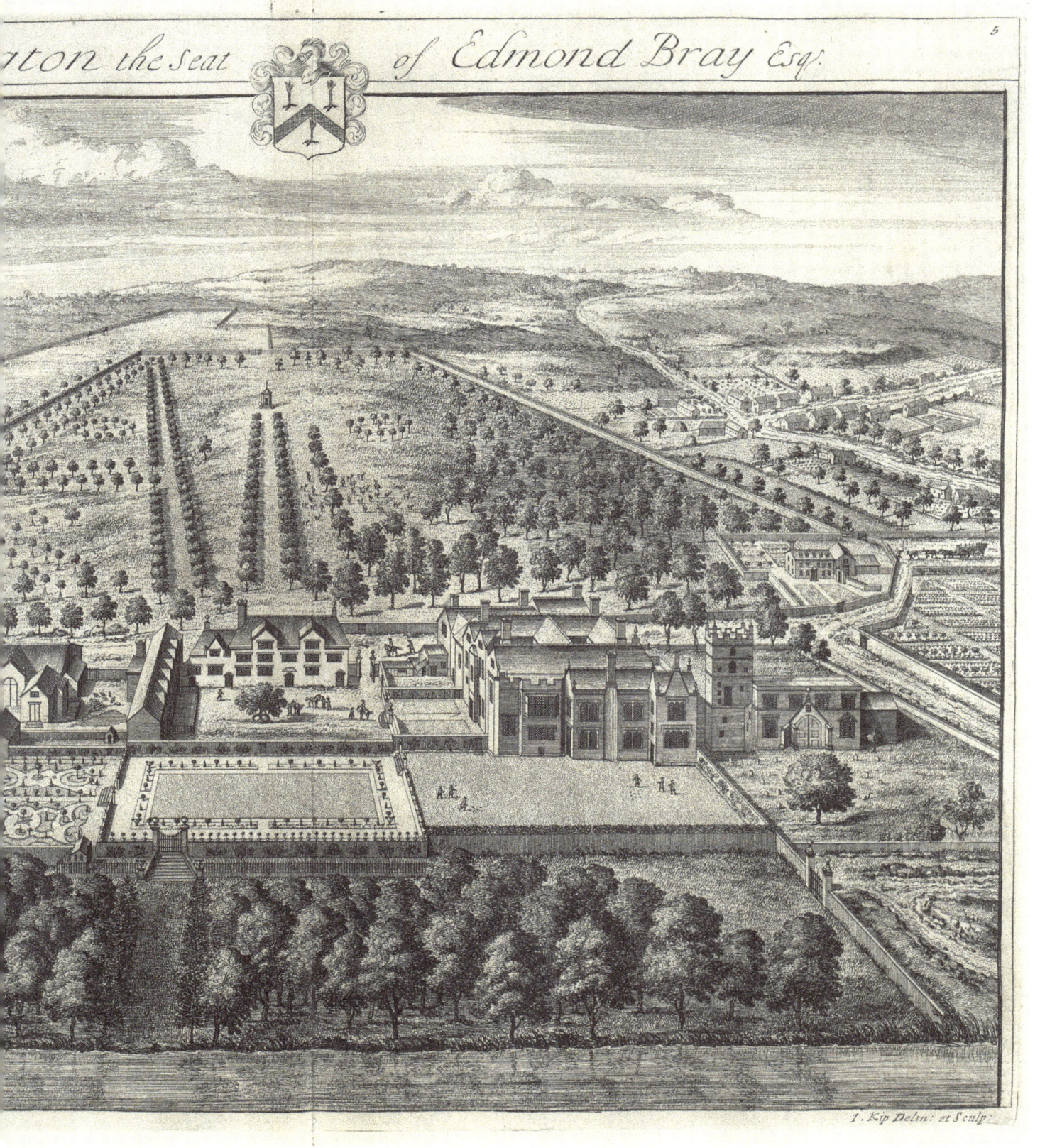

ton the Seat of Edmond Bray Esq.

I. Kip Delin: et Sculp:

14 Battsford the Seat of Richard Freeman Esq [Atkyns, Battesford, 256-257].

'Richard Freeman Esq has a very handsom pleasant seat in this parish, and a great estate. He is descended of an ancient family

Kip's view of Batsford House shows a multi-gabled house, to which a pedimented façade has been added to the south garden front, which faces geometric gardens with topiary and walks. The house appears to have had a number of additions. Barn, hayricks and dovecotes reveal a country enterprise (*qv*).

There were several plantations at a distance, and the gazebo-like building on a grass terrace at the head of a grove on a hillside north-west of the present house is now within the modern wood, Gilbert's Folly. Although not far away, Batsford village and church are not in the picture. However, Batsford parish boundary is strongly marked, to the left (north-west), and beyond it is a featureless stretch of countryside in Blockley. It was significant because this was also the county boundary; until 1931 Blockley was in Worcestershire.

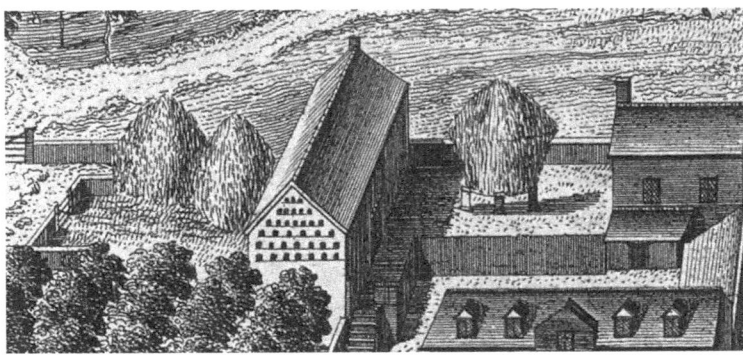

Batsford House was for many years the home of the Freeman family; the last Freeman died in 1808, but later descendants added 'Freeman' to their surname. Richard Freeman, named by Kip, died in 1710; he was succeeded by his son, also Richard, who transformed the surroundings of the house by 1748 into a semi-formal landscape. Plans to deformalise the landscape were complete by 1777, when Bigland commented that there was a 'Park and Plantations of great beauty, and correct taste'.

John Mitford, Lord Redesdale, who inherited the estate in 1886, built a new house in the Cotswold Elizabethan style in 1888-1892, about 100m to the south-east of the existing house; the Georgian predecessor was demolished in 1890 and the site planted with trees. The new gardens, which made Batsford well known from the 1890s, were laid out by A B Freeman-Mitford who had been influenced by the gardens, landscapes and flora of Asia Minor and Japan.

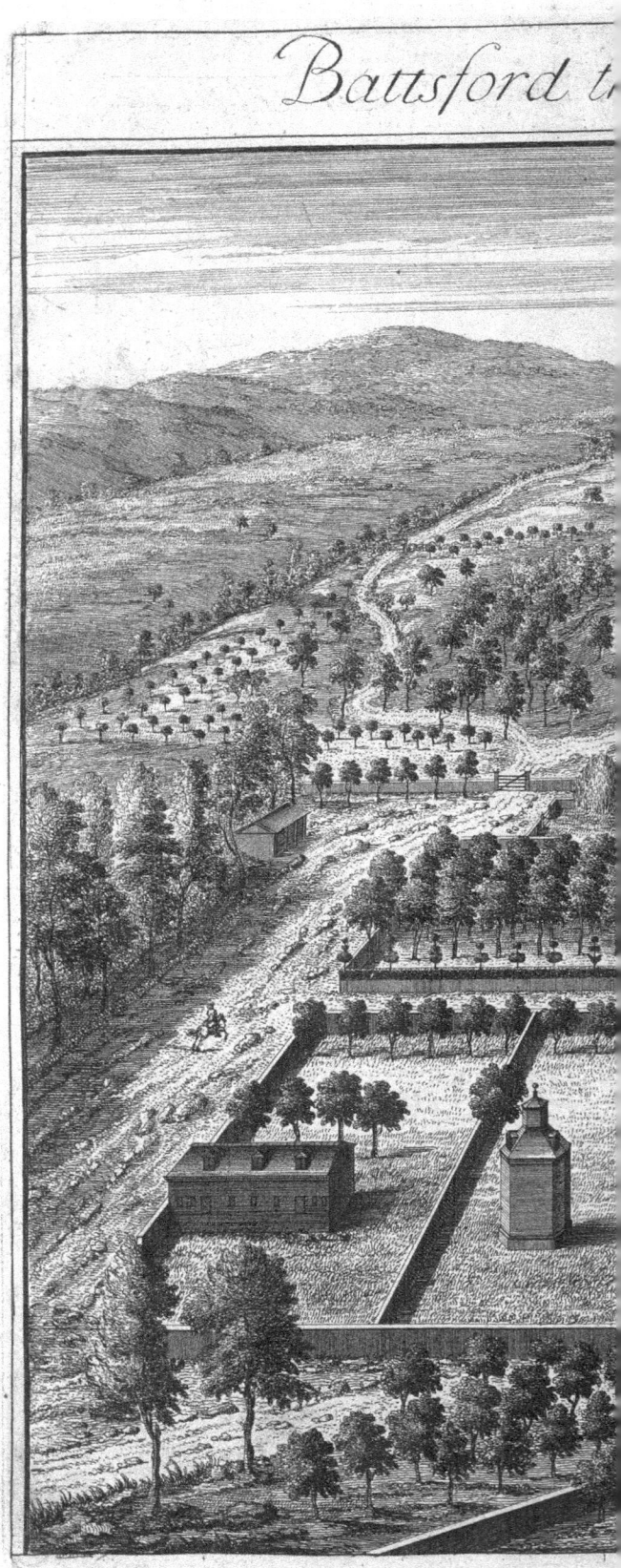

Battsford t

Postcode: Moreton-in-Marsh, GL56 9QE. NGR: SP 18264 33804.

which has long resided in this place. He was made Lord Chief Baron of the Court of the Exchequer in Ireland in the year 1706'.

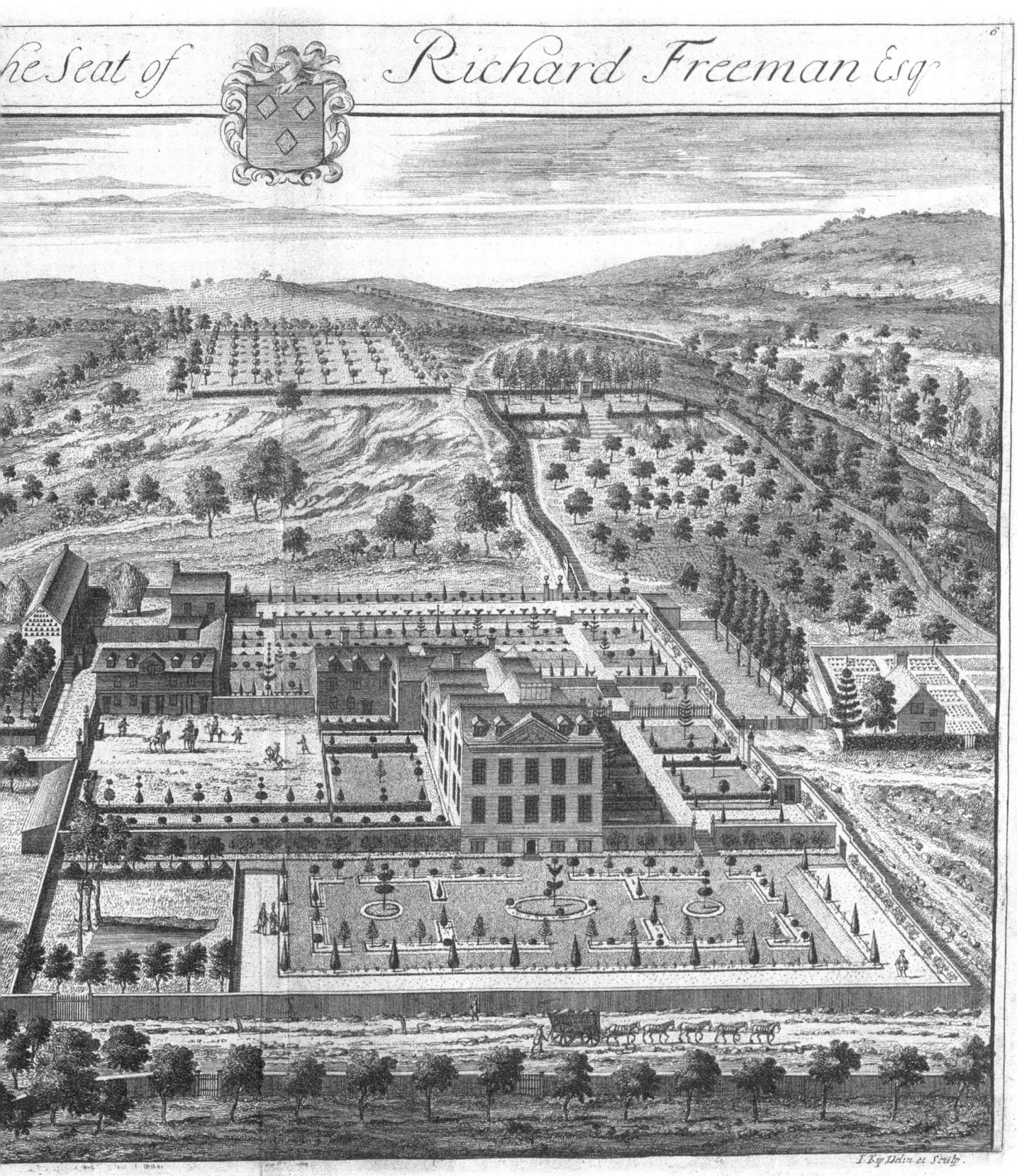

he Seat of   Richard Freeman Esq

15 Berkley the Seat of the Earl of Berkley [Atkyns: Berkeley, 260-261].

'Charles ... succeeded his father in the earldom of Berkeley ... He is the present Lord Lieutenant of the county of Gloster, and one of and has a stately castle joyning to the town, which has been in the family ever since it was granted by King Henry the second to

Sir Robert Atkyns' comment on the remarkably long period of ownership of Berkeley Castle by the same family can today be extended by more than 300 years, probably a unique achievement in the county: the present Charles Berkeley is the twenty-seventh generation of the family. Moreover the castle has been maintained and occupied since the efforts of the 2nd earl to restore it. Berkeley Castle was beseiged in 1645 during the English Civil War, and then slighted and the surrounding land ruined.

When Charles, the 2nd earl of Berkeley, inherited the estate in 1698, he set about renovating the ancestral home. Numerous entries in the beautifully written accounts, still held at the Castle, show the extent of the works undertaken between 1699 and 1707. A gatehouse, tower and various walls were demolished, trenches and military earthworks were levelled, extensive repairs to the roofs and windows were undertaken. The large orchard and kitchen garden in the foreground of the Kip engraving were planted during this time; artichokes, asparagus, melons and beans, as well as apples and pears were grown. The terracing to the immediate south of the Castle was

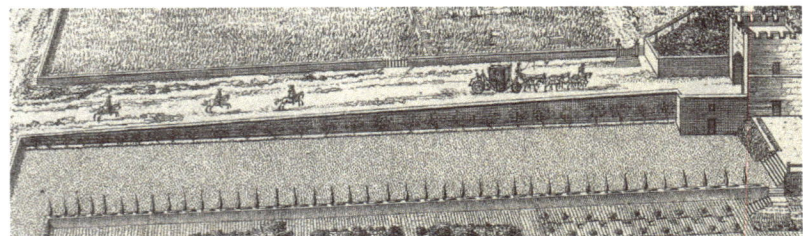

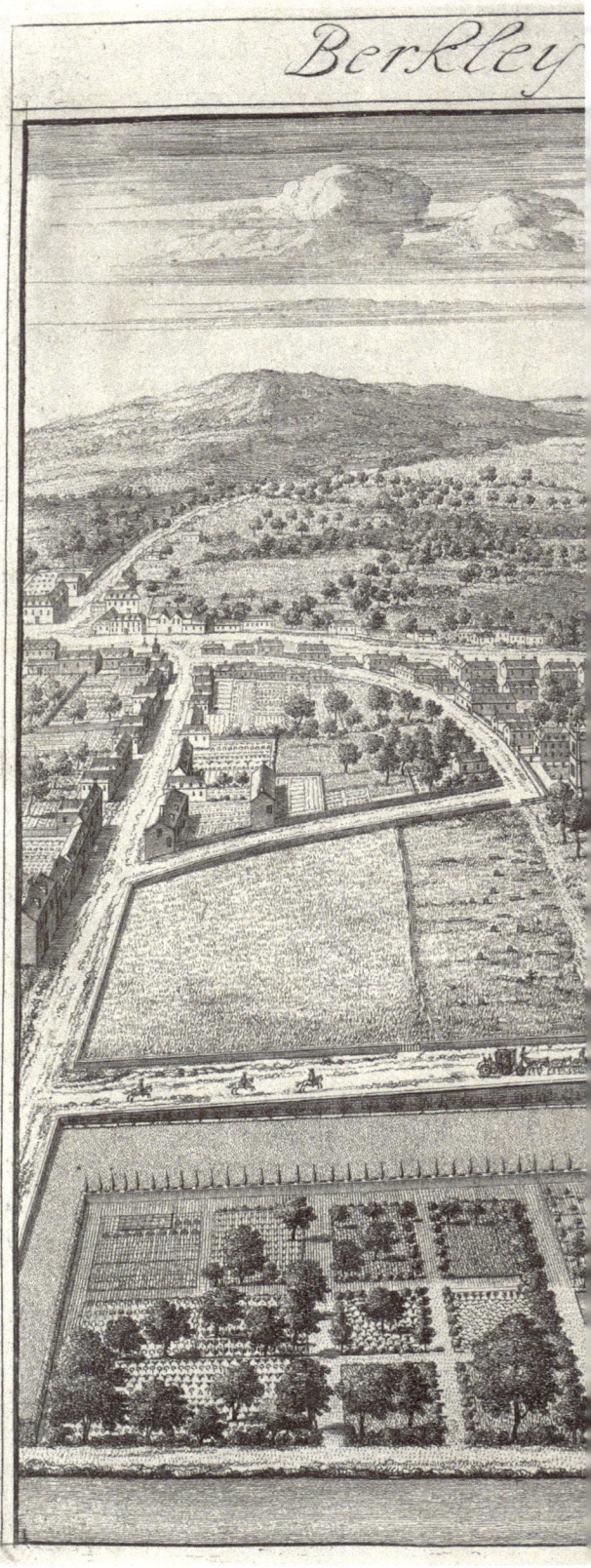

also built and still stands, although a second, lower terrace was added in the 1920s. The Bowling Green below the causeway of the Castle's western entrance was re-turfed in 1707 and exists today, along with its southern yew planting (*qv*). The yews were trained as an arcade, then as various forms of topiary, including elephants, cut down in the 1950s to make a solid continuous hedge. Kip drew two coaches arriving at Berkeley - one is approaching the gateway and one is in the courtyard beyond the archway.

The entrance was on the north-west side, dominated by the bastions of the Keep. Kip's view is from the south-west. The north-eastern bastion had previously housed the twelfth-century chapel of St John, which Kip's drawing shows had gone by 1708; it is identified by its three windows, one of which Kip would probably not have been able to see from the position he adopted for the drawing (*qv*). In 1756 the new Evidence Room was built in the empty bastion but in 1923 that was re-converted to a Norman-style chapel of St John.

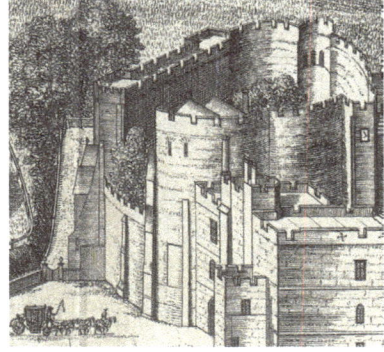

There was a dry moat between the castle and church, in part still visible, which involved a piece of the churchyard being used; it extended round the back of the castle to the east. Leland

Postcode: Berkeley GL13 9BQ. NGR: ST 68514 98984, ST 68520 98934.

er Majesty's most honourable Privy Council, and is the present possessor of the mannor of Berkeley, where he keeps a court-leet,
Robert the first Lord Berkeley, which is above the space of 600 years. He has large parks, and a very great estate in this county.'

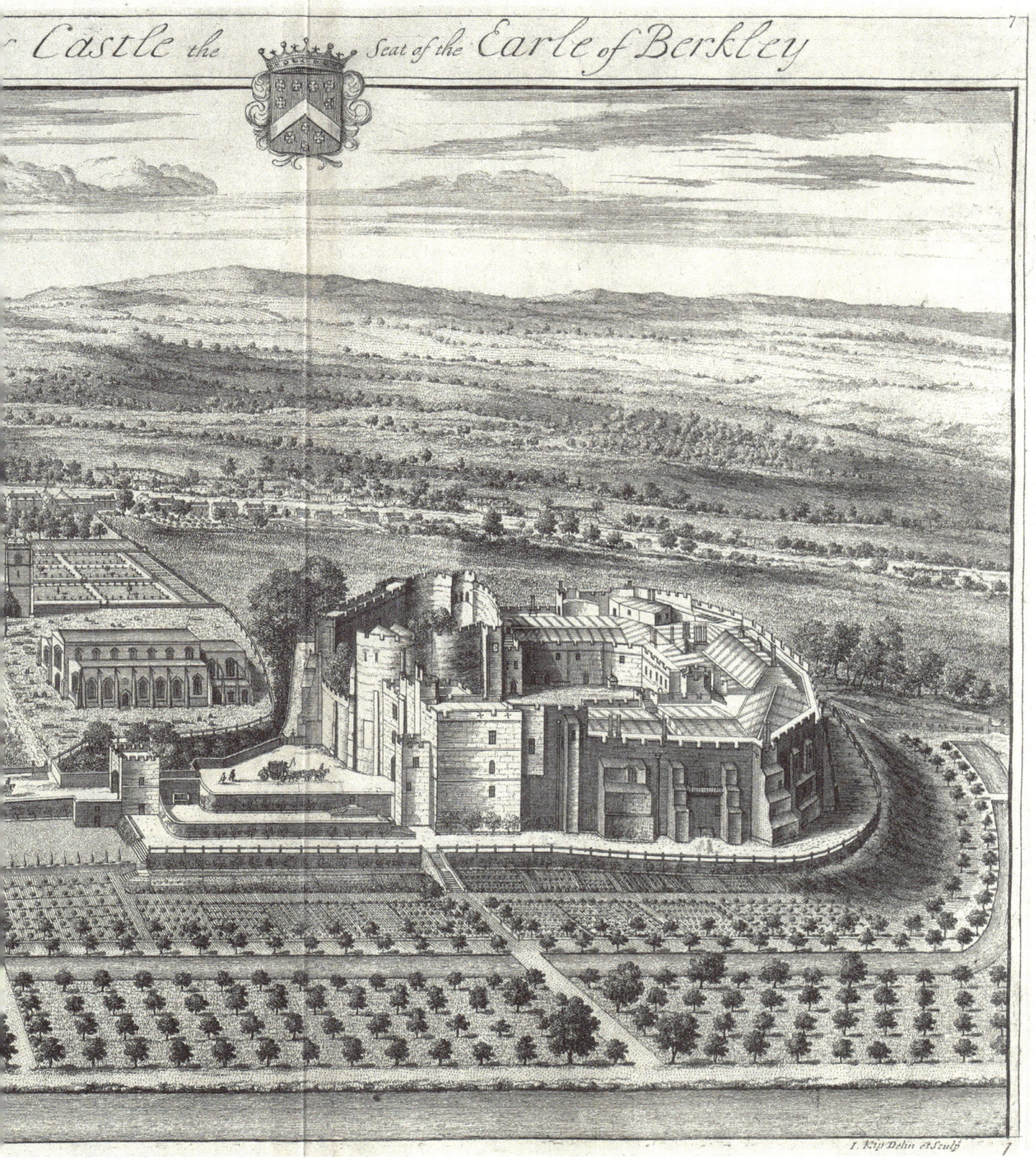

Castle the ... Seat of the Earle of Berkley

I. Kip Delin et Sculp

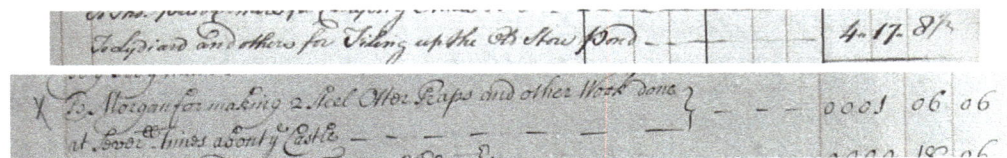

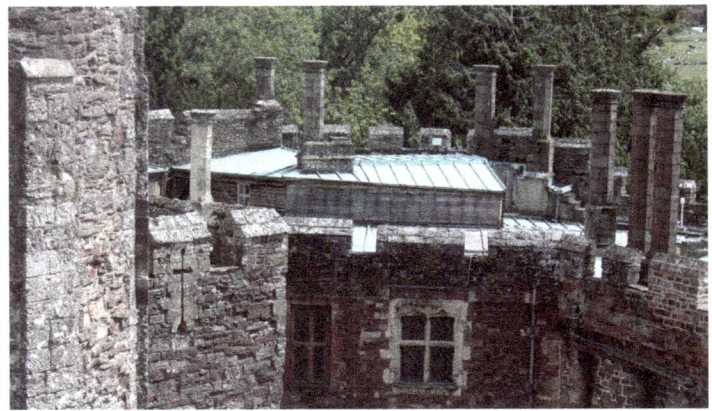

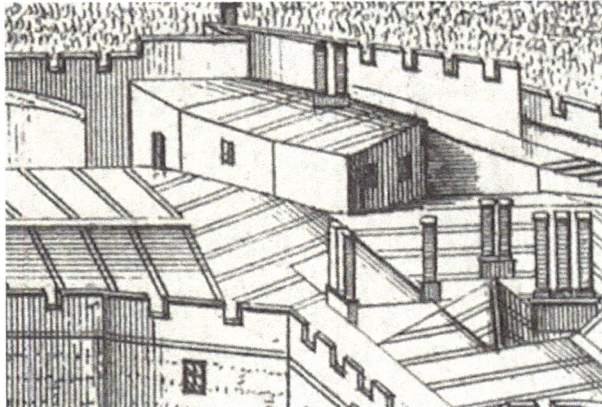

about 1540 mentions the bridge over the ditch to the first Gate. To the south the castle was naturally defended by the escarpment and the water meadows and drainage channels; 'rhine' or 'reen' was the local spelling and pronunciation. A system of sluices could be used to flood this marshland as a defensive measure. Half of the reen (Doverte Brook) is in the foreground of Kip's engraving, separated from the canal or fishponds by an area of careful tree planting.

Below the bluff on which the castle stands Kip drew what appears to be a canal, cut in two places by paths although without any bridges. Fashionable garden design in the late seventeenth century involved straight-sided canals. At Berkeley, the canal appears in fact to be a series of three straight-sided ponds, possibly fish ponds, rather than a continuous canal; two steel otter traps were made in 1707 to protect fish (qv). In 1758, however, a payment was made to fill up the 'old store pond', and from this time the canal was not a visible feature in engravings.

Kip's attention to detail is highlighted by the Castle's roofs. Now coated in copper, in 1708 they were lead. His depiction of the falls and watersheds is

approximately 80% as they are seen today, the remaining 20% may have been accurate at the time of drawing and have since been altered as internal alterations have necessitated structural changes on the associated roof. One area of note is above the Custodian's flat in the north-east corner. The pitches of the roofs and positions of the chimneys are incredibly accurate for a relatively insignificant building (qv). Other small details are there in the engraving: the well-head in the courtyard, and a sundial on the wall above for example (above on right-hand side of the keep).

While the castle is viewed from the south-west, the church has been slightly rotated to present its south side in full. The shape of the building, and the number and position of the windows, are as today although the detailing of the mullions is different. Looking along the south aisle, the rose window above the door and the raised sill of the window at the east end are, again, as today. There are numerous seventeenth century gravestones.

The tower is separate from the church (qv). Reputedly very ancient, it was once attached to another church which may have been a remnant of the early

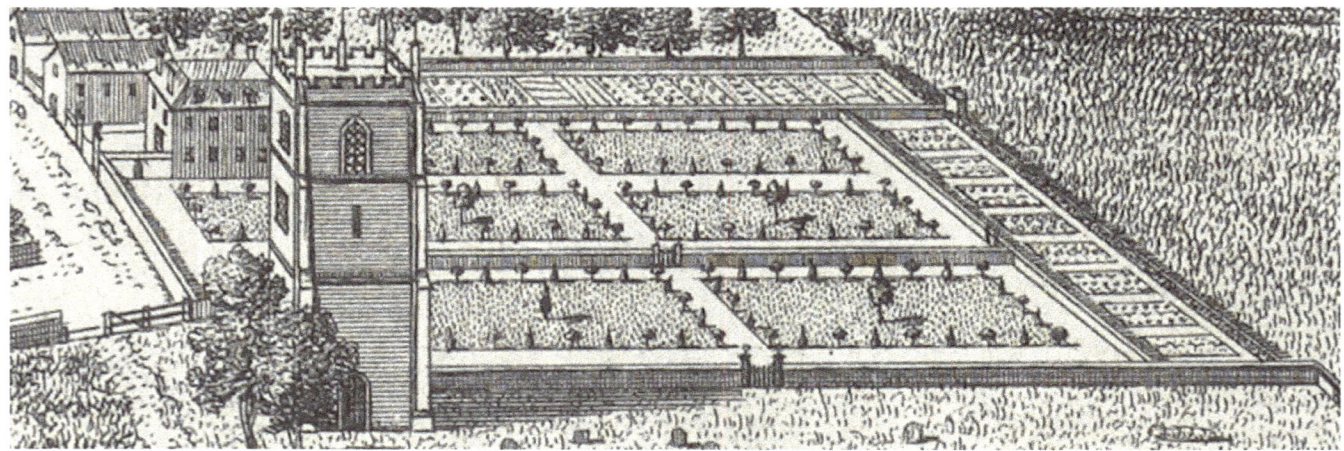

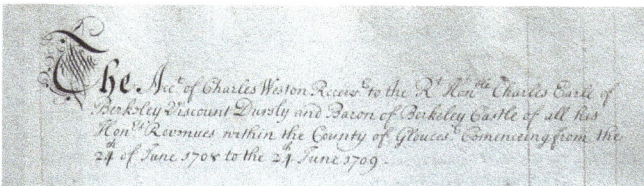

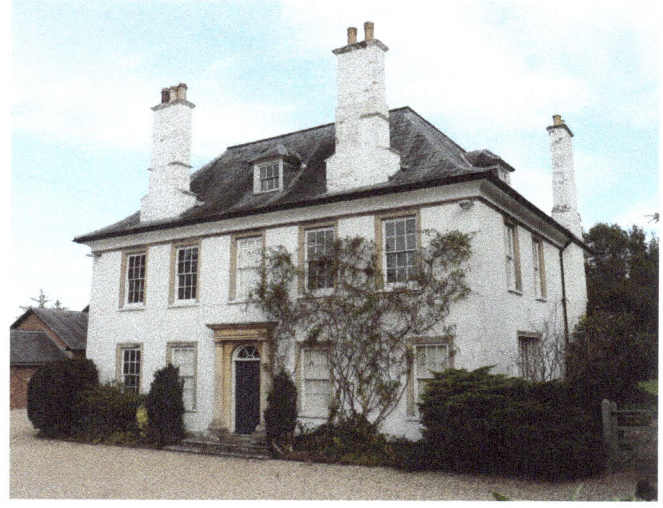

minster buildings on the site. In 1748 the 'Minister, Church Wardens and Principle Inhabitants' applied for permission to raise a rate to rebuild it. 'The tower had suffered much in the late Civil War at which time a great part of it was demolished. The south side thereof is cracked from the bottom to the top. The south east corner is bulged from the rest of the tower, and several loads of stone fallen out of the main wall.' Kip may have minimised the damage or the churchwardens may have exaggerated it; his drawing suggests some misalignment on the south-west corner. The rebuild was completed by 1753.

Kip also provides a record of the town. The only significant difference to the road layout is that Church lane has now been moved to the west, away from the front of the Chantry, so that a paddock was included in the curtilege. The Chantry (*qv*) is behind the church tower and the gate from the manicured garden into the churchyard still remains. Refurbishment had been completed by 1707; it was then the home of Charles Weston, the Berkeley castle 'receiver' or treasurer (*qv*). Later it became Dr. Jenner's home and museum. The chimneys in Kip's engraving are accurate but not the dormer windows.

It is believed Kip would have made some preparatory study of the Castle from a vantage point in Whitcliff Deer Park a mile to the south. While hills are visible, they are more distant than Kip indicates. The orientation of the church and the roads leading

northwards suggest that he drew high ground in the Forest of Dean and May Hill, leading on to the Malverns, rather than a view to the north-east appropriate to the castle orientation, which might suggest the Cotswolds.

In July 1708 'John Kip the Dutch engraver' was paid £5:07:06, 'by his Lordship's order for a drawing of Berkeley Castle'. This was the engraving published by Atkyns. It was so respected that the 4th earl carried a copy with him on his travels, and in a portrait, thought to have been painted by Gavin Hamilton in Brussels, his left hand drew attention to an image of Kip's engraving at the earl's side.

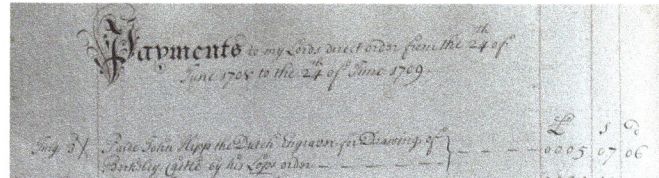

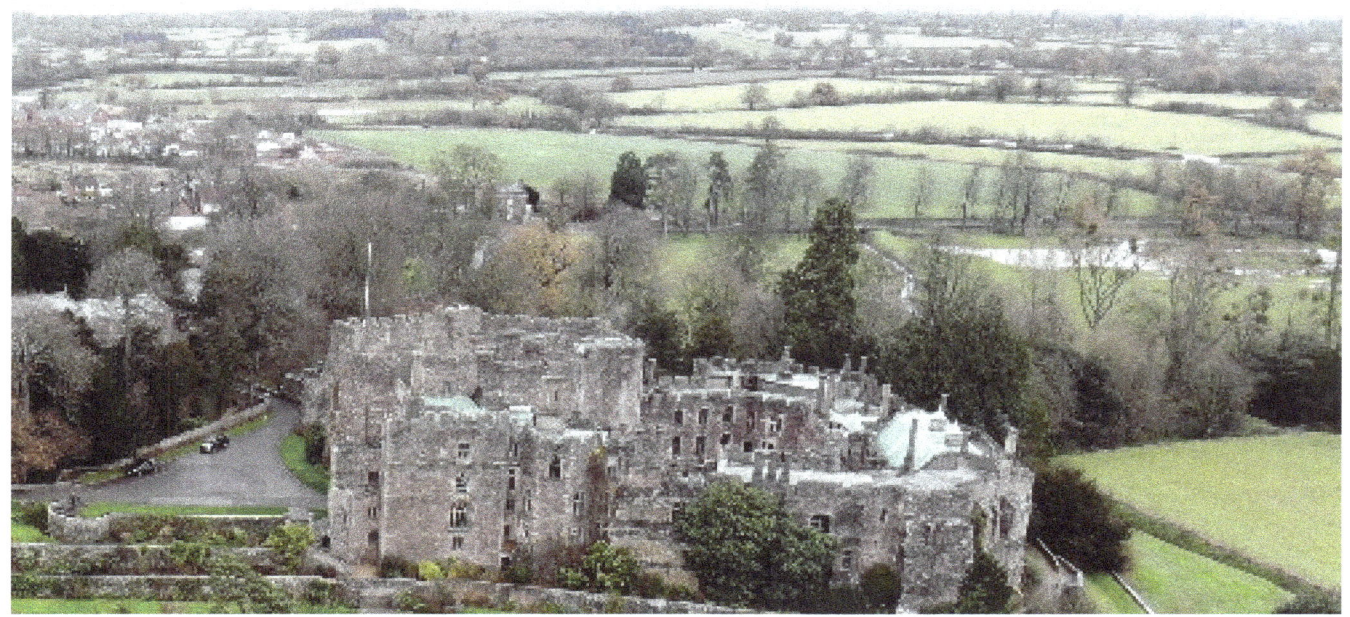

16 Broadwell the Seat of Danvers Hodges Esq [Atkyns: Broadwell, 300-301]

'Danvers Hodges Esq ... hath a large Mannor-house adjoyning to the church, and a good estate in this and other counties.'

Broadwell, like Maugersbury, was an early Evesham Abbey estate. About 1200 the abbot built a 'noble house', probably on the same site as the present house. Church and manor house are near a plentiful spring, indicated by Kip. They are also near the site of a Roman villa a little higher up the hill towards the Fosse Way. The road skirting church and barn joins the Fosse Way not far from Stow-on-the-Wold, and in the background Kip suggests the hill on which the town stands.

Following the Dissolution, the manor was broken up. Anthony Hodges and William Chadwell jointly bought the manorial demesne in 1619: Hodges retained the manor house. In 1672 'Mr Hodgis' was taxed on 12 hearths and 'William Chedwell esq' on 9 hearths. The Chadwell family built ostentatious tombs in the churchyard, some with bale tops (*qv*); Kip drew the family tombs at Alderley, but not these Chadwell ones in Broadwell. He did mark the ancient yew tree growing near the south aisle. The churchyard was later much enlarged to include the ground where a coach and horses are approaching the house.

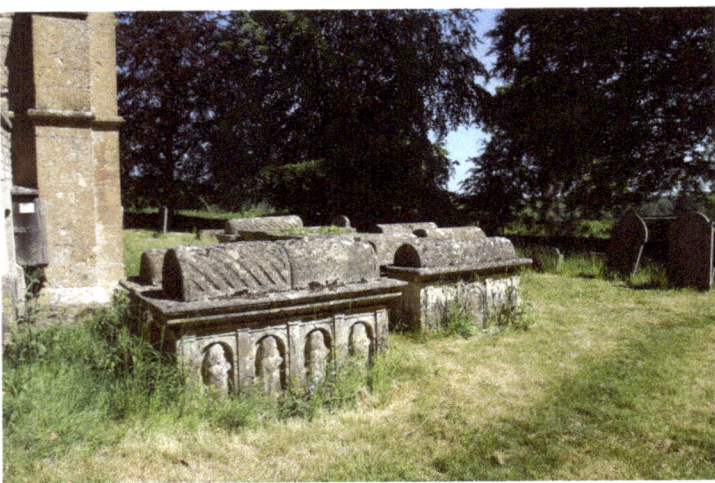

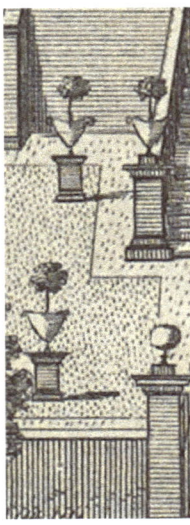

Broadwell Manor faces north-east but Kip has angled it to match the church. The land close to the house is terraced, and falls steeply to the south. A prominent stairway makes a grand approach to a first floor hall. There was a parterre and dovecote at the rear and a large barn; in the front some fashionable vases were planted with shrubs.

The manor house remained in the Hodges family, through sons and later daughters, for the next three centuries. Danvers Hodges' daughter married Dr Thomas Chamberlayne, and in 1757 he built a fashionable front block and a smaller rear block which exist today, encasing the seventeenth-century house.

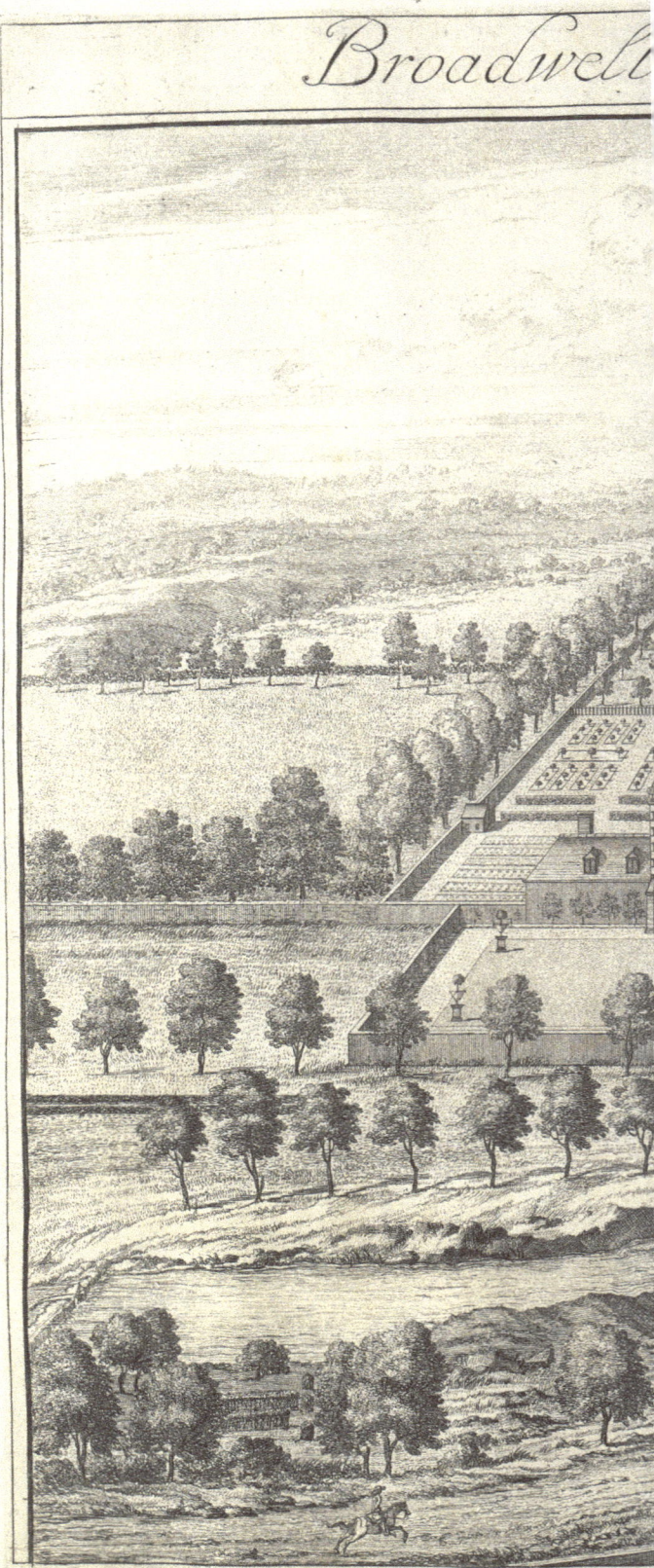

Broadwell

Postcode: Moreton-in-Marsh GL56 0**YD. NGR: SP** 20038 27631**. VCH VI** 49-59.

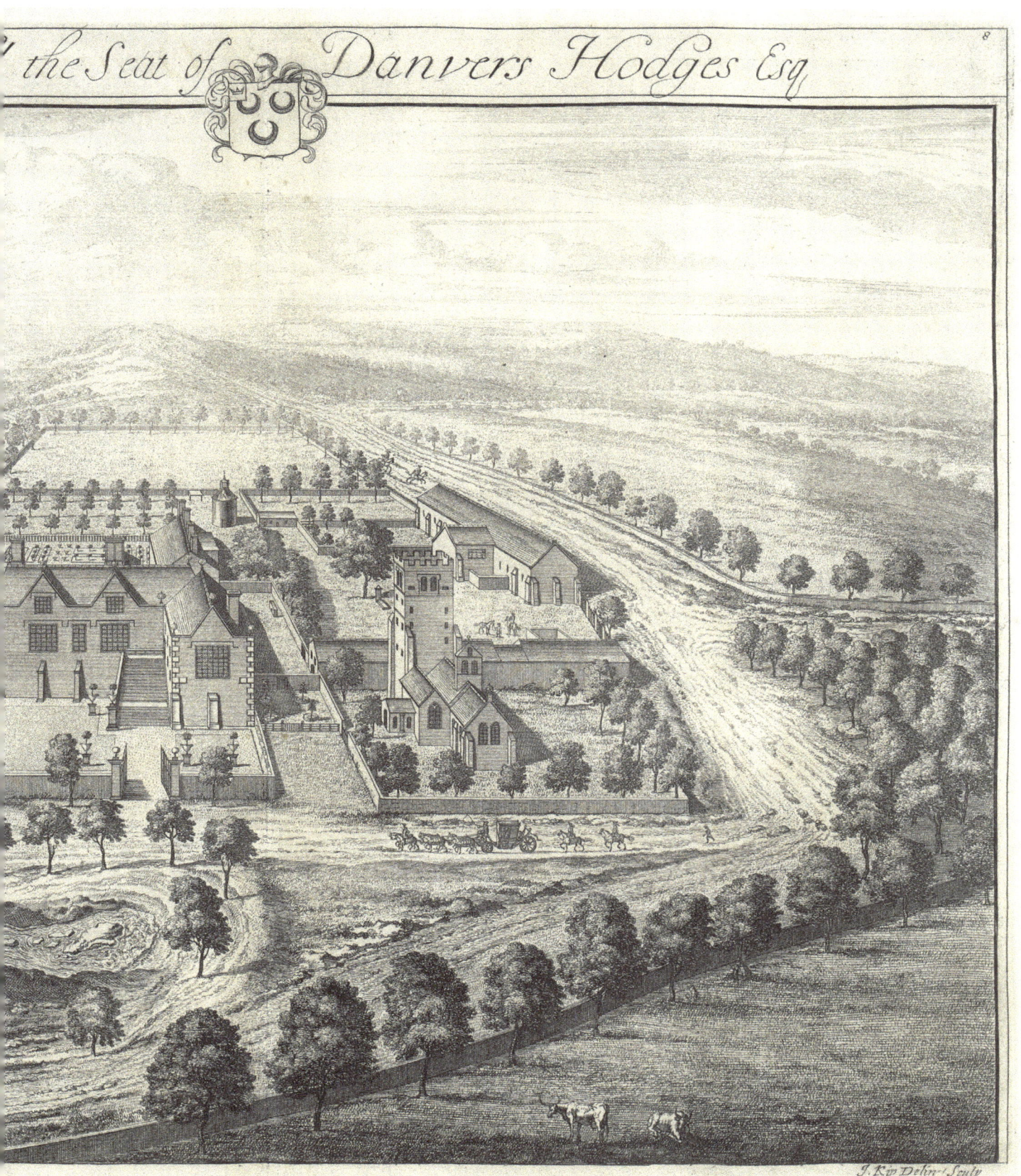

the Seat of Danvers Hodges Esq

J. Kip Delin-t Sculp

17 Cirencester the Seat of Allen Bathurst Esq [Atkyns: Cirencester, 344-345].

'Allen Bathurst Esq is the present Lord of the Manor. He hath a very large house in this town.'

Cirencester was the seat of two members of the county gentry. The first is now known as Cirencester Park, after Allen Bathurst built a new house and created a fine park soon after Atkyns' book was published. House and park exist today, and the park is open to the public by permission of Lord Bathurst. The second was the seat of the Master family, built on the site of the medieval abbey. This house was replaced later in the eighteenth century and a park created to the east. At the end of the nineteenth century the Chester-Master family ceased to occupy Abbey House, and when no tenant could be found, in 1964 it was demolished. A block of flats was built on the house site, and other land was sold for housing development, but extensive grounds, nearly 26 acres (10.4 ha), were presented to the town by R G Chester-Master in 1965 as a public park. Thus both the big houses now provide Cirencester's inhabitants with splendid recreational open space.

There is some overlap between Kip's two scenes. A small cluster of buildings and gardens at the lower end of the Market Place appears in both. When he was drawing Abbey House, Kip was positioned with his back to Cirencester Park, but within the view of the town which features the Bathurst's house, there is a small copy of the drawing of Abbey House.

Cirencester does not seem to have impressed Kip. He portrayed a small town with many open spaces, useful gardens and small, generally gabled and undistinguished houses. Although there was some rebuilding after the Civil War, it appears that many houses were old and that there was much refronting and some rebuilding during the eighteenth century. In this Kip may have been reflecting the economic difficulties with which the woollen industry in the town was afflicted. In 1698 the inhabitants petitioned parliament and stated that 'several hundred' poor people formerly engaged in yarn-making and wool-combing were unemployed. They blamed imports from Ireland through Bristol. Textile manufacturing did not recover but the corn market flourished.

It is interesting that the seat of Allen Bathurst is shown as the whole town of Cirencester rather than his house and grounds. A possible reason is that Allen Bathurst became M.P. for Cirencester in 1705 and represented the town until 1712; his rival Thomas Master at the Abbey House was not elected until 1712. Bathurst was also lord of Cirencester manor, which had been purchased by his father Sir Benjamin Bathurst.

The view is from the east. In the centre is the impressive parish church, very curiously drawn, with the famous south porch missing and the tower appearing to be in the middle of a much shortened nave rather than at the west end. An engraving of the church prepared by Thomas Bonnor for Bigland's Collections and published

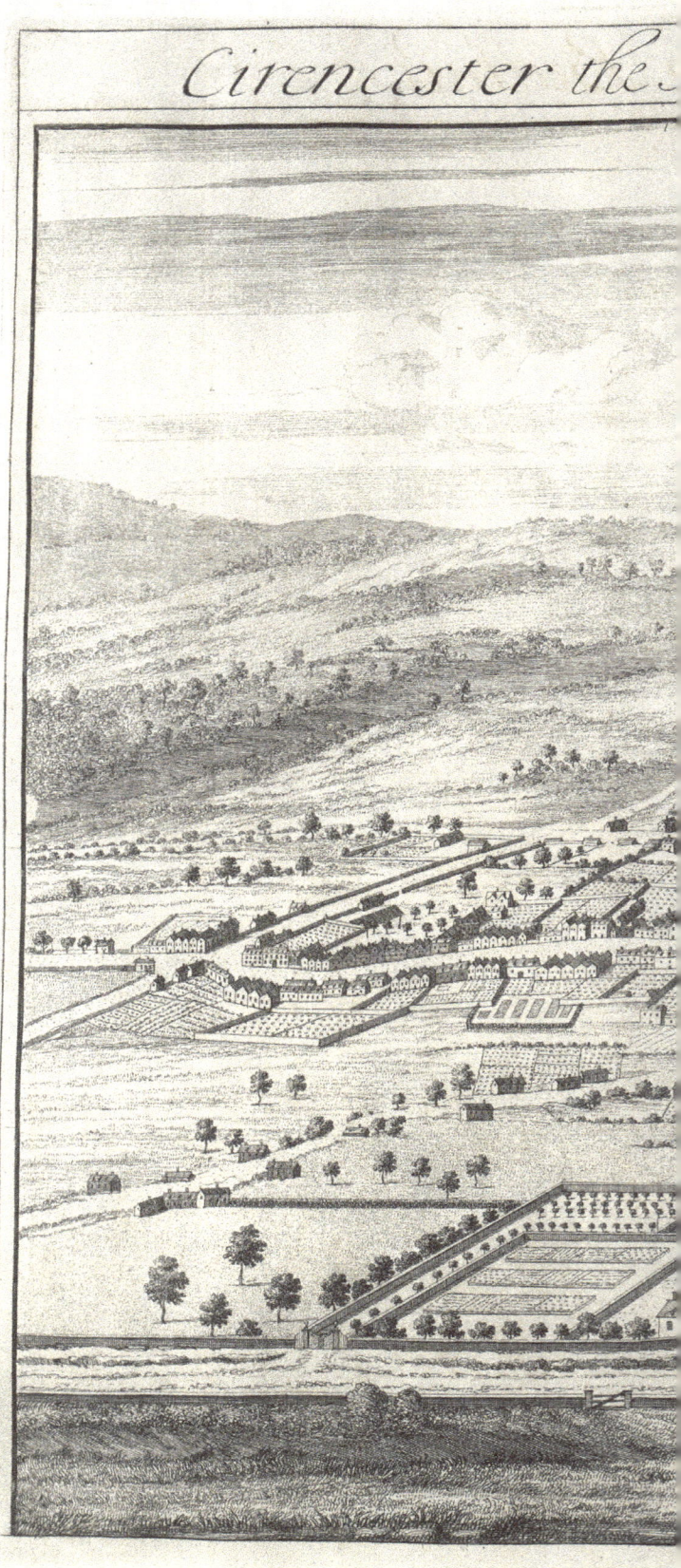

Postcode: Cirencester GL7 2BP. NGR: SP 02020 02032. **[VCH XVI forthcoming]**

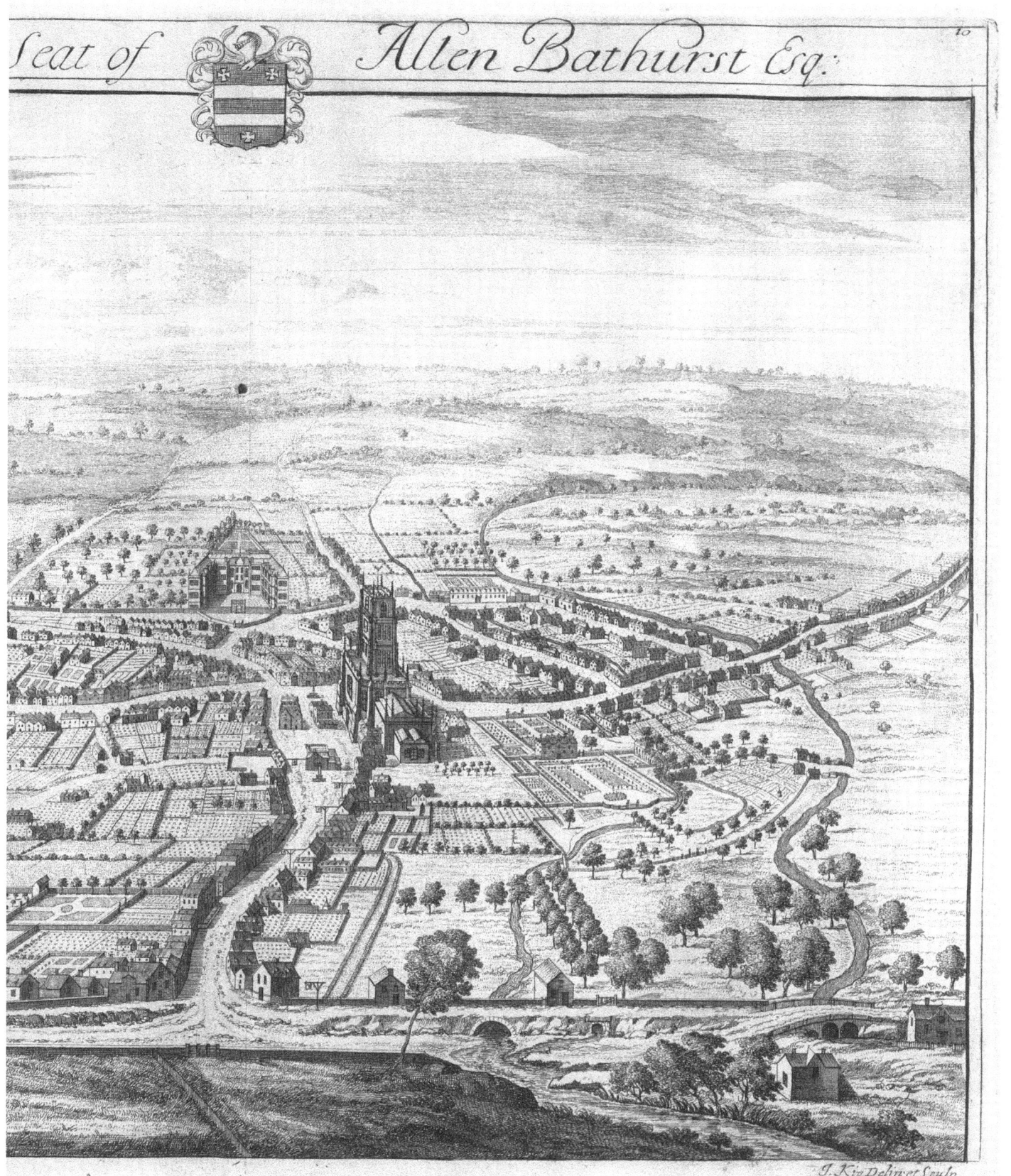

in 1781 illustrates Kip's strange failure. Was he short of time and made inadequate notes?

Allen Bathurst's house is behind and to the left of the church. It is a late Elizabethan and Jacobean house built for the Danvers family and purchased by Sir Benjamin Bathurst in 1695. Allen Bathurst was raised to the peerage in 1712 as Baron Bathurst and in 1714 retired from politics, devoting his time to rebuilding the house and creating one of the grandest landscaped parks of eighteenth-century England. The land behind the house is seen just before its development. The tactfully small Abbey House and its formal gardens are to the right of the church.

Kip drew another significant though smaller house

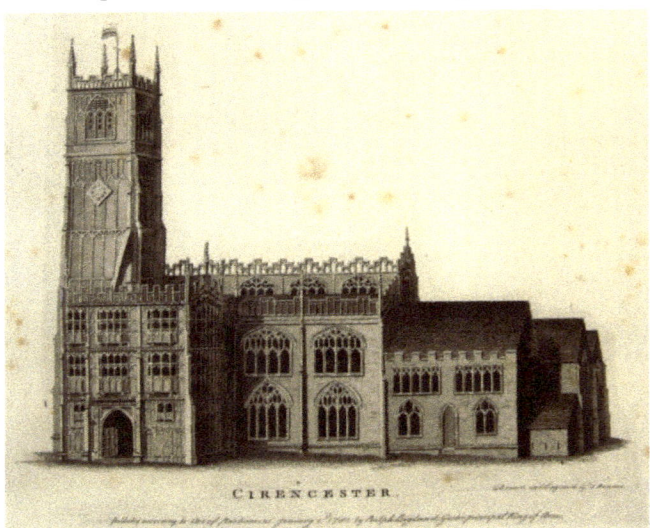

CIRENCESTER.

in the town, in Dyer Street, identified by a fashionable garden behind it, belonging to William George. After discussing the Master family, Atkyns noted 'There is also another handsome house and gardens in this town, late the possession of William Georges, of Baunton, esq whose family has long continued in this place'. The house was built about 1700, and William George died in 1707; the house was then occupied by his widow, Mrs Rebecca Powell, whose first husband he was. It faces north and the front is barely visible, but it is a 3-storey house of three substantial blocks, now called Gloucester House.

A wide carriage entrance from Lewis Lane led to the walled orchard. The house was substantially rebuilt in the late eighteenth century. The large walled vegetable garden was a nursery in the late nineteenth century but a school was then built on the site.

The long, many gabled house in the distance, at the end of Barton Lane (behind and to the right of the church) is Barton House, seventeenth-century and on the site of a Roman villa; it has been very substantially renovated. A very small Barton mill is in front of it with the river running under the house. The road immediately above the church tower is Cecily Hill which leads to Sapperton in the distance, whilst the Fosse Way is shown running from the left to right of the engraving. The buildings in the middle of the Market Place were removed about 1830 and the old high cross, at the junction of Cricklade street, Castle street and Gosditch street, was moved first to Cirencester Park and then, in 1927, restored and moved to the north-west side of the church (qv).

Six inns are flagged by Kip; there are three in the Market Place on the north side, with posts at the edge of the pavement supporting their sign boards, one of which is The Fleece. On the south side is the King's Head. Another inn is at the bottom of Dyer Street (qv George's house), and at the beginning of Castle Street there is The Ram, but none is pictured with very distinctive architecture.

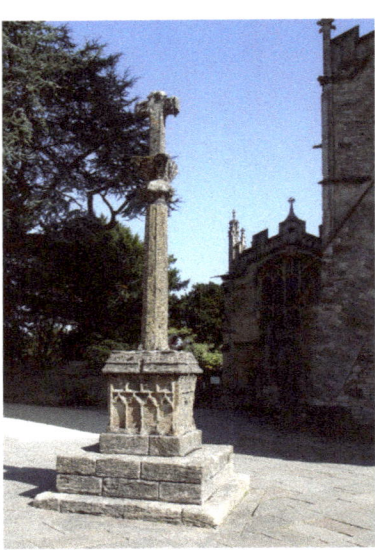

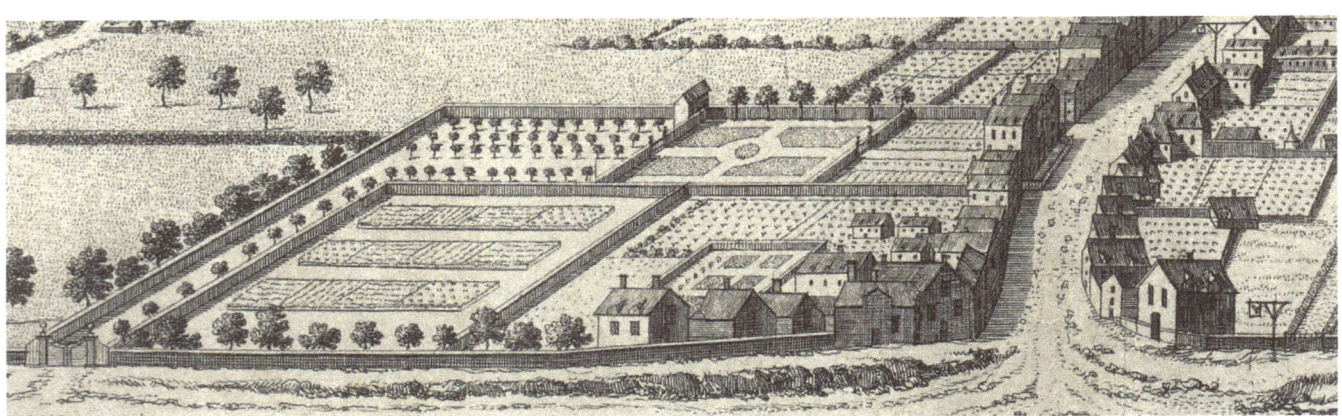

Cirencester Abbey

Cirencester Abbey surrendered to the king in December 1539. For the next twenty-eight years the site was leased, and the conventual buildings destroyed. Queen Elizabeth in 1568 granted the reversion of the site to Richard Master, her physician, and he bought out the previous tenancies. He probably built the house pictured by Kip before his death in 1588. It faced west and was approached from Gosditch Street. Neither this house nor the more fashionable one which replaced it in 1769, facing in the opposite direction, now exist. But 'The Abbey Grounds' are preserved, with many large trees, and features derived from the former gardens.

The grounds were defined by the parish church and churchyard on the south, relics of the Roman wall to the east and the river Churn (beyond which today is the ring road), and roads into Cirencester and the Market Place. The size of the formal gardens can be appreciated today from the long sweep of grass reaching to the lake. A little to the north-east of the parish or town church, grass overlies the foundations of the abbey church, picked out with paving stones (*qv*). Numerous urns were the conventional decoration of the long rear garden, which terminated in a decorative bowed gateway and gates. Beyond it is a more informal and wooded area, with an avenue running through it.

Kip presented a view eastwards suggesting a not very distinct Tar Barrows, a site with Bronze Age or Roman links, now separated from the Abbey Grounds by the ring road. A straight line or axis through the gardens was apparently focussed on the Tar Barrows but archaeological investigation has shown that the orientation of the ride was on a slightly different alignment, focussed on the Ice House a few degrees to the north of the Tar Barrows but within the Abbey House grounds. There is no sign of the Ice House in Kip's engraving.

Few remains of the wealthy abbey's buildings existed to be drawn by Kip, and only the Spitalgate still survives, a very small building in the distance in the north-east corner of the grounds; but comparison with Kip's view of Hailes might indicate that the owners of these houses on former religious sites did not wish ruins to be pictured, though a barn on the northern boundary of Abbey House grounds appears to be roofless. Close to the house was a building called the Abbot's Lodging, which possibly made use of an existing arcade, but no longer exists.

Few traces remain of the Master family's two grand houses either; the entrance gate piers are distinguishable within the present wall along Gosditch Street, and the curved line of the gateway leading to the ride through the grounds to the east is echoed in a terrace. Geophysical surveys and aerial photography have identified linear outlines which are possible vestiges of the gardens and

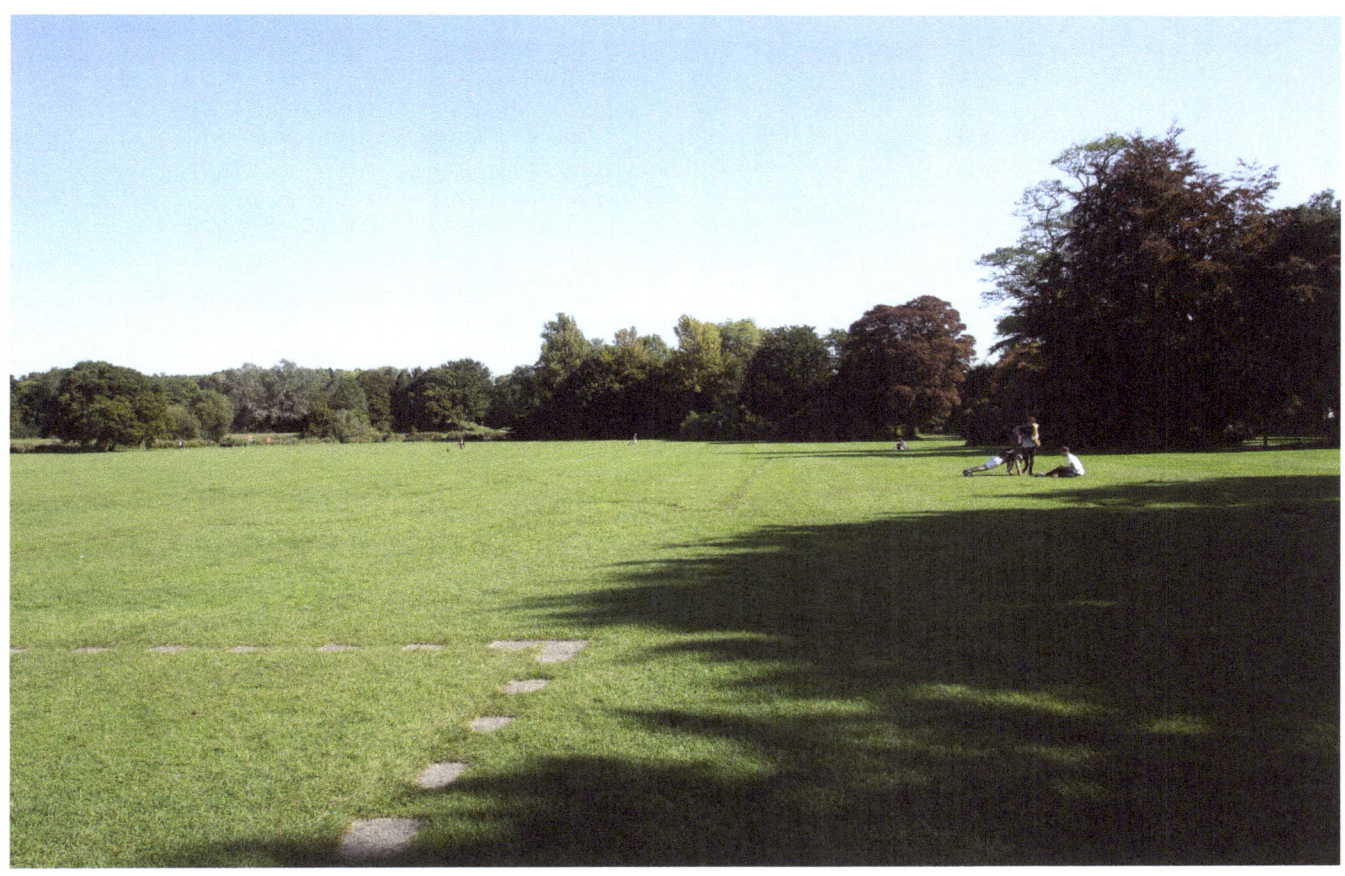

18 The Abbey in Cirencester The Seat of Thomas Master Esq [Atkyns: Cirencester, forthcoming]

[The Abbey is] 'a very pleasant large house in the town, with beautiful gardens, and a large enclosure of rich pasture'.

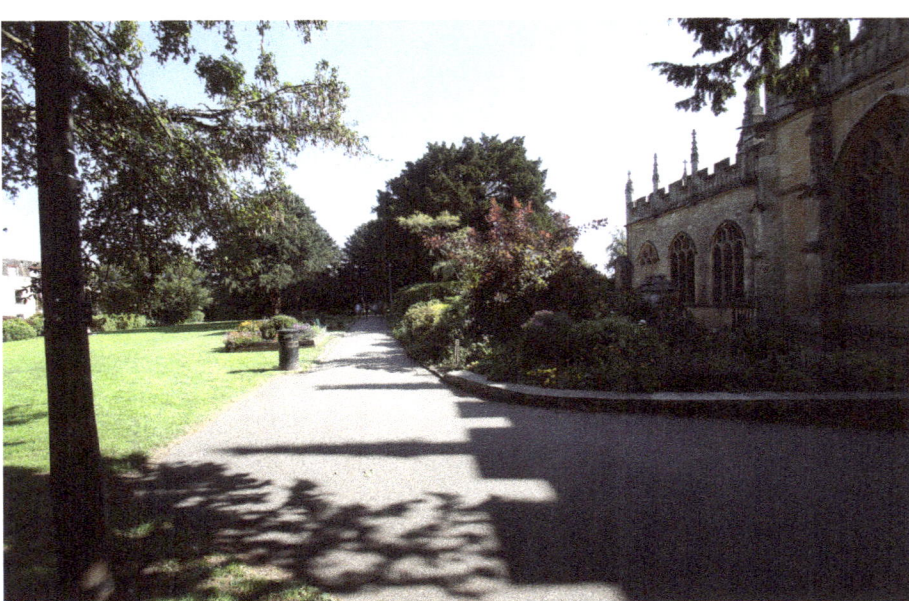

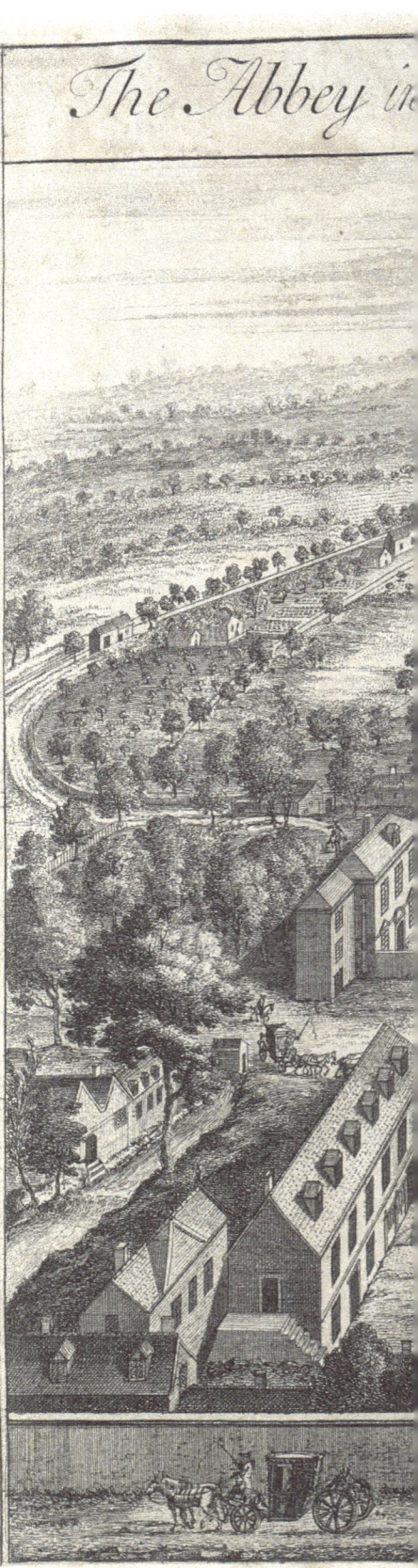

paths, and show that Kip accurately depicted the course of Gumstool Brook and its geometric relationship to the formal gardens. Kip's drawings naturally tend to distort the perspective at a distance from the great houses.

His viewpoint was from the entrance to the Abbey Grounds close to the north side of the church, where the main entrance to the Abbey Grounds is today. The narrow south garden is immediately in view, and to the left the flats built on the site of Abbey House (*qv*).

From here Kip could see into the churchyard, and he drew the wall separating it from Abbey House gardens. A large monument in the middle of the churchyard is probably the monument in that position today (*qv*). Bigland recorded inscriptions on a 'large raised tomb' to the Adye family, the first dated 1724, but the tomb would appear to be earlier.

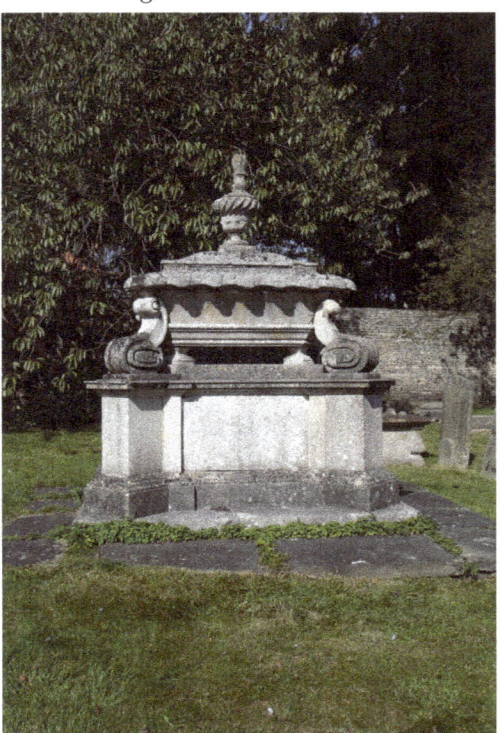

346-347]. Postcode: Cirencester GL7 2EG. NGR: SP 02329 02223. **[VCH XVI**

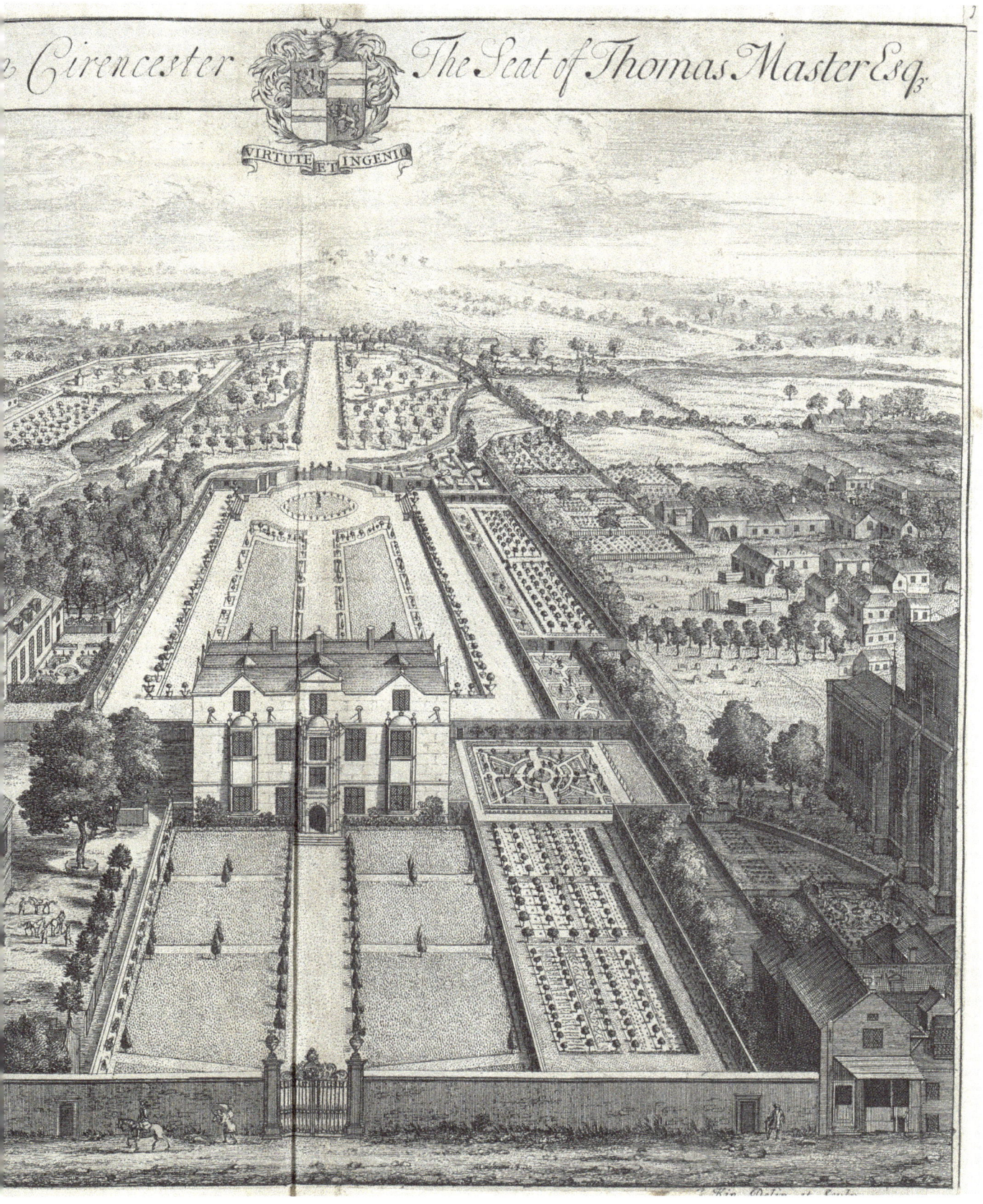

Cirencester   The Seat of Thomas Master Esq.

VIRTUTE ET INGENIO

19 **Southam the Seat of Kinard de la Bere Esq** [Atkyns: Cleeve, 356-357]

'Kinard De-la-bere is the present lord of this mannor. He hath an handsome large seat in this place, and a great estate, and is

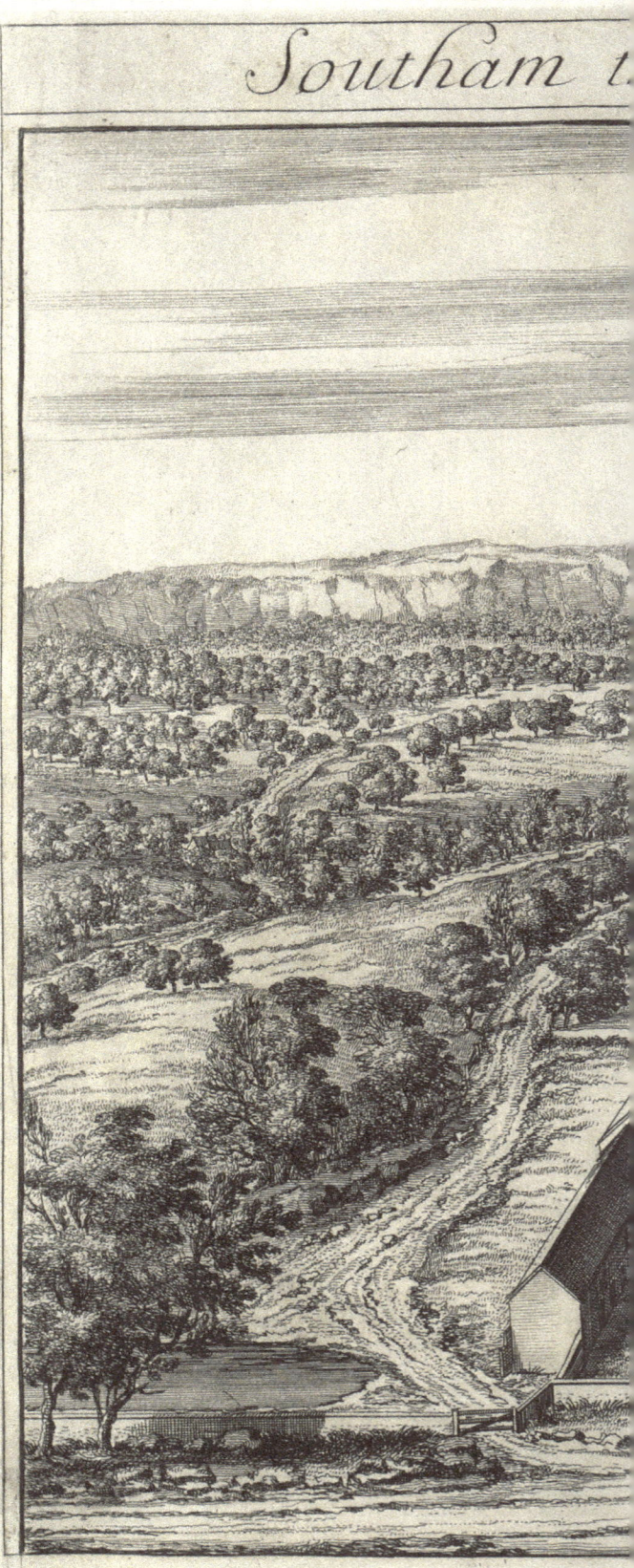

Kip dramatised the skyline east of Southam House. The long cliff edge of Cleeve hill, from 1484 if not before poetically named Cleeve Cloud (indicating the rocky cliff face as the result of quarrying), is clearly visible from the house though not quite as dominating as Kip suggested. Cleeve Hill is the highest point of the Cotswolds, 1,083 ft (340 metres). The lower slopes are equally, if not more wooded today than Kip indicated.

On the north side of the house is Southam Lane, which runs through the village; from it a turning, now a footpath, led to Southam House. The lane wound to the top of Cleeve where it linked with the ancient White Way. The road over Cleeve was turnpiked in 1792, but in 1823 surveyors found a lower, less daunting route to Winchcombe, and access to Southam house is now from the new road to the east of the house. Southam village, with the church and former manor house, was behind Kip, as also is an extensive view; Richard de la Bere, already the owner of Southam House, bought Southam manor in 1609.

Southam House was entered through a simple courtyard, leading to the early sixteenth-century great hall and the solar range with the two-storey battlemented bay window. It is 'one of the largest sixteenth-century houses to remain in the county' and this part is substantially unchanged since Kip drew it.

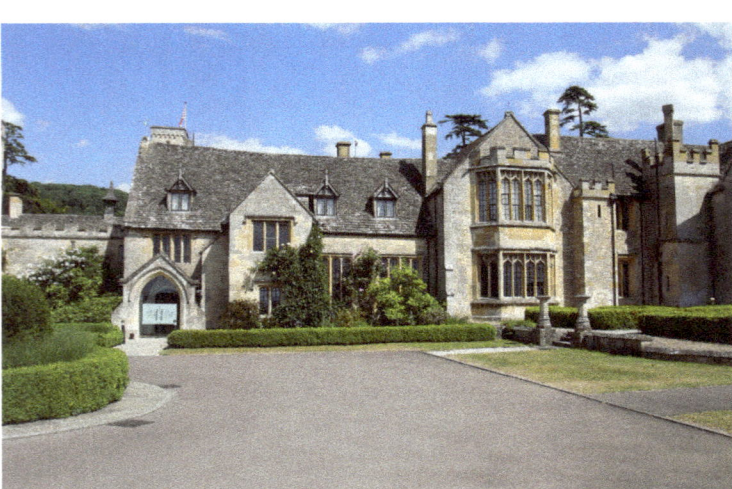

On the north side he drew a square building which appears to be a free-standing kitchen (*qv*), and on the garden side the wing is seventeenth-century. The layout of the gardens is much simpler today but the overall footprint is unchanged.

Southam House was greatly extended with buildings on all sides in the nineteenth century by Lord Ellenborough, hence the modern name of 'Ellenborough Park'.

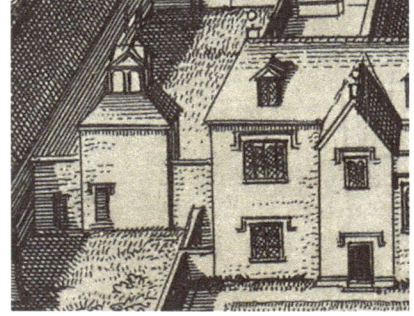

Postcode: Cheltenham GL52 3NJ. NGR: SO 97229 25350. **VCH VIII** 2-25.

descended from a very ancient family'.

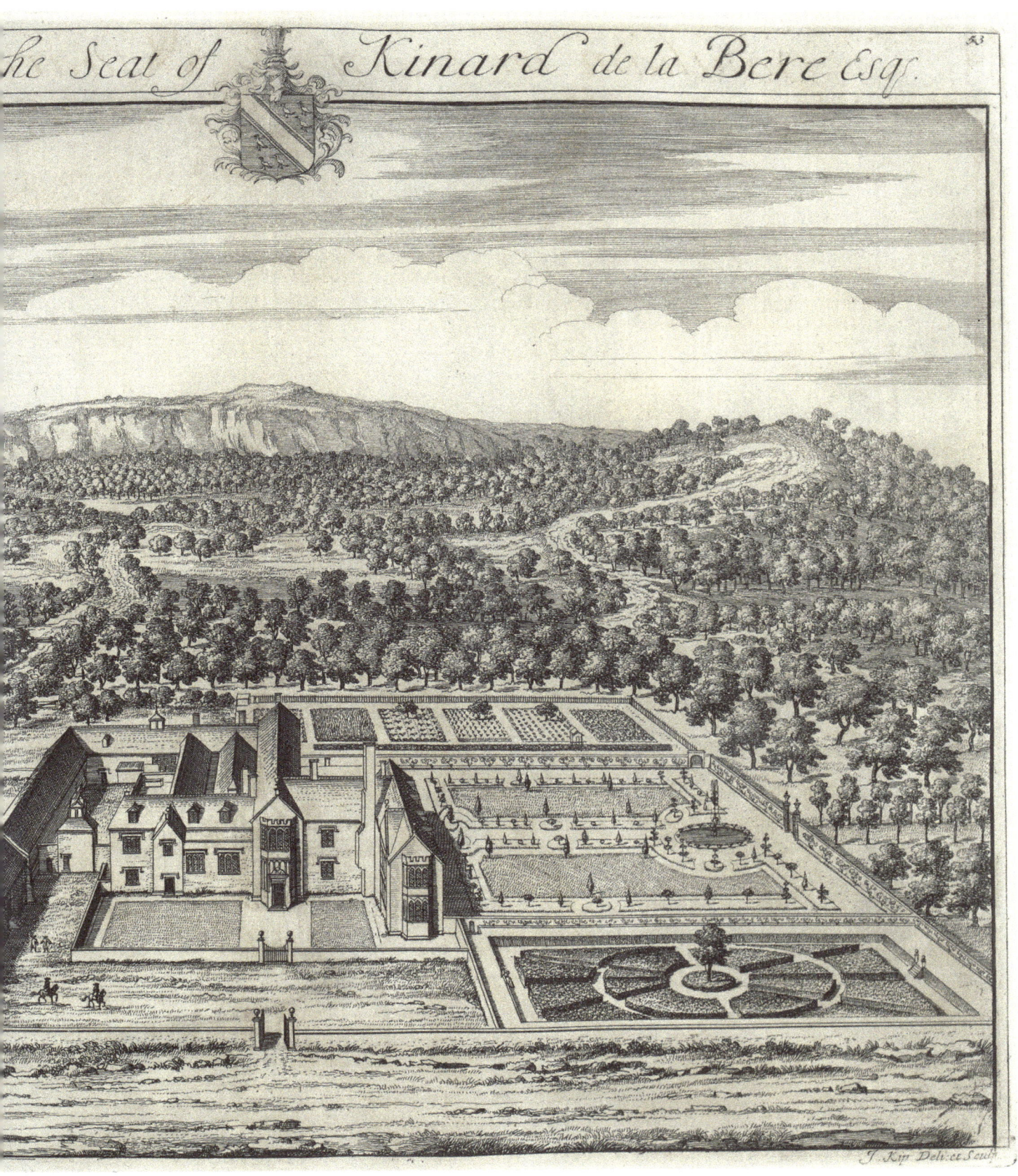

20 **Williamstrip, the Seat of Henry Ireton Esq** [Atkyns: Coln St Aldwyns, 364-365]

'He hath a very handsome house, and large beautiful gardens, and a great estate in this and other places.'

Henry Ireton died in 1711, the same year as Atkyns himself. Kip's engraving shows the west front of the house, and extensive formal gardens to the north-east. It was unusual for Atkyns to comment so specifically on gardens, but at Williamstrip it seems to reflect the notable development which Ireton had undertaken. George London, a famous plantsman of Brompton Nursery, may have laid out the fruit garden designed on a St Andrew's cross; London is known to have been at Williamstrip in 1696. He and Henry Wise had abridged a book by Jean De La Quintini, translated by John Evelyn, which contained a plate showing just such a garden layout.

Henry Ireton's wife had inherited Williamstrip in 1692 and garden development went with the rebuilding of the house which Ireton had also undertaken. Kip also drew a building to the north-west of the new house, linked to it by a covered way; it has the appearance of being an older house which was retained while being reduced in height, possibly while the much grander house was being built. It consisted of three blocks in a zigzag and had a large number of chimneys. It stood beside a gateway leading to parkland later called 'The Great Lawn'. A strong boundary separated it from the gardens. The park has since been enlarged.

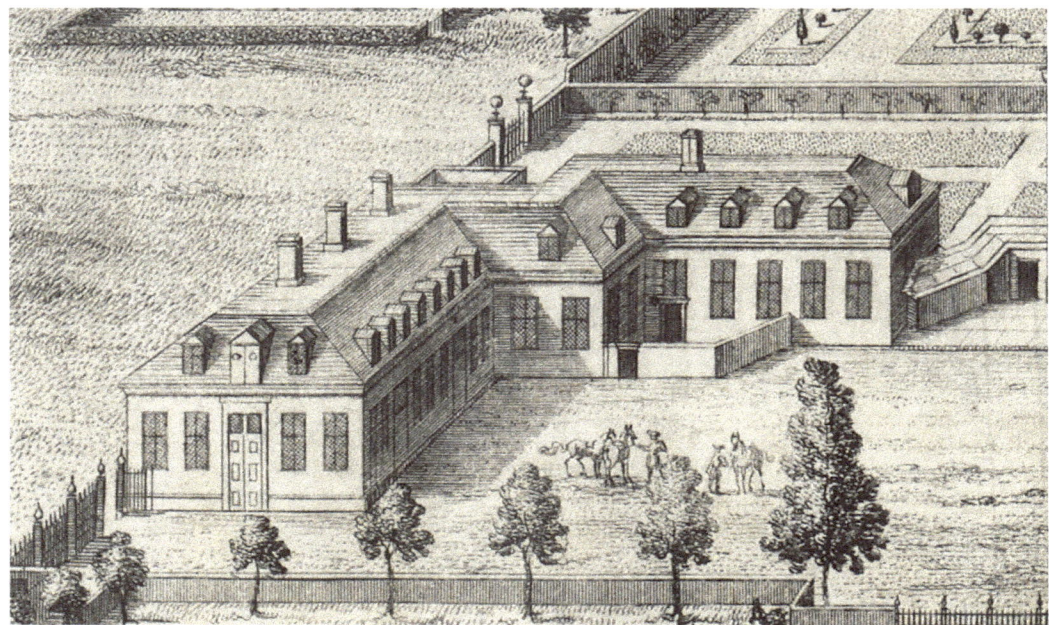

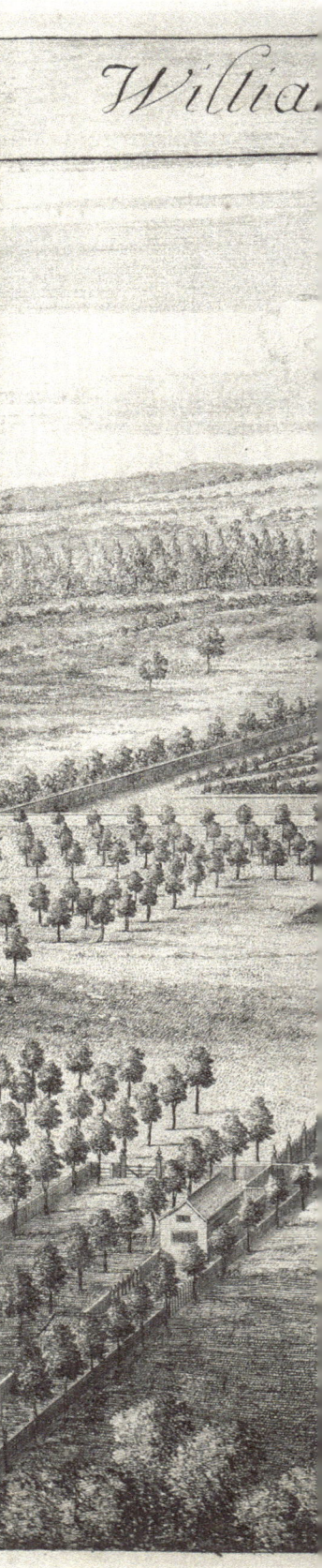

Kip placed himself at an angle to the west front of Williamstrip so that while the house is in the middle, more land was sketched to the east, where it was owned by Ireton, than to the south, which was Hatherop land. The main entrance was on the Hatherop road. A road crossing Kip's view joined Akeman Street which may be visible climbing to the hilltop on the horizon. These roads were later closed or moved further from the house.

Postcode: Coln St Aldwyns GL7 5AT. NGR: SP 15545 05407. **VCH VII** 44-55.

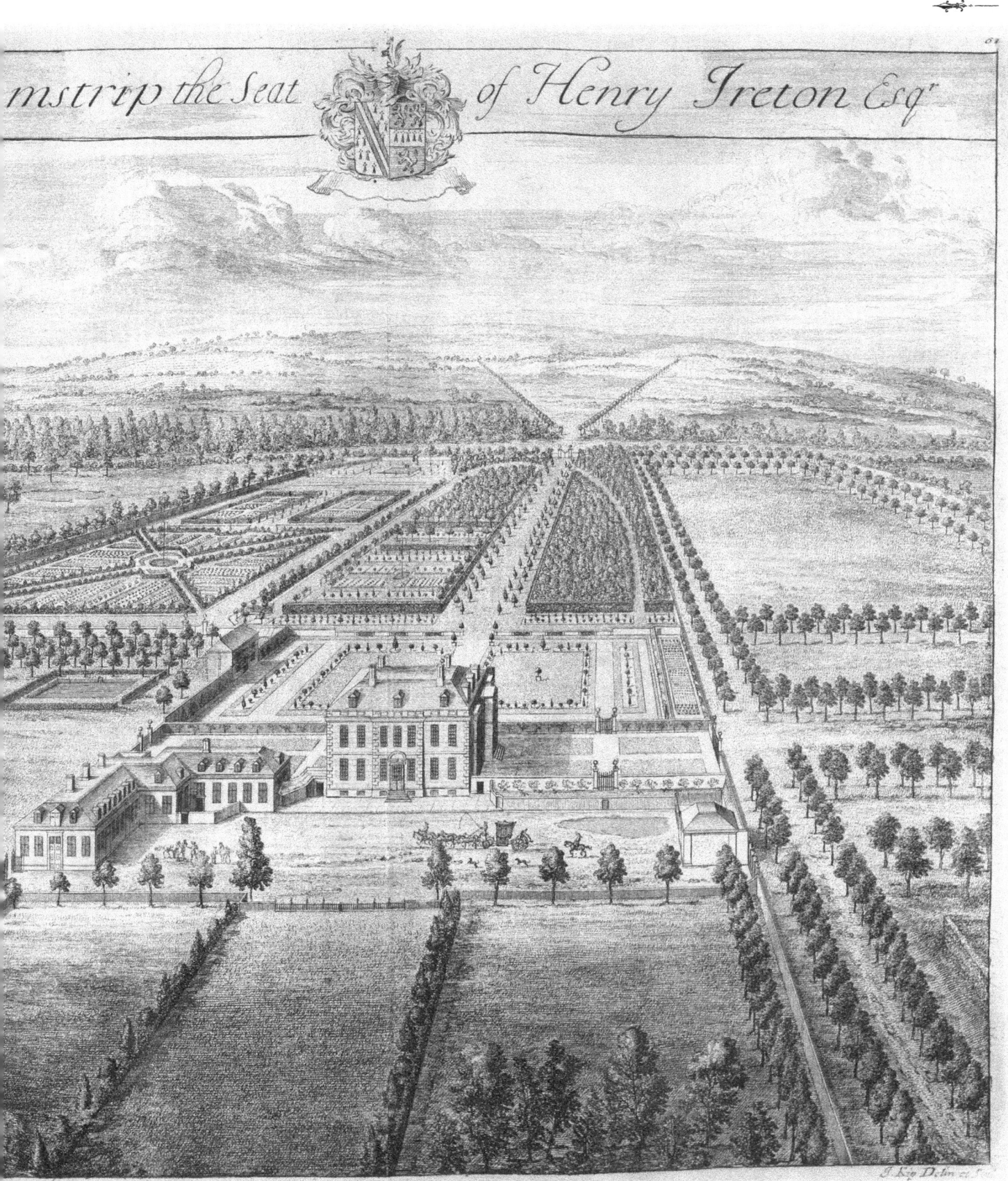

21 **Little Compton the Seat of Sr Richard Howe Bart** [Atkyns: Compton Abdale, 366-36*

'[Sir Richard Howe] hath a large new built house, with delightful gardens, and a pleasant river running thro' them, with an

A great deal of the attractive scene at Little Compton portrayed by Kip can be enjoyed today. The main part of the house, which faces west, still stands; additions have been made on the north side, but the one major change is the demolition of the south wing. It stood beside the Coln which was canalised on the south side of the house, as it still is.

The elaborate gardens behind the house have gone, but the sloping field to the east has a raised bank through the middle corresponding to the sections of the garden shown in the engraving. The dovecote on the stable block remains and the bowling green, on which Kip drew a game of bowls in progress, remains as a flat area partly enclosed with old yew trees.

Immediately beyond the house, on the far side of the river Coln, Kip indicated parkland with the symbolic deer grazing (*qv*). As Atkyns observed, the park was of 'great extent', 356 acres (144 ha) in 1805, and three centuries later, Compton Great Park and Little Compton park remain open pasture with scattered trees. The decorative gate into the park is replaced by a farm gate but even the recess leading to the gate is as Kip showed it. Extensive woods still clothe the hills towards Chedworth but rides through the Star Wood are less prominent (*qv*).

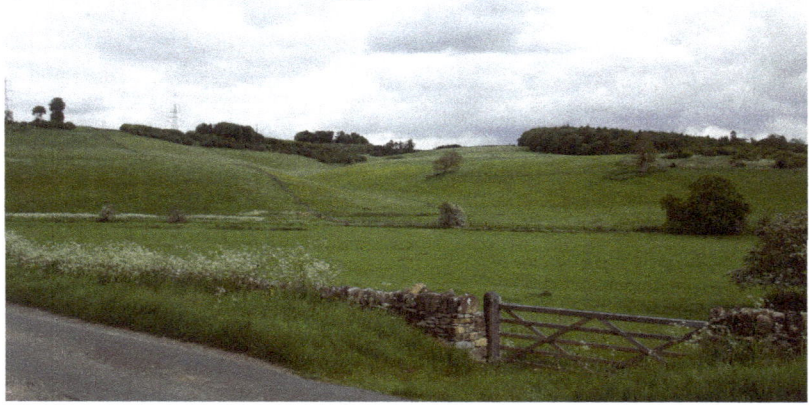

Atkyns placed Cassey Compton house as the manor house of Compton Abdale, even though it is in Withington parish, but he entered the description of Cassey Compton hamlet and the early history of the Cassey family under Withington. Withington parish boundary followed a stream from Compton Abdale which joins the Coln below the house.

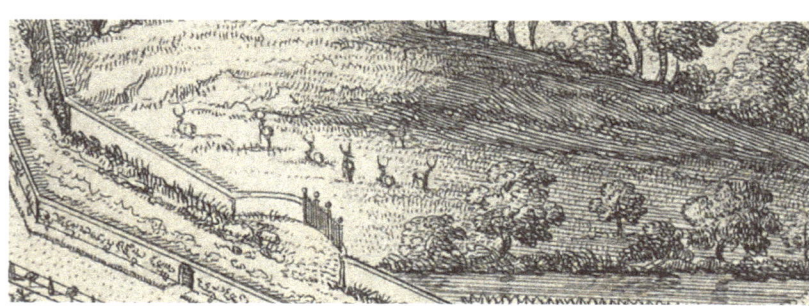

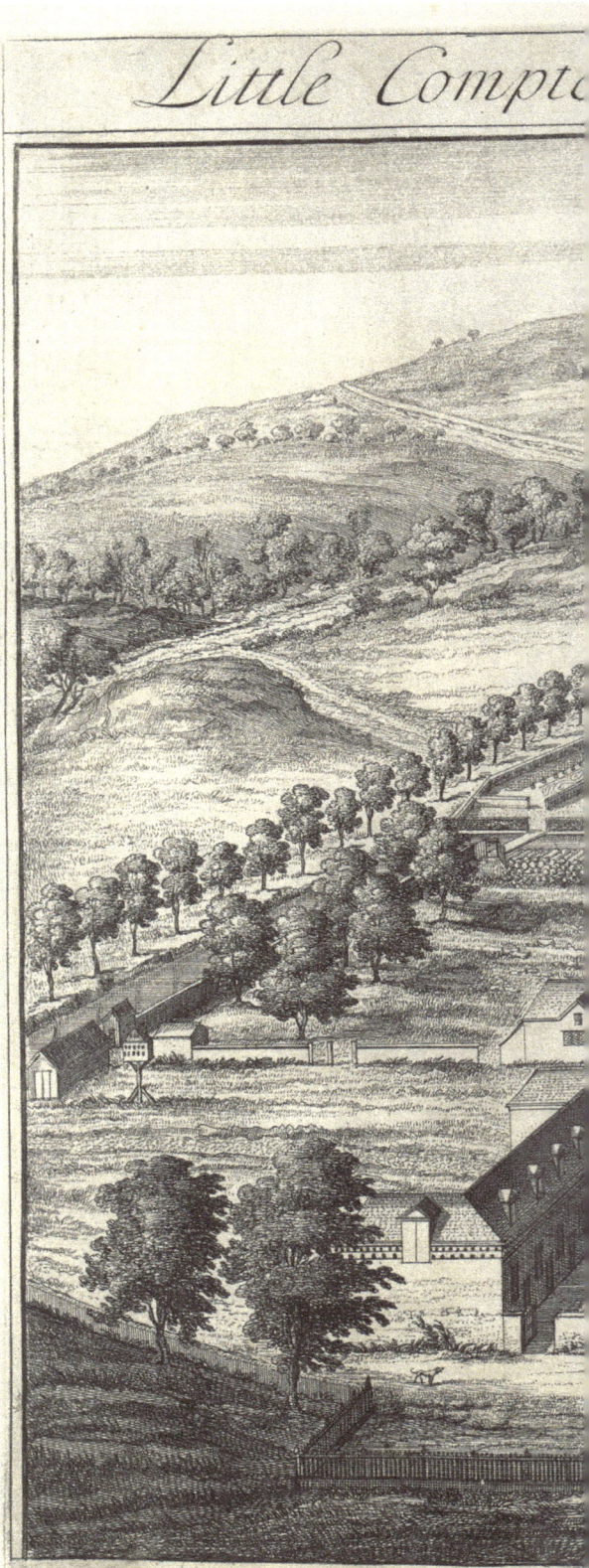

Postcode: Withington GL54 4DE. NGR: SP 04982 15015. **VCH IX** 261-63.

greeable prospect on large woods, and on a park of great extent'.

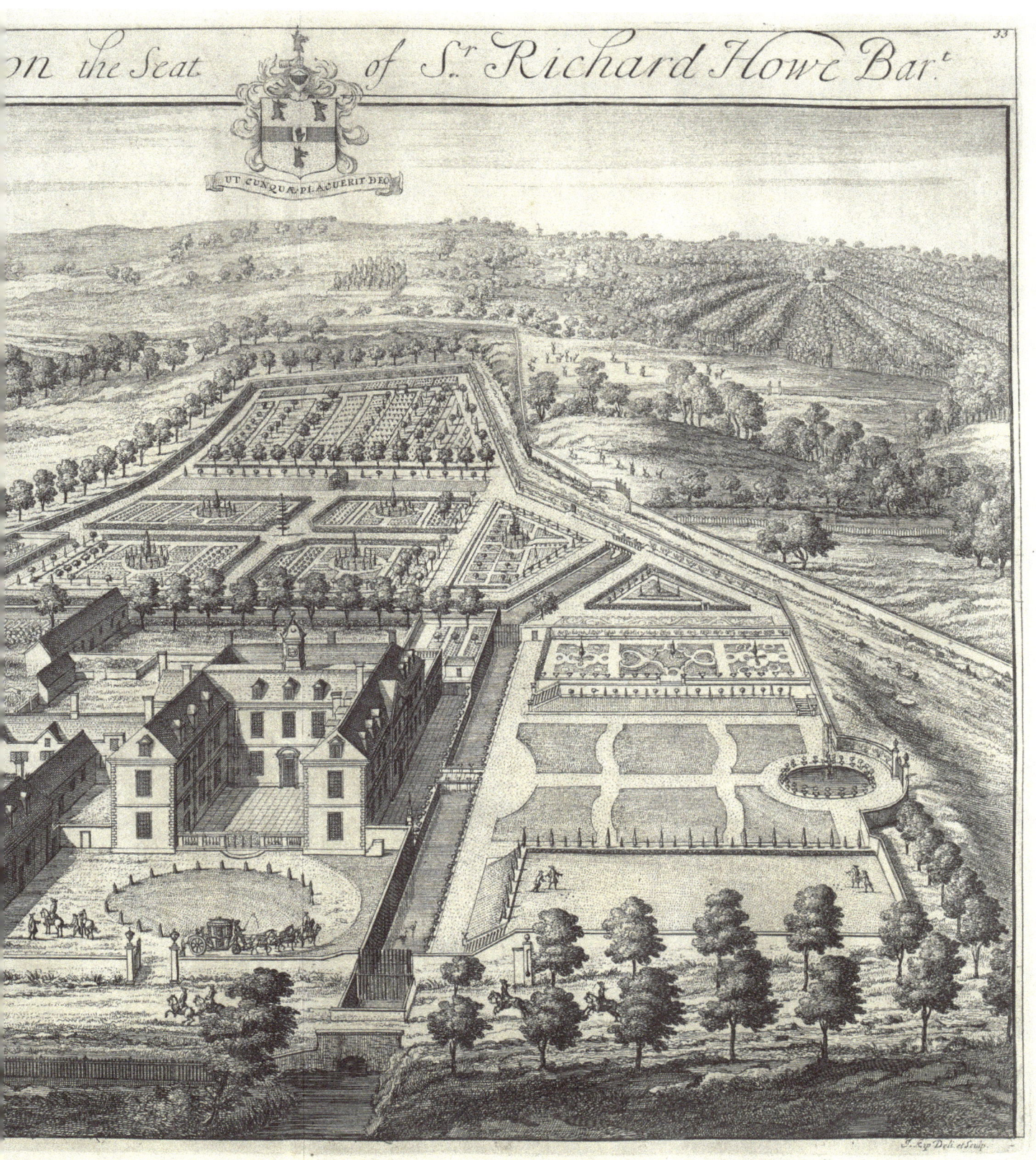

22 Coberly the Seat of Jonathan Castelman Esq [Atkyns: Cubberly, 376-377].

Jonathan Castleman Esq is the present lord of the mannor, who hath a large house near the church, with handsome gardens

Coberley Court was demolished about 1790; the stone was carted away and the site is now a grass field. A house fronting the road was built for the farmer. But many details of the site today correspond closely with Kip's observation.

Kip's view is from the north. A striking feature is the church completely surrounded by the manor grounds. It is reached by a carriage way through buildings including a large listed barn, and a path then runs through a private garden. The old house was on the south side of the church. One range appears like a medieval Great Hall, and beyond it was another range which may have been older.

The Gloucestershire Way follows the line of the former road to the east of the house, leading to a causeway retaining the upper pond or lake (*qv*); Kip drew a boat on the far side of the island, on which there was a gazebo.

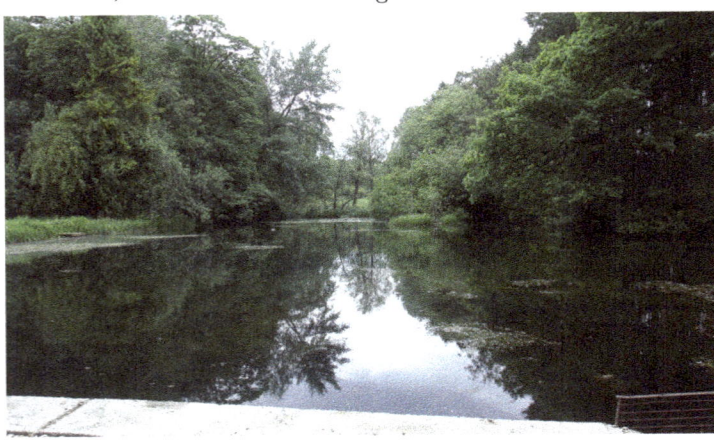

The pond below the causeway is today a surprisingly deep ravine; Kip drew a pavilion on the bank.

Beyond the causeway the road forked as the footpath does, but went along avenues of which there is now no sign. The kitchen garden close to the upper pond is mainly grassland, as is the formal garden adjoining the churchyard. The walled area once an orchard remains; the wall once separating church and manor house and the crenellated wall on the east side of the churchyard are listed.

Coberley Court was sold to Paul Castelman in 1660, and in 1672 he paid tax on twenty-six hearths, which suggests the size of the house. His son Jonathan inherited in 1678 and retained it until he sold in 1720. Thereafter the house ceased to be occupied by the owners, and gradually fell into disrepair.

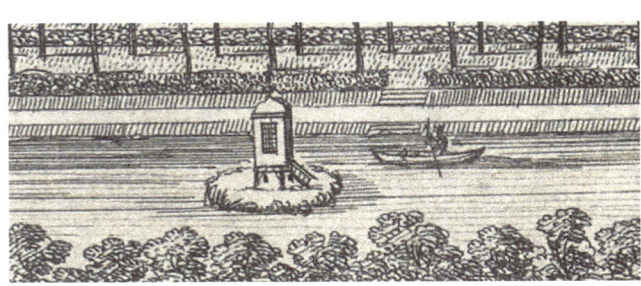

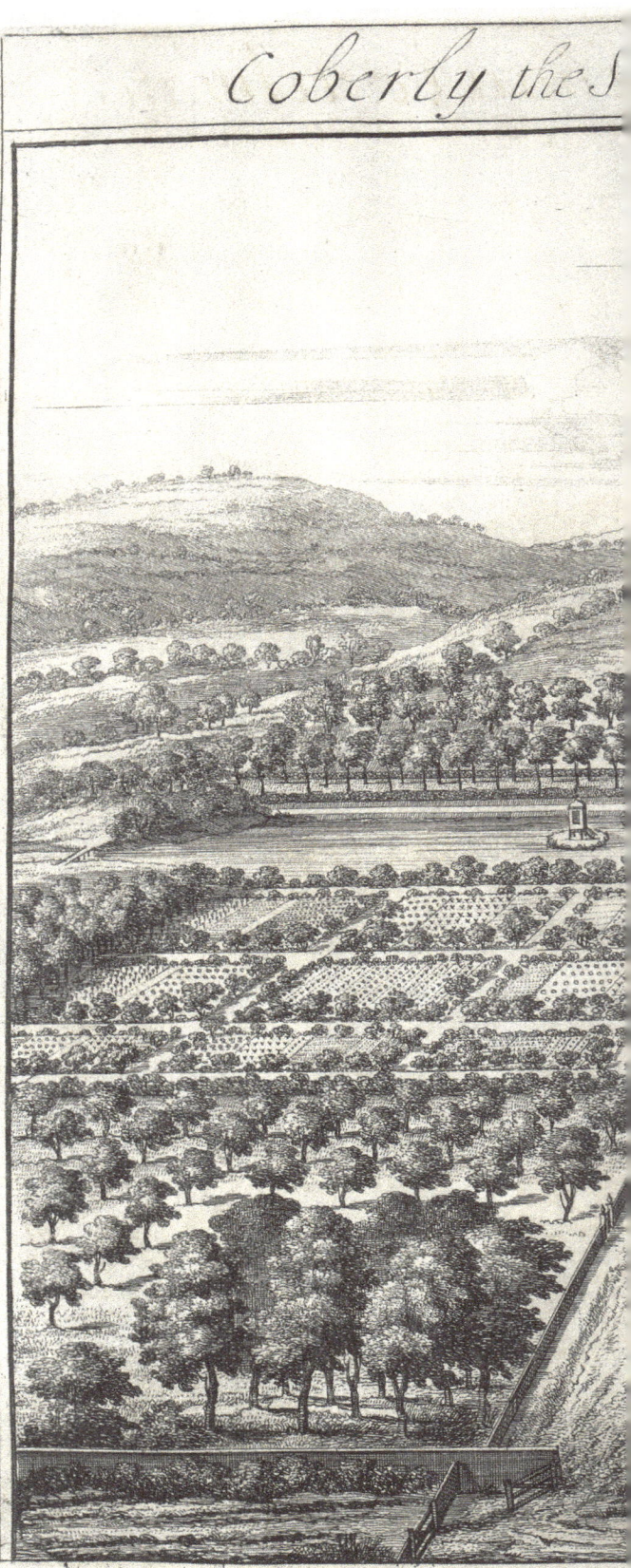

Coberly the S

Postcode: Cheltenham GL53 9RA. NGR: SO 96565 15816. **VCH VII** 174-183.

and ponds, and hath a great estate in this parish'.

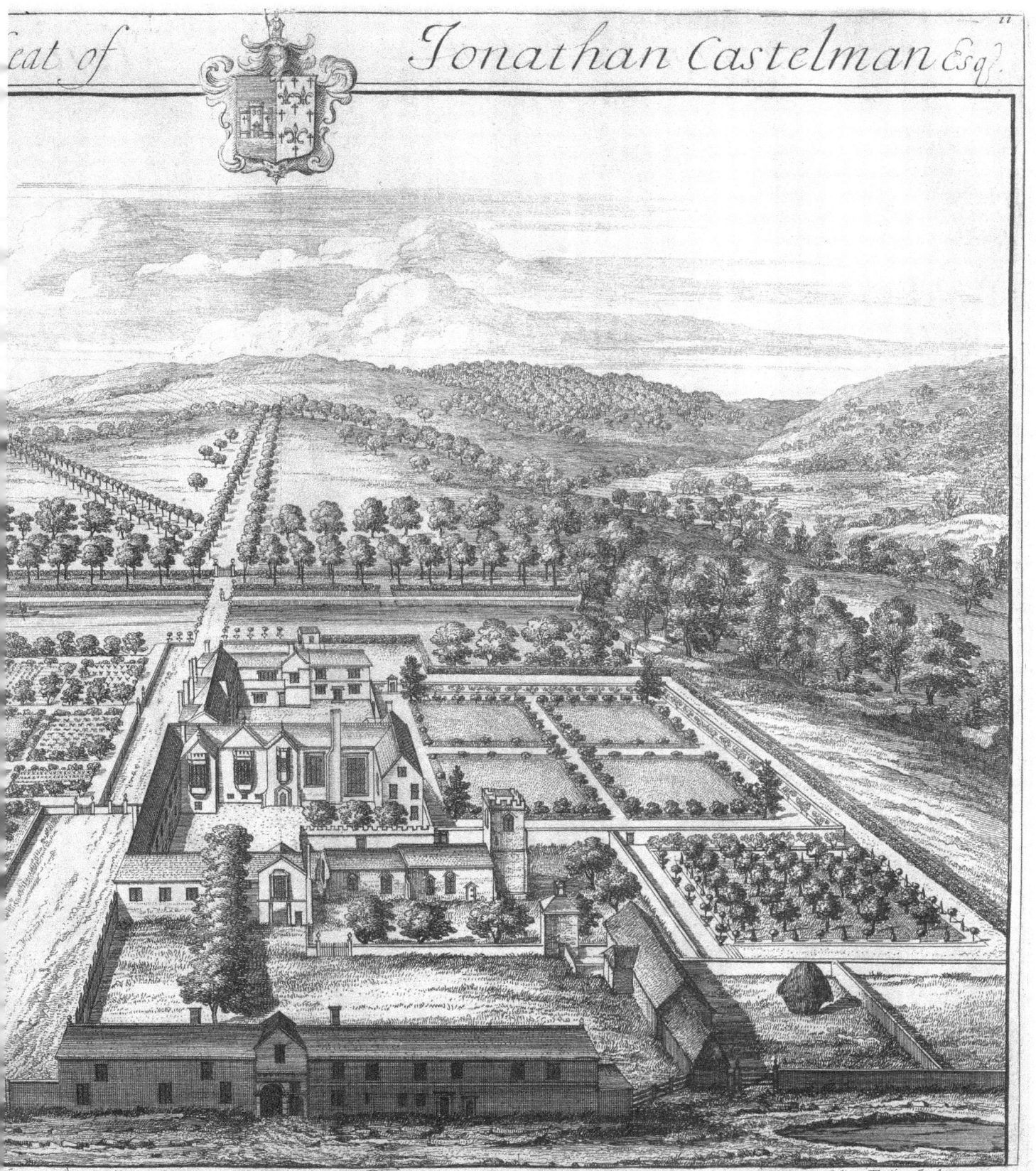

23 Didmarton the Seat of Robert Codrington Esq [Atkyns: Didmarton, 390-391].

'Robert Codrington Esq … has a large house near the church, with pleasant gardens, and a great etate in this and other places

The story of Didmarton is unusually complicated. The house, with its two projecting wings and courtyard facing east, was similar to Toddington manor and was built about the same time. Simon Codrington had acquired Didmarton through marriage in 1571 and his great-grandson held it in 1712. Much more of the house has survived than at Toddington: a block behind the southern gable, together with the south wing cut back to be approximately level with the front (*qv*). The footprint of the simple formal gardens to south and west remains as Kip indicated; to the south figures are apparently dancing, one in each of the eight squares. The barn has been rebuilt.

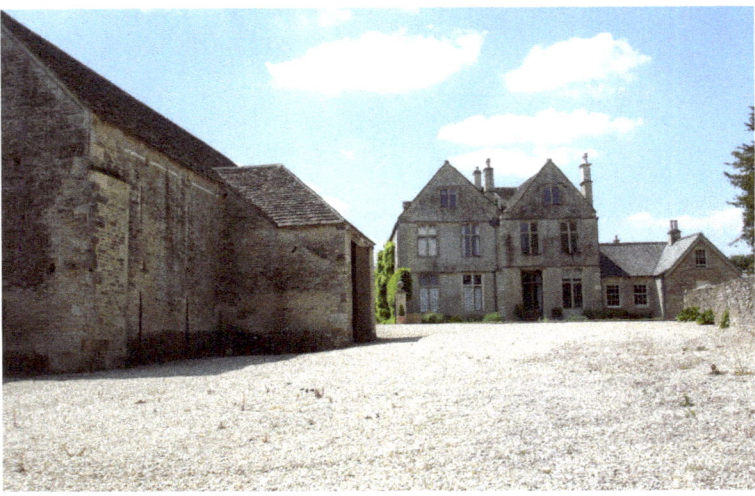

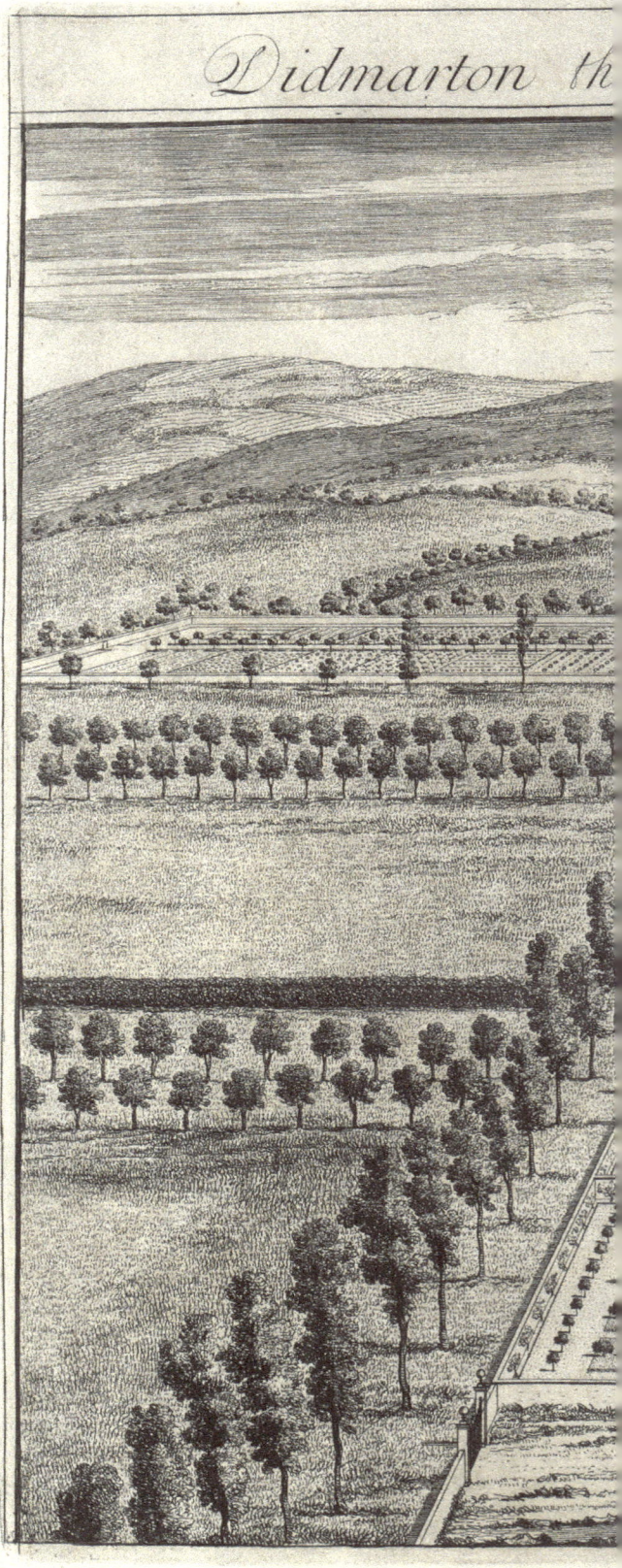

House and small church are close to an important road. In Atkyns' time this was the highway between Bristol and Banbury, recorded in John Ogilby's Britannia road atlas published in 1675 (*qv*). Ogilby's symbol for the church, however, was misleading; the church today is much as Kip drew it, a single cell Norman building and a fourteenth-century north transept. Atkyns noted that 'the church is small with a small wooden turret', as Kip also noted.

The boundary between Didmarton and Oldbury-on-the-hill to the north ran along part of the road; to the south, a continuous line drawn by Kip, just one long field away, was the Wiltshire boundary. Didmarton's name meant Dydda's boundary settlement. Kip drew arable strips in the fields especially to the north, which were common to Didmarton and Oldbury.

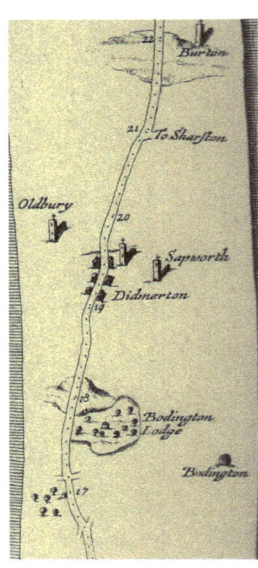

The Duke of Beaufort acquired Didmarton in mid-eighteenth century. He demolished a large part of the house and after repairs, gave it as the rectory house of the combined livings of Didmarton and Oldbury. It was sold by the Church Commissioners in 1950 and reverted to private ownership.

Postcode: Didmarton GL9 1DT. NGR: ST 82179 87420.

of this County'.

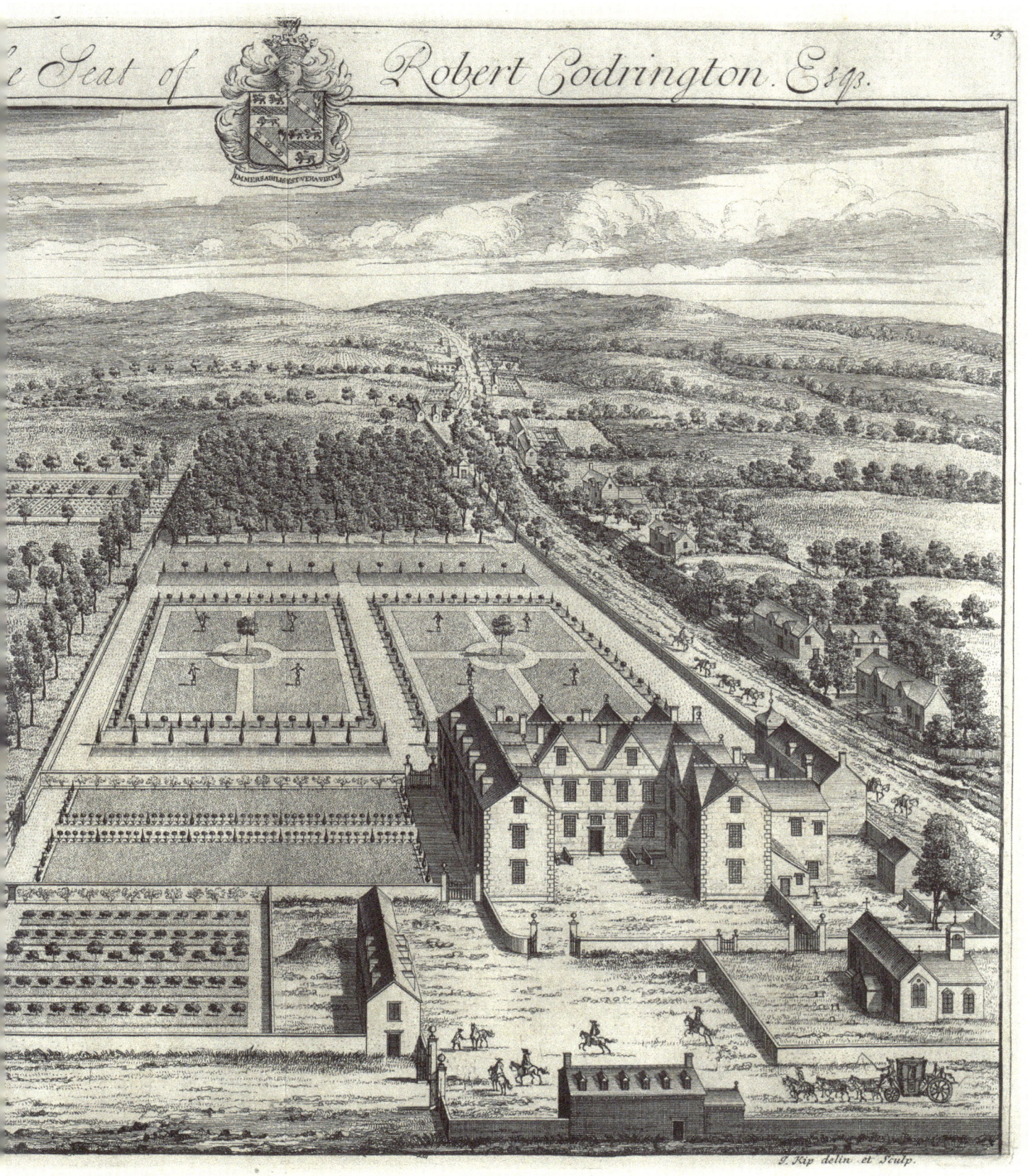

24 Upper Dowdeswell the Seat of Lionel Rich Esq [Atkyns: Dowdswell, 400-401].

'Lionel Rich Esq, son of Sir Edward Rich, is the present lord of the manor of Upper Dowdeswell, and hath a good seat and a

Dowdeswell

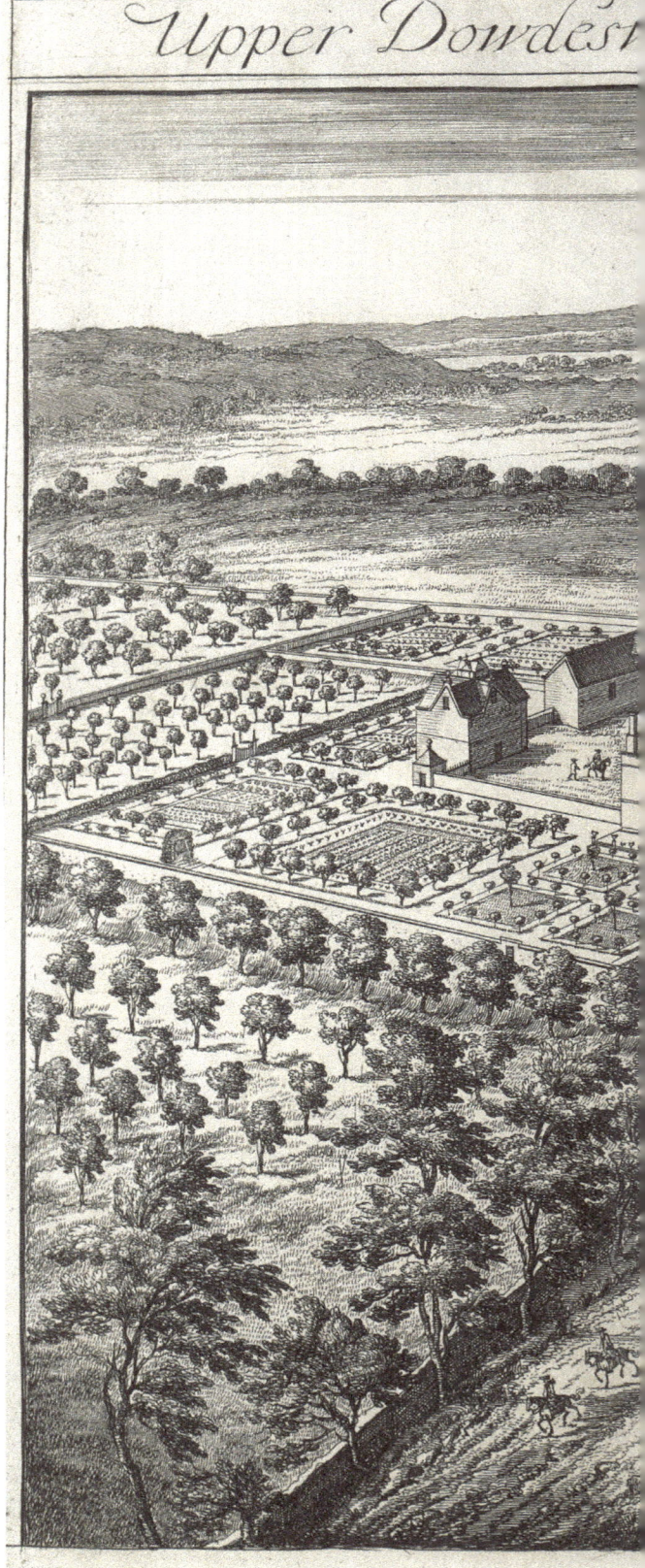

Dowdeswell is well-known because of the reservoir in a deep valley in the parish, holding the water of the river Chelt which rises near Sandywell. Sandywell, however, is on a watershed, and to the east of the house small streams flow into the Coln. Dowdeswell is familiar to historians because linked with the estate recorded in the eighth century as the inheritance of one abbot Headda. There are two settlements in the parish: Lower Dowdeswell, the larger of the two, which has the parish church, and Upper Dowdeswell.

Upper Dowdeswell house is near the top of the hill where there is an iron age hill fort; it is on the right-hand side (to the west) of Kip's engraving. He indicated the great view from near the house, drawing boats on a distant river Severn and five church towers on the flat land. He also showed the steep fall of the ground, and on the right-hand edge drew a small sketch of the old manor house and church in Lower Dowdeswell (*qv*).

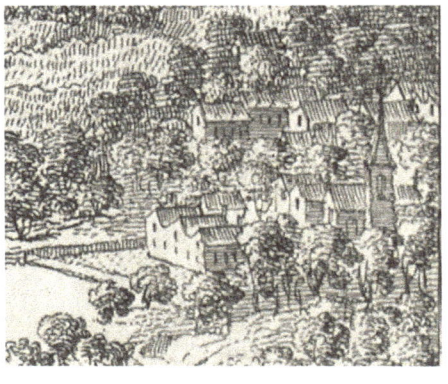

Upper Dowdeswell house was built in the late sixteenth century, probably by Anthony Abington, whose grand-father had bought the estate in 1549. It was sold a hundred years later to Edward Rich, whose grandson was the owner when Kip visited. This family retained the estate until 1774. The house was taxed on 13 chimneys in 1672, the largest house in Dowdeswell. The Rich family claimed that Upper Dowdeswell was a manor and eventually the prestigious title was accepted.

The house faces north and this front range survives. The buildings on the other three sides of the small courtyard, the roofs of which are evident in Kip's drawing, were later demolished; in the twentieth century the west wing was rebuilt. The house is now divided into three.

Typical formal gardens were on the east side of the house; walls and a gazebo north-east of the house (*qv*) remain. To south and west a small park of some 30 acres was grazed by deer later in the eighteenth century. The widening in the road before the first gate and by the barn is still evident.

Postcode: Cheltenham GL54 4LT. NGR: SP 00519 19169. VCH IX 42-69.

large estate'.

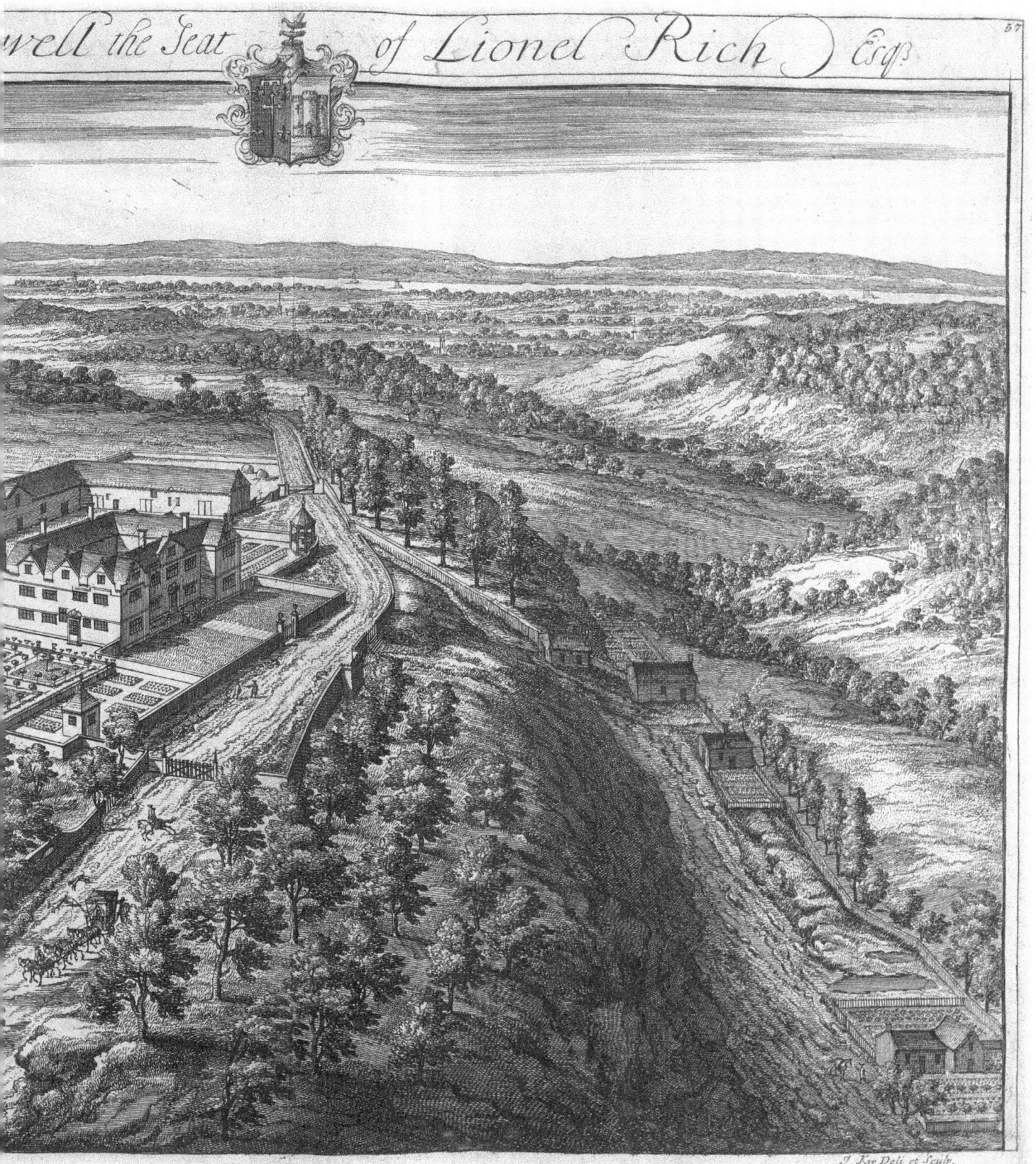

25 **Sandywell the Seat of Henry Bret Esq** [*Atkyns: Dowdswell*, 400-401].

'Henry Bret Esq has a neat pleasant seat at Sandywell, and a new-built house, with pleasant gardens, and a park: he is

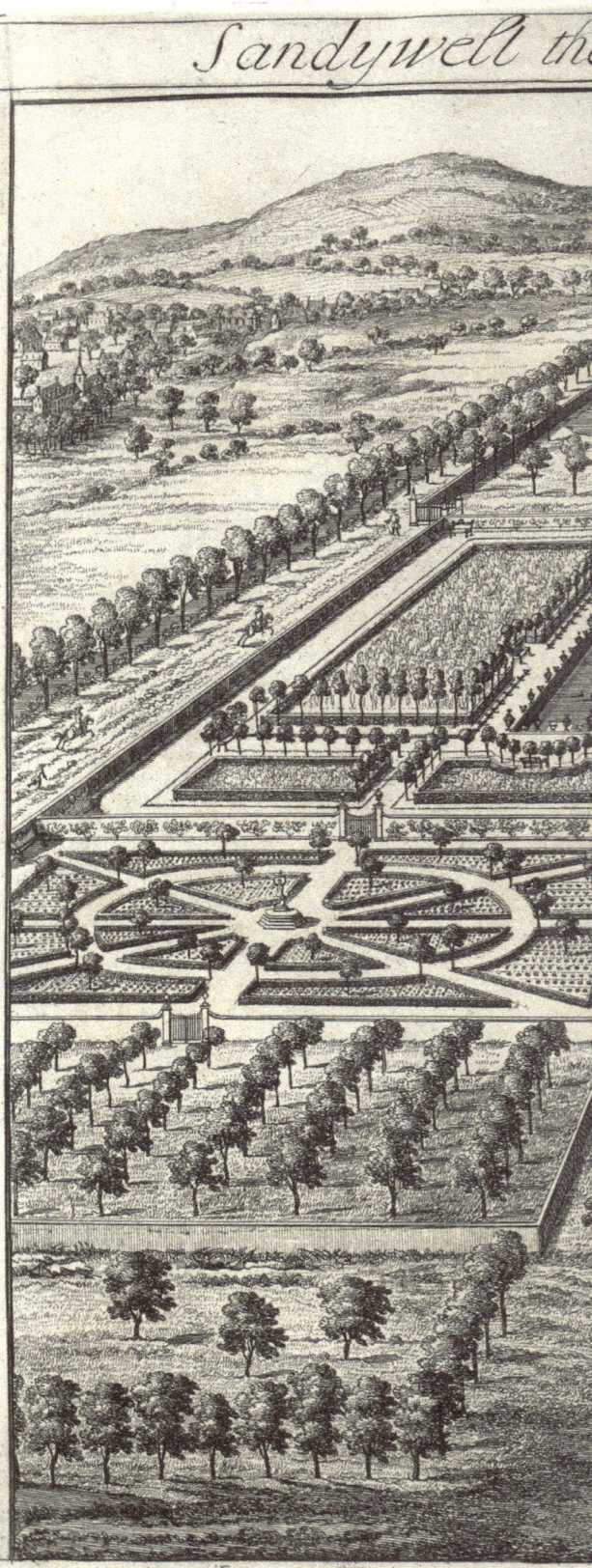

Sandywell is close to Andoversford village, once also within Abbot Headda's estate. The ford was over the Coln, into which water drained from the garden ponds and water features drawn by Kip at Sandywell.

The house is situated on gently rising ground and faces west. When Kip visited it was newly-built by Henry Brett, who had acquired the estate in 1704. In 1712 he sold it to Lord Conway, who two years later bought nearby Whittington Court. A small but distinct Whittington Court can be seen on the northern edge of Kip's engraving (*qv*).

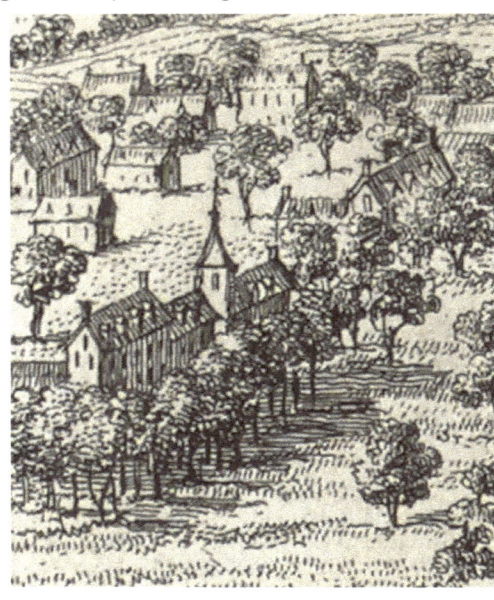

On the roof of the new house Kip drew a viewing platform surrounded by a balustrade, and a strange gazebo which perhaps held the stairs (*qv*). From here the view will have been a beautiful and extensive one of the surrounding hills: Hannington Hill to the north-east and Foxcote Hill to the south-east, both sketched in by Kip.

With ten hearths in 1672, the house which Brett demolished had not been a small one. The formal gardens decorated with statues and urns on tall pillars were most likely the work of previous owners, as also the walled park with its elaborately arranged tree planting and the frisky set of deer. There were seats in the gardens and two seats round trees in the park (*qv*). Brett did enlarge the park on the north side with an exchange of land with Whittington.

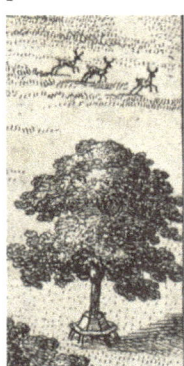

The entrance to Sandywell was on the Upper Dowdeswell to Whittington road, where a fine wrought iron gate was later erected by Lord Conway, one of several on the estate. A coach and horses is driving along the avenue towards the entrance. A lime avenue is on the same line today but the entrance is now on the main road, the A40.

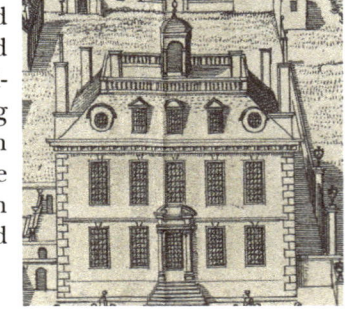

Lord Conway enlarged Sandywell significantly with flanking wings and his son owned the house until 1748, since when Sandywell has had a succession of different owners. It is now divided into twelve flats.

Postcode: Whittington, Cheltenham GL54 4HF. NGR: SP 01372 20243. VCH IX 42-69.

descended from the ancient family of the Brets of Bret-Hall in Warwickshire'.

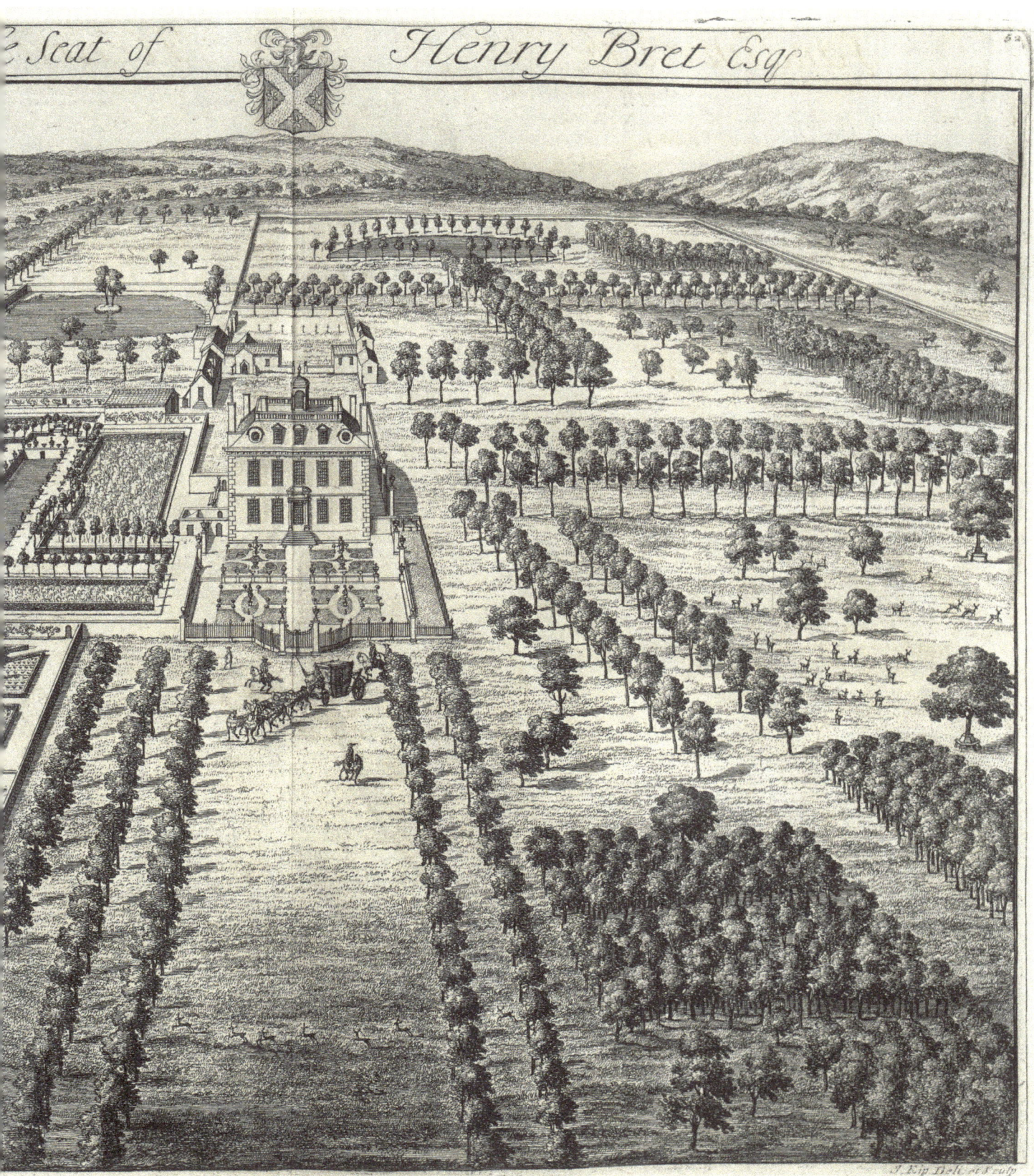

26 Dumbleton the Seat of Sr Richard Cocks Bart [Atkyns: Dumbleton, 405-407].

'Sir Richard Cox Baronet is Lord of the mannor, and hath an handsome seat near the church: the whole parish belongs to him

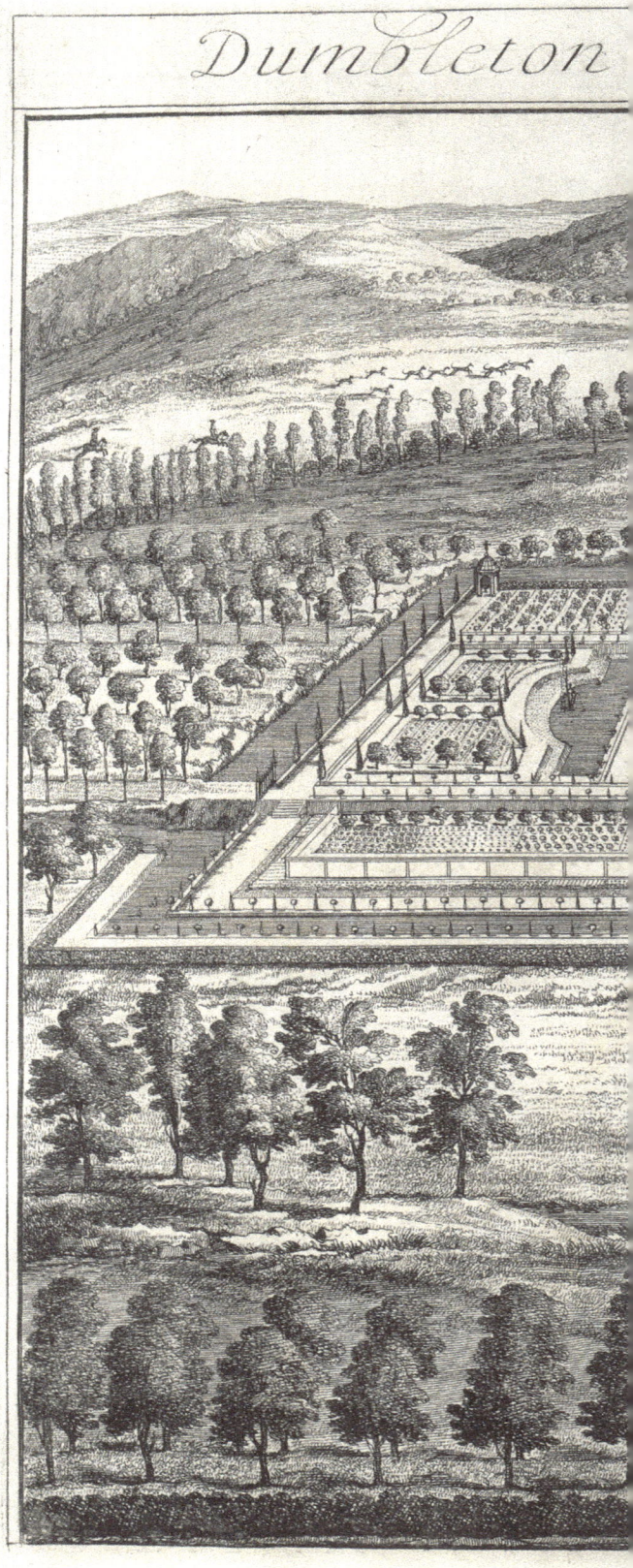

The house illustrated by Kip was constructed during the late 1680s or 90s for Sir Richard Cocks who inherited the estate in 1684. It was south-facing with a small inner courtyard and two projecting wings. After 1767 the family lived elsewhere and the house was partially demolished and remodelled as a farmhouse. It was completely demolished about 1830, the ground levelled and grassed.

From the house a long avenue led to the entrance gates. Another avenue to the north led the eye towards the tower of Ashton-under-Hill church, though the view is foreshortened and liberties have been taken with the representation of Bredon Hill. Note the hounds and riders in full cry in pursuit of their quarry. Three other churches are in Kip's view.

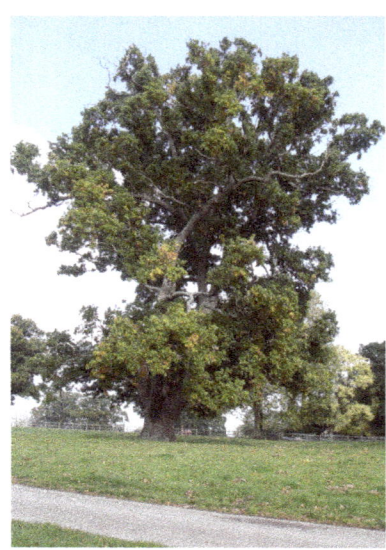

To the west of the house Kip drew an ornamental garden. This too has disappeared under grass but substantial earthworks remain, notably the 'D' shaped embankment framing the pool which Kip showed was decorated with a statue and fountain. Also clearly seen on the ground are the twin parallel raised walks framing this pool. A more subtle depression south of the modern drive coincides with the Kip canal whilst several ancient oaks (*qv*) may be survivors from the original planting.

Nineteenth-century maps chart the demise of Kip's encircling canals; a resistivity survey and exercise in map regression written up for *Glevensis* in 2003 correlates with the outlines of these features and provides evidence of the accuracy of Kip's composition.

A new house, now a hotel, was built in mid-nineteenth century on a site sheltered by Dumbleton Hill. The long range of service buildings north-west of the manor house survive in residential use, also the Rectory house to the north of the church, occupied by Sir Richard Cock's brother, which Kip marked with an elaborate but smaller garden.

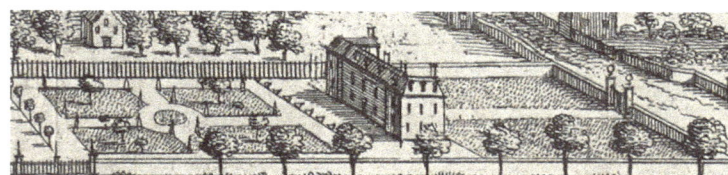

Postcode: [St Peter's church] Evesham WR11 7**TL. NGR: SP** 01650 35761.

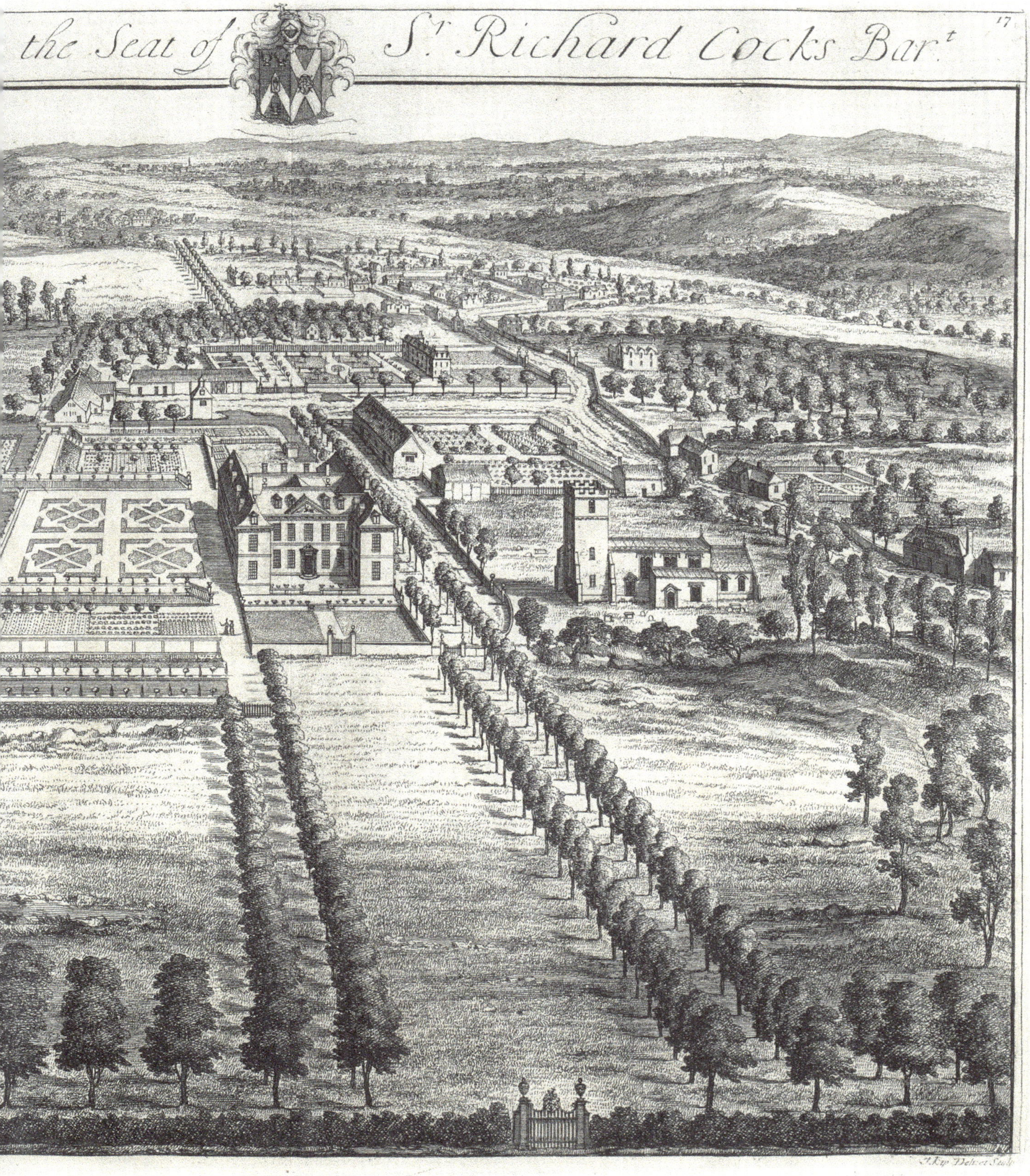

the Seat of   S.ᵗ Richard Cocks Barᵗ

27 Dyrham the Seat of Willam Blathwait Esq [Atkyns: Dyrham and Hinton,414-415].

'William Blathwayt Esq … hath a large handsome new-built house near the church, and beautiful gardens of a great extent, Kingswood. He hath a large park and warren which joyn to his gardens.'

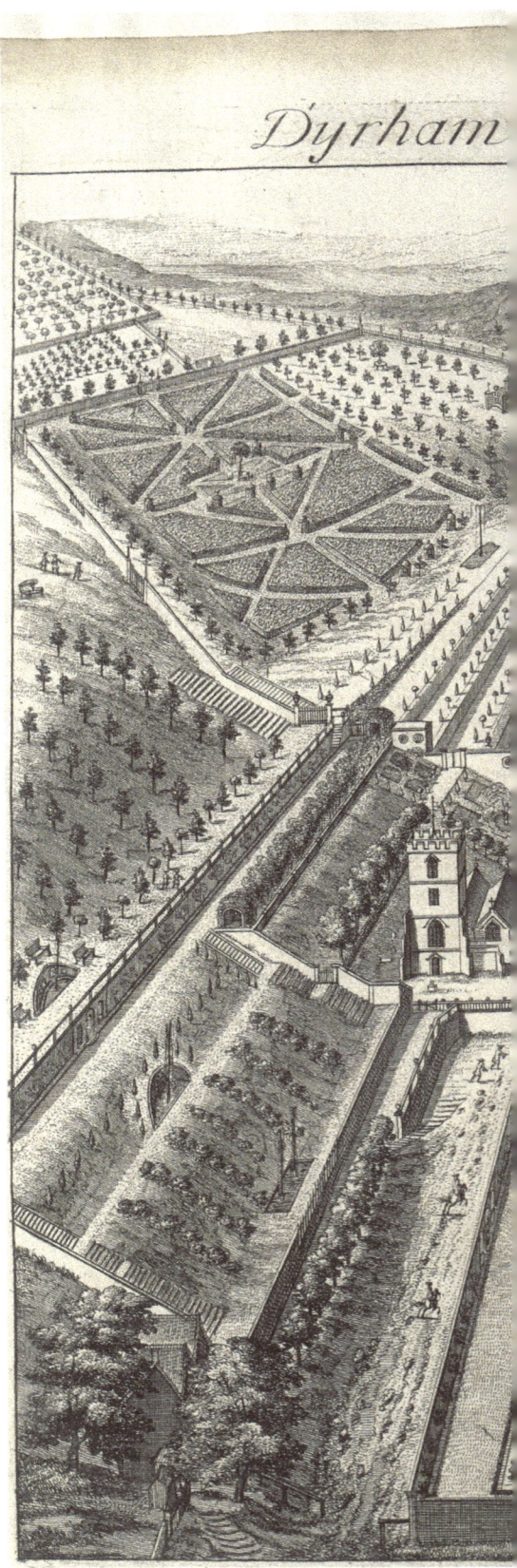

Kip must have found his task at Dyrham very pleasant. If he talked with William Blathwayt it could have been in his own language, as Blathwayt spoke fluent Dutch; he had lived in The Hague between 1668 and 1672, where his uncle Thomas Povey had placed him as a clerk in the embassy. This was the foundation of his career. When William of Orange came to England, he became a trusted assistant. The garden designs, too, would have had echoes of gardens in Kip's own country. Blathwayt became exceptionally interested in water features: fountains, cascades, water spouts and pools were all created at Dyrham. Kip had another unusual advantage in drawing Dyrham: letters and plans sent between Blathwayt and his chief gardener, Thomas Hurnall, while Blathwayt was with William III in Flanders, may have given Kip very precise and up-to-date knowledge. Blathwayt married the heiress to Dyrham, Mary Wynter, in 1686. The estate had been owned by the Wynter family since the later sixteenth century. John Evelyn noted Blathwayt was 'a very proper handsome person', and 'married a very great fortune'. Mary's father died in 1688 and Mary died in 1691. Blathwayt erected a monument in the church to his 'most dearest and most beloved wife' and to her father and mother. He did not marry again and died in 1717, just after his daughter Anne who died in childbirth. Anne had married the son of Sir Robert Southwell, a mentor to her father, and so went to Kingsweston, also engraved by Kip. Two Blathwayt sons survived, and the family continued to own Dyrham until 1956.

Once in control of the estate, Blathwayt commissioned a survey from Christopher Jacob. The map, dated 1689, shows that the main features relevant to the later gardens already existed (*qv*). Blathwayt's designs involved some earth-moving and culverting of the stream, and the building of walls, but mainly were ambitious schemes of planting.

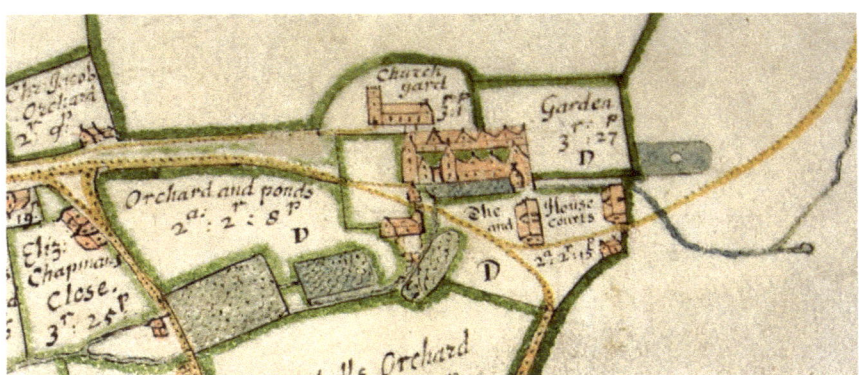

The old house faced south; it was about 200 years old, and Blathwayt thought it needed expensive repairs. After Mary's death he started to build a new house, on the same site but facing west. It was finished in 1694, an unostentatious but balanced design by a little-known Huguenot architect, Samuel Hauduroy. This is the house in Kip's engraving (*qv*). The beds in front of the house had clearly been recently planted. The National Trust, which became responsible for this property in 1961, has recreated gardens on this side of the house inspired by the engraving, and in the spirit of Blathwayt's design. Painted iron poles with gold knobs supporting young shrubs were used originally, and have been reintroduced.

Postcode: Chippenham SN14 8HW. NGR: ST 74424 75821.

with curious water-works and pleasant walks, which have distant prospects on the City of Bristol, and Forest of

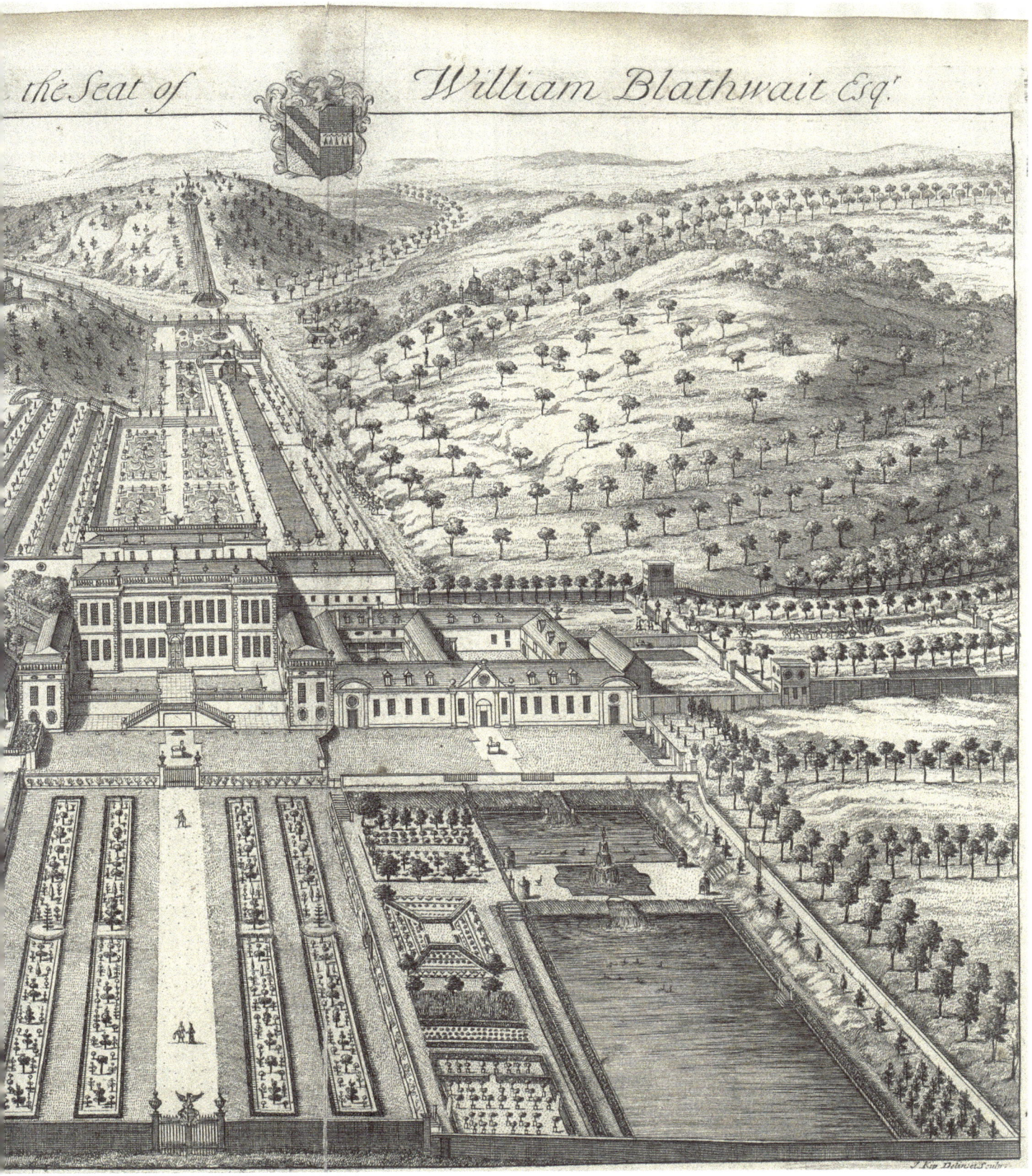

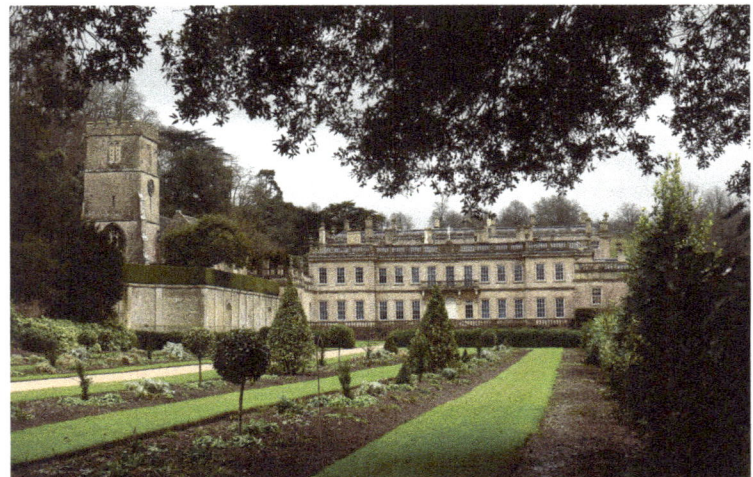

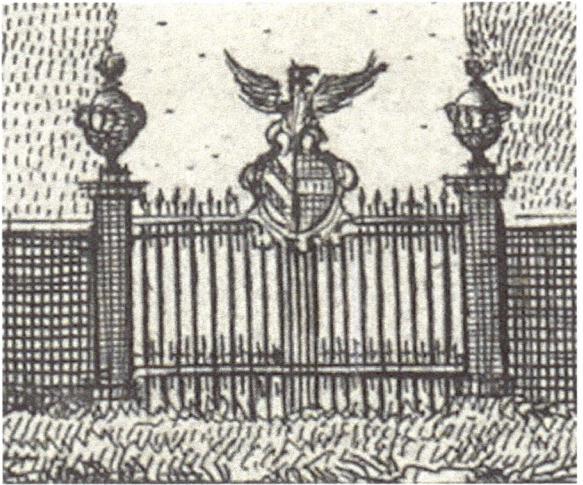

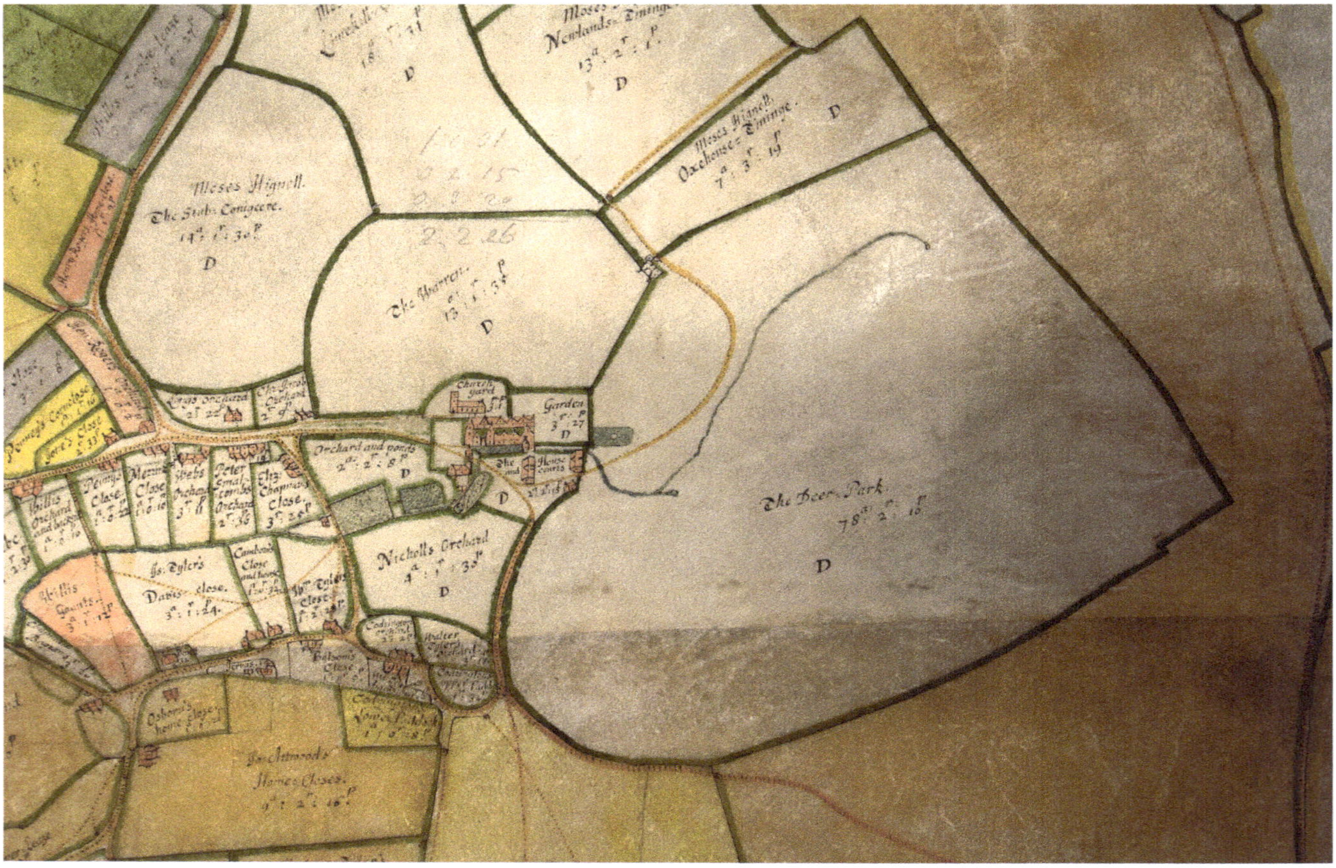

Four years later an east-facing building was started, designed by William Talman, comptroller of the Royal Works. By tilting the drawing Kip was able to show gardens on the east side though not the façade. These are not being recreated; only the statue of Neptune remains on top of the hill facing the east front (*qv*), which once stood above the long cascade of water – 224 steps - now a steep grassy slope. The cascade required elaborate works to bring water to the top of the hill, and Blathwayt did consider abandoning it and using the stone elsewhere. The cascade or cataract attracted much admiration. Strangely, although within the deer park, Kip did not draw deer, as he usually did to indicate a park. Jacob's map labelled the area and noted that it was 78½ acres (32 ha) (*qv*); it has since been extended. Sir George Wynter created the park in 1620. Jacob's map also indicates to the south-east an 'old park' and further south a large former park around a lodge; both were probably medieval. In 1710 there were 38 'antlers' and 72 'does, teags and fawns' at Dyrham, and Blathwayt received deer as a gift from Germany. Possibly they had been moved away from the cascade.

The park was bounded on the south side by the curve of the drive from the Marshfield-Cold Aston road and a carriage and horses are shown approaching house and stables. The drive was re-routed when the road to Bath was improved. On the other side of the house Kip drew a new entrance from Dyrham village; previously the road to the church also led to the house. He made the wrought iron gates look more grand than they really were with an over-sized eagle on top (*qv*), a copy of the one above the east front.

The church, dating at least from the thirteenth century, stands close to but higher than the house and a tall retaining wall supports the terrace on which it stands. Above the church the land rises steeply to Hinton Iron Age hill fort. The 1689 map labels the wooded slope 'The Warren' where rabbits were reared for the table, and next to it a 'Conigeere' or rabbit garden. On the slope of the hill four narrow terraces were created, planted with dwarf pear trees; veterans are still growing there. Semicircular niches in the terrace walls, seen in Kip, contained fountains, one with seats arranged round it. Other niches contained paintings.

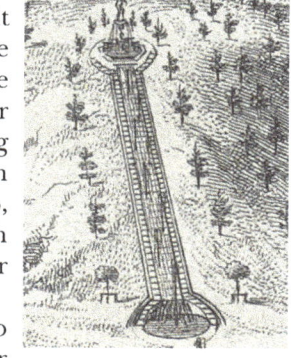

In the lower garden to the south-west is the smaller pond, fed by a cascade from the culverted stream under the stable block, and below it the larger pond. Both existed in 1689, shown on the map as formal straight-sided rectangles. They were not purely decorative, but contained fish for the table, as did other pools with fountains. There were swans on the lower pond.

Between the two ponds Kip drew a much smaller round pond with a statue in the centre, no longer existing though a dry summer reveals its footprint. Archaeology has revealed the base of one of the four small pavilions set in the corners around it. Similarly the base of one of the sphinxes in front of the house has been found, also

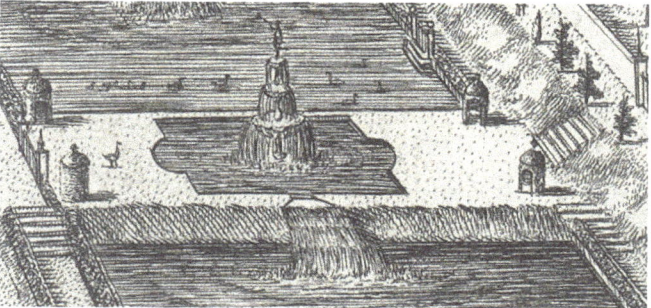

confirming Kip's drawing. The gardens were embellished with numerous statues and small pavilions.

The gardens were an elaborate essay on the topography of the site. The house is surrounded on three sides with rounded hills (*qv*), while open on the west to Dyrham village and a longer view. The constraints of an etching meant that Kip could not capture the beauty of the scene, but did give an accurate picture. Many details of Kip's engraving are confirmed by visitors' descriptions, and by a whole chapter devoted to 'A description of a beautiful rural garden' in the third volume of Stephen Switzer's *Ichnographia Rustica*, published in 1718.

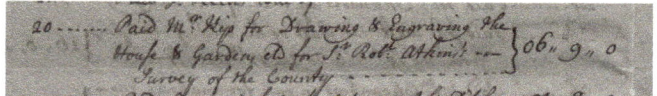

On 20 September 1710 Blathwayt's meticulous accounts record 'Paid Mr Kip for Drawing & Engraving the House and Garden, etc. For Sr Robert Atkins's survey of the County. 06. 09. 00'. The entry (*qv*) shows that owners of houses illustrated in Atkyns' book paid Kip directly, as implied also in the Berkeley accounts. Furthermore, Blathwayt's papers contain an 'Account of Dirham' which, apart from a few omissions and additions, is almost word for word the same as the account in the *The Ancient and Present State of Glostershire*, owners were seemingly given a fair copy of a draft for comment.

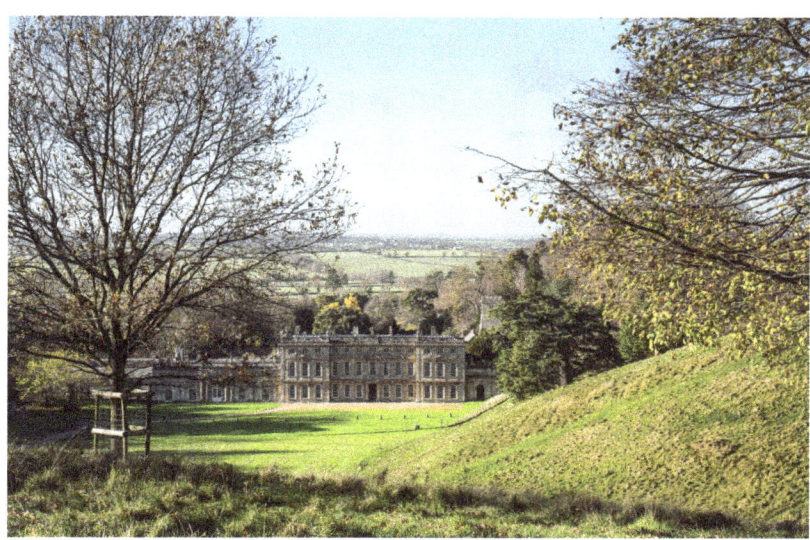

28 Easington the Seat of Nathaniel Stevens Esq [Atkyns: Easington, 418-419].

'Nathaniel Stephens … is the present lord of the mannors of Easington and Alkerton … He hath a beautiful stone house near

Of the buildings in Kip's engraving, only the church and the two-storey cottages to the west remain. The site was a constricted one, bounded by the river Frome and several cuts flowing from it, as well as a moat, part of which survived when Kip drew the scene. Hence the manor house was a compact, tall, square three-storey building of ashlar stone with a porch on the north side rising the full height. There was limited room for gardens. Standing almost in the moat, Kip drew a timber-framed dovecote, and very unusually a pigsty with two curly-tailed pigs in the yard (*qv*).

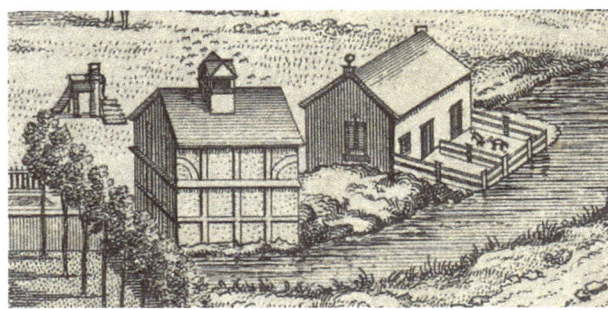

Richard Stephens bought the chief house and site of Eastington manor in 1569. His brother Edward built the new manor house about 1578. The Stephens were associated with the cloth industry. In 1672 Richard Stephens Esq paid tax on nineteen hearths. Soon after Kip had drawn the house the family moved to Chavenage and Eastington manor became a farmhouse. It was in poor repair when demolished in 1778 and the materials sold. Millend Lane now follows the drive which once led to the big house.

The site resembles an early manorial 'bury' with a rounded boundary inclosing manor house and church, though the church is not recorded until 1291. The church tower seems too big for the modest size of the nave but Bigland's engraving suggests how exact was Kip's drawing of nave and chancel (*qv*); the roof has since been raised. The former rectory on the far side of the road to the east is now the site of the primary school. In the distance hills, appearing much closer to the church than in reality, might be the rising ground at Frocester.

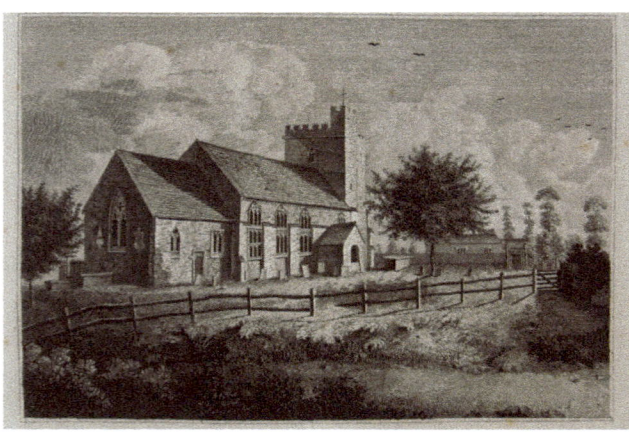

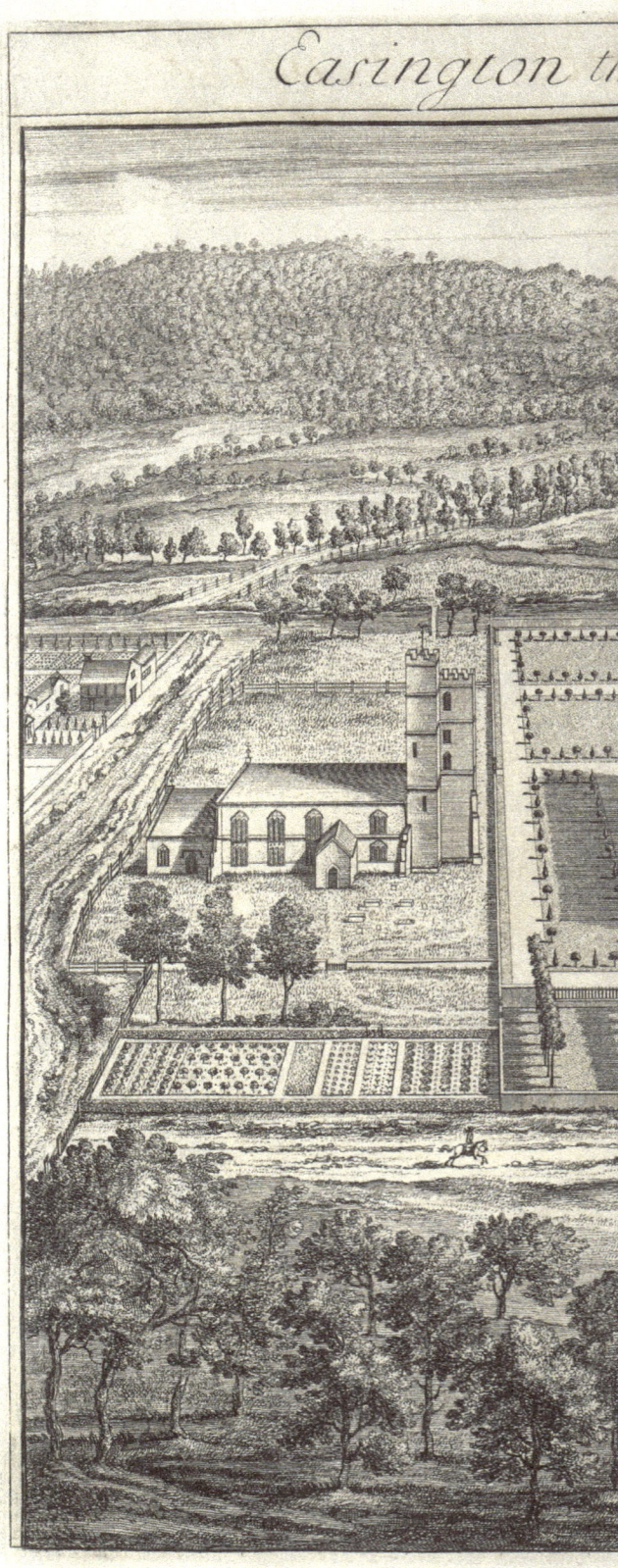

Easington t

Postcode: Stonehouse GL10 3SB. NGR: SO 78182 05756. VCH X 123-139.

the church, and a very great estate in this, and other places of this county'.

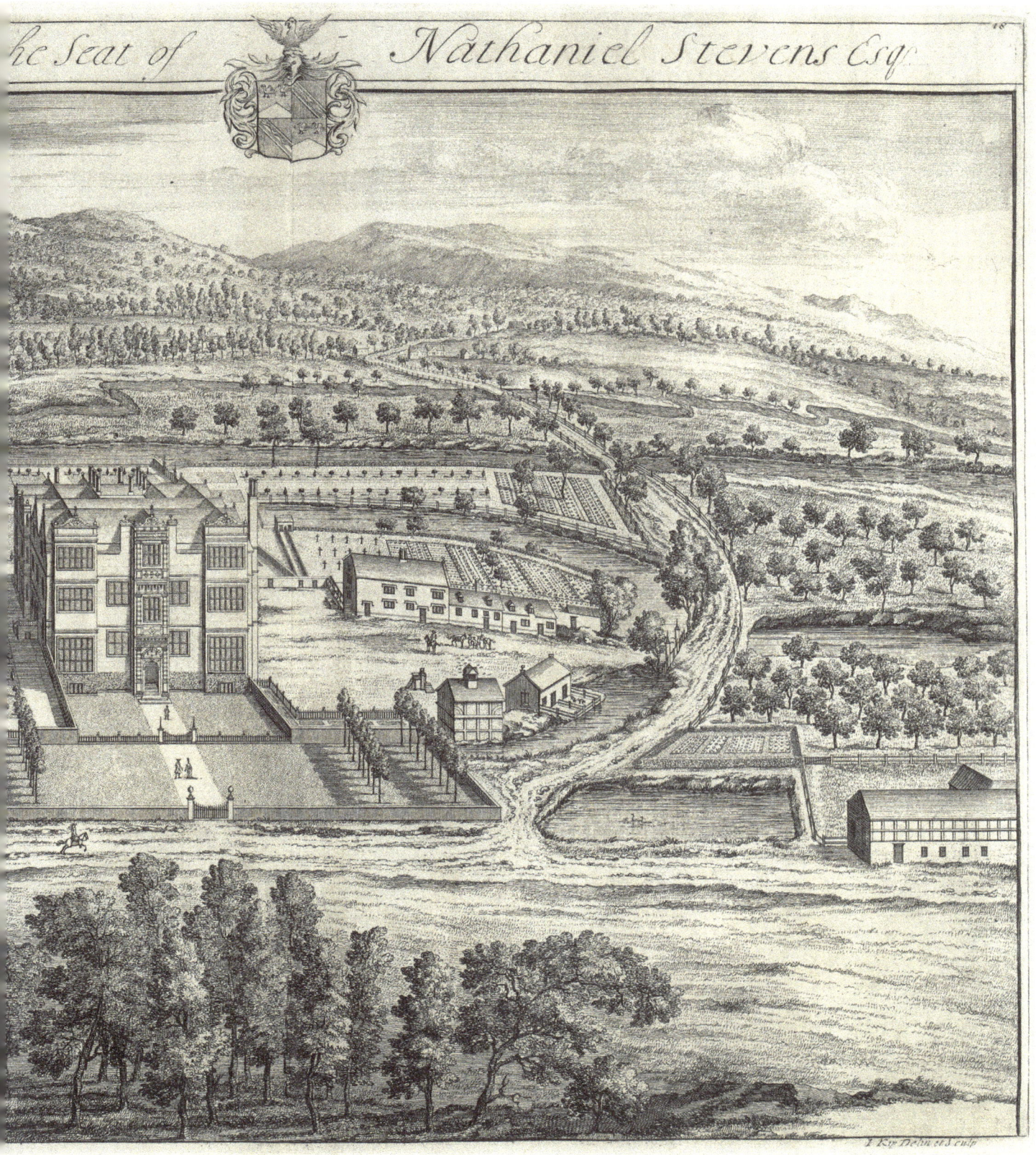

29 Wotton the Seat of Tho: Horton Esq [Atkyns: Elkstone, 428-29]

'Mr Horton of Comb-End has a very handsome new-built house in this place; Mr Blanch has also a good house and estate here

This plate was mistakenly inserted with the pages relating to Elkstone (Thomas Horton had a country estate at Coombe End) but the text, quoted above, is on page 586 under the appropriate heading of North Hamlets.

Wotton House was an example of stylish suburban development. Wotton was a hamlet outside the North gate, in the Gloucester parish of St Mary de Lode, one of seven places grouped together as the North Hamlets. Kip's view is from the east, and the house faces what is now Horton Road. Built for Thomas Horton in brick in the fashionable Queen Anne style, it has a date stone 1707. Kip drew the right number of windows on the front façade but today there are only three dormers. It is presently an international school.

To the north-east, not drawn so boldly, was Wotton Court (demolished about 1900); it was owned in 1712 by John Blanch, whose daughter Mary was Thomas Horton's wife. Possibly he had made the site for Wotton House available to his daughter and son-in-law. Wotton Court's garden was in the fashionable style, but appears to have been quite small (*qv*).

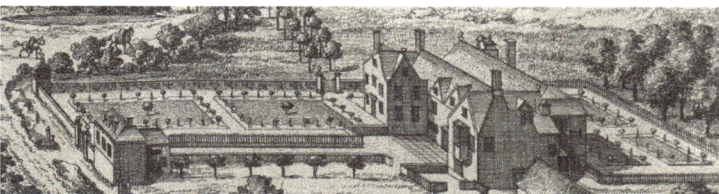

Wotton House garden is extensive, being described unusually in *The buildings of Gloucestershire* as a 'fine garden'. It is remarkable that it has survived, situated so close to the centre of Gloucester. The layout today is simple (*qv*) and a large residential block has been built on the former orchard and garden to the north, but with walls on the south and west sides, the overall site appears unchanged since Kip's visit.

In the background Kip engraved the north side of Gloucester cathedral (involving some artistic licence to view the whole north side) and the towers and spires of city churches.

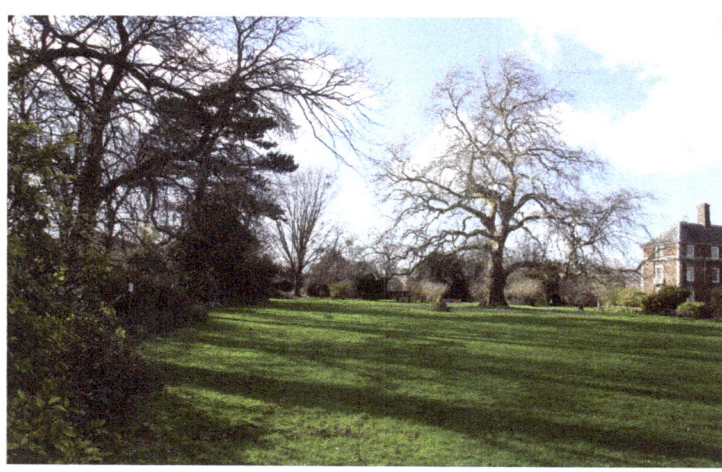

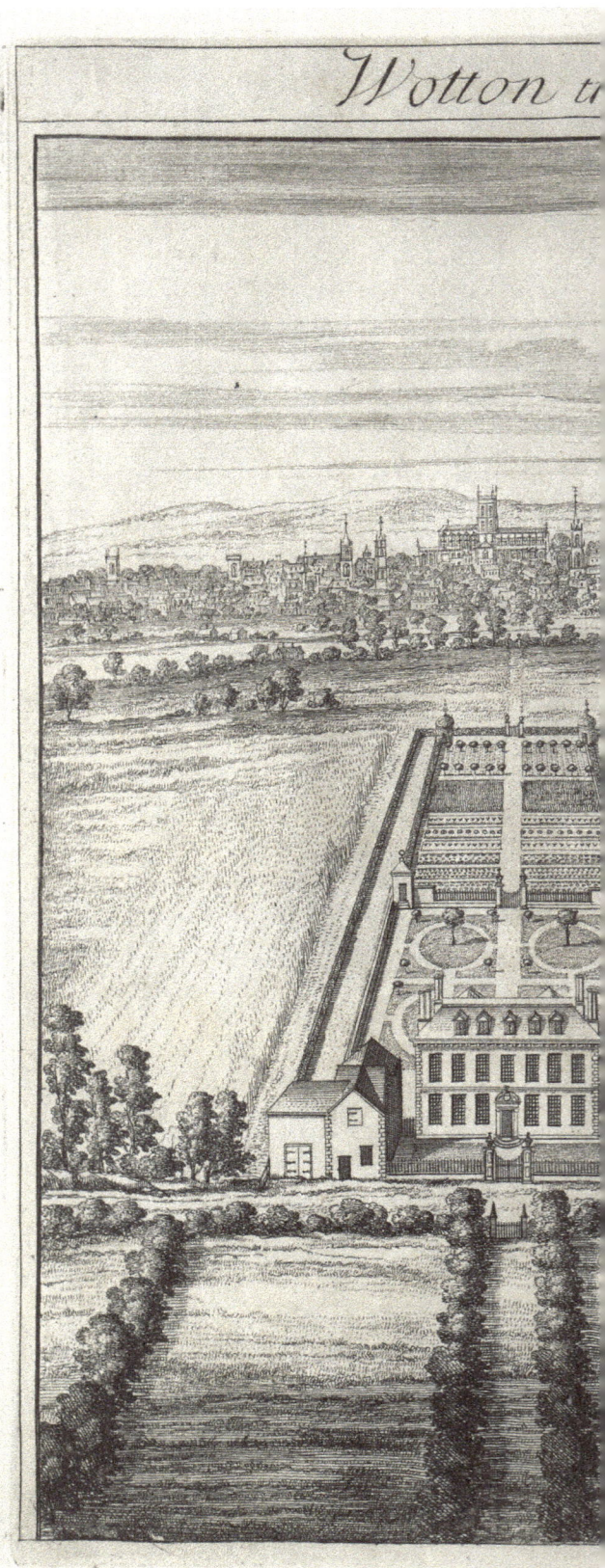

Postcode: Gloucester GL1 3PR. NGR: SO 84468 18813. **VCH IV** 382-410.

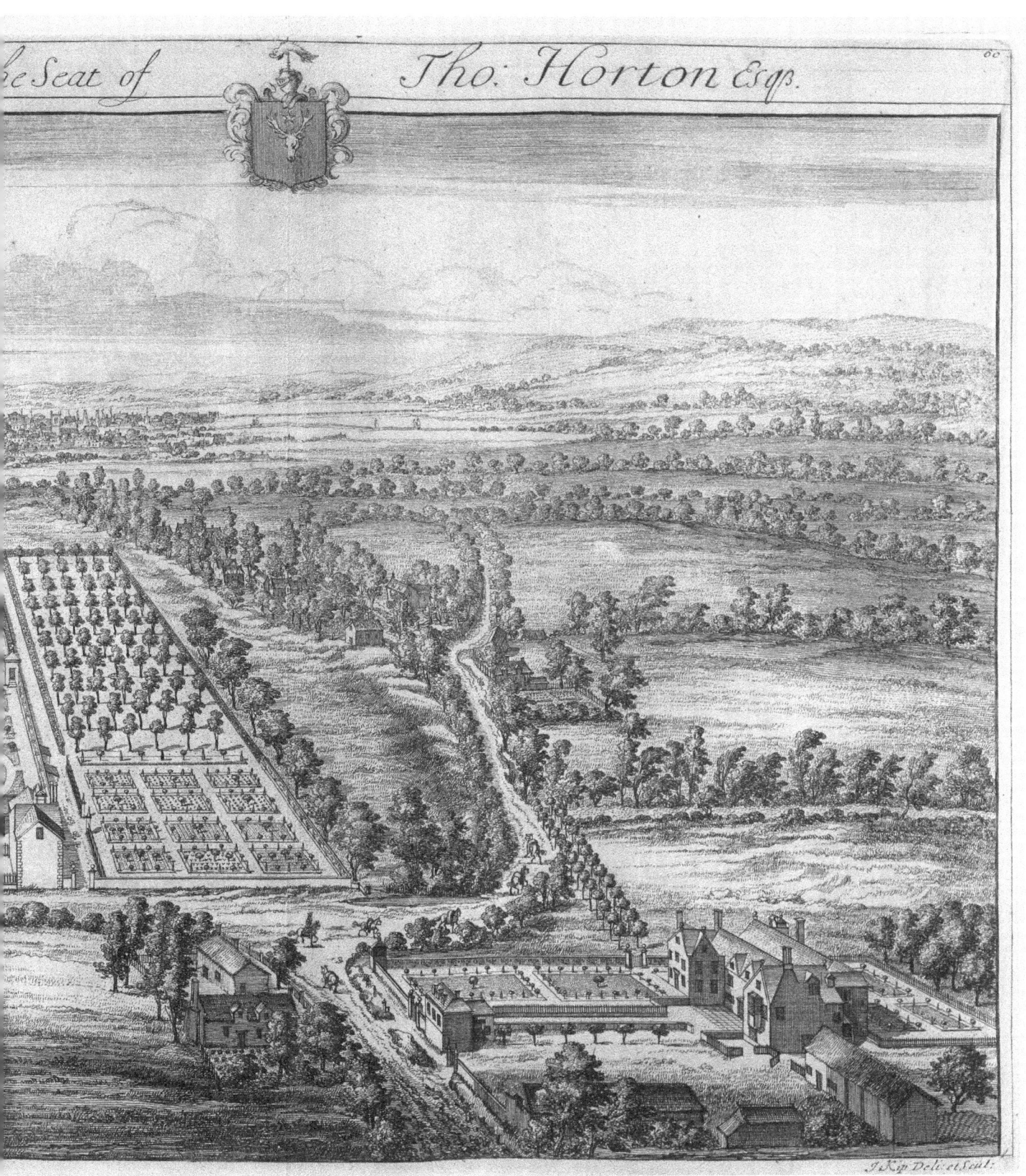

30 Fairford the Seat of Samuel Barker Esq [Atkyns: Fairford, 430-431].

'Samuel Barker … left two daughters, infants, coheiresses. They have a new built house, at a convenient distance from the tow

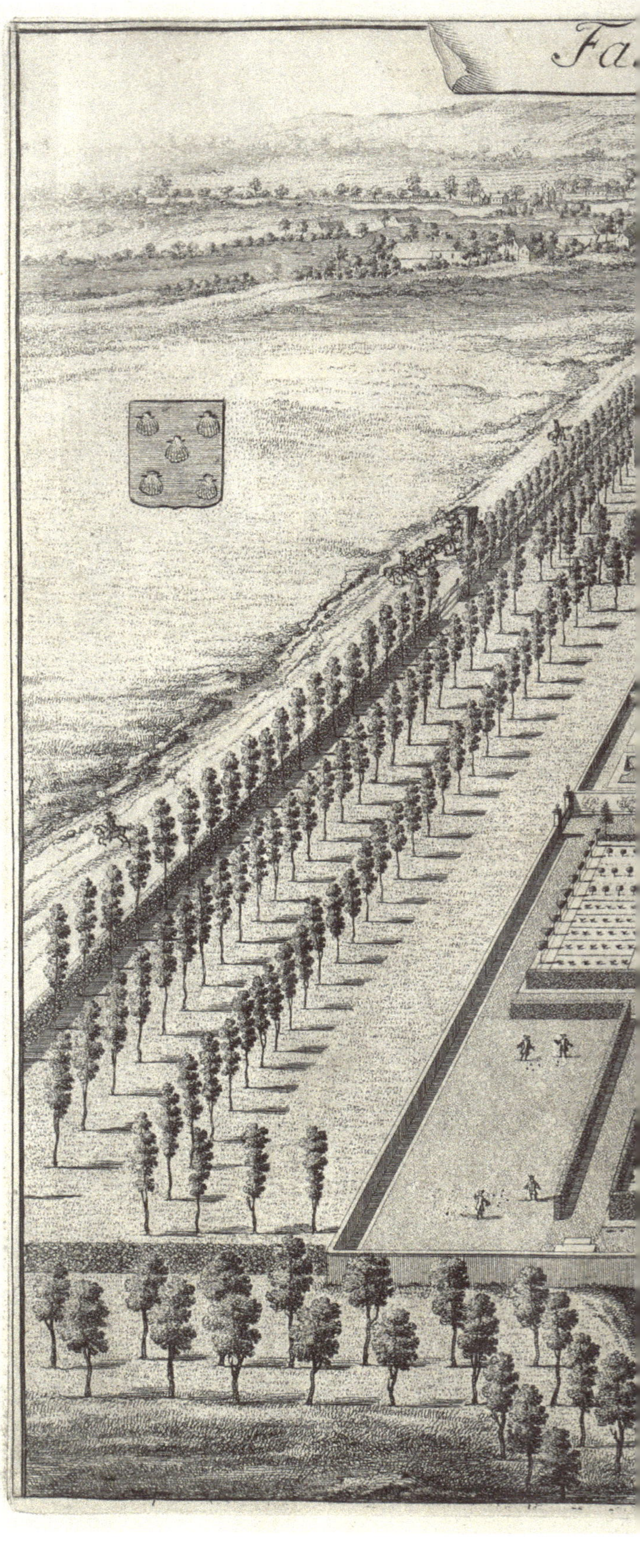

Fairford manor was bought in 1650 by Samuel Barker's father; Samuel inherited it in 1700 and died in 1708, apparently soon after Kip's visit. The family remained there until 1945. The mansion erected in 1661-62 was demolished in 1957, described by Pevsner as 'the most tragic loss amongst seventeenth-century Gloucestershire country houses'. It had been built by the Strongs, father and son, masons from Taynton, and in Kip's engraving resembles Coleshill, Oxfordshire, also lost. Fairford Park's site is now occupied by a secondary school.

Kip's view shows the north front and the stylised grounds which closely match a map of about 1690 (*qv*), before extensive landscaping in the mid-eighteenth century; even those gardens have gone but the general layout survives as a park occupied by a charitable trust. Behind Kip's back the long avenue led northwards into the later deer park. On the east side Kip hinted at the open field strips in Hoppers Furlong (see map).

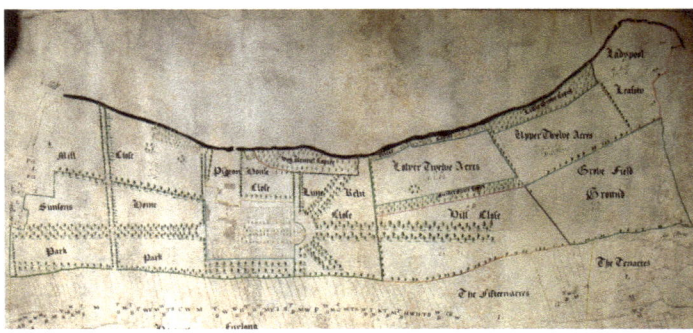

The house and gardens are given extraordinary prominence and the town is shown as a very small backdrop, only the church given any presence. Kip thus emphasised the size of the park beween house and town. No maps or illustrations of the town exist from Kip's day but unfortunately his representation seems unreliable. The arrangement of the streets, notably the east-west route from Gloucester to London, is approximately correct and two bridges over the River Coln are in the right positions but implausibly rendered. Known medieval buildings in the market place are not identifiable. In the High Street a huddle of houses gives the impression of a settlement near the church separate from the market burgages; the High Street seen from the park gate today (*qv*) is quite different.

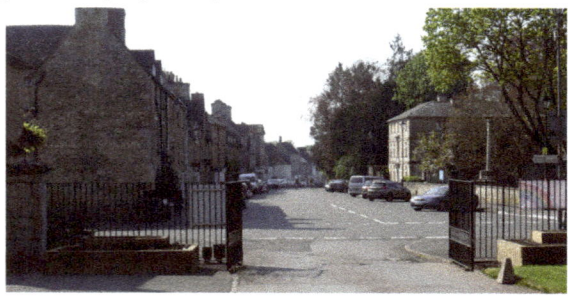

Postcode: Fairford GL7 4JQ. NGR: SP 15198 01798. **VCH VII** 69-86.

with large and beautiful gardens, and many pleasant long walks of trees, and a large estate in this and other places.'

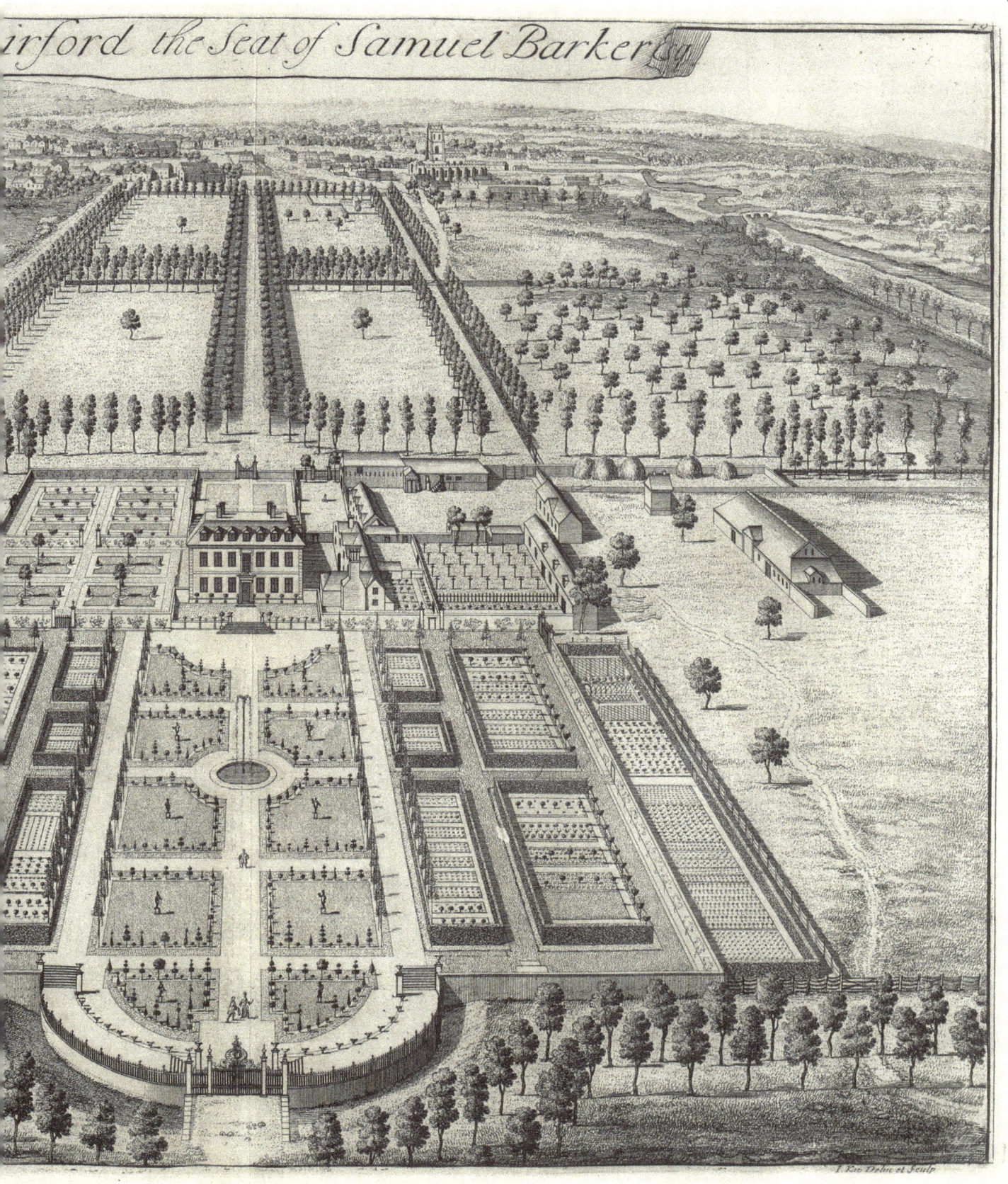

irford the Seat of Samuel Barker

I. Kip Delin et Sculp

31 Flaxley the seat of Mrs Bovey [Atkyns: Flaxley, 436-437].

'William Bovey dyed 1692, whose Widow is the present lady of the mannor. She hath an handsome house, and pleasant

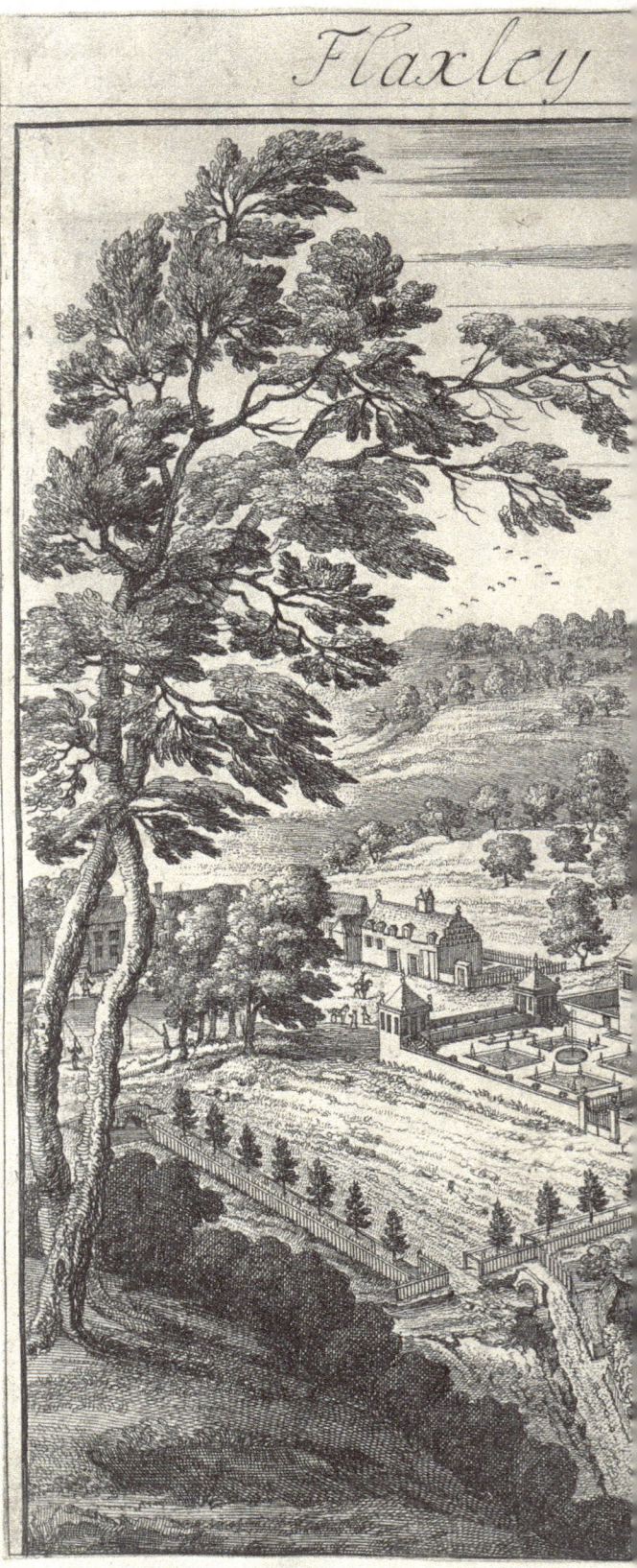

The survival of a conventual building from the small Cistercian monastery of Flaxley Abbey, occupied as a domestic residence, is unique in Gloucestershire. The plan of the abbey has been revealed by archaeological investigation, and clearly related to the house and garden drawn by Kip. The house was the abbey's western range; Kip's view is from the west. The house today is completely recognisable from Kip's engraving despite various changes: the leaded lights in the front windows have been changed, the northern end was destroyed by fire in 1777, and a new south range was built between 1777

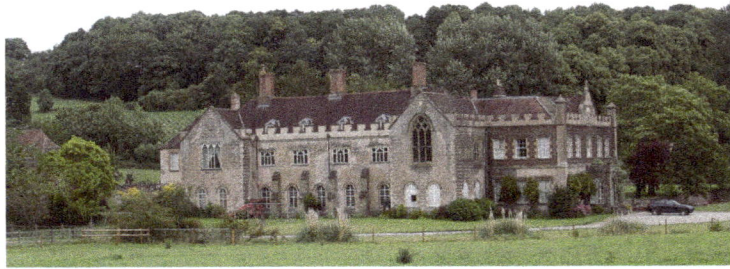

and 1783 (*qv*). Behind the house the parterre set out by Kip almost matches the cloister, and on the north side, partly hidden by a chimney, the still-existing Orangery backs onto the south wall of the abbey nave; Kip drew a line of ruined masonry beyond it. Two canals possibly utilised monastic cellars and walls, while the wall beside the river remains. The ride through woods leads eastwards to a terrace with a wide view. Catharina Bouvey and her husband were members of London's Dutch community. She was 22 years old in 1692 when William Bouvey died and requested her to finish the garden - it might with justice be called a 'Dutch' garden.

A coach and horses are approaching the house in Kip's engraving, passing the villagers' church, which matches Atkyns' description of 'very smalll' with a 'low wooden tower'; a new church now stands further from the house. To the north-west were farm buildings, one with characteristic 'Dutch' gables (*qv*). To the south-east was a watermilll, and beyond it a furnace for smelting iron, with smoke billowing out of a tall chimney (*qv*).

Dominating the engraving is a sweet chestnut; the abbey was endowed with tithe of sweet chestnuts in the Forest of Dean and with land known by the trees.

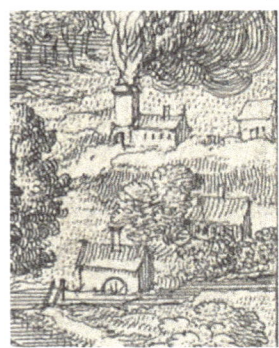
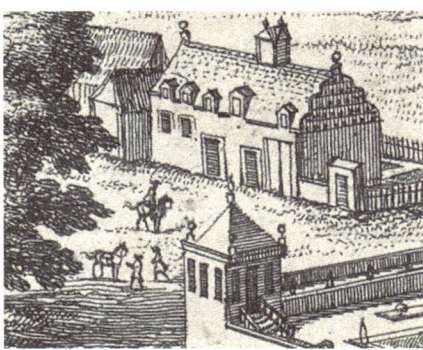

Postcode: Newnham GL14 1**JR. NGR: SO** 69011 15420. **VCH V** 138-150.

gardens, and a great estate; a furnace for casting of iron, and 3 forges.'

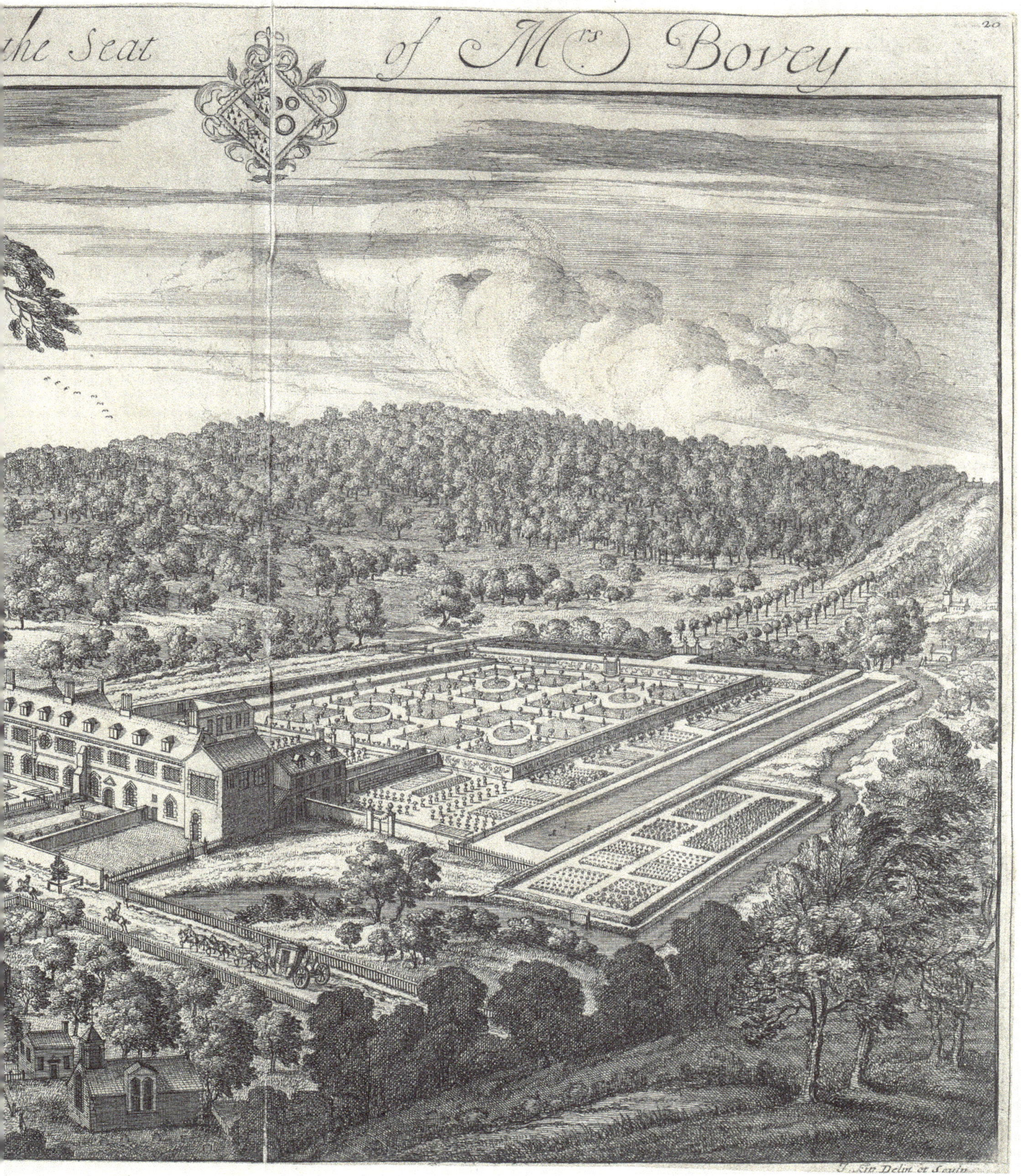

32 Hampton the Seat of Phillip Shappard Esq [Atkyns: Hampton, 451-453]

'Philip Shepard is the present lord of the mannor of Minching Hampton, and keeps a Court Leet. He has a large house near th

Kip recorded a scene which is much changed. Known as Minchinhampton because the manor was once owned by the nuns of Caen, *myncen* being the word for nuns in Old English, in 1656 it was purchased by Philip Sheppard (or Shepard). The house appears to be medieval, and nearby were barns and other farm buildings, and a round dovecote. It ceased to be occupied by the Sheppard family from 1774, when Edward Sheppard moved to his new house at Gatcombe, and was apparently demolished about 1827, when a short-lived owner started to build a new house where the school now stands.

To west and north of the house was a walled park, said to be distinguished by a noble stand of trees. Beyond were the sheep downs. Kip did not draw the westward sweep of the Common, presumably because it was not privately owned; from the early twentieth century the Sheppard's park became part of the Common. A few great trees survive.

Kip's view is from the south, and it appears he might have been at the top of a building in the High Street. The new Market Hall, built in 1698, is just visible, though today it does not have dormers in the roof (*qv*); also visible to the right is Butt Street, skirting round an area of market gardens.

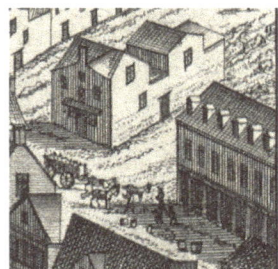
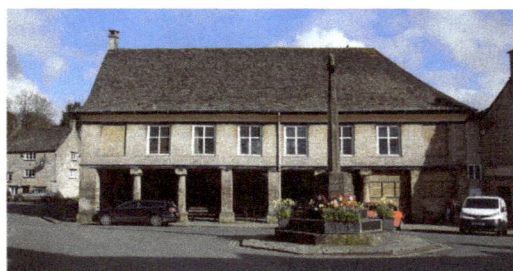

In his drawing of the church Kip closely followed the main features, though tidying up the outlines. Although the external staircase was moved, its trace is visible in the later engraving by Thomas Bonnor prepared for Bigland's Collections about 1790. The church was rebuilt in 1842-3, apart from the transepts and tower with its distinctive truncated spire.

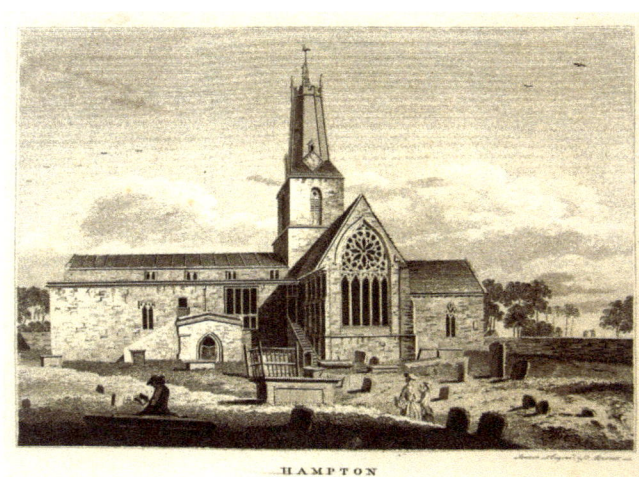

HAMPTON

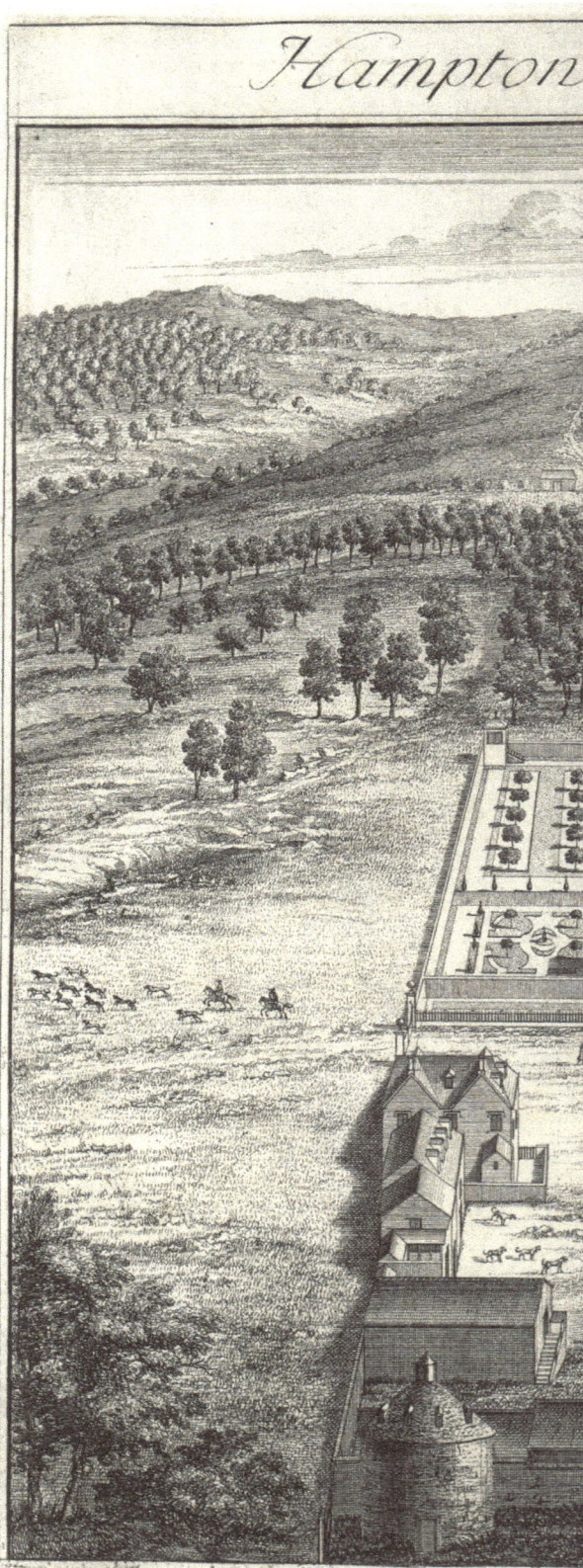

Hampton

Postcode: Stroud GL6 9BP. NGR: SO 87256 00749. **VCH XI** 184-207.

hurch, and a spacious grove of high trees in a park adjoyning to it, which is seen at a great distance.'

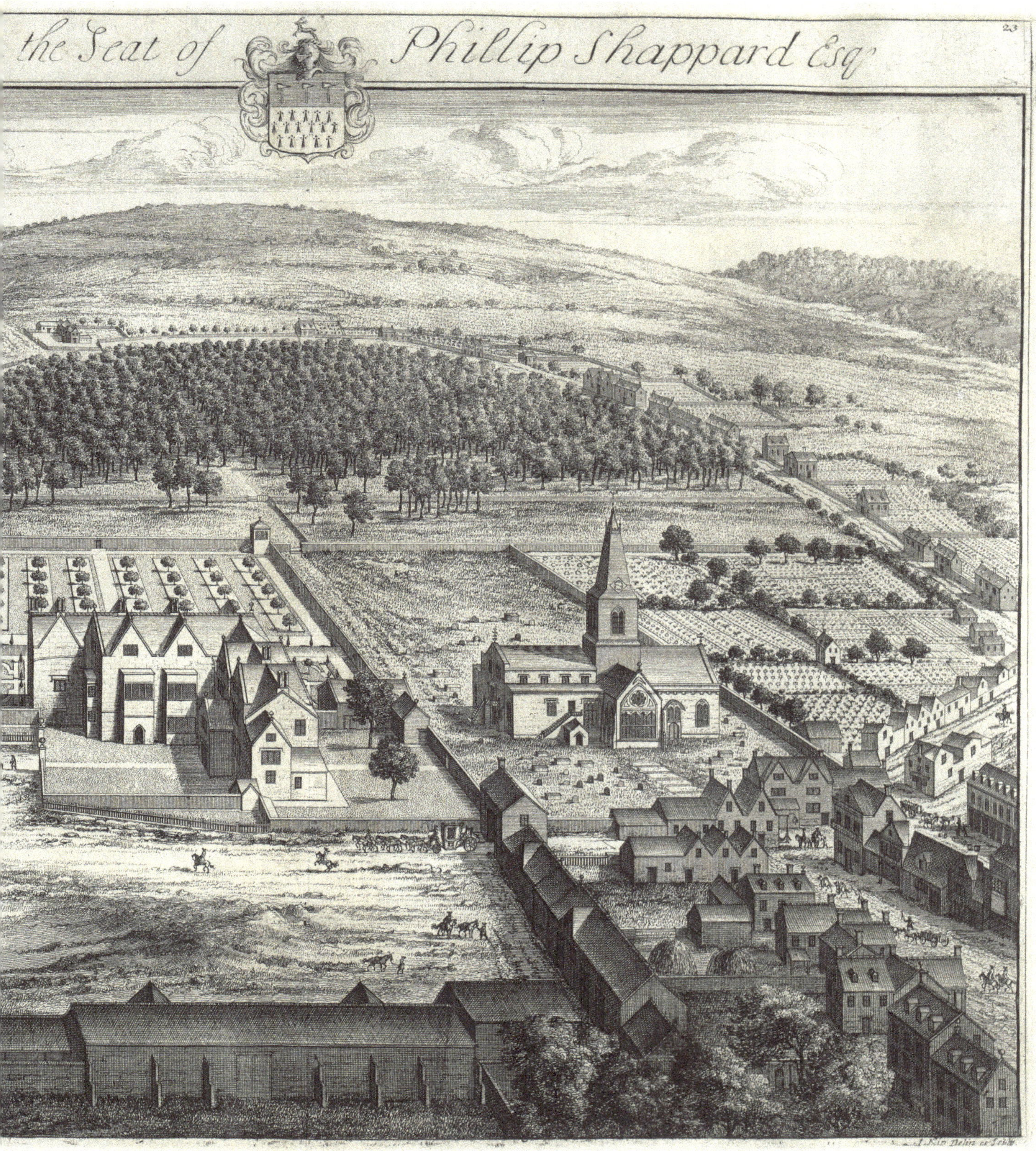

33 Hardwick Park Court the Seat of William Trye Esq [Atkyns: Hardwick, 456-457].

'William Trye Esq is lord of the mannor, and hath a very handsome house, moted almost round, and a pleasant park and can

The Trye family first came to Hardwicke Court (as the house is named today), when John Trye married the heiress, Isabel, who inherited the estate in 1397. William Trye, named by Atkyns, inherited the estate in 1681; his descendant, Thomas Trye, sold the estate in 1727 to Philip Yorke, who took his title from Hardwicke when created first a baron and then an earl.

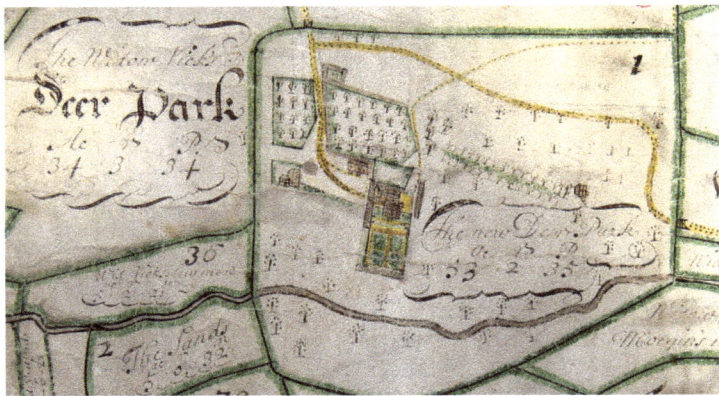

A map made for William Trye in 1699 (with north at the top) shows Hardwicke house surrounded by deer parks - it was probably originally the Park Lodge; a park was recorded at least 200 years earlier. Kip's engraving is from the west side of the house and shows 'the New Deer Park' (*qv*), which was mainly to the east of the house. It was a little under 54 acres (22 ha). He made sure of the identification, drawing a herd of deer dangerously close to the large kitchen garden (*qv*). A swathe through the trees led to a gate on the Gloucester to Bristol road. The view was thus opened up to Haresfield Beacon; Kip took liberties with the perspective here. The older 'Deer Park' marked on the 1699 map was behind him.

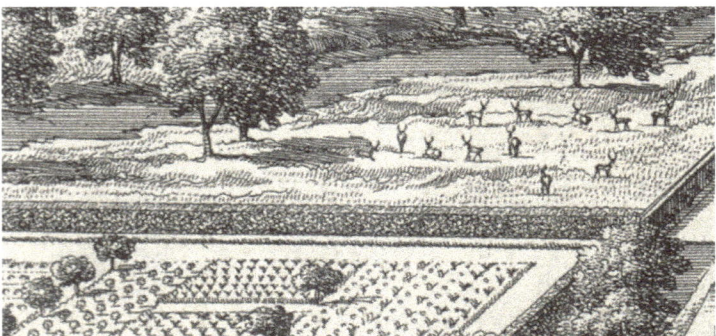

Hardwick Court appears U-shaped in the engraving, probably built in the sixteenth century, and moated; two swans are visible. The gatehouse could be the one referred to in the late twelfth century. There was a formal garden on the south side of the house, confirmed by the map though more primitively drawn. On the terrace at the rear Kip drew the urn fountain which still stands there. The house was pulled down after 1815 and a new house designed by Robert Smirke built on the site.

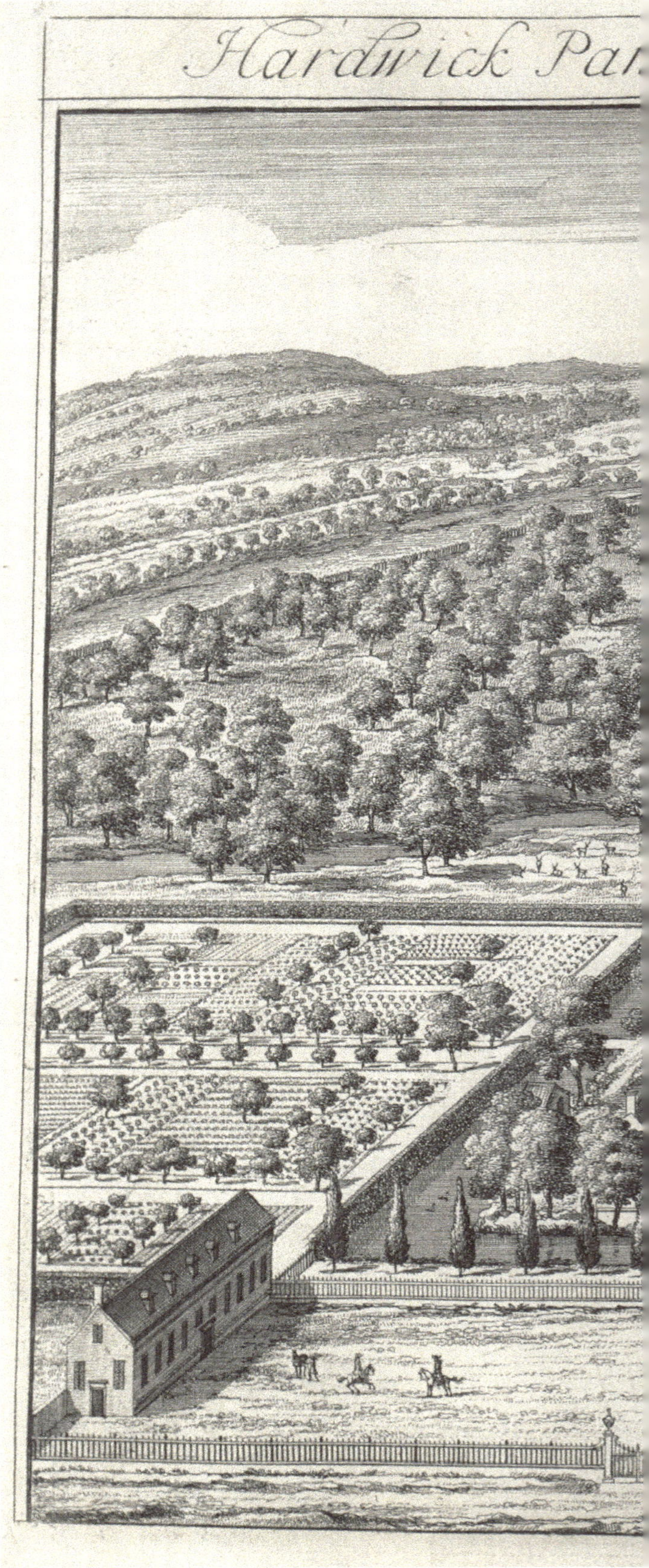

Postcode: Gloucester GL2 4RS. NGR: SO 78786 11712. **VCH X** 178-188.

nd a large estate in this parish.'

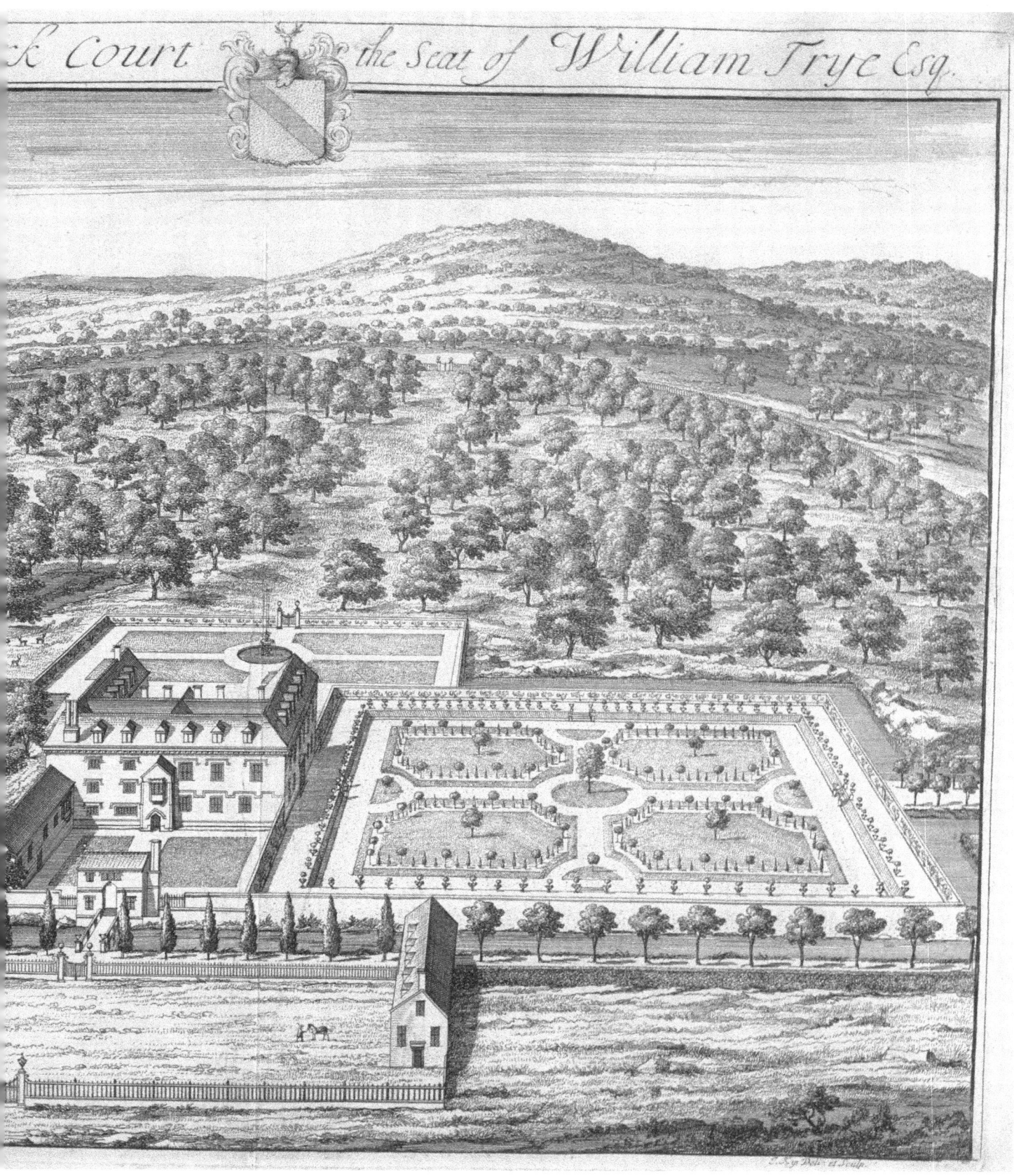

k Court *the Seat of William Trye Esq.*

34 Hatherop the Seat of Sr John Webb Bart [Atkyns: Hatherop, 464-465].

'Sir John Webb … keeps a Court-Leet. He has a large house and gardens near the church, and a very great estate in this and

Kip placed Hatherop house in the middle distance, allowing him to draw a wide view of the countryside. The long ridge to the right (west), densely wooded, is Netherton Ridge. It divided the parish of Hatherop from Quenington. A steep descent leads from the ridge to the river Coln and a water meadow, which significantly Sir John Webb did not own. The village of Coln St Aldwyns is further to the west, Netherton mill to the south, the well spaced out houses of Hatherop village to the east, and beyond them, arable fields on gradually rising ground. Kip indicated that the fields were cultivated in strips (*qv*), where tenants' lands were intermixed. A track led across the pasture

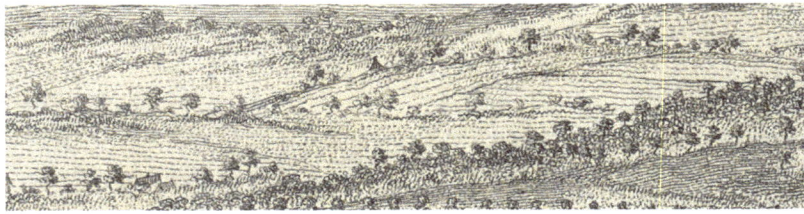

from Netherton, and still exists, but the few houses there were later taken into Hatherop estate.

Hatherop house was approached, as it is today, along an avenue. Decorative gardens were mainly on the south side, although a large walled kitchen garden was in the front; the brick walls are mainly rebuilt, but on the same footprint. An ancient yew walk runs close to the wall, supposed in 1906 to be about three hundred years old (*qv*).

To reach the small church, Hatherop villagers walked through Church Furlong, in which Kip drew a small herd of cattle. The church had a west tower and nave but no separate chancel; both Dr Richard Parsons about 1700 and Ralph Bigland before 1791 commented on this, confirming Kip's observation. A larger church was built in 1854-5, shortly after the house was rebuilt following a fire in 1844, its north front possibly inspired by Kip's engraving. Now called Hatherop Castle, it is used by a school.

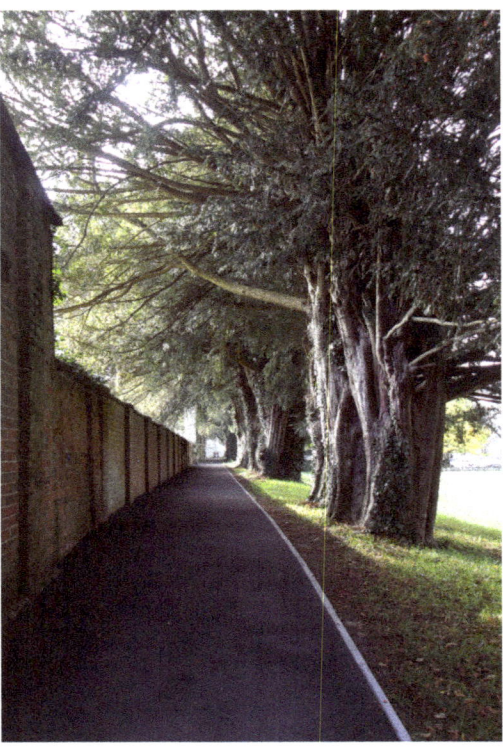

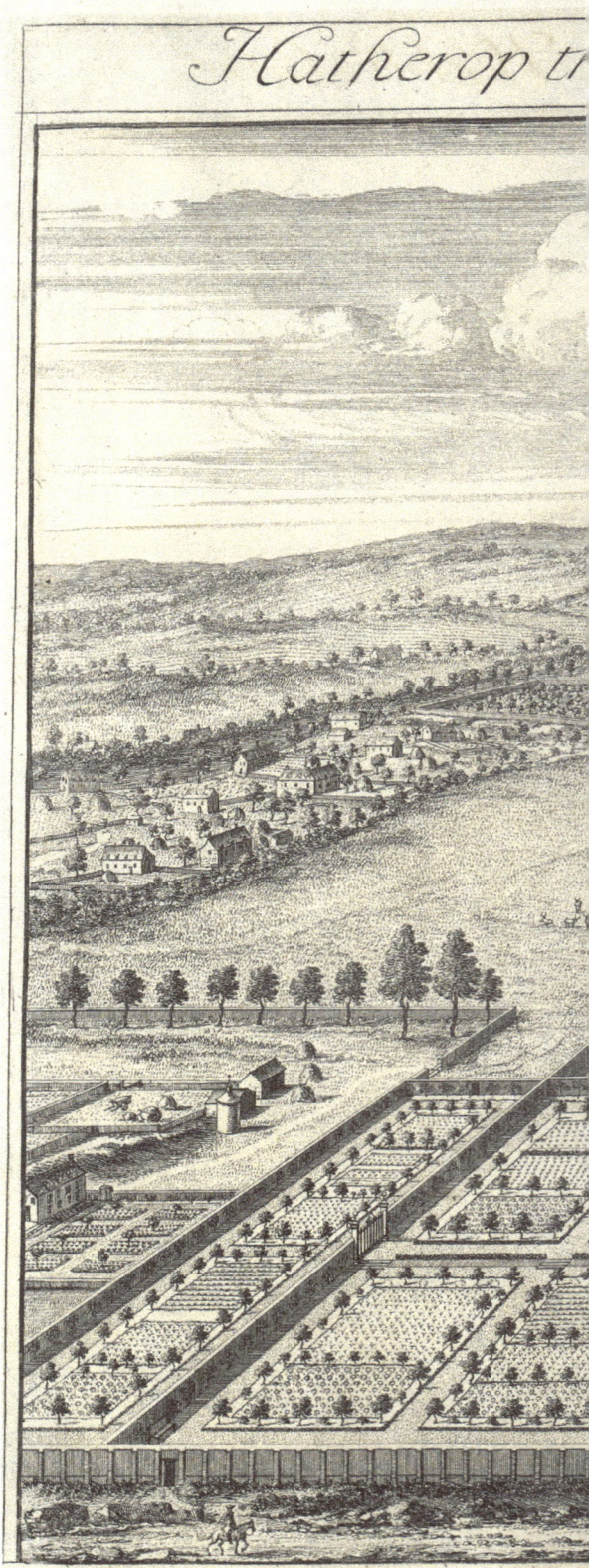

Hatherop tr

Postcode: Cirencester GL7 3NB. NGR: SP 15317 05126. VCH VII, 86-96.

other counties.'

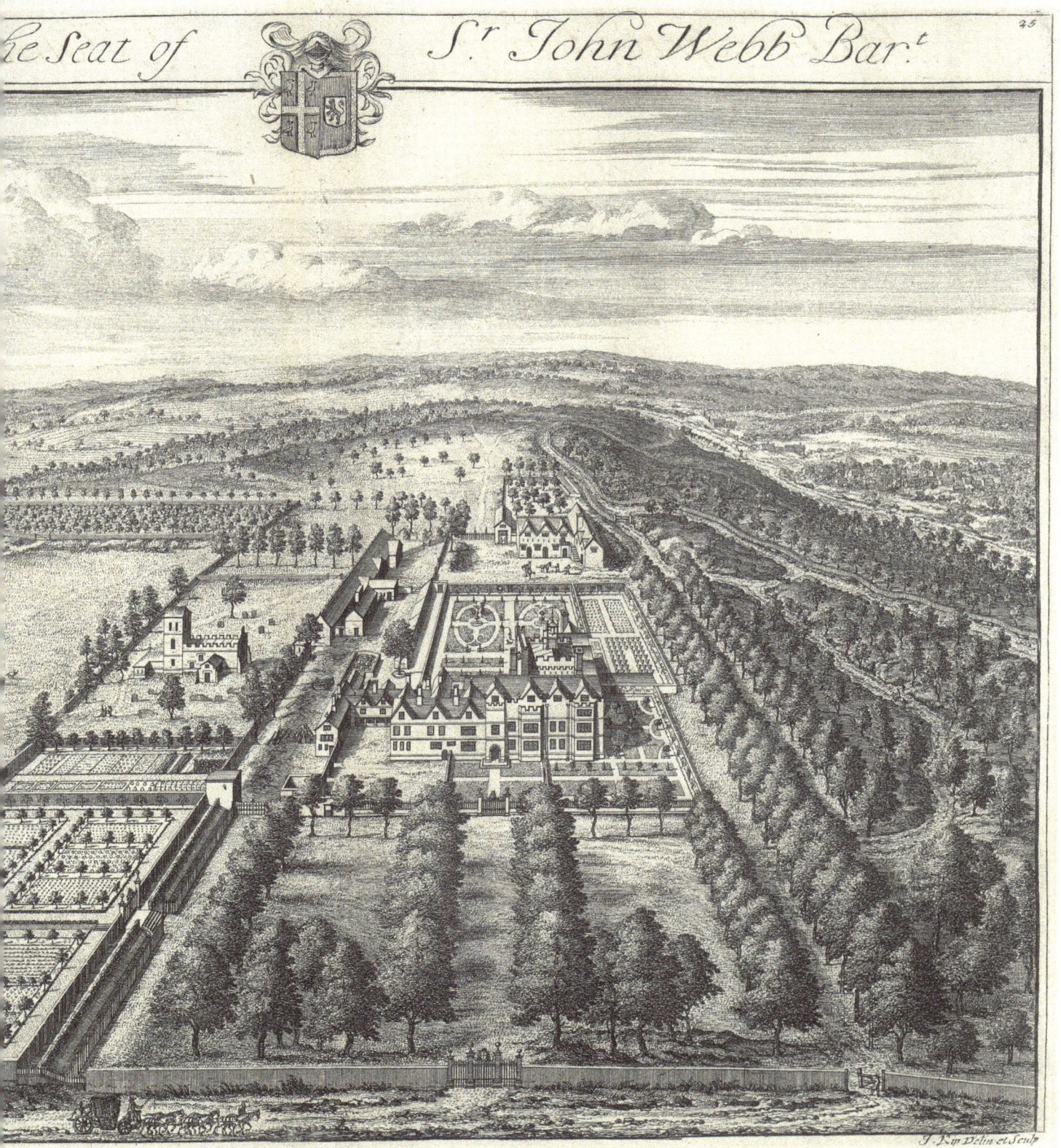

35 Hales Abbey the Seat of the Lord Tracy [Atkyns: Hayles, 470-471].

'One of the cloysters is yet remaining … The Lord Tracy, of Toddington, is the present lord thereof, who has a very large house in this

Despite Atkyns' comment, Kip did not draw a cloister nor any monastic ruins. On the other hand, the steeply rising hill to the east, with the road winding up it, is readily recognisable, the laden hay waggon needing five horses to negotiate it.

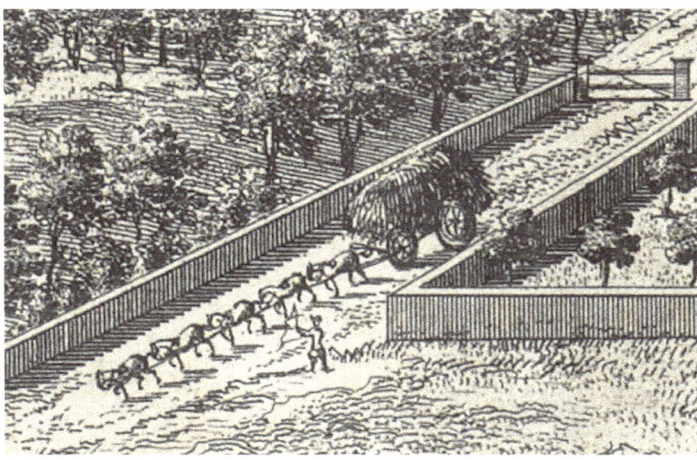

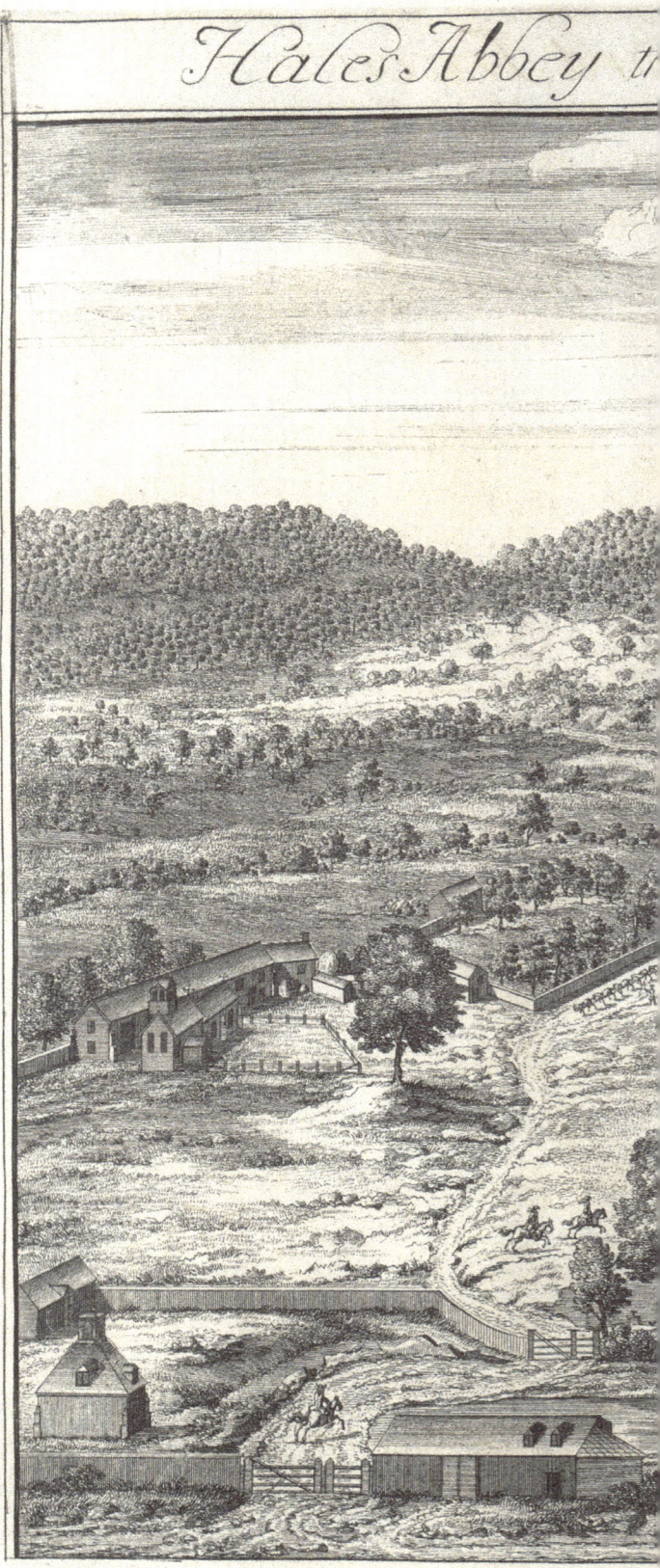

The abbot's house at Hailes had been converted in the late fifteenth century from the lay brothers' wing on the west side of the cloister; new-built were the tower at the south-west corner and, projecting, the 'pretty Chappel with a gallery for people of quality to sitt in,' as Celia Fiennes noted. The gables which can just be seen above the front roof related to an eastern range, shown more romantically in a painting by Thomas Robins the elder dating to the 1730s.

Kip's view is from the west, with extensive formal gardens to the east. A map of the 1580s has a comparable picture of the house but suggests some ruined masonry though no gardens. Robins' painting, from the east side of the house, shows a formal parterre in a courtyard defined by surviving cloister arches, but no surrounding gardens. It seems that Lord Tracy required Kip to leave out ruined masonry but enlarge the gardens. The Tracy family no longer occupied the house after 1686, preferring Toddington; in 1794 Samuel Lysons drew some cloister arches half-buried in the ground, and others attached to the few parts of the house still standing.

The small, partly fourteenth-century parish church to the left is largely unaltered, except for the top-heavy bellcote at the west end, now replaced with a more modest-sized one; interestingly, the walled enclosure round the church corresponds precisely with the fenced area drawn by Kip, but the building behind has gone.

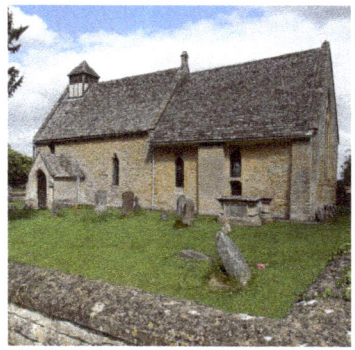

Postcode: Cheltenham GL54 **5PB. NGR: SP** 05044 29999.

ace, which was heretofore the habitation of the abbot, as appears by many religious figures and inscriptions in the rooms of the house.'

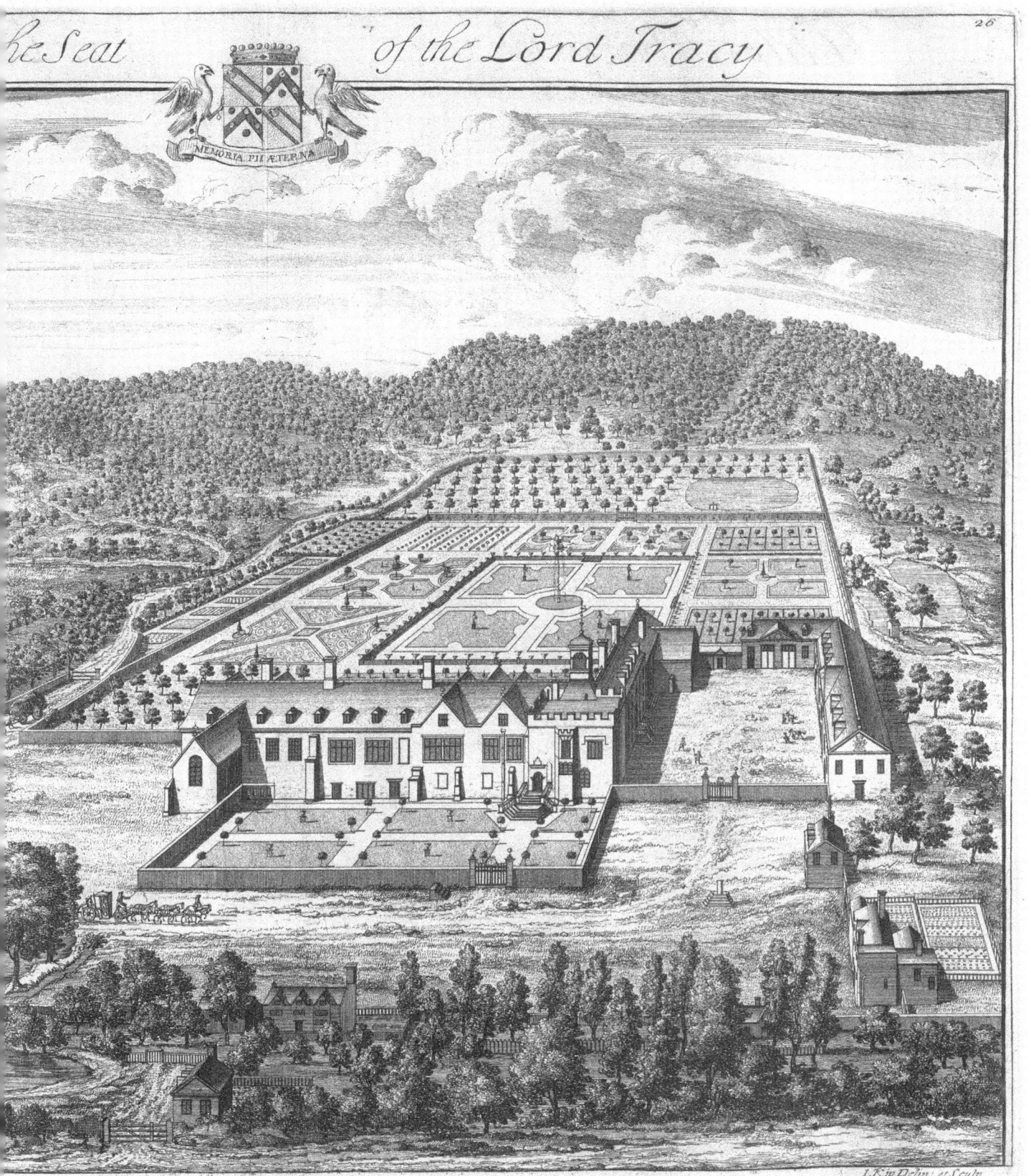

he Seat *of the Lord Tracy*

MEMORIA PII ÆTERNA

26

J. Kip Delin: et Sculp

36 Henbury the Seat of Simon Harcourt Esq [Atkyns: Henbury, 472-473].

'Mr Harcourt hath an handsome new-built house, and a very great estate in this and other places of this county'.

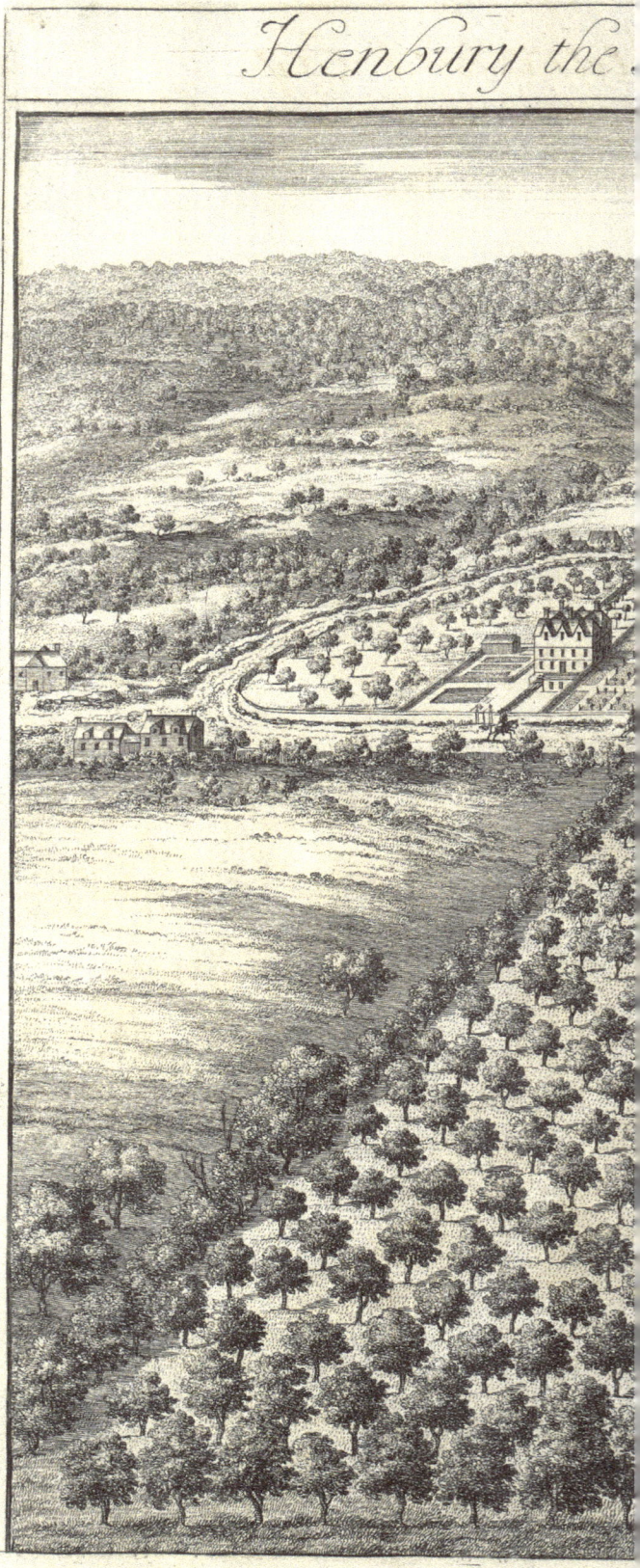

Kip made engravings of three houses in Henbury parish, one at Kingsweston, two identified simply as 'Henbury'. His engraving of Kingsweston was published just as the house was demolished, to be replaced with one designed by Sir John Vanbrugh, which though relatively small has been described as one of his finest (Grade 1). The two Henbury village houses appear twice, small in one engraving, large in the other as appropriate. The houses were near neighbours and were village houses rather than 'country houses'. One, known as 'The Great House', was demolished before 1809, to be replaced with Blaise Castle House on a new site, now a museum; only a ruined orchard of the old house is visible over a wall. The other, known sometimes as 'The Awdelett', more recently as Henbury Manor, survives; since 1950 it has been owned by Bristol City Council and adapted as a special school. Proximity to Bristol brought the prosperous to Henbury and has now worked to substitute many houses for the few. Henbury was incorporated into Bristol city in 1935.

Simon Harcourt, named by Atkyns as the owner of the Great House, had recently acquired it through marriage with the heiress, the widow of Sir Samuel Astrey. Astrey was probably the builder of a new house on a site owned by George Morse, whose daughter he had married. He was a wealthy barrister, who steadily increased his Henbury landholding and in 1680 bought Henbury manor with the advowson of the church. He was knighted in 1683. George Morse died in 1688. When Astrey died in 1704, he left his property to his wife.

Kip drew the crenellated north side of the house, with a handsome pair of wrought iron gates on the roadside on the south side, beyond which, leading up Blaise Hill, is an avenue which Sir Samuel Astrey planted. Gardens stretched northwards parallel to the road, and the house was also close to the road which wound its way to Weston. In the distance is a windmill at Kings Weston, and beyond it again the river Avon. The windmill also appears in the second Henbury engraving (*qv*).

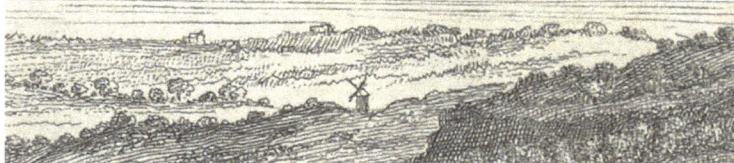

Thomas Farr, a wealthy Bristol sugar-merchant, bought 110 acres (*c* 45ha) of the estate in 1762, comprising the old gabled Manor House, depicted in one of Repton's Red Book paintings, Blaise Hill, the land between the Hill and the village of Henbury, and Hazel Brook in its spectacular gorge; he built the 'castle' on the top of the hill and started to create an elaborate park and gardens. At the end of the eighteenth century J S Harford bought this estate and Blaise Castle House was built for him on a new site between 1795 and 1799. It is now owned by Bristol Corporation and is a museum. The Great House thus became redundant. It was acquired by Edward Sampson and by 1809 he had demolished it, ostensibly to use the materials in extending The Awdelett.

Postcode: Henbury BS10 7**QS. NGR: ST** 56199 78725.

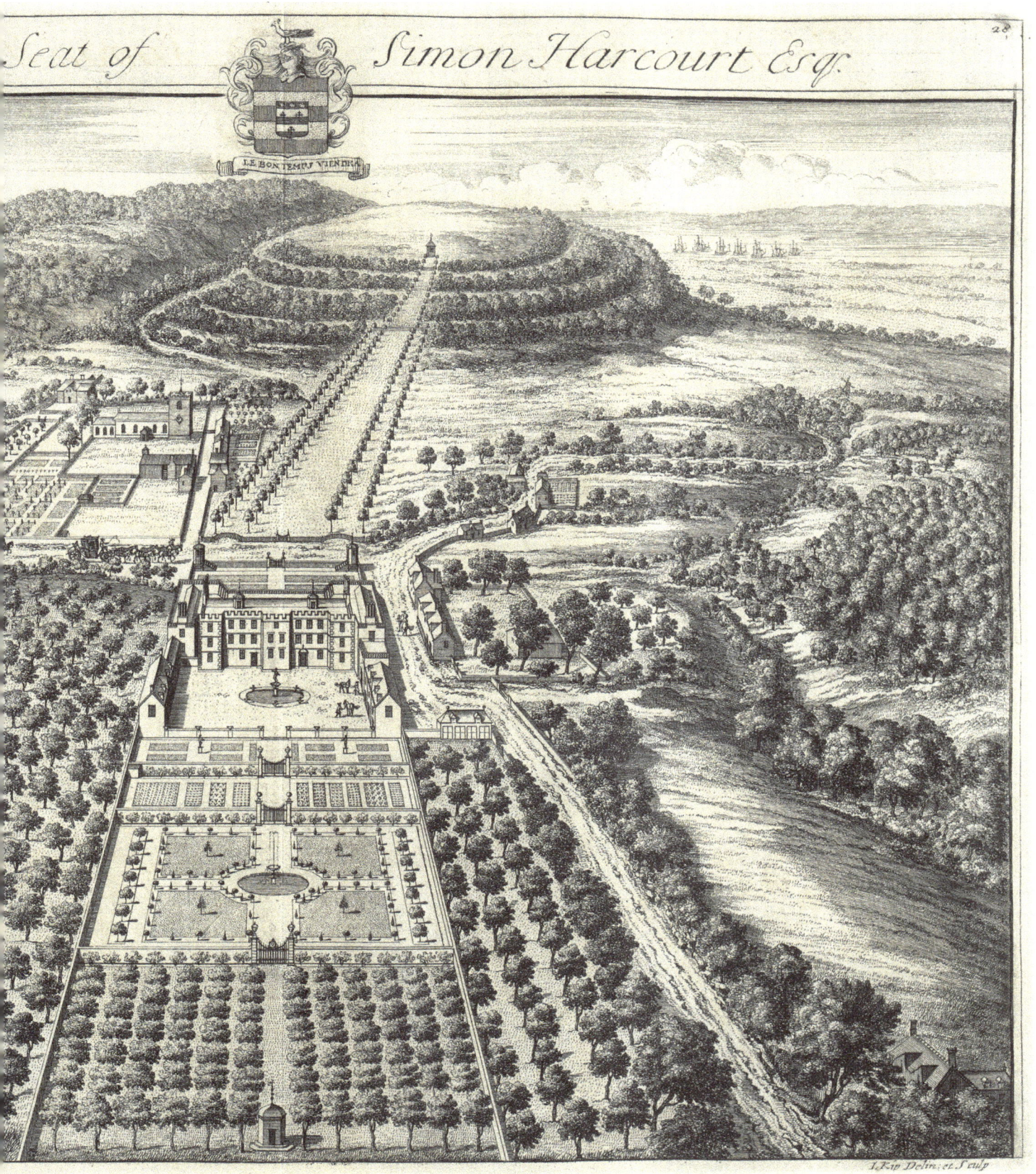

37 Henbury the Seat of Mr John Sampson [Atkyns: Henbury, 474-75].

'Mr Sansome has likewise a very handsome new house, and a good estate in Henbury'.

The Awdelett was the earlier and smaller of the two houses in Henbury, though Kip has presented a bolder view of it and of the village. It was built on land that had been a Westbury-on-Trym college prebend. Although close to Henbury church, it was a detached part of Westbury parish, as were scattered parcels of land making up the estate. The connection between this estate and John Awdelett is not known, but was sufficiently strong for his name to be attached to it. The surname Awdelett or Audelett was unique in this country and rare in northern France, from where one John Audelett came to England in the early sixteenth century. He was the last steward of Abingdon abbey and a crown surveyor concerned in the dissolution of the monastery; he died in 1536. As a wealthy wool merchant, this estate of 1200 acres (486 ha), alternatively known as 'Henbury Saltmarshe', would have provided significant amounts of grazing for the sheep.

A descendant of John Audelett's daughter sold this estate to Edward Sampson of Henbury in 1627; later John Sampson, who acquired sugar plantations in Nevis in 1663, built a new house which carries the date 1688. It appears as an uncluttered almost classical design though with vernacular gables. Note the rooftop platform surrounded by a balustrade (*qv*); two people are standing on it, one with a fowling piece or perhaps a telescope.

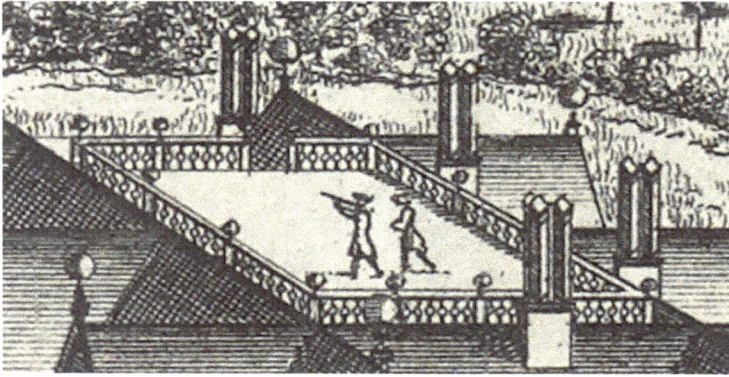

The garden was organised in a number of walled compartments and appears to have been next to the village pond. A coach is travelling the road past the Great House towards Weston.

Henbury

Henbury was a large parish, not far short of 10,000 acres (4,000 ha) with a substantial area of saltmarsh. At one time it contained 12 vills or townships. Henbury and Aust appear to have been granted to the bishop of Worcester at the end of the seventh century, and some Henbury land was later allocated to support canons of Westbury-on-Trym college. The college

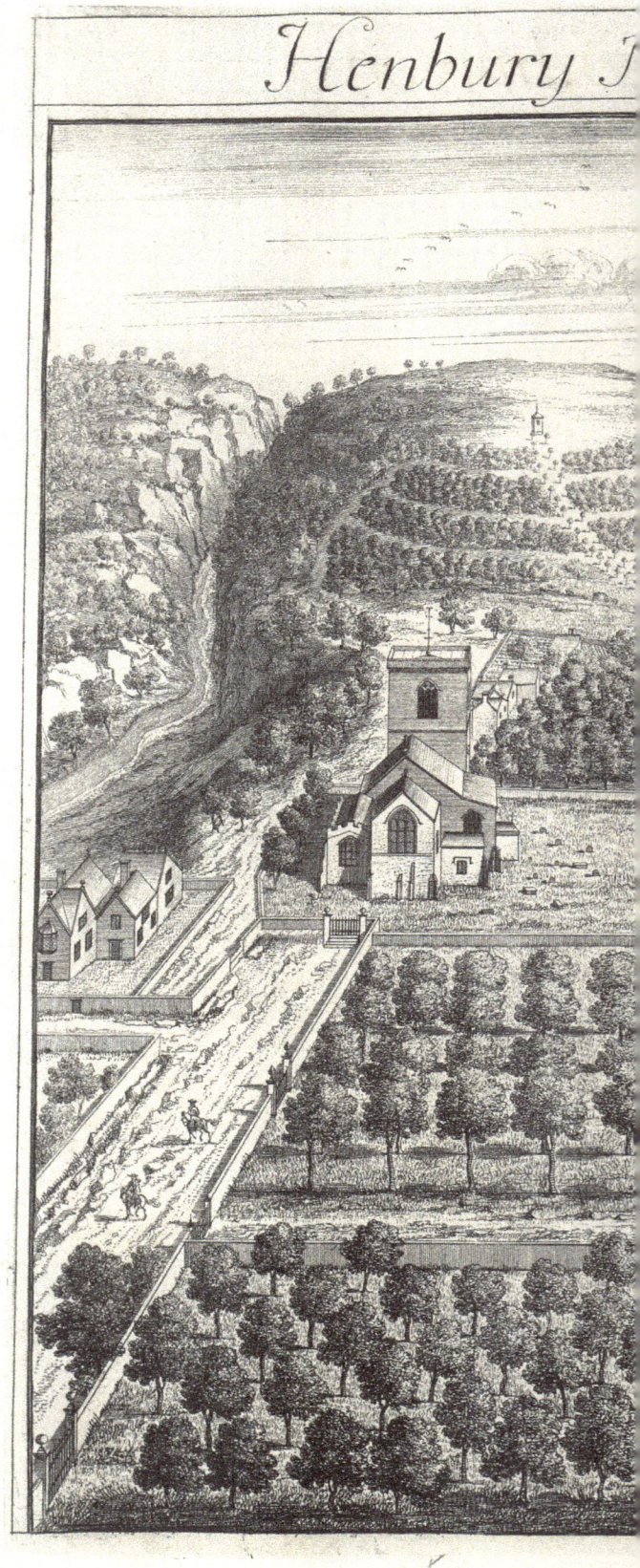

Postcode: Rectory Gardens BS10 7**AH. NGR: ST** 56347 78879.

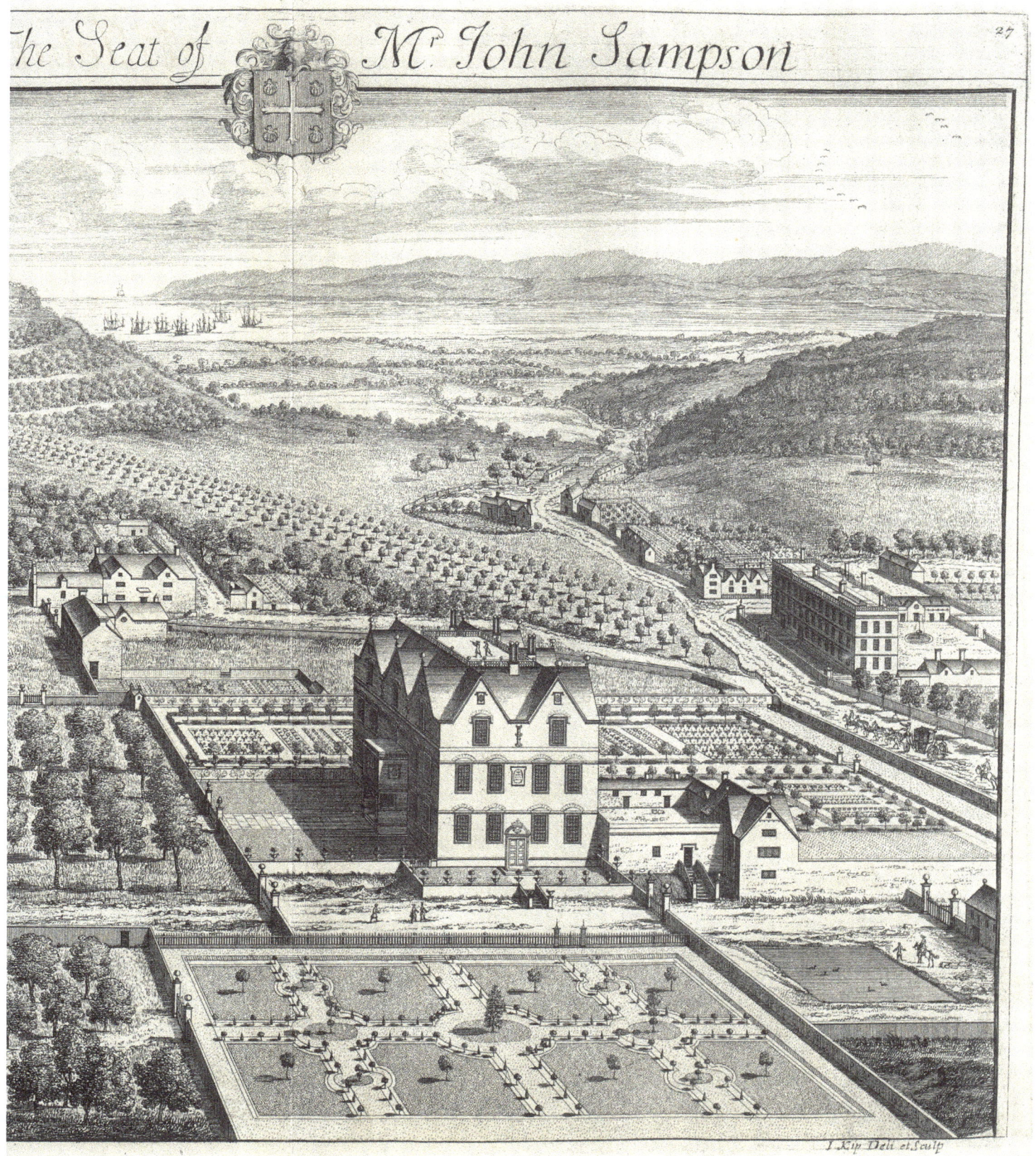

surrendered to the crown in 1544 and the bishop was forced to surrender the manor in 1547. Although the two estates were quickly united by Sir Ralph Sadleir and subsequently passed through several generations of the

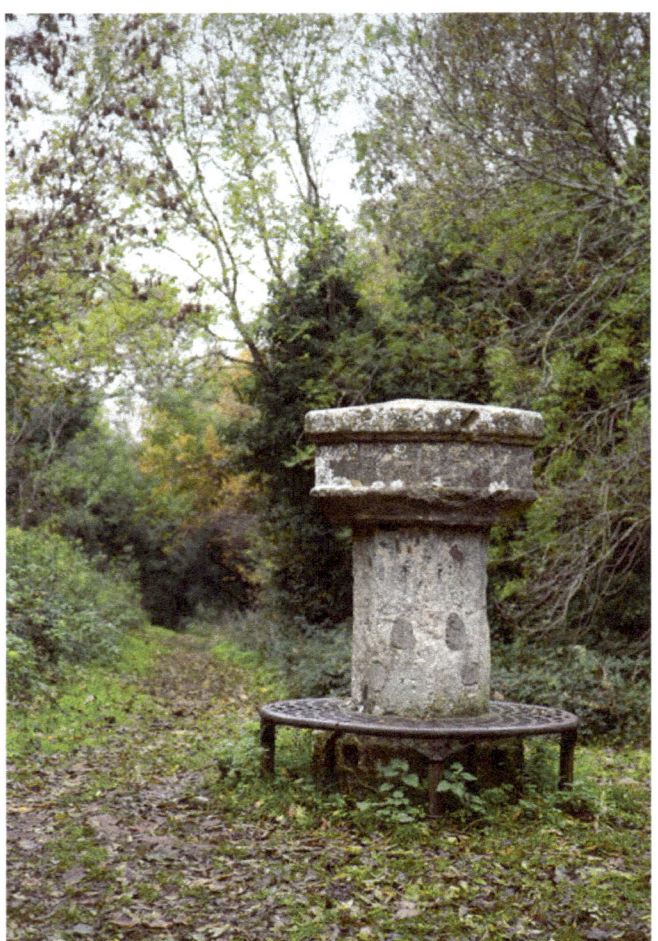

family, from 1675 they were sold off in lots. This history explains two equally prestigious estates in the village of Henbury. Kingsweston, as its name implies, was not an early ecclesiastical estate but the king's, and there has been an estate here since the third century, pointed up by the scheduled remains of the Roman villa which can be visited.

Views of shipping on the Avon and Severn are the only features common to all three engravings. Kings Weston is the closest and has the best view; there is a mariners' compass on Penpole headland (*qv*), a point from which both Avon and Severn are in view. The two Henbury village engravings, however, have an unusually large degree of overlap. Kip drew two houses in several parishes: Almondsbury, Cirencester, Dowdeswell, Shipton Moyne and Westbury-on-Trym, as well as the three in Henbury, but the common features are few. Only in Cirencester is there a small overlap; there Kip placed himself with his back to the first house when drawing the second. In Henbury, two views are angled at 90 degrees to each other.

The iron age hill fort is the most prominent common feature, and the banks and ditches on the north and west are still considerable. Henbury almost certainly was named from the 'high bury'. In the sixteenth century there was a chapel on the hill reputedly dedicated to St Blaise, an early fourth century bishop and martyr known for his healing abilities, hence the name Blaise Castle. Atkyns recorded that some foundations were 'dug up' in 1707 and 'many modern coins, as also ancient Roman coins, and other Roman antiquities', which suggests people were still seeking healing there. Kip shows the round hill rising above a dramatic gorge through which the Hazel Brook runs to join the Trym. An avenue of a double rows of trees and then single, leads up Blaise Hill

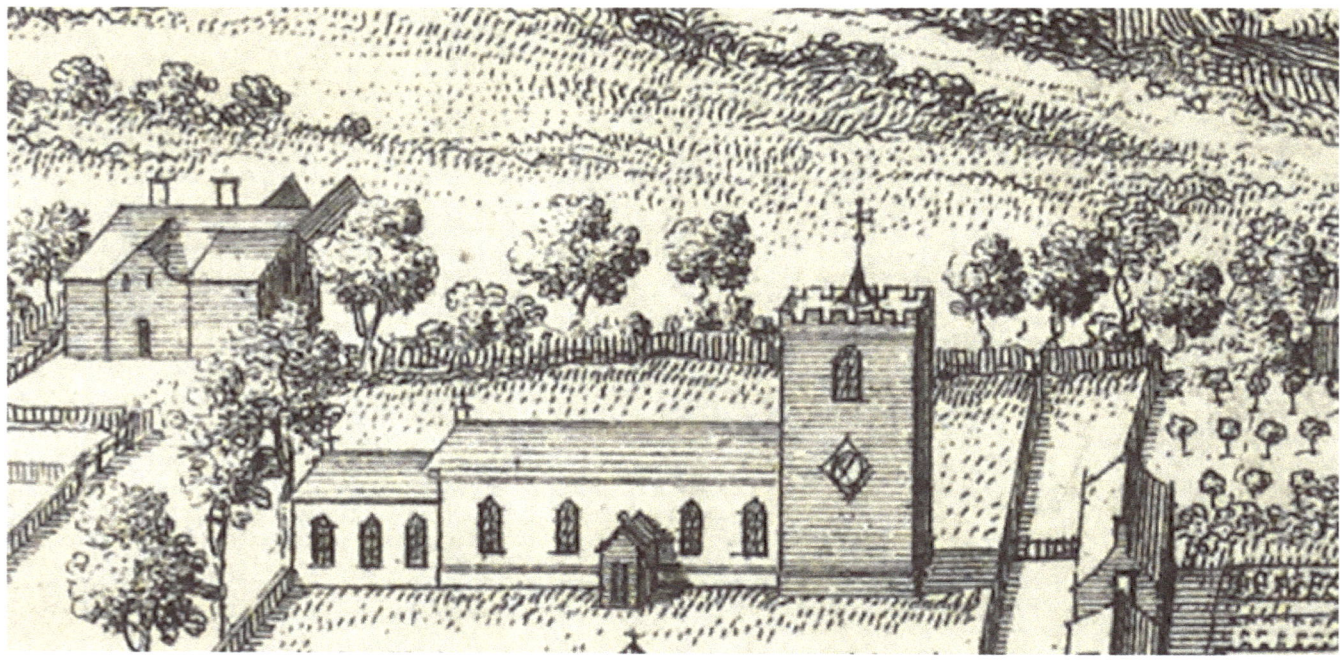

from the Great House. Part of the avenue was marked on the 1841 tithe map and some veteran trees survived in 1911. The castle or folly on the hill today was built by Thomas Farr between 1766 and 1768. The hill is a public park.

The church is another important common feature, which Atkyns noted was 'large, and hath an isle on each side, and a large flat tower at the west end, and a smaller chancel at the south side of the greater chancel.' The east end is clearly drawn on the second Henbury engraving, John Sampson's house, and matches Atkyns' description. In the first engraving, Simon Harcourt's house, the view is of the north side and the tower is not flat but crenellated; moreover it hardly implies the two aisles nor their position relative to the tower (*qv*).

Church, vicarage to the south-west of the church, Great House and the Awdelett are placed accurately in both engravings, as also the relationship to the hill, though the view is foreshortened. Thomas Robins the elder painted a somewhat similar view of Henbury, probably about 1740 when he was working in Bath; the picture is now in Bristol Museums. It also shows how close together the two houses were and confirms the major features, though Robins made the Weston windmill rather more prominent.

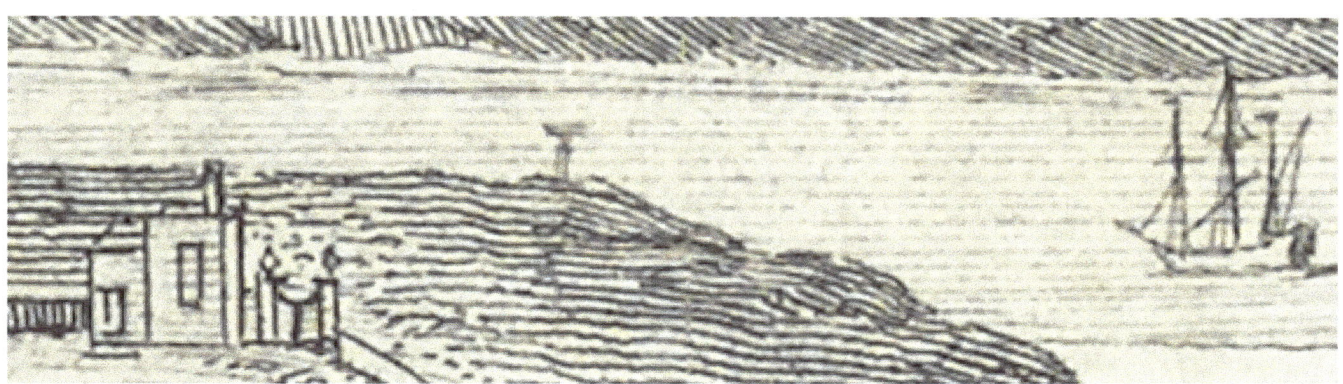

38 Kingsweston the Seat of Edward Southwell Esq [Atkyns, Henbury, 476-77]. Post Code: Kings Weston BS11 0UR. NGR: ST 54173 77481.

'Edward Southwell Esq. … has a pleasant seat in this place, with delightful gardens, and a full prospect on King Road, the harbour to the City of Bristol, and over the Severn sea into Wales. He has a great estate in this and other counties, and in the kingdom of Ireland.'

Kingsweston estate occupies the western edge of a steep limestone spur, cut through by the River Avon near its junction with the Severn, both waterways in the background of Kip's engraving busy with ships. Kip's viewpoint was Kingsweston Hill, rising darkly and steeply from the road. While his engraving is focused on the strongly patterned Tudor parterre, echoed in the regular garden front of a seemingly much augmented Elizabethan manor house, it sweeps the eye westward along corridors of trees towards Penpole Point and its mariners' compass. Kip included small drawings of Penpole Lodge and the compass (*qv*).

Kingsweston house is drawn so that both the north and east facades can be seen. Two tall stair turrets in the internal angles of its entrance front are very similar to those at Siston. The U-shaped house seems too small for its three hundred acres, although on the north a jumble of ancillary buildings spills out. To the east there is an orangery and walled fruit and vegetable gardens typically espaliered. In the entrance court are what appear to be seven dog kennels. In the north-east corner is a banqueting house. The site is bounded on the north by the rutted carriage road.

Humphrey Hooke, merchant ex-mayor of Bristol, sold Kingsweston to Sir Robert Southwell, a self-made post-Interregnum diplomat from Ireland, in 1679; Sir Robert died in 1702, and was succeeded by his son, Edward, similarly a diplomat. He had married a wealthy heiress who died in 1709, perhaps enabling him to build a new house; building work began on 16 June 1712. In 1716 Edward married Anne Blathwayt of Dyrham but she died the following year. The surroundings were later made fashionable and the estate is Grade II; it is mostly opened to the public by its owners, Bristol Corporation and the National Trust, although the southern part is leased to Shirehampton Golf Club.

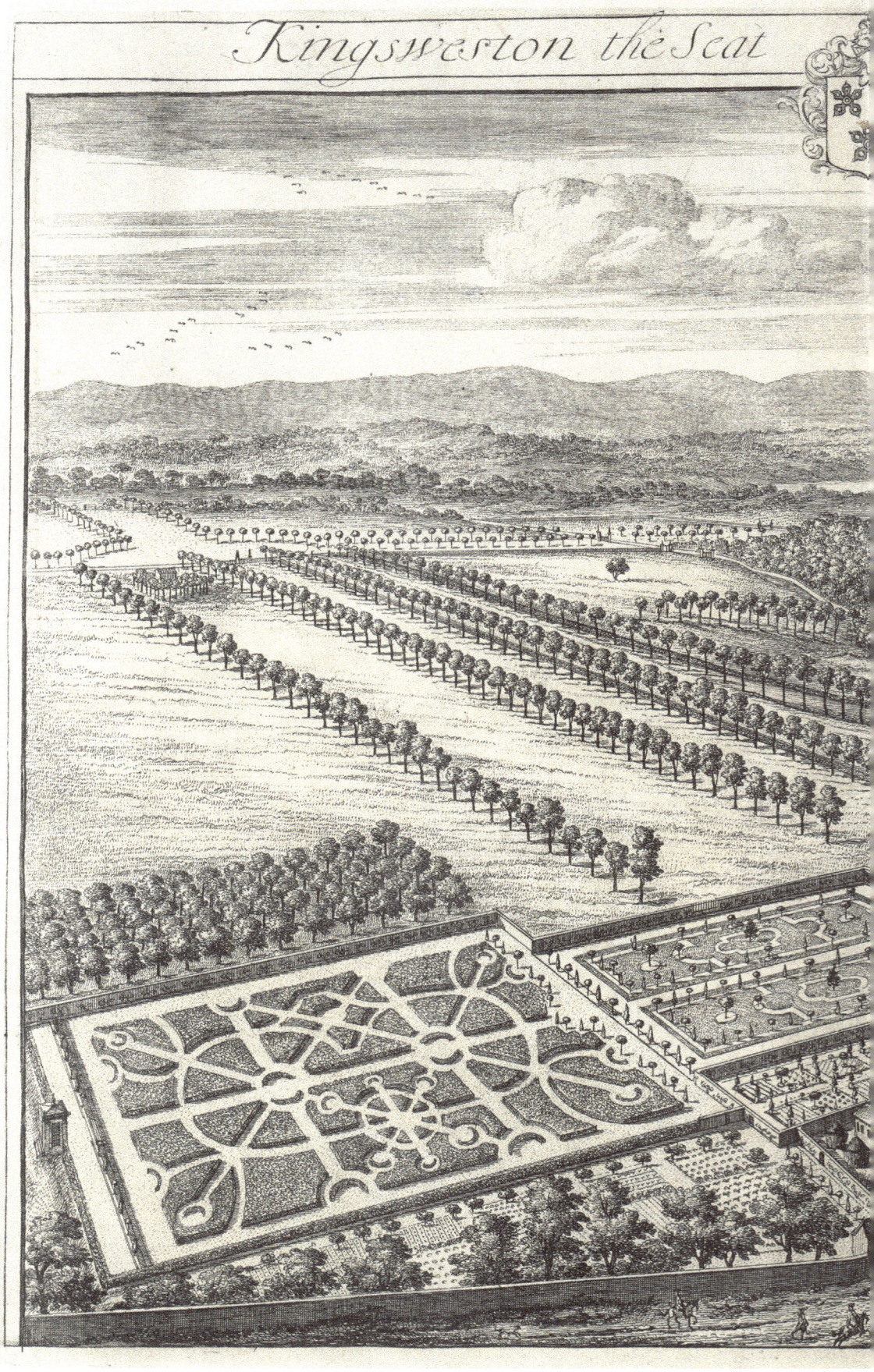

Kingsweston the Seat

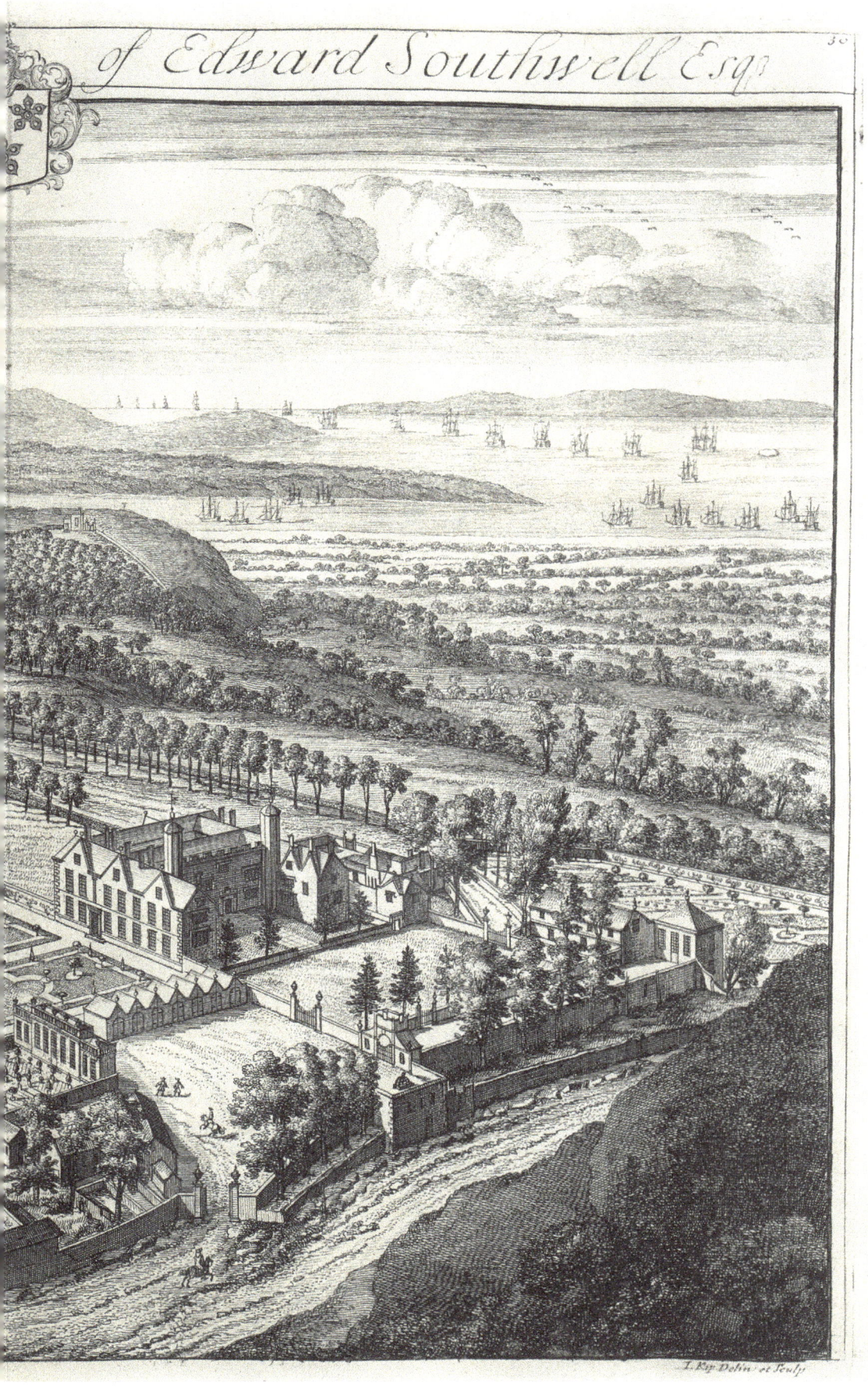

of Edward Southwell Esq.

I. Kip Delin. et Sculp.

39 Hull als Hill the Seat of Sr Edward Fust Bart [Atkyns: Hill, 478-79].

'Sir Edward Fust … was High Sheriff of Glostershire 2 An. 1702. He is the present Lord of the Mannor, and keeps a Court-Lee *Fust has lately built a small chancel on the south side of the other, which is the burying place of that family.'*

Hull and Hill were variously recorded until the late eighteenth century, when Hill became the accepted name. Kip's engraving shows what seems to be a medieval hall, possibly the lodge within a medieval 90 acre (36 ha) park, but with numerous later additions. The walled site rises gently along the Severn Vale ridge, and the entrance front faces approximately west to the Severn at Shepperdine. Kip chose a view looking inland rather than to the village which is to the west of Hill Court.

Steps leading down to a courtyard with double walls terminate in small summer-houses; Kip drew the urns commemorating Fust family marriages on the tops of the lower walls to left and right (*qv*). A similar set was commissioned for Dyrham.

A broad path through kitchen gardens and orchards leads to the outer gates. The stables are on the north side, and a carriage is departing down the road. The formal gardens to the east accommodate a large duck pond very close to the house.

The church is near the house, and the tower with its three stages and elaborate bellcote still exists. It has been extensively repaired and part rebuilt, and the west window has been restored to its original shorter dimension as drawn by Kip, an example of the influence a Kip engraving can have.

Hill manor was first owned by a Fust in 1609 and remained with direct descendants for two centuries. Sir Edward Fust, named by Atkyns, died in 1713. Subsequently the house was extensively altered, entirely changing the entrance front, although service ranges were kept. By 1853 it was extremely dilapidated and was demolished. The present house was built on the same site in 1863-64. Now a wedding venue, the remaining formal gardens are an attractive feature.

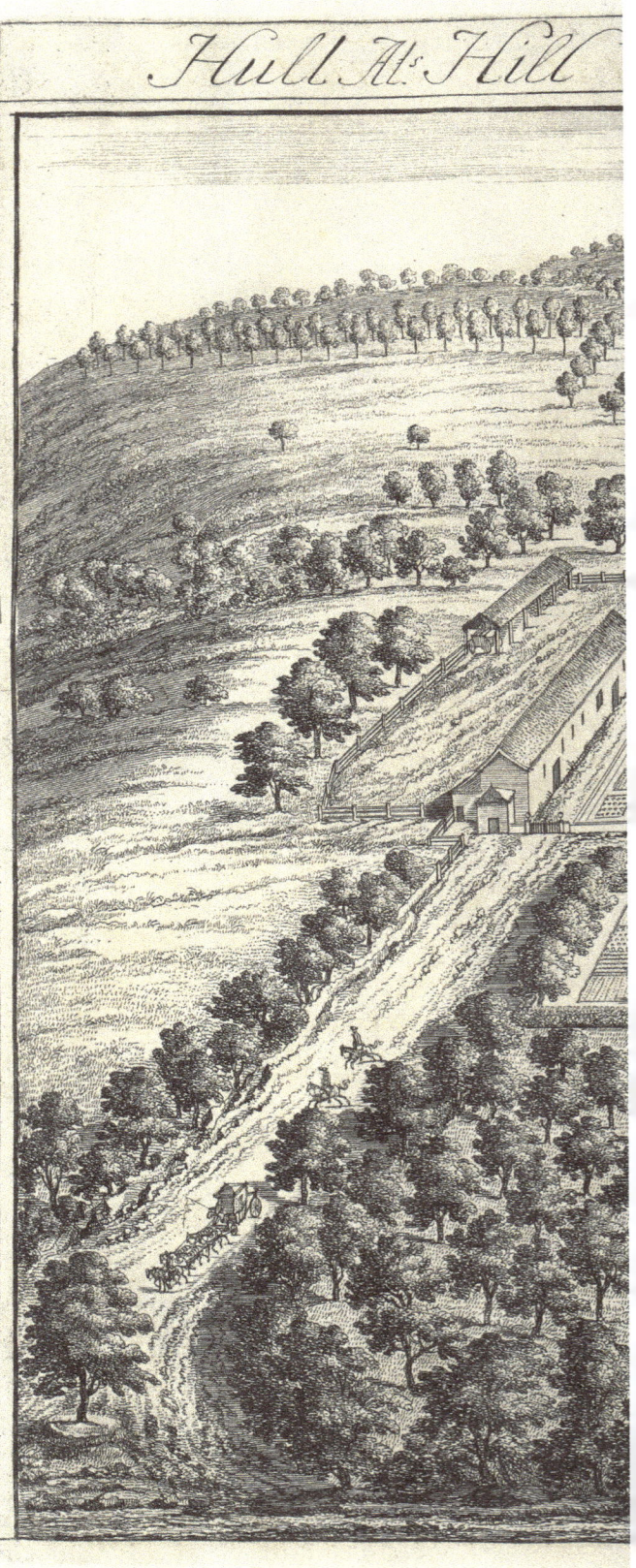

Hull Als Hill

Postcode: Hill, Berkeley GL13 9EB. NGR: ST 64978 95256.

has an ancient seat near the church, and a large estate. … The church is small, and hath a low spire at the west end. Sir Edward

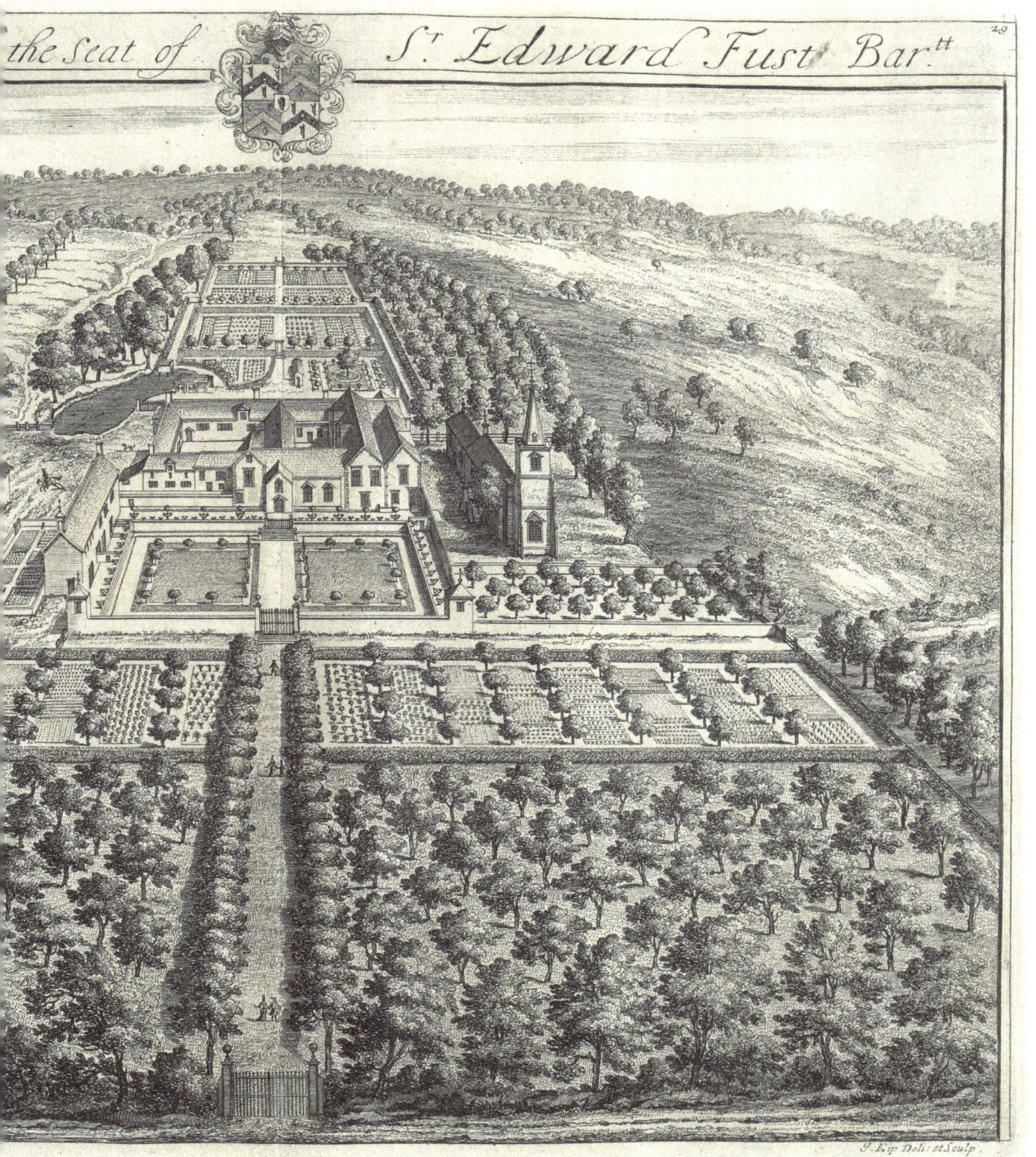

40 Kempsford the Seat of the Lord Viscount Weymouth [Atkyns: Kempsford, 490-91].

'Lord Viscount Weymouth … is seized of the mannor of Kempsford … and has a large seat near the church; and by the death to their great estates … He is a person truly honoured for his virtue, loyalty and generous charity.'

The Thynnes' great manor house has vanished as if a bomb had been dropped, with the usual effect of blast: peripheral fragments. The house was ranged round a courtyard; the north range had stepped or 'Dutch' gables, the front range was simpler. It was finished by 1639. There was a walled garden and a terrace walk beside the Thames along the rampart of an earlier fortified manor house. But in 1682 Sir Thomas Thynne inherited Longleat and the family ceased to occupy Kempsford. Nonetheless it was the subject of a Kip engraving.

The house was demolished by 1784, and some of the stone used to front Manor Farm, and some purportedly used at Buscot Park, Oxfordshire. All that survived in 1976 was part of the terrace walk with the ruins of a summer house within the Old Vicarage garden, given the name 'Lady Maud's Walk' and now listed (grade II), and most of the farm buildings (*qv*).

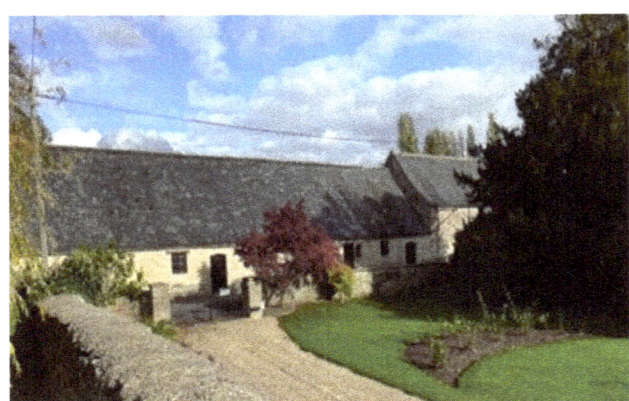

The church, with its gigantic fifteenth-century central tower, was close to the house; the south side is exactly as Kip drew it, except for the Lady Chapel added in 1858. North of the church Kip drew the old vicarage.

More interest attaches to Kip's detail of cottages in the long, winding village street, adjacent hedged fields in the flat landscape, and (impressionistic) view towards the Cotswolds. An early seventeenth-century estate survey at Longleat described the houses as mainly mud and thatch, and Kip's drawing of roofs in many cases suggests thatch, as in the first, possibly medieval house along the village street within its walled toft (*qv*). Kip also shows in the street a cross whose base is preserved in the new cemetery.

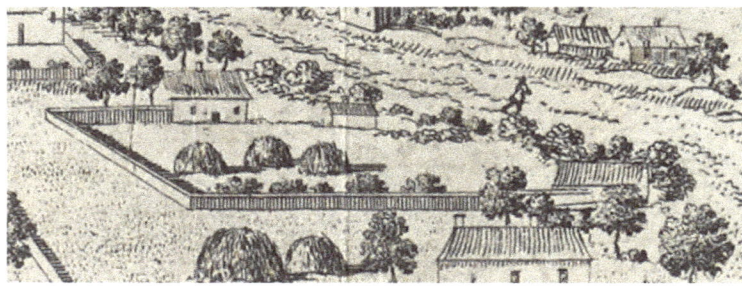

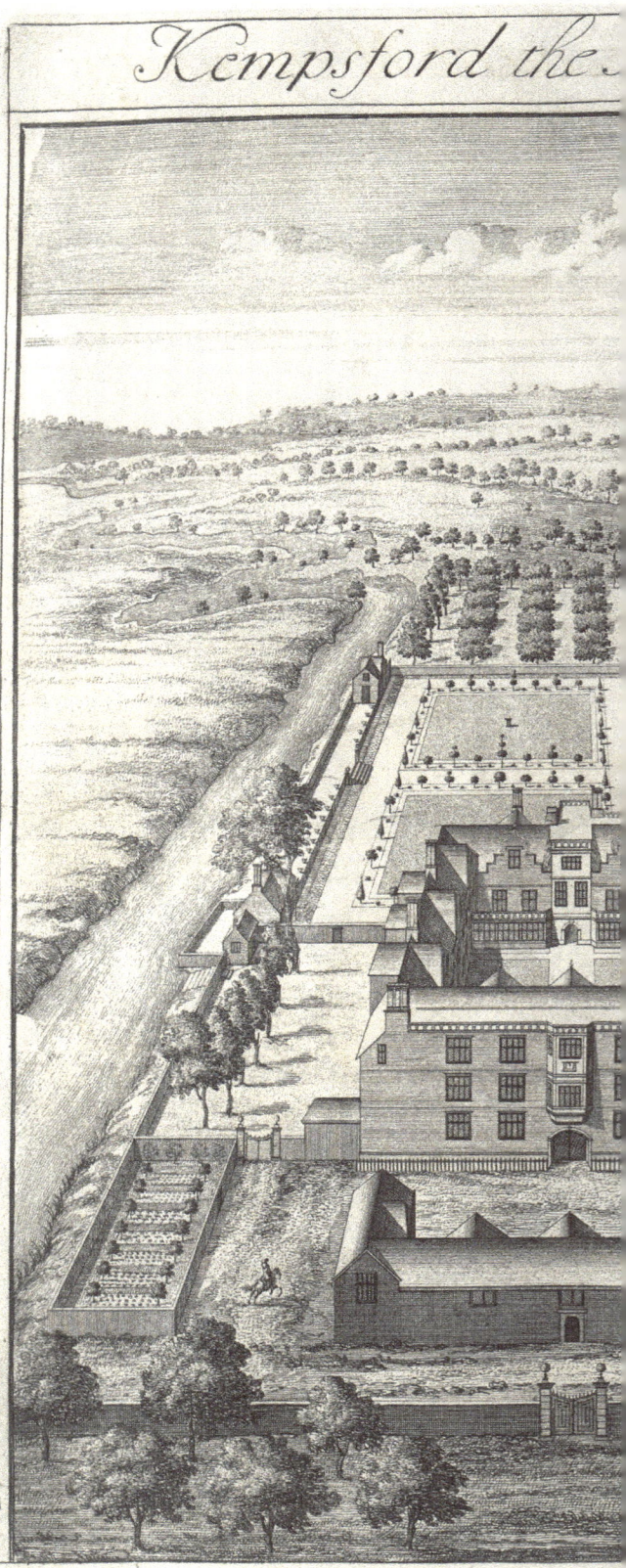

Kempsford the …

Postcode: Fairford GL7 4 ET. NGR: SU 16211 96489. VCH VII, 96-105.

of his uncle Sir James Thynn, without issue, and of Thomas Thynn, Esq, villainously murdered … he likewise succeeded

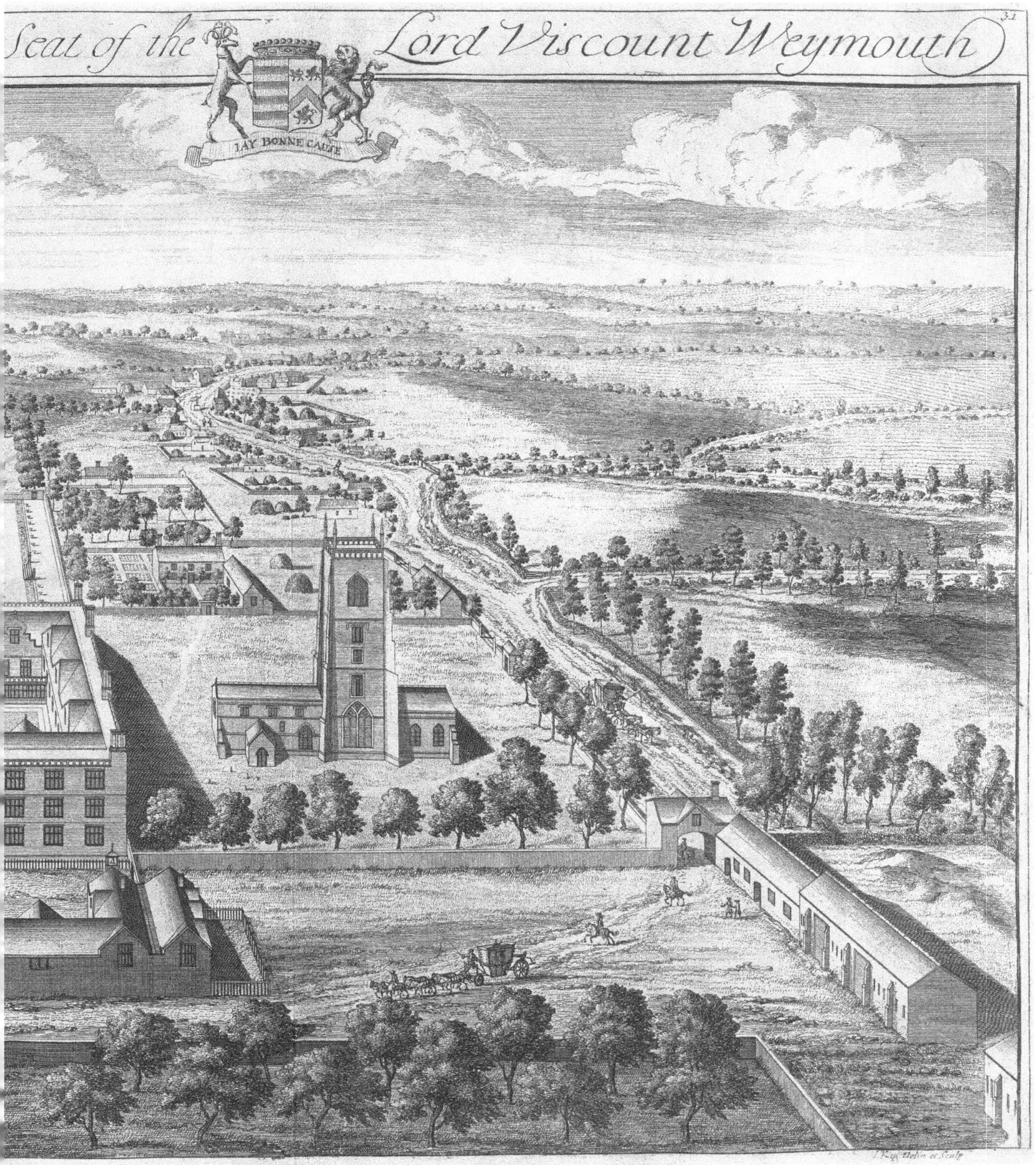

41 Leckhampton the Seat of the Revd Thomas Norwood [Atkyns: Leckhampton, 532-33

'The Reverend Thomas Norwood … is the present owner of Leckhampton … He has a large ancient house near the church,

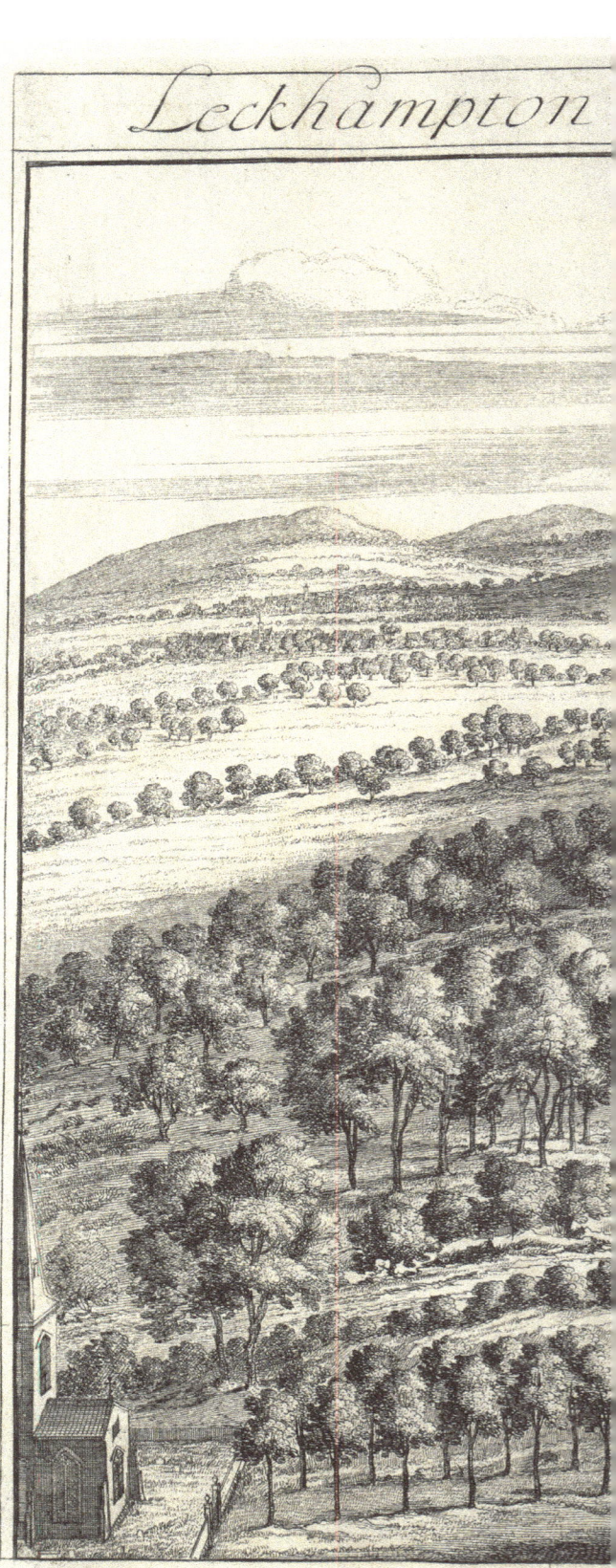

Atkyns must have seen the 'large prospect' from Leckhampton Court: from the front of the house, which faces west, and from the north side, the view stretches from the Malvern Hills to Cleeve Hill and Leckhampton hill. Kip lightly sketched Leckhampton village, Cheltenham church and houses, and further away Elmstone Hardwicke and Bishop's Cleeve.

Much of the house today also reflects Atkyns' observation, preserving early fourteenth-century features, notably the great hall on the north side of the front range, and the battlemented two-storey porch. Kip suggests the timber-framing of the south wing, and behind it the small walled garden, both surviving. The north side of the house has been altered several times, but the building closest to the viewer is early sixteenth century.

Leckhampton Court is on a terrace on the hill side, and the footprint of the gardens today reveals the structure in Kip's

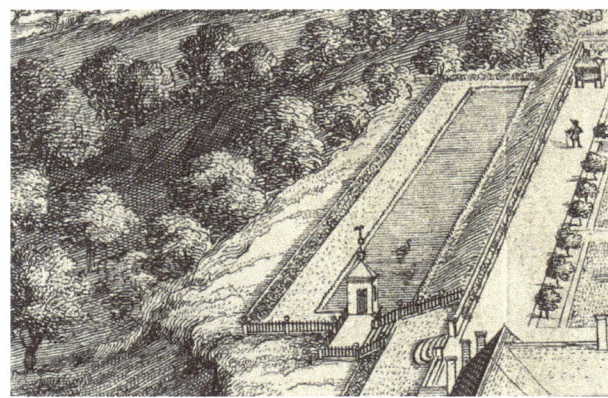

engraving. Behind the house, a lawn covers the paths, but the steps at the far side remain, though not the gazebo; two raised grass walks once led to it. The sloping vegetable garden has

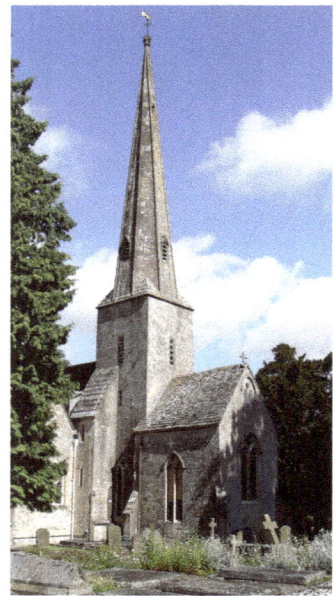

become a car park. To the north there are traces of the canal and the walk beside it, and the ground falls steeply from here as Kip indicated (*qv*).

There are traces of the avenue of limes which led to the Revd Thomas Norwood's church of which he was rector. The early fourteenth-century chancel is tucked into the corner of the engraving; Kip noticed the window on the upper floor of the unusually tall chancel (*qv*), though its shape has been altered.

Today Leckhampton Court is a Sue Ryder Hospice and the founder's imagination saved the near-derelict house by extensive restoration in 1979-81.

Postcode: Cheltenham GL53 0**QJ. NGR: SO** 94499 19338. **[VCH XV forthcoming].**

with a large prospect over the Vale, and has a great estate in this and other places.'

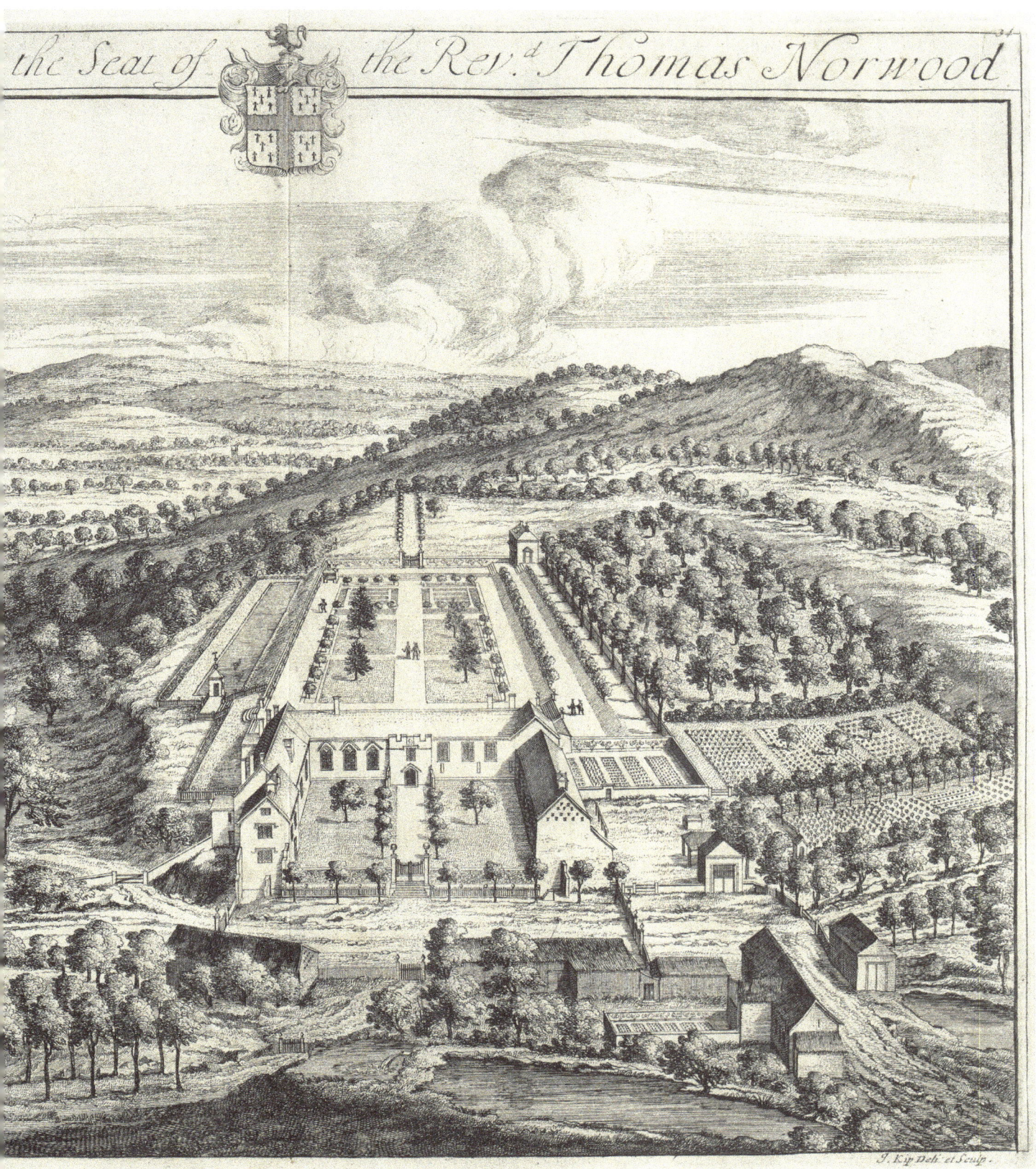

42 Cleeve Hill the Seat of William Player Esq [Atkyns: Mangotsfield, 546-47].

'William Player Esq is the present owner thereof, who has an handsome seat, with large walks and plantations. The royalty

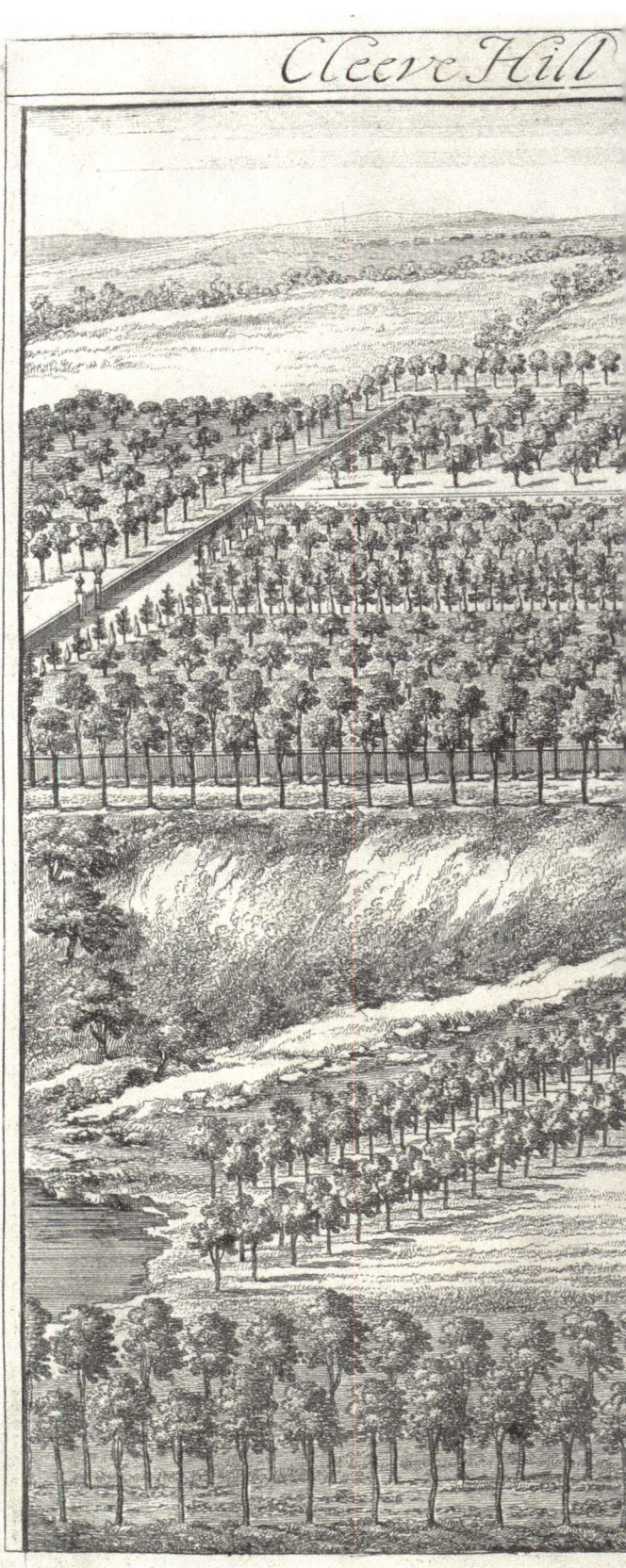

The Cleve Hill estate was bought by William Player's ancestor in the early seventeenth century, and the house constructed about 1627 was home to his descendants until the later eighteenth century. Kip shows it occupying the crest of a south-west to north-east escarpment, the cliff which gives the locality its name, which he has indicated separating the house from the three converging avenues.

Devoid of movement, the picture is dominated by the three avenues of large trees. The house hardly seems to justify Atkyn's description of 'handsome'. Kip presented an unprepossessing rectangular facade, two storeys, gabled attics, and very modest gardens. The two-bay entrance front with single-storey wings east and west, faced south across a plain lawned courtyard. To the west there was a second lawned courtyard, and the ground then falls to the Frome Valley with a view to Stoke Park; the avenue to the north, leading towards Cleve Hill Farm, which Kip did not draw, formed the eastern boundary of Bromley Heath with the collieries whence came Player's wealth.

Between 1730 and 1750 the house was extended and re-cased in Classical style, much of its original structure being retained, and new gardens laid out. Used as a hospital during World War I, the house was demolished in 1930 and the estate sold for housing. The modern road names all employ Kip's spelling of Cleeve. Of the site as engraved by Kip almost nothing remains, except for some substantial estate boundary walling. There are some survivals amongst the modern housing of later garden buildings, including a rare semi-octagonal roofed wooden arbour known as a Kent seat, after Georgian designer William Kent, listed Grade II, dated to approximately 1750. Perhaps it replaced the small arbour drawn by Kip at the back of the parterre.

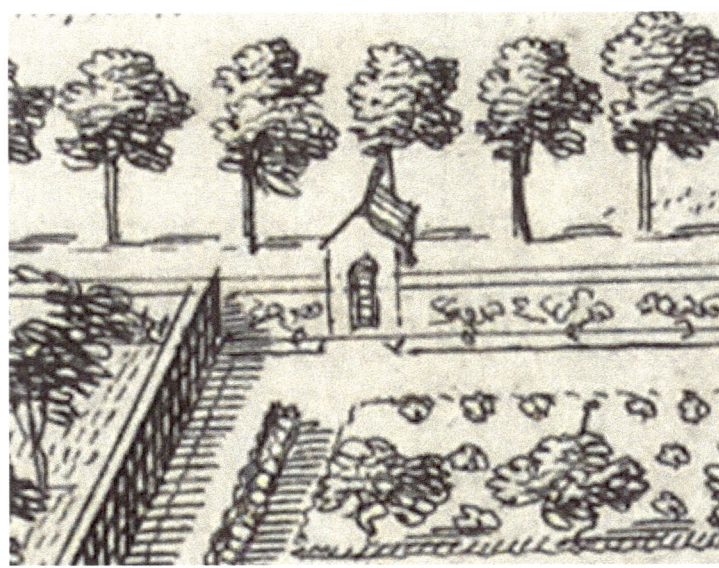

If he had drawn Cleve Hill farm there would have been a more substantial survival to the modern day.

Postcode: Cleeve Court BS16 6DL. NGR: ST 64883 77173.

and wasts, and a great part of Kingswood Chase, are within this mannor, wherein are many profitable coal-mines.'

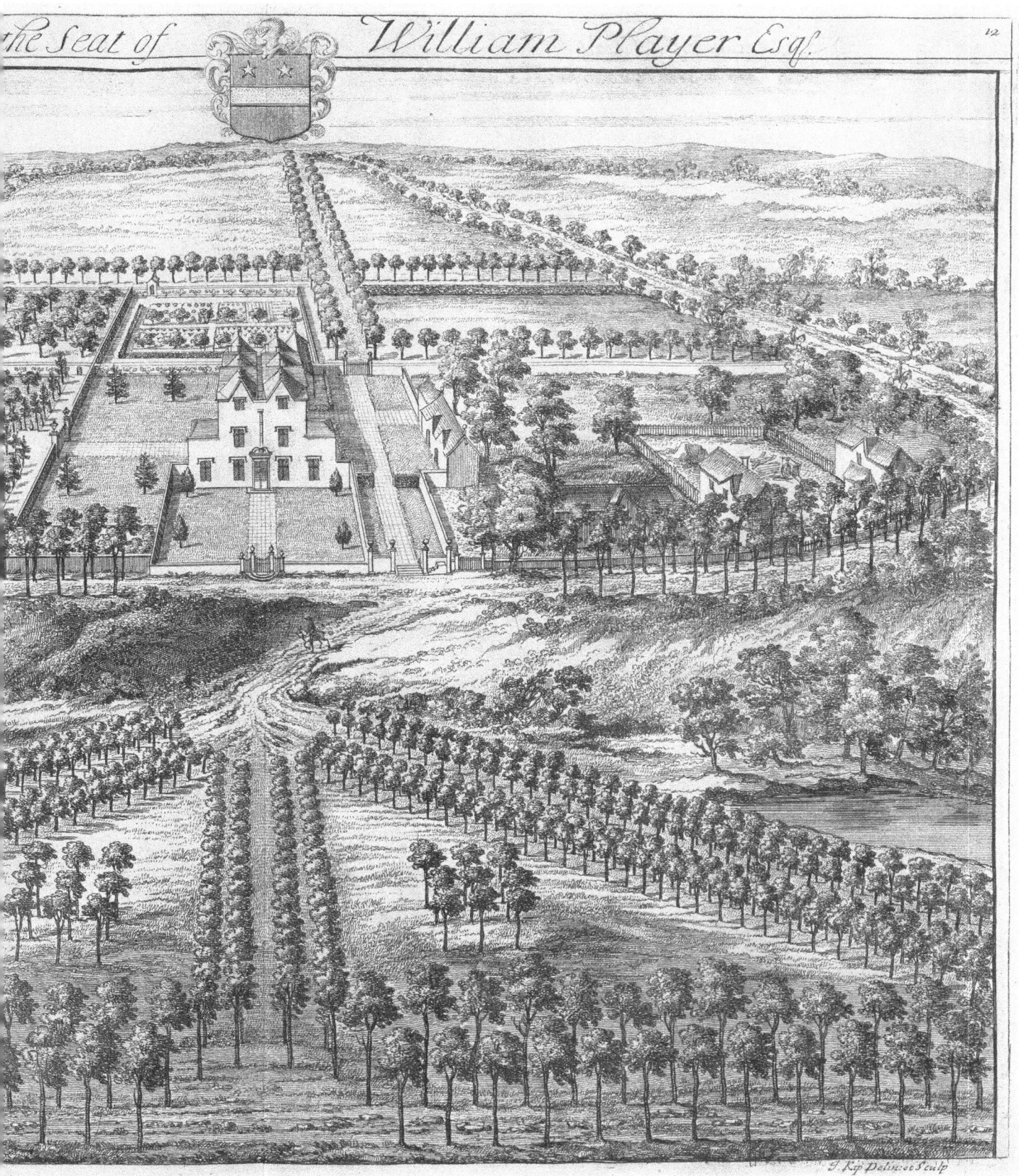

43 Miserden the seat of William Sandys Esq [Atkyns: Miserden, 560-61].

'William Sandys.....is present lord of the manor. He hath a good stone house and a large park adjoining it, and a very great

The engraving of Miserden is unlike most of Kip's Gloucestershire work. The house is small, set in the middle of a wide sweep of countryside, with formal gardens to rear and front not very strongly characterised, but with the deep valley of the Frome brook dramatically emphasised. The view is from the south-east. It apparently reflected the estates the Sandys family owned in Brimpsfield and Winstone as well as Miserden Park, bearing out Atkyns' comments. A Sandys' ancestor had acquired all three estates by 1623. Miserden park, which was recorded as early as 1297, extended eastwards across the Frome brook into Winstone. Kip has drawn the wall quite clearly on the far side, also Winstone church to the east, and Brimpsfield church on the skyline; although very small, both are placed reasonably accurately. The very meandering course of the river Frome is also approximately right and the lake is today a noted attraction (*qv*); Kip added a man fishing, a rowing boat and lots of ducks.

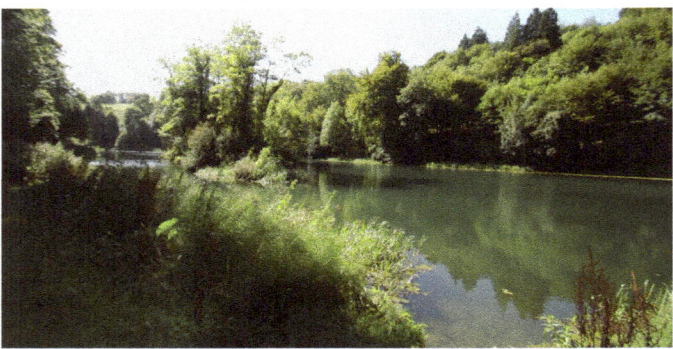

When Kip visited Miserden Park, it was held by the widow of Miles Sandys, who had died in 1697, during the lifetime of her son, William. Perhaps this explains why the house is so far away, and why no deer are recorded in the park. After William died in 1712, park and house in turn passed to his widow. Significantly also, Kip made the village houses very small; Sandys did not own most, and the drawing of the church is curious: Kip shows a tower separate from the nave and chancel (*qv*).

Today parts of the seventeenth-century Miserden Park house survive, with many alterations and additions, the most important being after the Sandys family's ownership ended in 1832, together with ownership of Winstone.

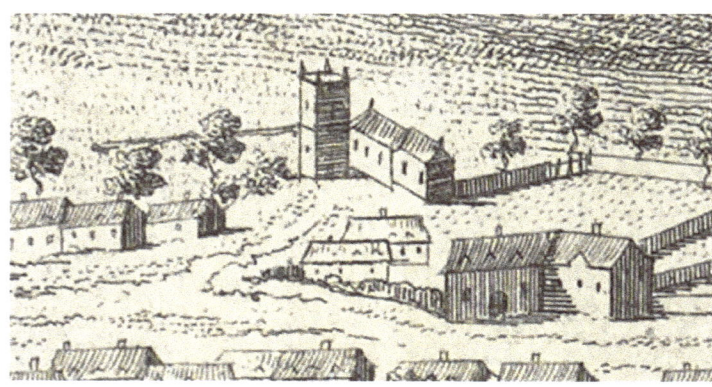

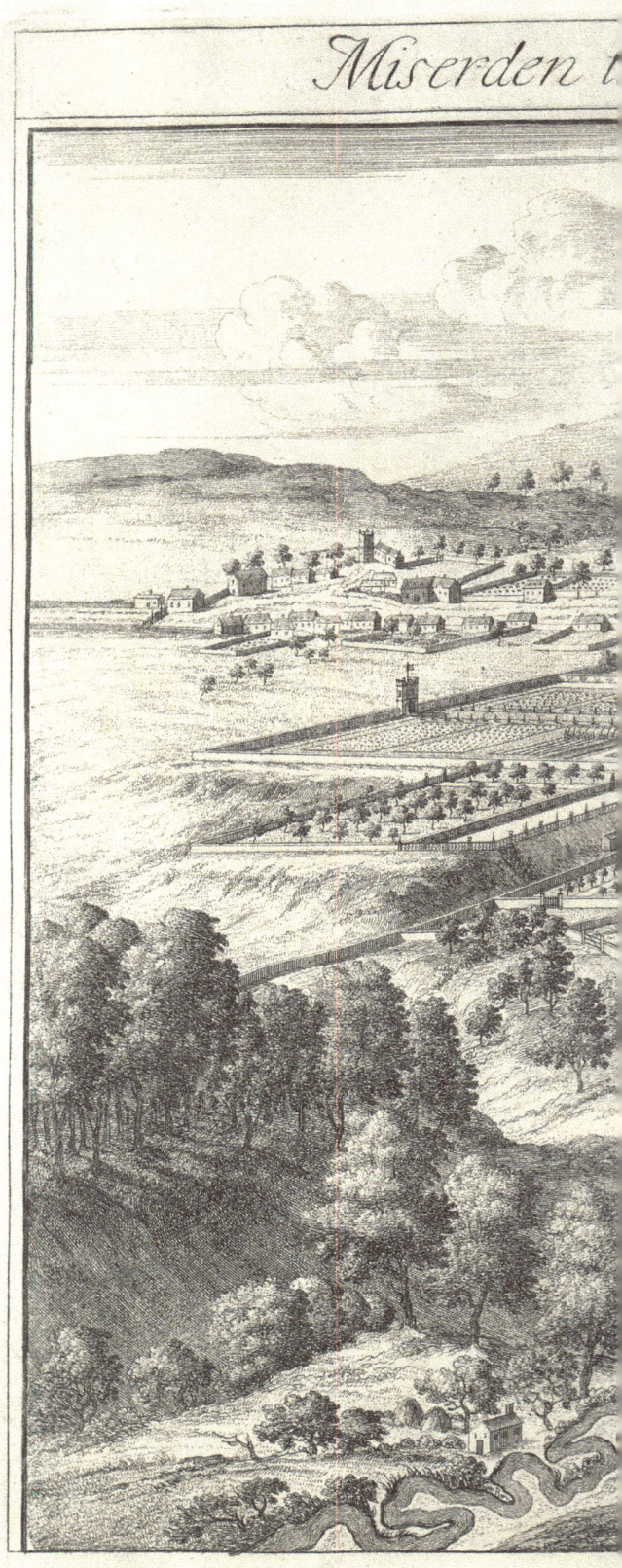

Miserden t

Postcode: Stroud GL6 **7JA. NGR: SO** 94324 09064**. VCH XI** 47-56.

estate in this and many neighbouring parishes.'

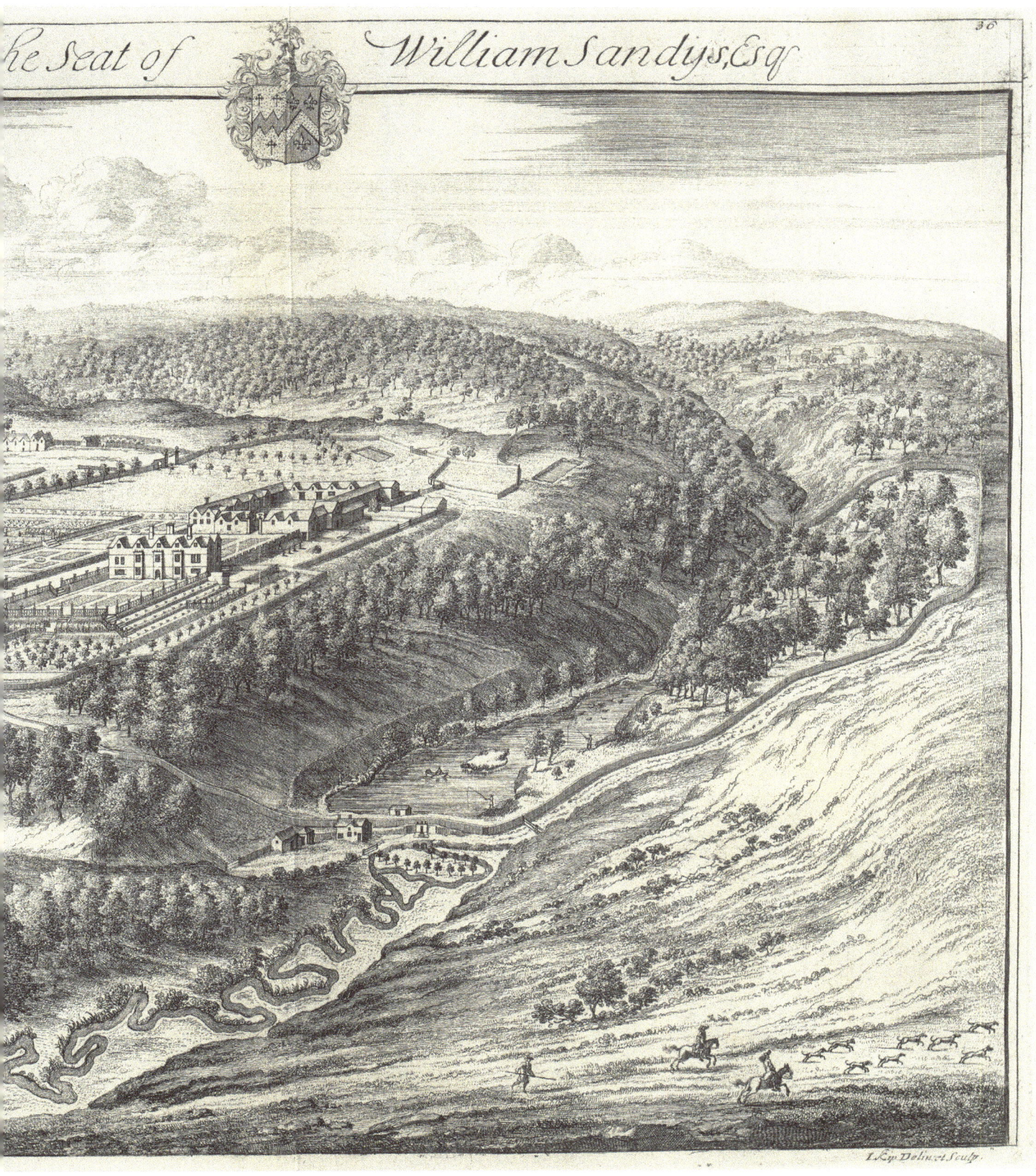

44 Clower-Wall [Clearwell] the Seat of Francis Wyndham Esq [Atkyns: Newland, 574-75]

'[Clearwell] is now the seat of Francis Wyndham Esq. He is descended from the ancient family of the Wyndhams in Somersetsh

'Clowerwall' was the form of the place-name into the seventeenth century, and Kip suggests into the eighteenth century too, not Clearwell as today. It was one of the larger settlements in the extensive parish of Newland, the new land cleared from the forest. On the western side of the Forest the hills are gentle (*qv*), as Kip shows in his engraving.

The Clearwell estate was associated with the Baynham family from 1484, by which time it was known as the manor of Clearwell, and remained their possession for 130 years. The large Elizabethan-style house in the Kip drawing was probably built by Thomas Baynham, who inherited Clearwell in 1580 and died in 1611. It faced north towards Clearwell village. It is likely that he created a small deer park to the west of the entrance avenue, where Kip drew deer (*qv*), and the rabbit warren on high ground west of the house.

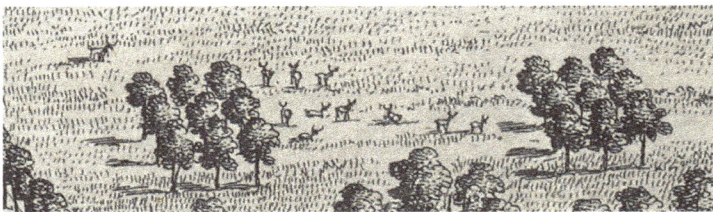

Through his daughter the estate came to the Throckmortons; as royalists they suffered in the Civil War and after the younger Sir Baynham Throckmorton died, Clearwell was sold in 1698 to Francis Wyndham. He probably extended the park to surround the house and gardens on three sides, including in it the rabbit warren. The parkland was embellished with regular clumps of trees, of which a few survive. Kip shows part was walled and the walls too survive though much of the former park is now arable land.

In 1725 Francis Wyndham's grandson pulled down the old house and replaced it with a Gothic Revival castle, one of the earliest in England, designed by Roger Morris, with a grand castellated gateway. While almost nothing remains of the Kip house or formal gardens, the overall area, a square of nearly 100 acres (39 ha), preserves the historic boundaries and is registered grade II.

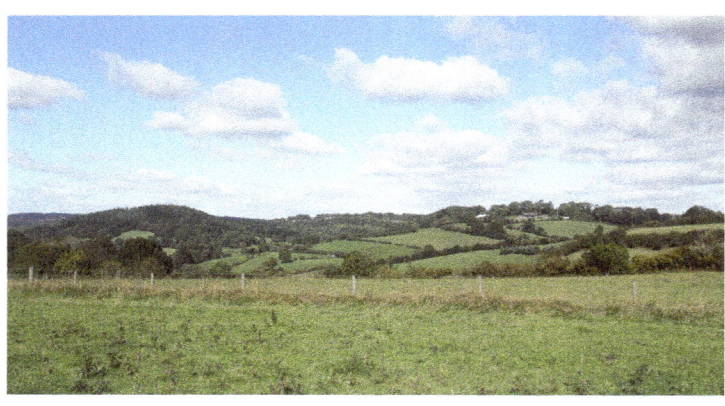

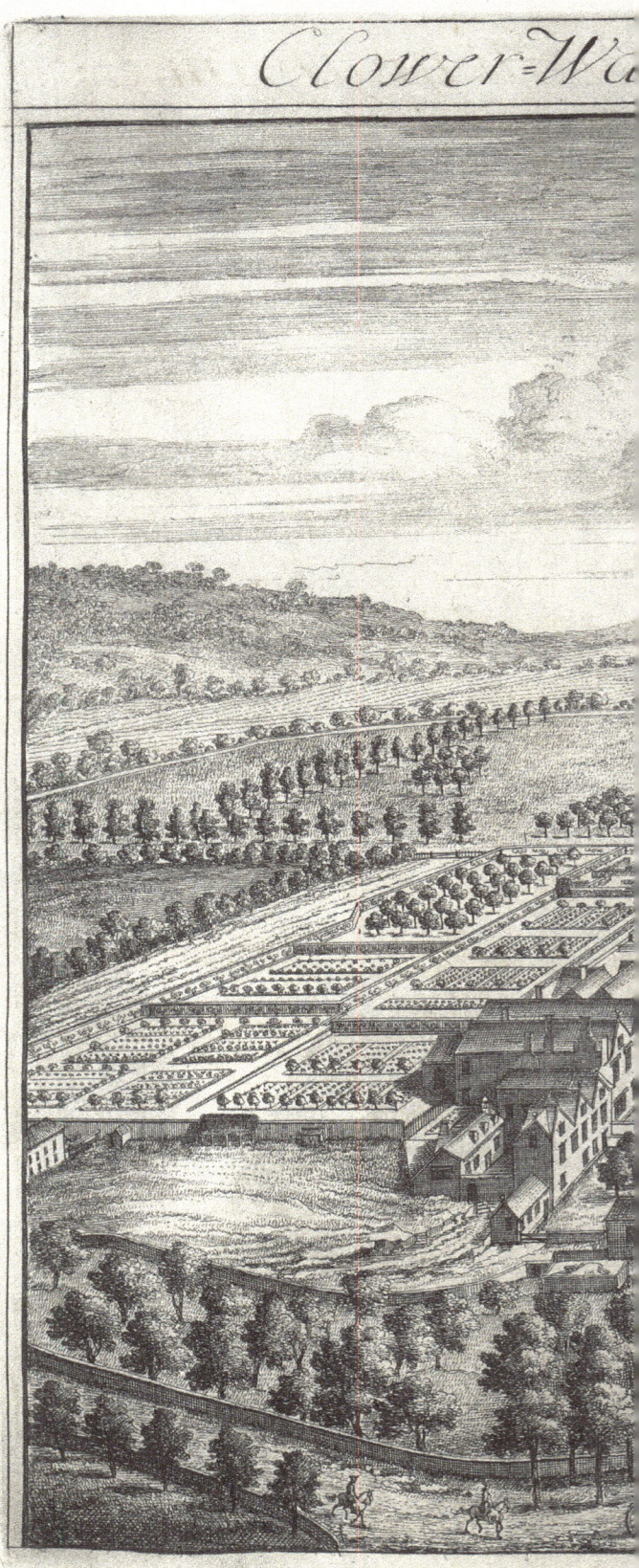

Postcode: Coleford GL16 8LG. NGR: SO 57009 07745. **VCH V** 195-231.

and has a large handsome house, with beautiful gardens, and a very great estate in this and other places.'

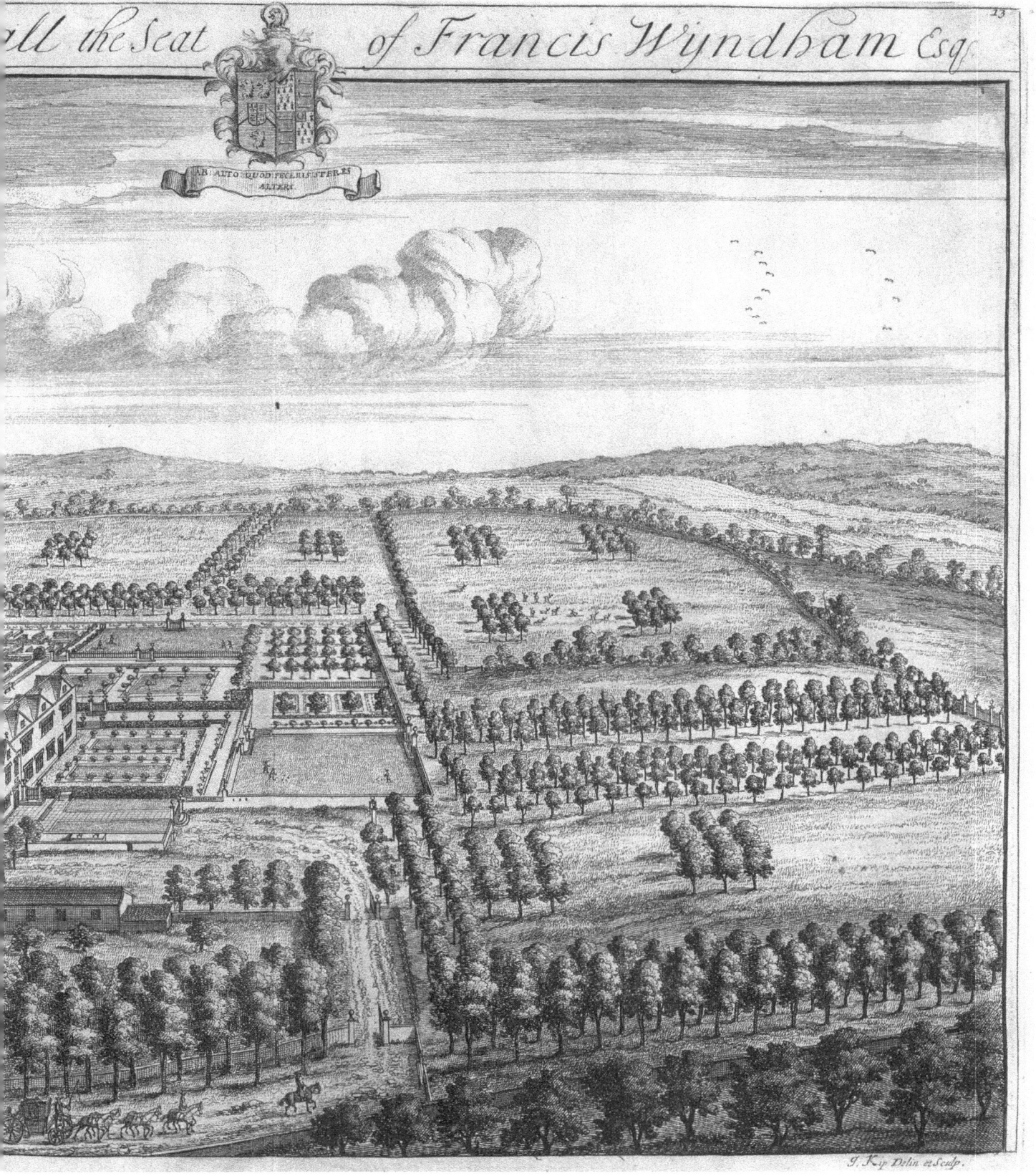

ll the Seat *of Francis Wyndham Esq.*

J. Kip Delin et Sculp.

45 Nibley the Seat of George Smyth Esq [Atkyns: Nibley, 578-579].

'George Smyth Esq has two very handsome seats in this parish, near one another, adorned with gardens and groves, and has Berkeley's family, with great judgment and industry … the whole county does at this day stand indebted to his memory'

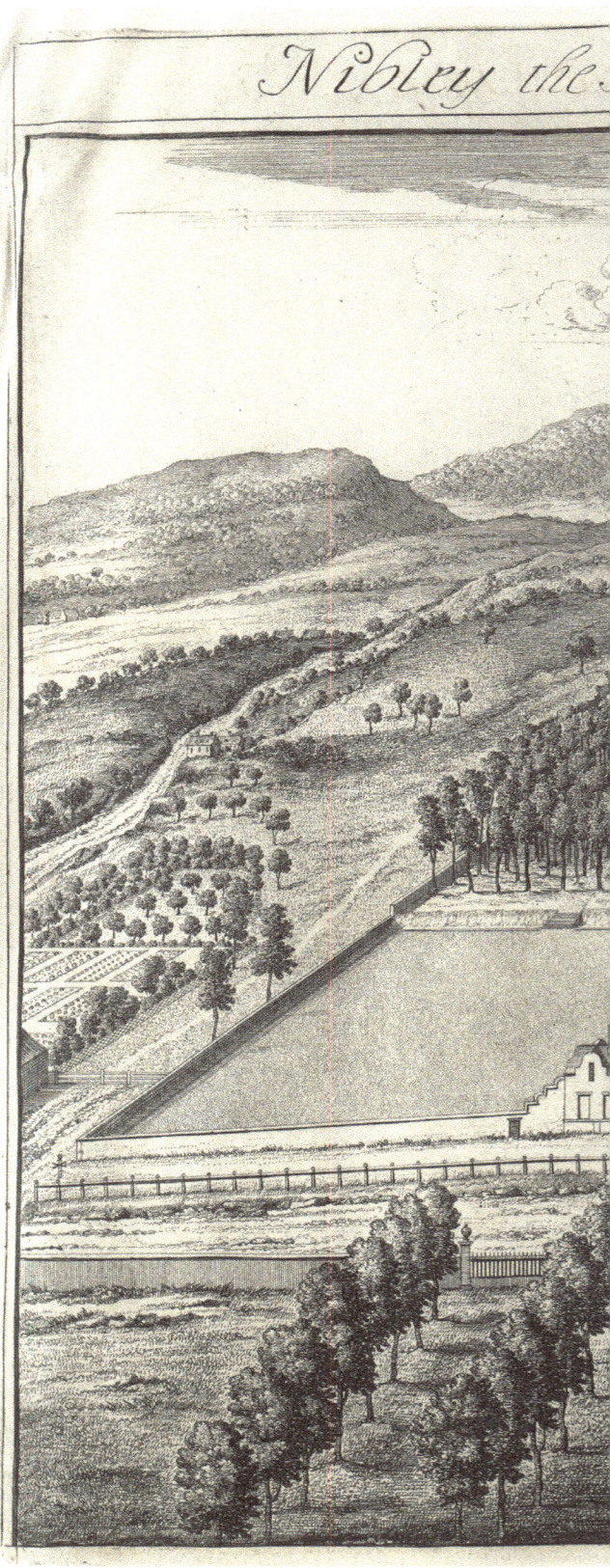

Kip drew the north front of Nibley house, and in the background the nib or Knoll which is the origin of the name, since 1866 topped with the William Tyndale monument. His drawing suggests that the house was in the country, but nearby to the east was Nibley village, and to the north the church and Smallcombe Court. This was John Smyth junior's house, built by his father in 1607 (demolished 1807), the second 'handsome' seat referred to by Atkyns, where he lived his whole life. His eldest son, Edward, who earlier had built the four-gabled triple block engraved by Kip, inherited Smallcombe in 1692. Both properties (A1 and L1 on the map, *qv*) after his death in 1700 came to his son George, named by Atkyns.

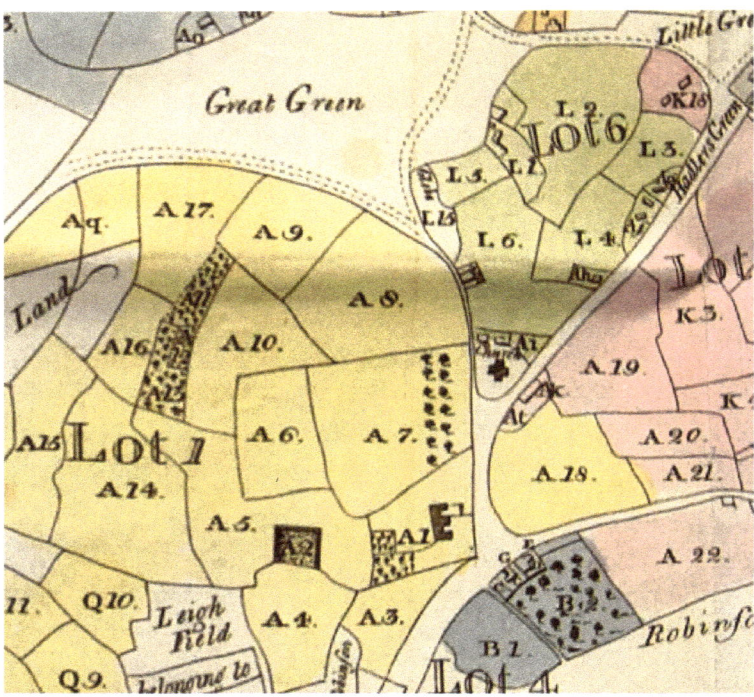

When Edward married in 1659, Warren's Court, an old house with a gallery and many chambers, was settled on him, but his grandmother, Mary, remained there till her death in 1667. Then Edward was able to build. Some fabric remaining in the neo-classical house built by a later Smyth in 1763 fits the date of Edward's building. The two pavilions or lodges also point to a mid-seventeenth century date; there is no trace of them in an engraving of 1779 or on early maps. The gardens were quite small, and a diminutive summerhouse was almost hidden in the centre of a grove of trees to the east. It was a farmhouse and to the south were stables, a barn and other offices.

The house and its land was a foundation endowment of Katherine Lady Berkeley's school in Wotton. Generations of the Smyth family leased the charity estate. Their estates were sold in 1798, and the lease was extinguished, possibly accounting for the later name of Nibley House, or The Great House.

Postcode: North Nibley GL11 6DL. NGR: ST 73754 95969.

a large park well wooded, and a great estate in this and other places. ...His great-grandfather wrote the history of the Lord
   [also for Men & Armour for Gloucestershire 1608 *(published* 1980*)]*

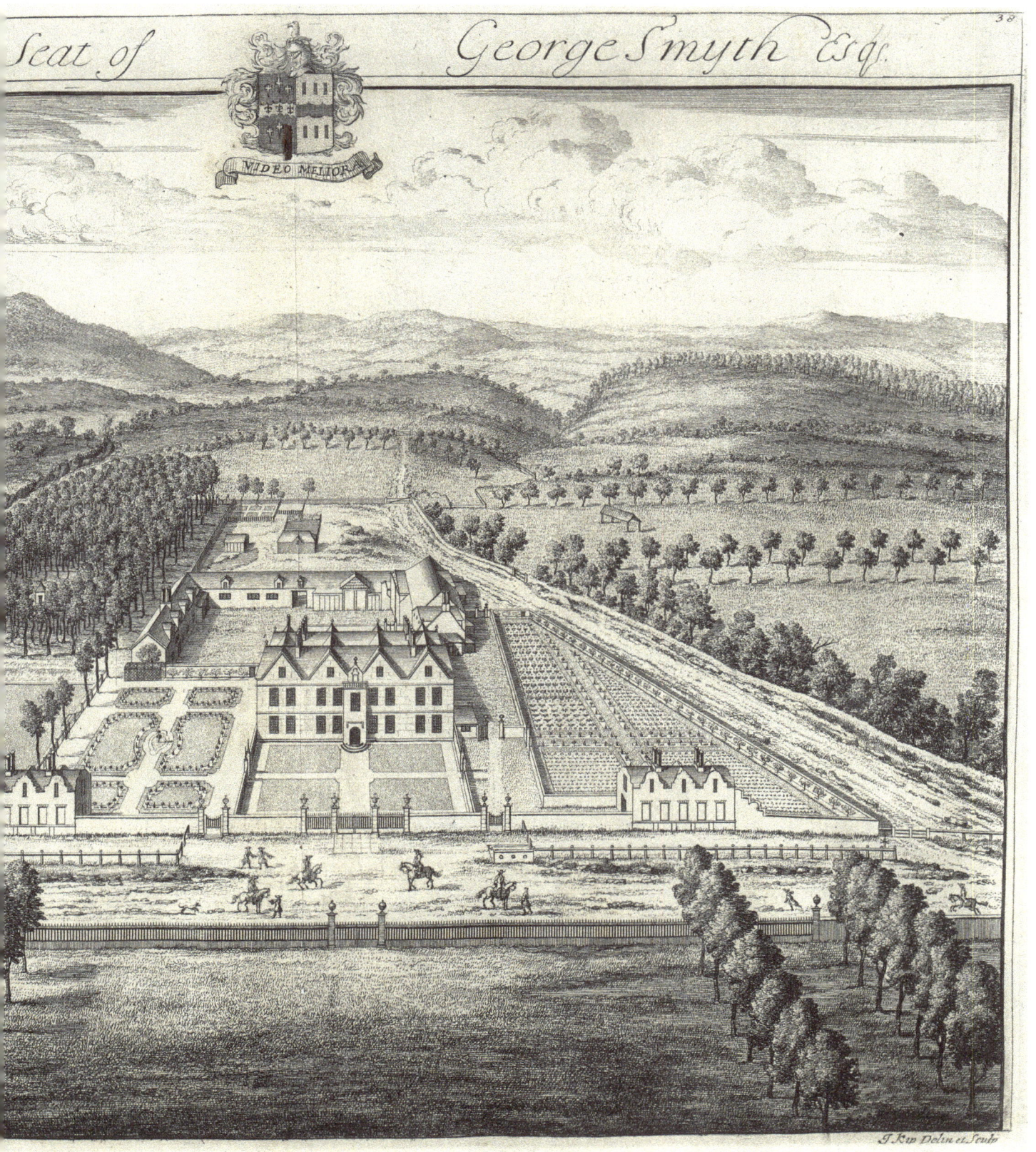

46 **Rendcomb the Seat of Sr John Guise Bart** [Atkyns: Rendcomb, 618-619].

'Sir John Guise …has … served as Knight of the Shire in several Parliaments: he is the present lord of the mannor of

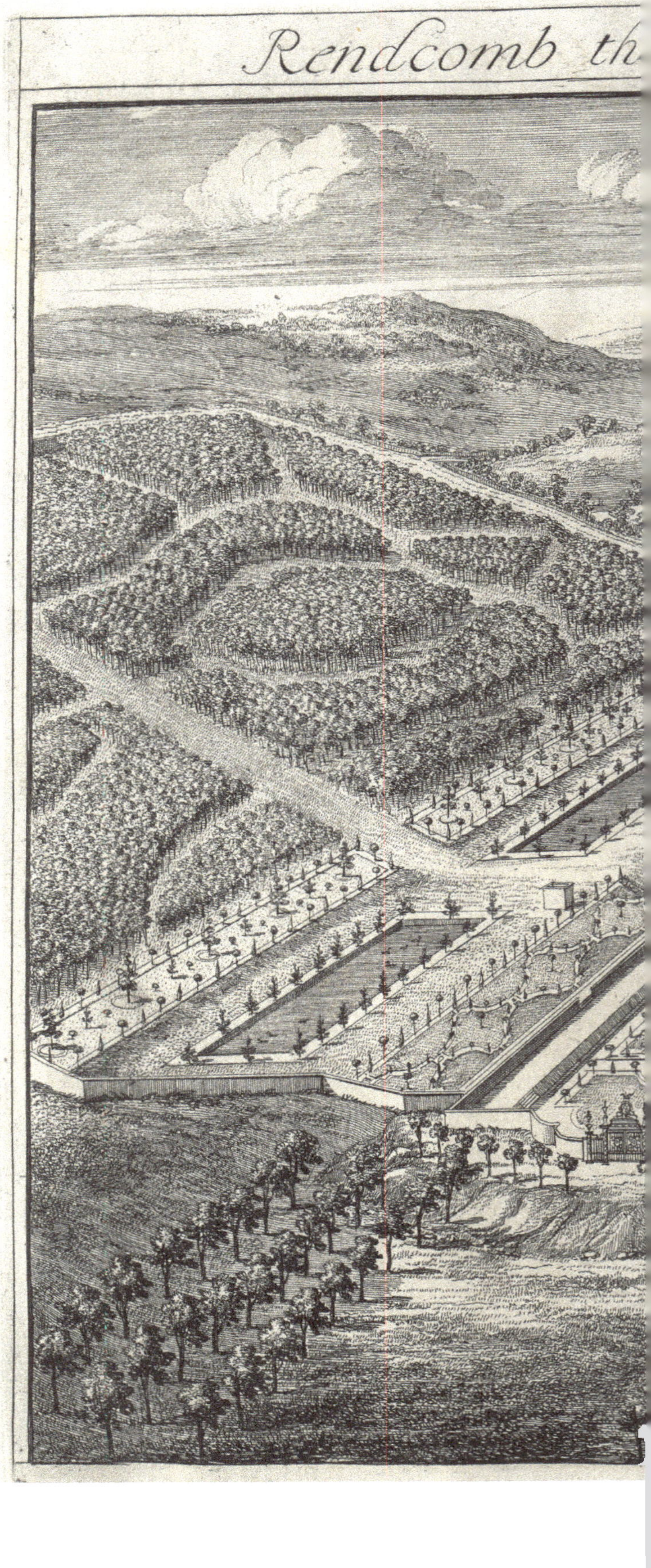

Rendcomb manor house was new-built about 1685. Sir Christopher Guise had bought the reversion of Rendcomb manor in 1635, but had to wait twenty-six years to take possession. His son, Sir John, built the house which became the family's principal residence during the eighteenth century; his grandson, named by Kip, succeeded to the estate in 1695.

The house was indeed neat and square, in the fashionable style of the period; the north-west front is well-lit and the view is slightly angled. In mid-nineteenth century it was again replaced by an Italianate house on the same site as previous houses, the best vantage point on the plateau within a steep-sided valley or combe. The gardens have been altered several times, but the terraces close to the house provide a basic structure and the wilderness to the north-east remains, bounded by the road to Marsden. Church, churchyard, and Rendcomb village are to the south and east of the house. The church appears without south aisle or porch.

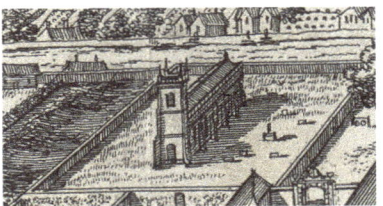

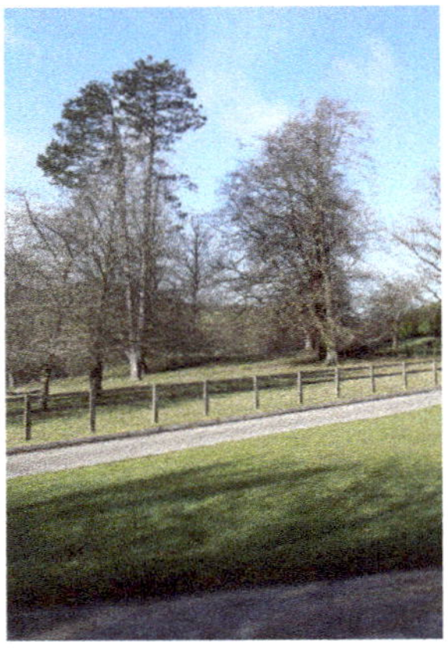

Kip seems to have enjoyed the huge panorama in this engraving. He was apparently standing in the park, to which ornate gates gave access, though it stretched a long way to the left. There are deer in the park today, also remnants of the avenues which Kip showed leading into it, and some very old trees (*qv*). The Churn flows south-eastwards through a deep valley, and widens out; Kip's drawing gives a disturbing sense of it flowing in the opposite direction. From the village the road descends to a bridge as it does today, where there was a corn mill (*qv*).

On the further side of the river is the wooded hill of Old Park; the Cirencester turnpike cut through a corner.

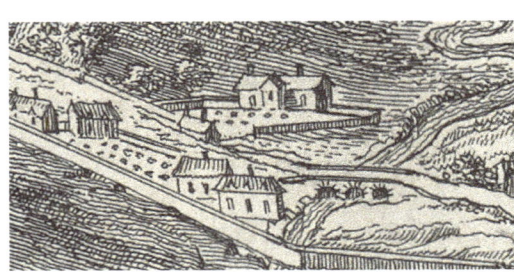

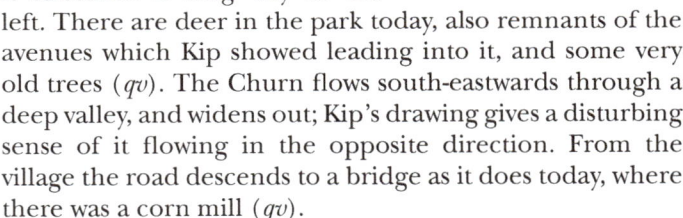

Rendcomb th

Postcode: Cirencester GL7 7HA. NGR: SP 01721 09853**. VCH VII** 218-227**.**

Rendcomb and has a large handsome new-built house, with pleasant beautiful gardens, and a large park adjoyning.'

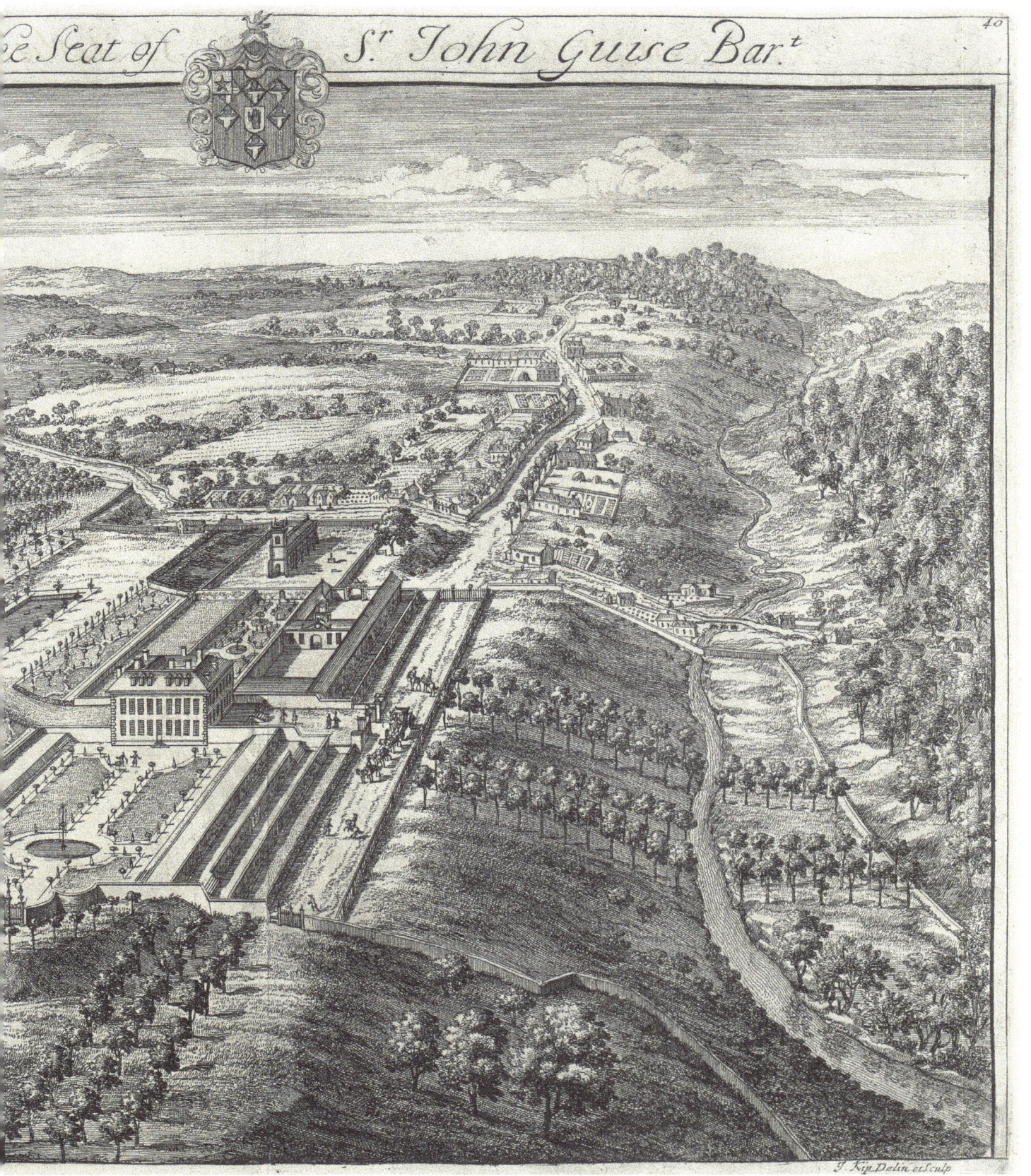

e Seat of St *John Guise Bar.ᵗ*

J. Kip Delin et Sculp

47 Saperton the Seat of Sr. Robert Atkyns [Atkyns: Saperton, 636-639].

'Sir Robert Atkyns … is the present owner of the mannor of Saperton … There is a large stone house near the church.'

The bold façade of Sapperton House, where Sir Robert Atkyns senior lived, dominates Kip's view. Sir Robert Atkyns junior made the briefest of comments on it, though giving a detailed history of the family, whereas on Pinbury Park (mainly in Duntisbourne Rouse) where he lived, he was rather more expansive, describing it as 'a pleasant seat in the midst of a large park'. Sir Robert Atkyns senior had bought both estates. Kip put a very small image of Pinbury in the Sapperton engraving (*qv*).

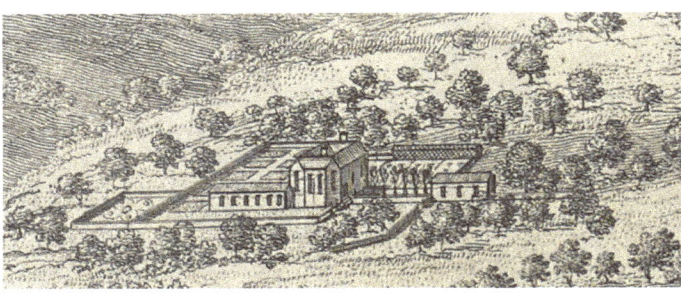

Sapperton House faced approximately south and stood close to the church. To the west is the river Frome in a deep valley, the ground falling sharply from near the house; some garden has since collapsed. Behind the house (near the coach and horses) are two cottages, rebuilt by Ernest Barnsley in 1902-3 as Upper Dorvel House. Sapperton House was pulled down in mid-eighteenth century. Some wood panelling was reused in the church and other material used to build Alfred's Hall in Cirencester Park. Traces of the garden terrace in front of the house are still visible but nothing remains of a long avenue leading away to the north, nor of the formal gardens to the rear. The long straight avenue to the right, known as 'Bishops Walk', does remain, and leads to Cirencester Park; the countryside in the vicinity now forms part of the Bathurst Estate.

The shape of the church matches Kip's engraving, with central tower and unusual spire (*qv*). Inside is the memorial to Sir Robert Atkyns, shown reclining on his left elbow, with an elaborate carved structure above and a long inscription at the back. His hand is placed on a closed book - doubtless *The Ancient and Present State of Glostershire*.

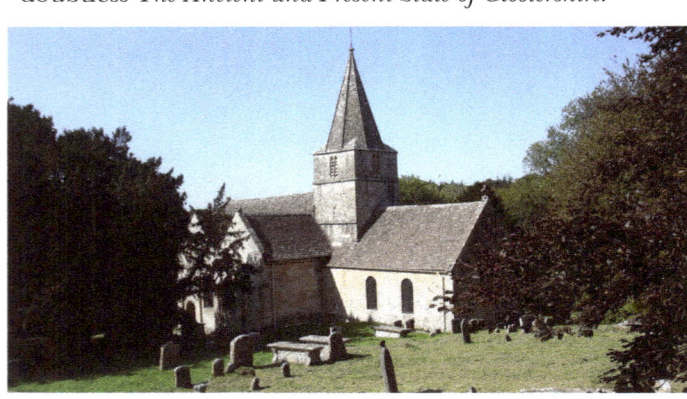

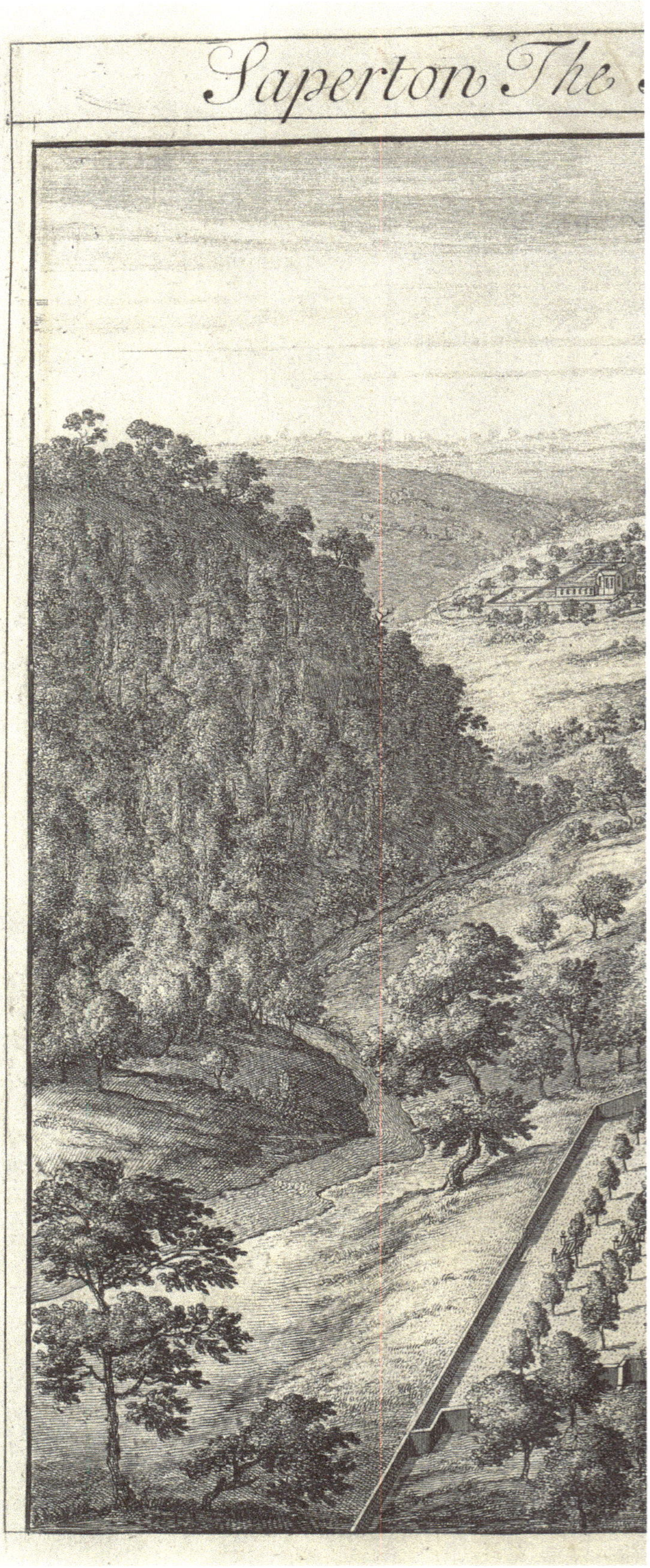

Saperton The

Postcode: Sapperton GL7 6LG. NGR: SO 94759 03382. **VCH XI** 87-99.

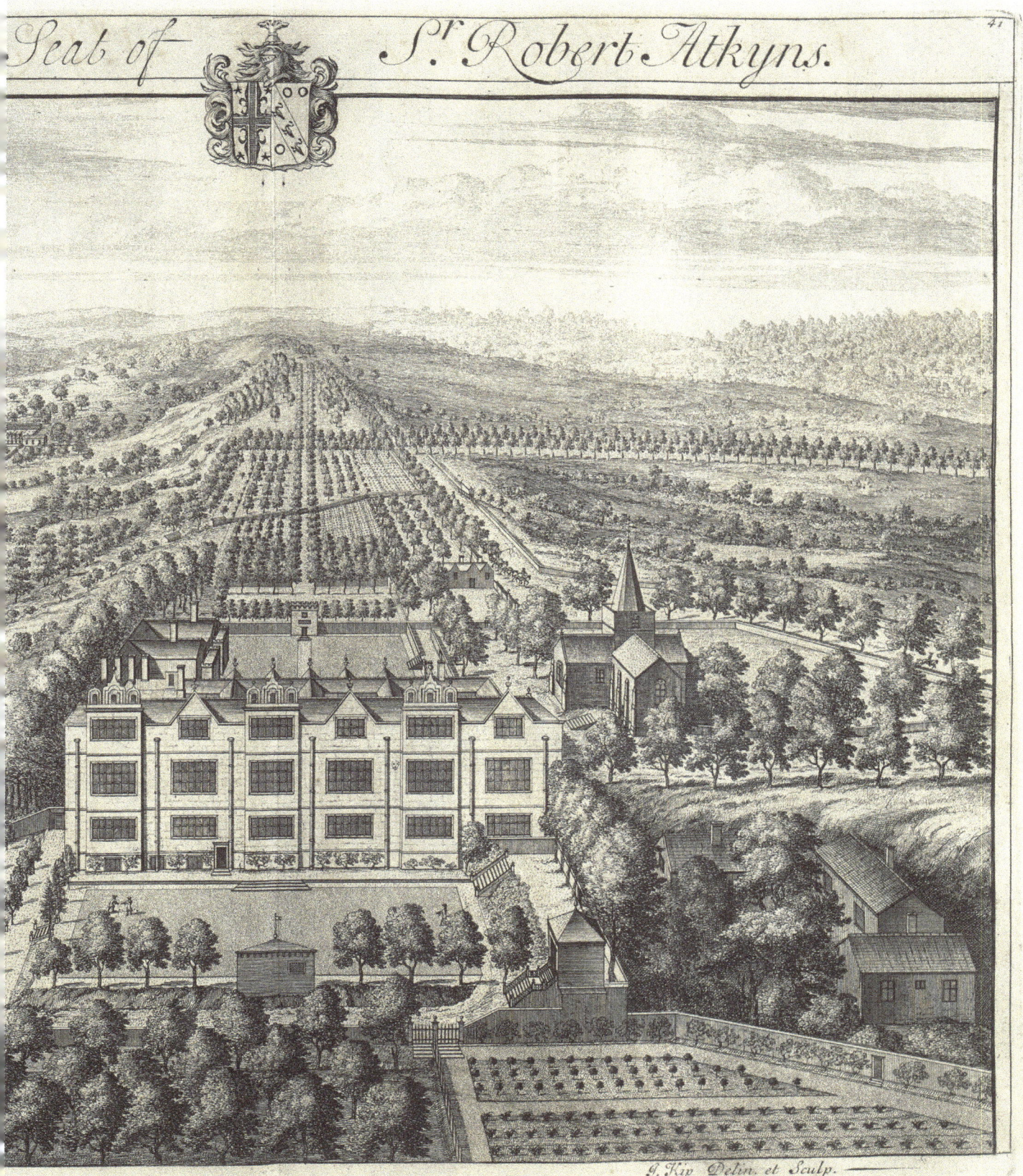

Seat of Sr. Robert Atkyns.

I. Kip Delin. et Sculp.

48 Sherborn the Seat of Sr Ralph Dutton Bart [Atkyns: Sherborne, 644-645].

'Sir Ralph Dutton … is the present possessor of this mannor. He hath a large stately house by the church, with large parks and a pleasant steeple at the west end.'

Sherborne became the centre of one of the two largest estates in Gloucestershire; the other was Berkeley. Sherborne had been acquired by Thomas Dutton in 1551, following the dissolution of Winchcombe Abbey which had held this manor at least from 1086 and probably for rather longer. Sir Ralph Dutton, named by Atkyns, was the 1st Baronet (cr. 1678); in 1710 he made over his estate to his son John, who died in 1743, and he was the last in the direct male line of the Duttons.

Kip's view from the west shows what a grand house Sherborne had become. It was drawn when the two wings were at their greatest extent and the church (very close though slightly differently aligned) was tucked behind the south wing. Kip drew this slight misalignment, indicating considerable care over detail. The main house had been greatly enlarged in 1651-53 by Valentine Strong of Taynton (in Oxfordshire) who a few years later was working at Fairford, and has been reworked at least twice since Kip drew it – in 1820 the wings were about half the length Kip indicated, and today the south (right) wing is gone, and the north (left) wing is back a step or two behind the church tower. Each reworking has taken inspiration from the seventeenth-century house, rather than creating a completely new design (*qv*).

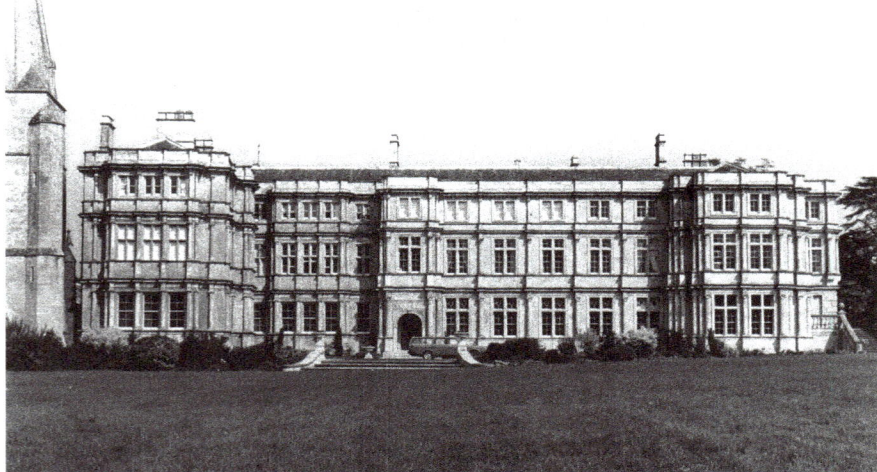

The church was rebuilt in mid-nineteenth century, enlarged and slightly repositioned further from the house, but tower and spire remain as drawn by Kip.

An important feature in the engraving is the old Deer Park, complete with deer, with the Sherborne Brook running through it. It had been inclosed in the late sixteenth century from common land. A map of the Sherborne estate of 1820 matches Kip's engraving to a large extent, though the Deer Park had become the Cow Park, reckoned to be 121 acres (49ha) - the deer had been removed to Lodge Park, created in mid-seventeenth century (*qv*). Kip's field with deer is number 25 on the enlarged map section below, amounting to 44 acres, but it's extent on the left side of the engraving is not visible. On the near side of the stream, number 18, an integral part of the park, was 31 acres in 1820.

North and east park boundaries remain where Kip drew them; they were walled about 40 years later, replacing what appear to be palings. Oaks and elms were planted in mid-eighteenth century and now mature oaks alone dot this landscape (*qv*).

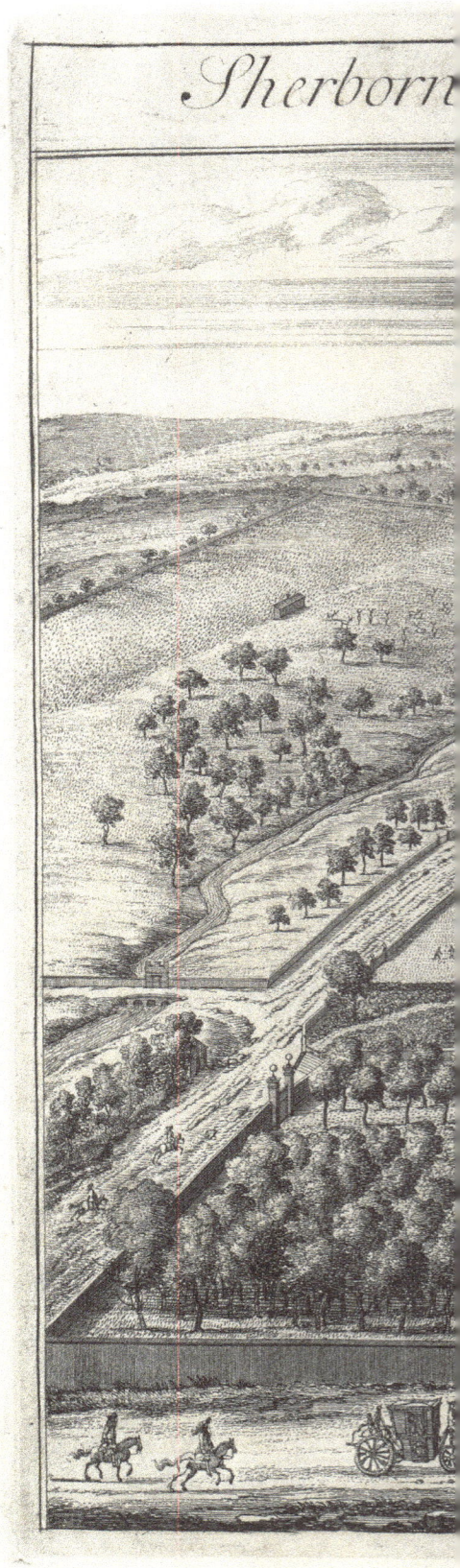

Postcode: Sherborne GL54 3**DZ. NGR: SP** 16889 14701**. VCH VI** 120-127.

paddock course, with a beautiful lodge-house … The church … has an isle as large as the body of the church, and a large spire

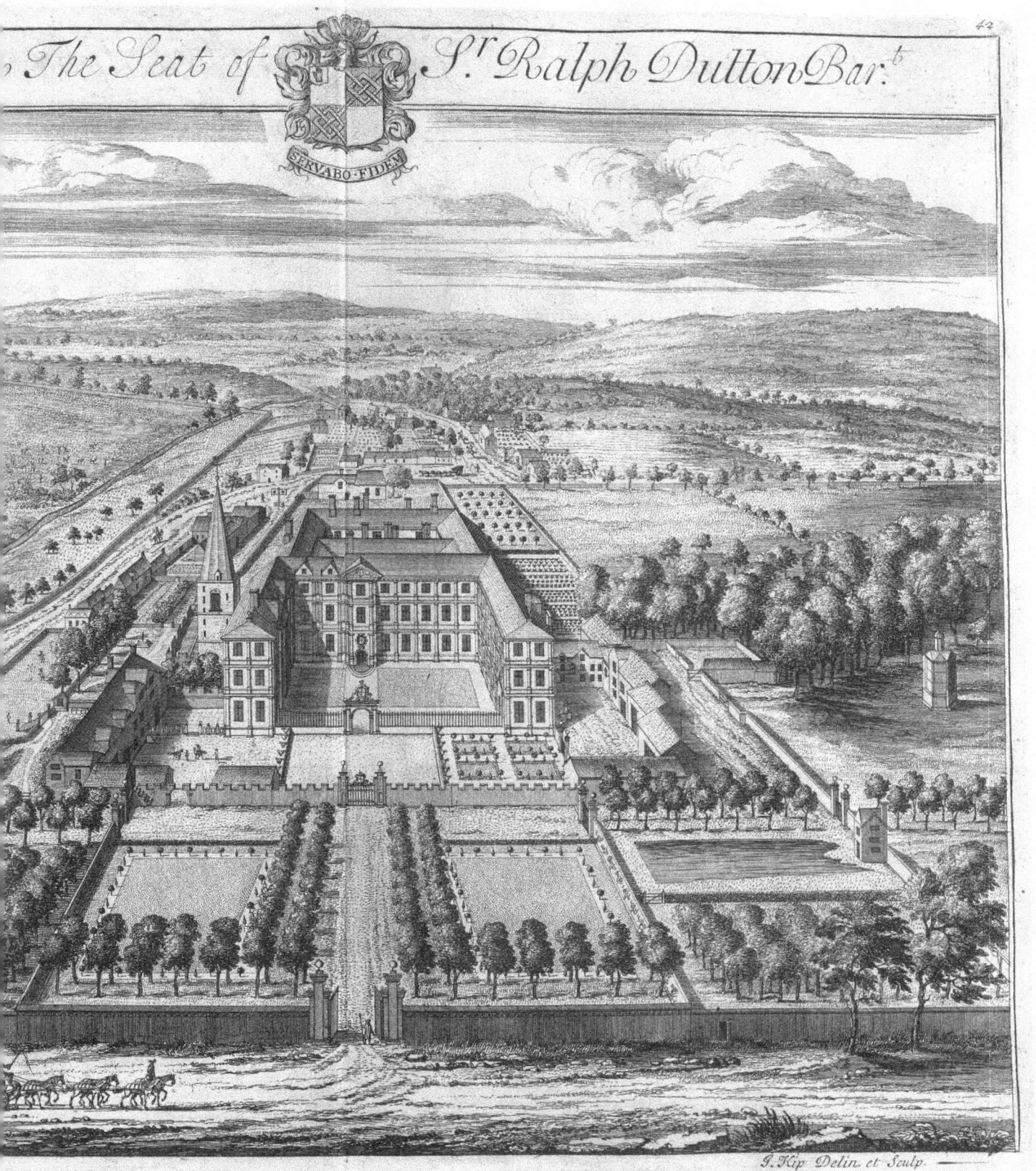

The Seat of Sr *Ralph Dutton Bar.*^t

SERVABO·FIDEM

I.Kip Delin. et Sculp.

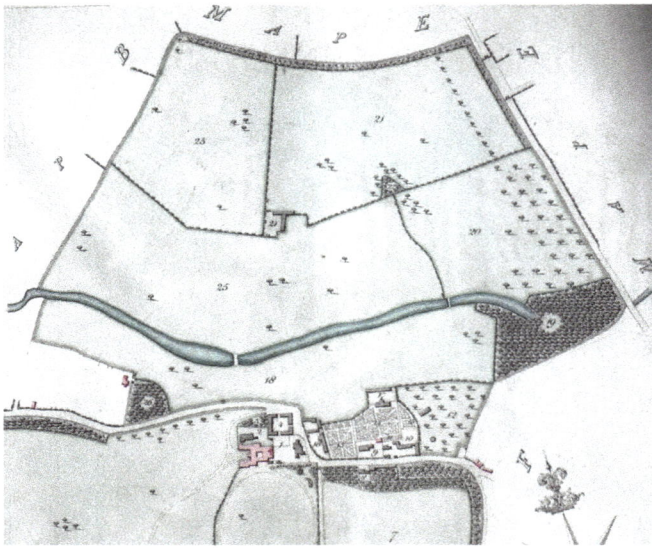

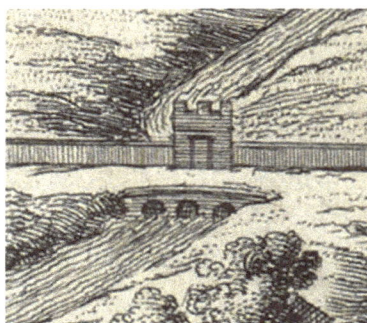

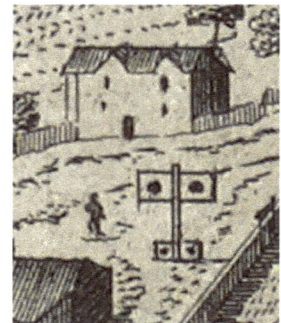

Kip's drawing is the only record of the line of the brook before it was widened in the eighteenth century. A weir penned the water, presumably originally to create a pool for washing sheep; today there is a lake. Kip suggests a noticeable difference in water levels and an impressive mechanism for raising and lowering a gate (*qv*). To the south of the house the land was pleasure grounds and parkland all the way to the Northleach to Burford road. The square field in the engraving is matched exactly in the 1820 map.

The road through the village no longer follows the course that Kip drew. Most obvious is the re-routing where Kip shows the road sweeping round behind the house. It was still in this position when the 1822 map was made, so separating kitchen gardens from the house, but it had been moved by the time of the Ordnance Survey of 1881.

To the west, as the road passes the house, it effectively now runs in a 'haha' from the bottom left corner of Kip's engraving to beyond the (now absent) bowling green, where a discussion about the distance of the bowls from the jack appears to be taking place (*qv*).

An image of a pillory is also seen where the road widens out before turning southwards behind the house (*qv*); it was close to where the large and stylish square stable block was built in mid-eighteenth century (4 on the map above). The pillory appears to be designed for two grades of sinner, or two at once, one with legs in the stocks, one with arms.

Little sign remains of the road running left to

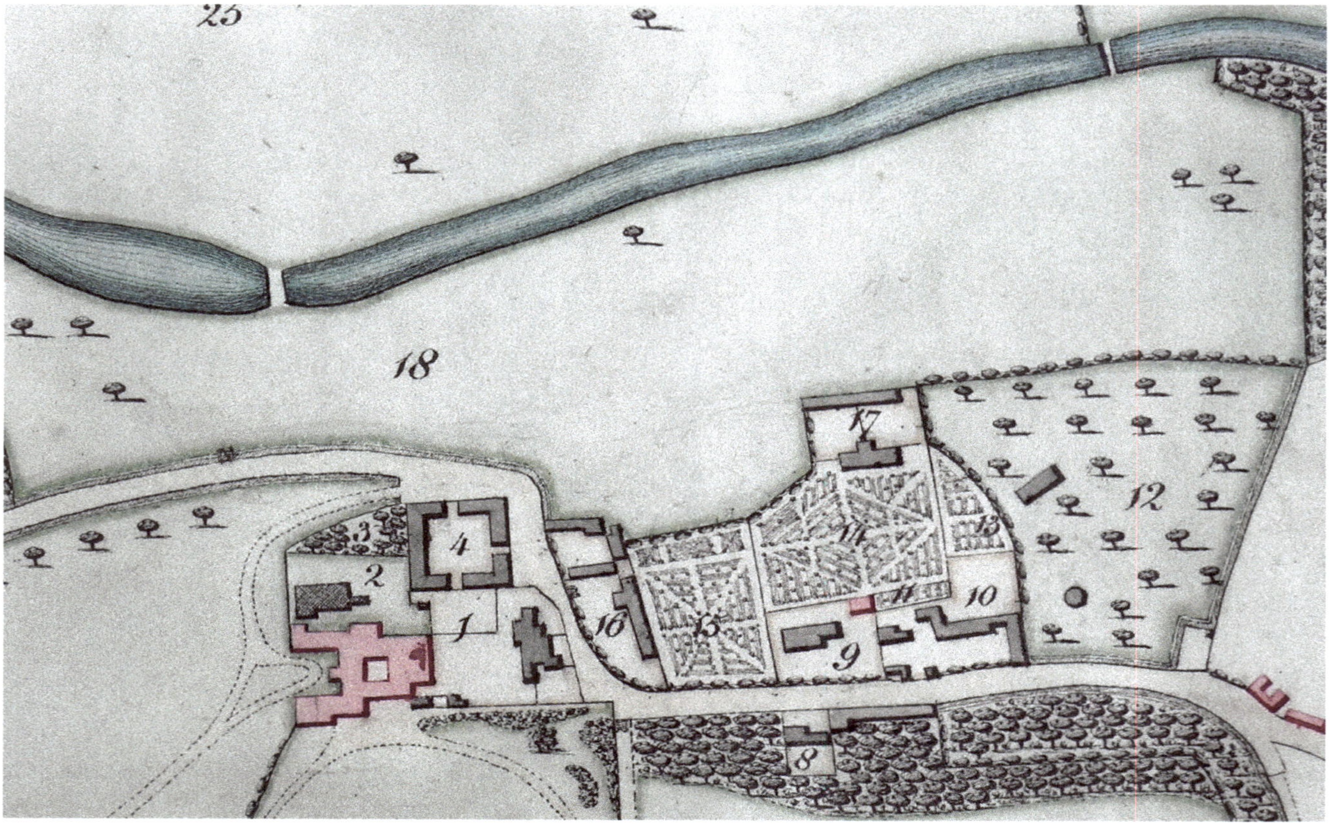

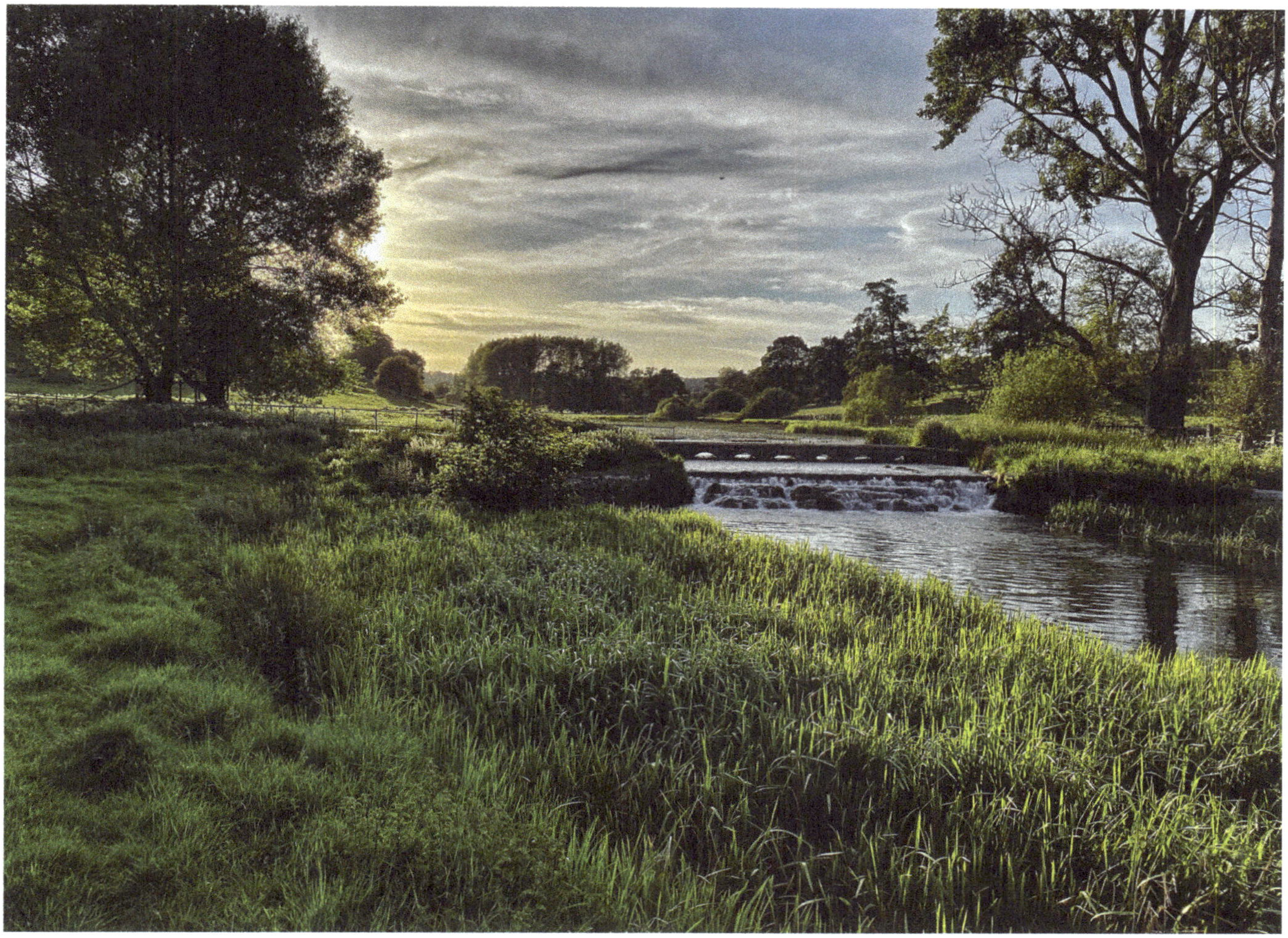

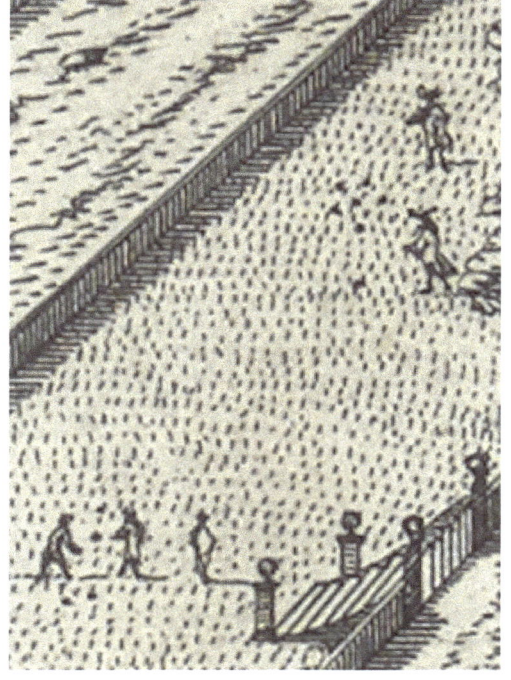

right across the front in Kip's engraving, giving access to the house, though the map shows a private driveway running all the way to the Northleach to Burford road; today the entrance drive to the house is further west along the road from Sherborne West End. The houses in this half of the village were behind Kip, while the buildings of the East End were largely replaced in the early nineteenth century by model village cottages.

Much ancillary building around the house has gone: removing the stables in the left foreground opened up views over the old park, and buildings around the south wing went along with the wing itself; the hexagonal dovecot was rebuilt in the yard behind the new stable block. The formal garden and wall at the front of the house is today an informal lawn. Rudder claimed, some sixty years after Kip drew Sherborne, that some artistic licence had been employed, and the 'pallisadoes, gardens and other decorations in the plate are all imaginary, and never had existence'. More recent scholarship is less dismissive of Kip's work.

The main buildings of Sherborne House were converted into apartments in 1981-83, and the parkland is managed by the National Trust. The church remains as the village church, and is listed Grade II*.

Sir John Dutton's financial accounts for 1710, about the time of Kip's visit (and ten years before Sir John became Baronet), indicate that he was already spending money on the estate at Sherborne, and include this item of expenditure: '*Nov 20. At ye Coffee house & at Sr Robt Atkins. £0. 3s 5 ½ d.*' Did the meeting relate to Kip's engraving?

49 Shipton Moyne the Seat of Mrs Hodges Relict of Tho: Hodges E[sq] [Atkyns: Shipton] 89729. VCH XI 247-257.

'Thomas Hodges Esq was lord of this manor in the year 1608, and was High Sheriff of Glostershire 20 Jac. 1622, and it still continues in

There were two Shipton manors in Domesday Book. From the early twelfth century one was held by the Moyne family; their manor house was probably near the church, on the same site or near the Hodges' house illustrated by Kip. Dovel was a settlement in the west of the parish. The other manor was centred in the east of the parish, the 'east court' from which the Estcourts were named; that house was further from the church. Estcourts became the major landowner in the district in the late eighteenth century and had a great influence over the development of the village.

The former Moyne manor was sold to John Hodges of Malmesbury in 1544 and remained with the Hodges family until 1794. A manor house was mentioned in 1224 but the one in the Kip engraving dates from the early seventeenth century. It seems to have faced south-west and the avenue running into the distance led to the Estcourt house. The Hodges were apparently noted for horses, an unusual Kip detail in a field (*qv*).

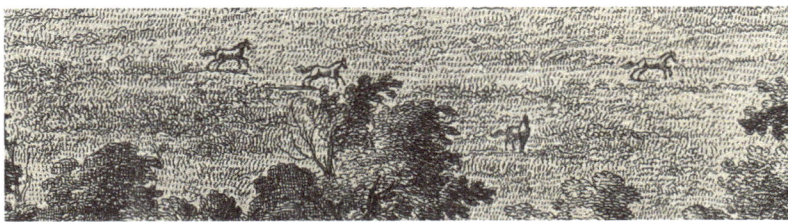

Atkyns named Thomas Hodges as lord of the manor, but he was a minor and died in 1708; his father had died in 1696. Kip named Edith, Thomas Hodges' widow. After her death in 1717 the house was demolished and a new house built a little further to the east. This too was demolished by 1838 but had ceased to be a manor house after 1794, when most of the estate and the manor were sold to Thomas Estcourt. Hodges Barn, converted into a house in the 1930's, is all that remains. The field between the church and Hodges Barn is very uneven and in a drought it is said the outlines of an old garden can be seen. There is very obviously some archaeology to be explored.

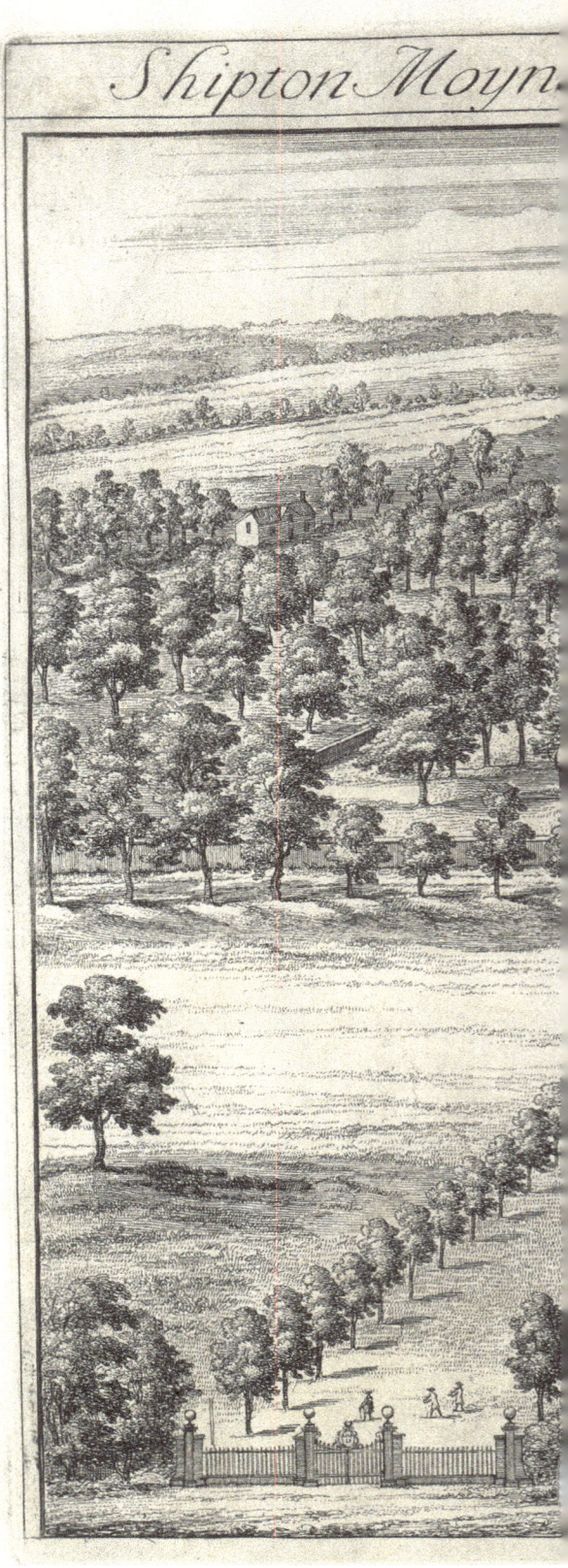

-Moign and Dovell, 646-647].   Postcode: Tetbury GL8 8PR. NGR: ST 89528

the same name and family. Thomas Hodges is the present Lord of it, and hath an handsome seat near the church.'

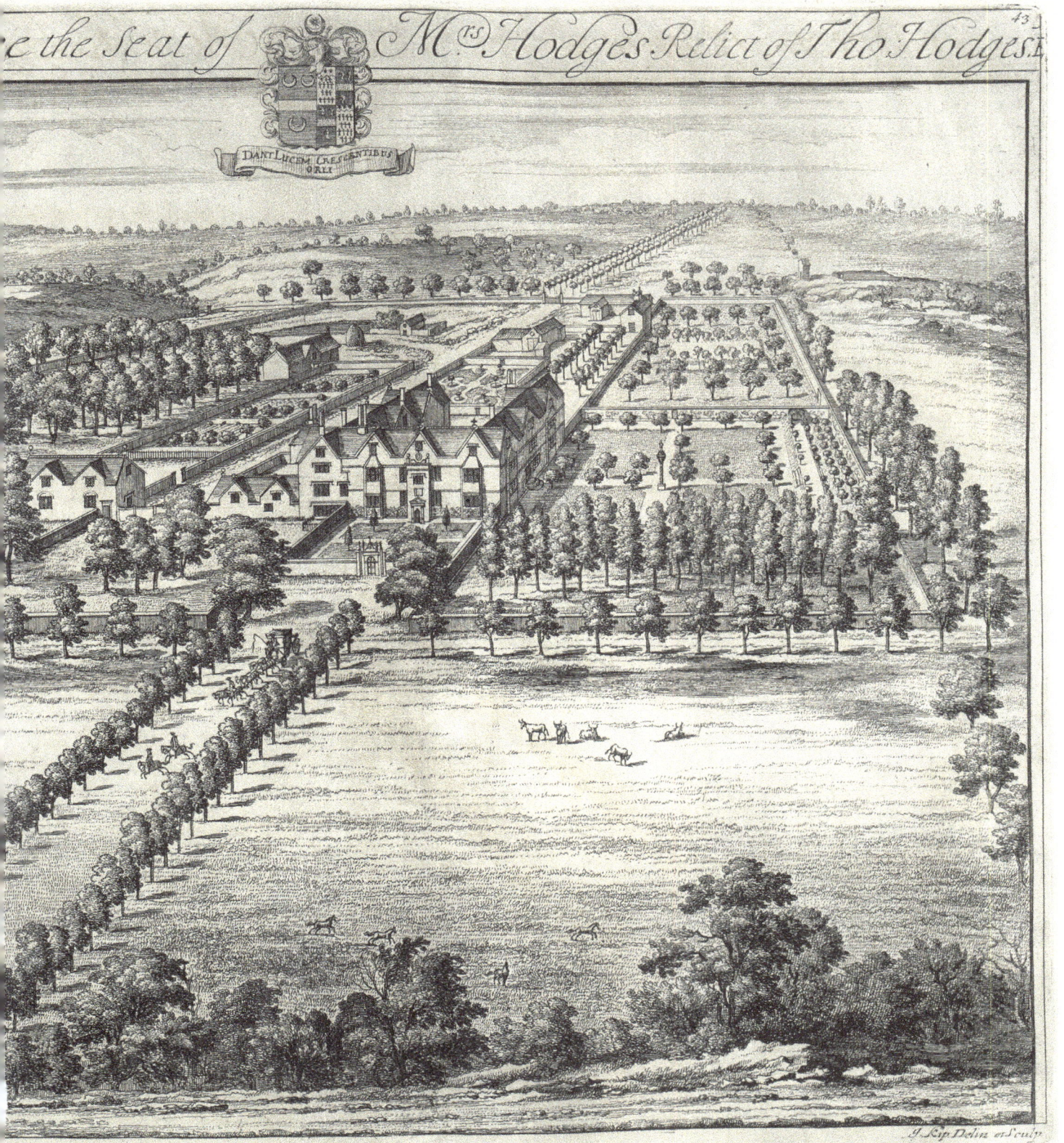

50 Shipton Moyne the Seat of Walter Estcourt Esq [Atkyns: Shipton-Moign & Dovel,

'There is another great seat, and a large estate in this parish, belonging to the ancient family of the Escourt's, who have resided in this place pleasant park adjoyning to it.'

The Estcourt manor house was in close proximity to Hodges' but neither drawing shows the other one, as Kip does in Cirencester and Henbury. Do these things say something about the owners at that time that we may never know? A manor house existed in 1359 but the one in Kip's engraving was built in the mid-sixteenth century. It was a characteristic U-shape, with rear gabled wings; the front faced south towards two entrance courtyards. The outer one had an ornamented archway through which a coach and horses had just passed, and the long building on the west side was perhaps for visitors in the same way as the wings at Siston. A detached twin-towered gatehouse was added in mid-seventeenth century at the entrance to the inner courtyard; it was unusual for Atkyns to comment on a detail like a gatehouse – he did not mention the one at Hardwicke. Typically there was a parterre and formal gardens. The small park (49 acres, 20 ha) was created by 1515; Kip drew the deer.

A map which accompanied a survey dated 1774 almost exactly matches the Kip engraving and identifies its position (*qv*). It confirms the shape and detail of the park, the courtyards and the gatehouse; it reveals that the small building to the east of the house was the forcing house in the melon garden (*h* on the map).

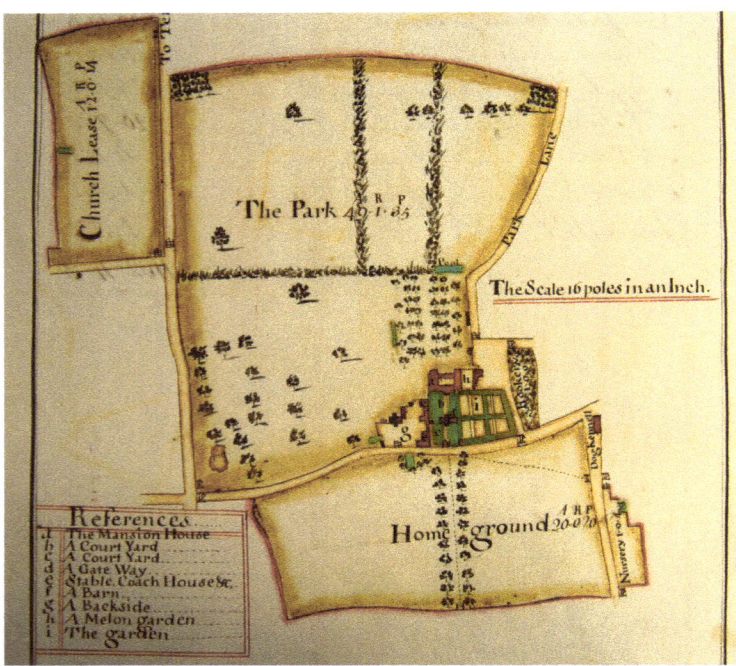

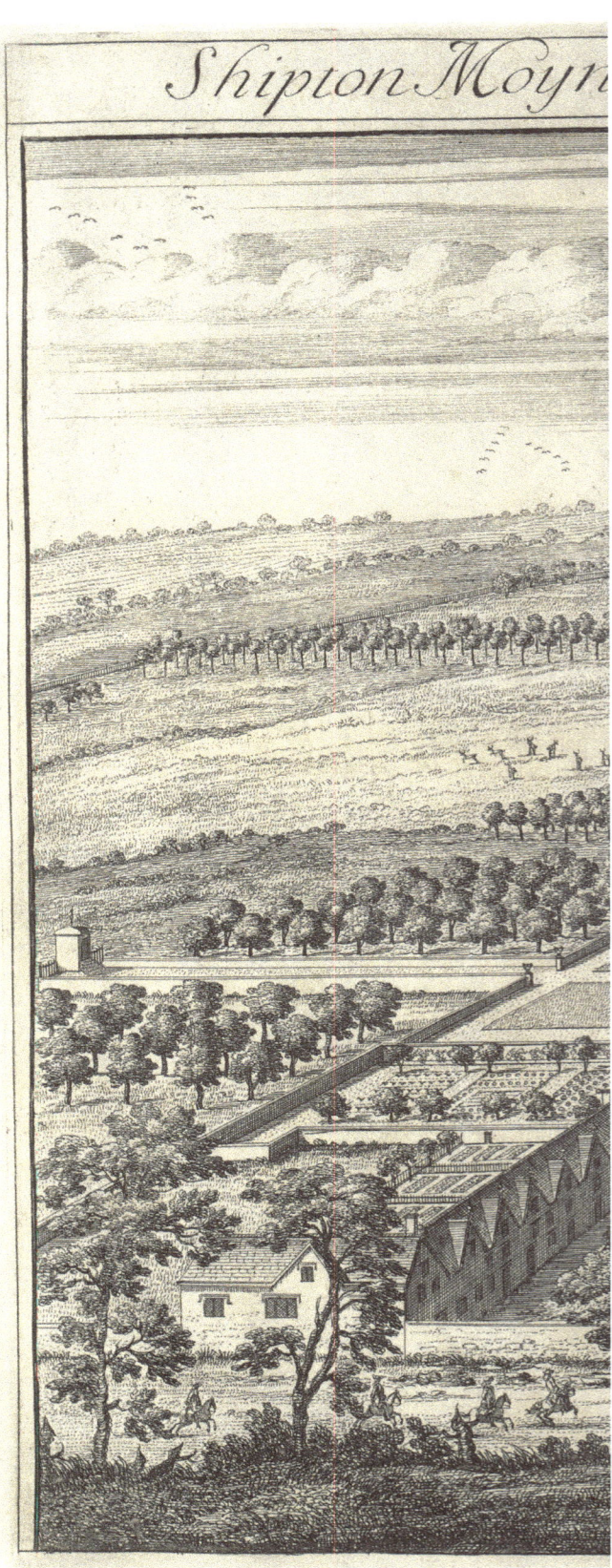

The house became very dilapidated and liable to collapse; after Estcourt built a new house, part became Park Farm and is now a private house. The new house, built in 1776-9 on higher ground to the north, was demolished in 1964, with only the stables dated 1781 and the coach house surviving.

These two sites at Shipton Moyne are not straight-forward to understand, as so much of what Kip drew has completely disappeared.

646-647]. **Postcode: Tetbury GL**8 8**PR. NGR: ST** 89731 90074. **VCH XI** 247-257.

300 years … Walter Escort … has a large house, with a very handsome gatehouse, with towers on each side, in this place, and a

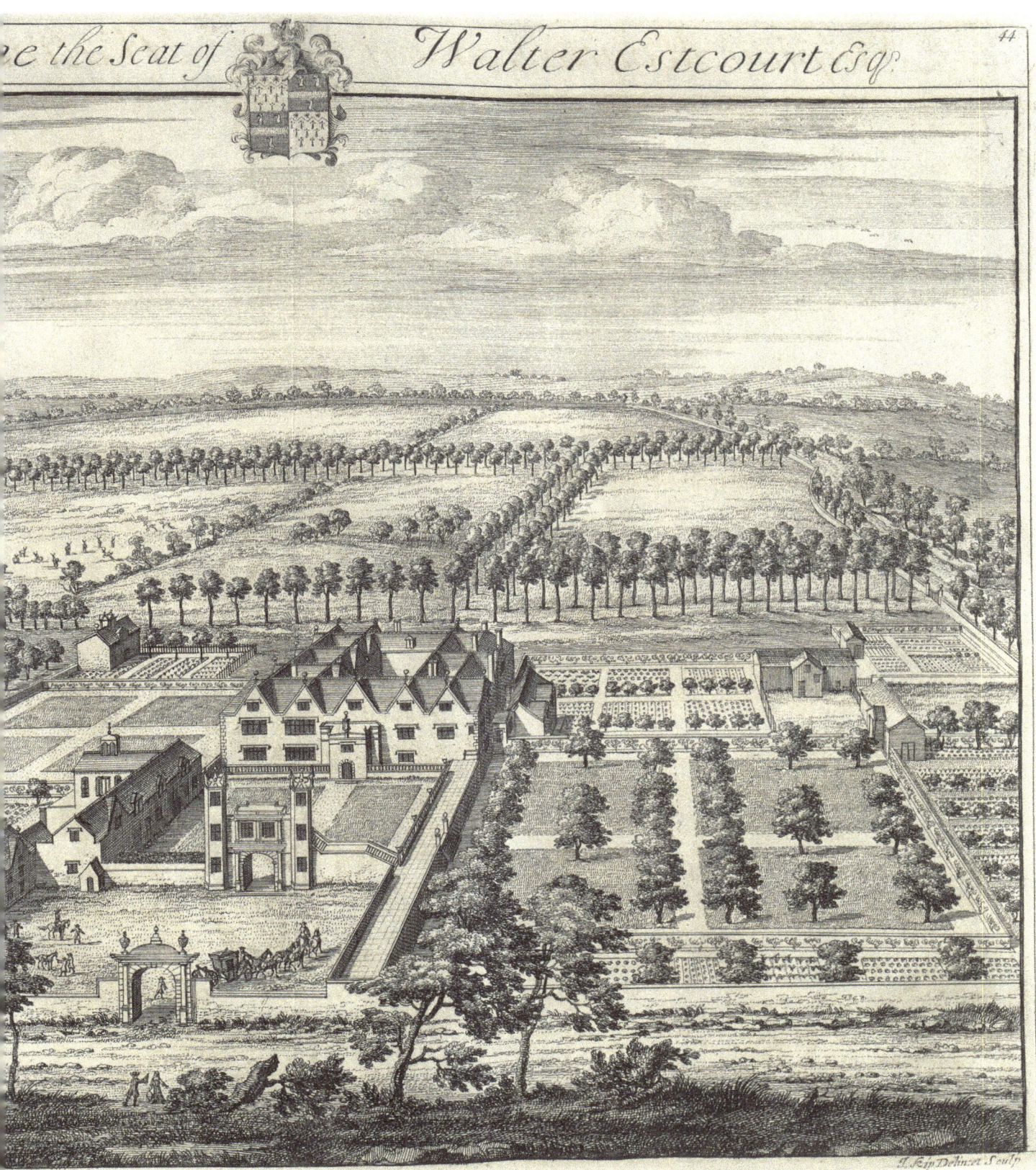

the Seat of *Walter Estcourt Esq.*

44

J. Kip Delin: et Sculp

51 Syston the Seat of Samll Trotman Esq [Atkyns: Siston, 654-655].

'Samuel Trotman Esq is the present Lord of the manor of Siston. He has a very large handsome house … built by the Denniss's.'

Siston Court is almost unchanged since Kip drew it about 1710, and indeed since a more romantic drawing was made by Georgina Chester-Master about 1916 (*qv*). They both pictured the house from the east but not its park to the south, in 1607 allegedly housing a thousand fallow deer.

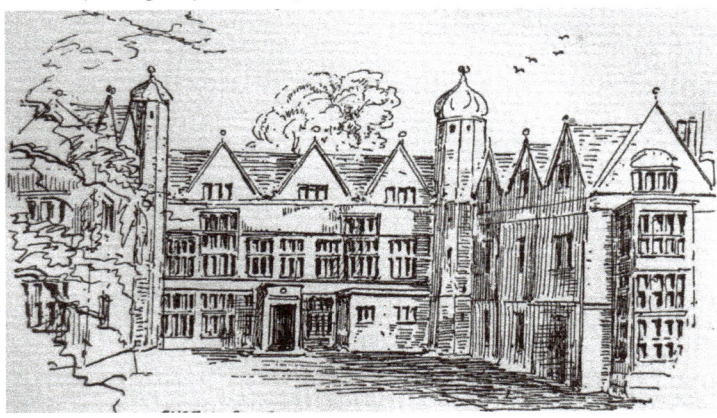

The house is an early example of a large Elizabethan mansion, moving away from fifteenth-century fortified manor houses. It was a 'U' rather than an 'E' shape in plan, each section two storeys with three attic gables, and tall stair turrets with ogee-shaped roofs in the corners. The north and south wings were designed for guests, each with two entrances with further symmetrical annexes, witness to the peripatetic nature of country house life.

The Denys family owned Siston from at least the fifteenth century until 1598; the first Samuel Trotman bought it in 1651 and his family remained for over 200 years. Kip shows extensive formal grounds occupying south-facing and steeply sloping land. A bowling green to the rear led out to the dower house and the hills beyond, the distinctive Shortwood Hill to the north-west. On the north side were stables and kennels, a walled fruit and vegetable garden, barn and rickyard of a typical working estate. Little remains of these planned grounds, the site now being largely lawns and parkland, with a ha-ha, pond, and avenue of limes leading to the entrance with its nineteenth-century lodges; lining the driveway in Kip's engraving are Portuguese laurels, introduced to this country some 50 years earlier, pruned to look like parasols (*qv*). Close to the north wing was a mounting block (*qv*).

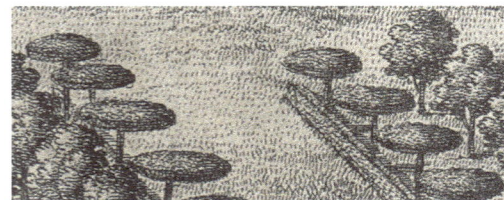
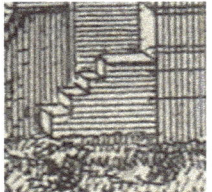

The Court was subdivided into six homes about 1950, but retains the flavour of a sixteenth-century manor house, close to Bristol but safe in the Siston conservation area.

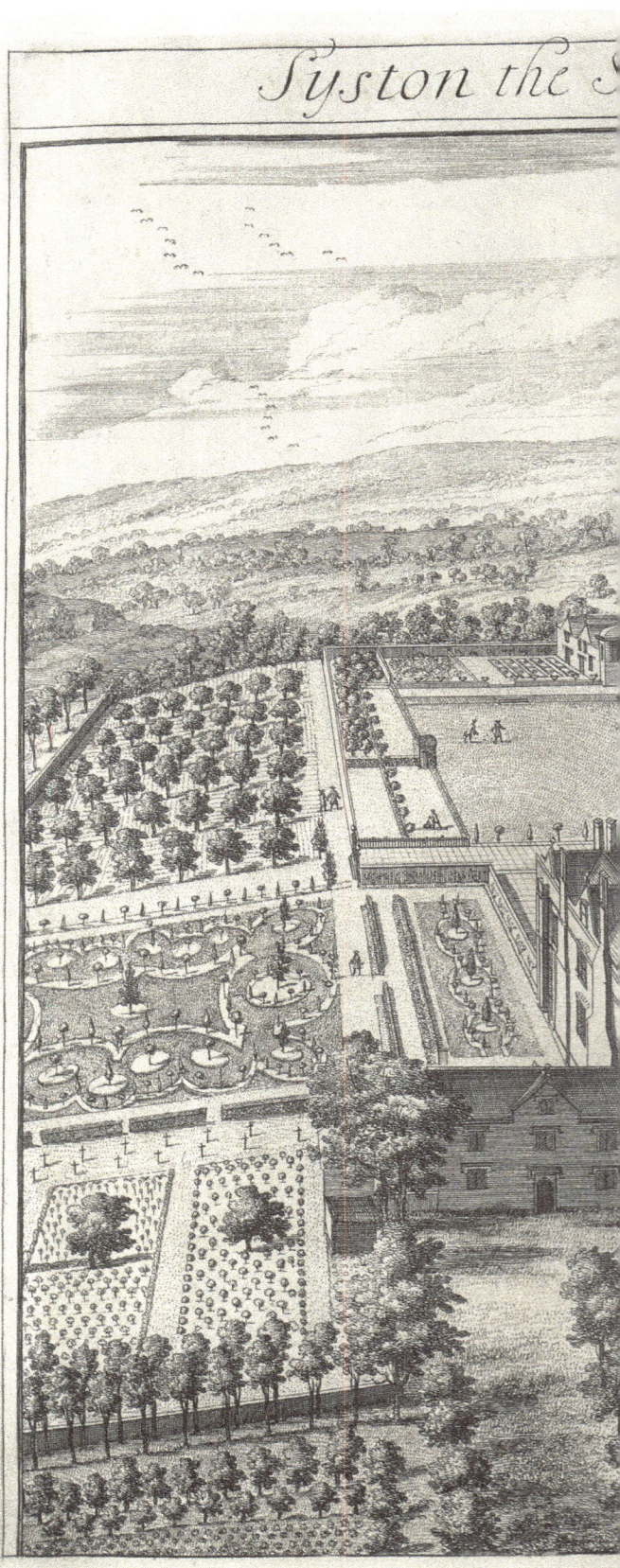
Syston the S...

Post Code: Mangotsfield BS16 9**LU. NGR: ST** 68661 75361**.**

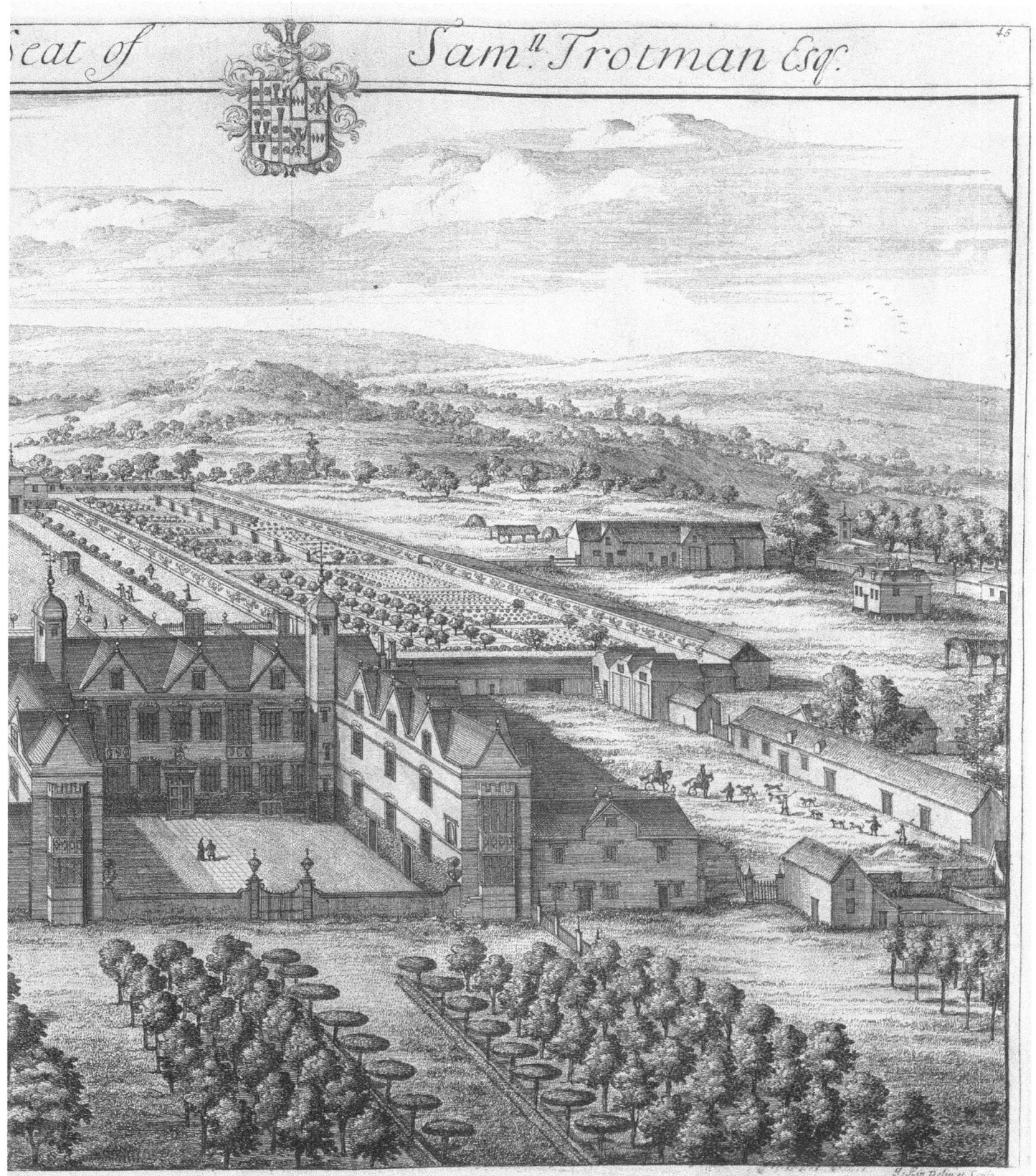

52 **Stanway the Seat of John Tracey Esq** [Atkyns: Stanway, 684-685].

'John Tracey Esq … is the present Lord of the Mannor of Stanway, and has a large handsome house near the church and a great estate in

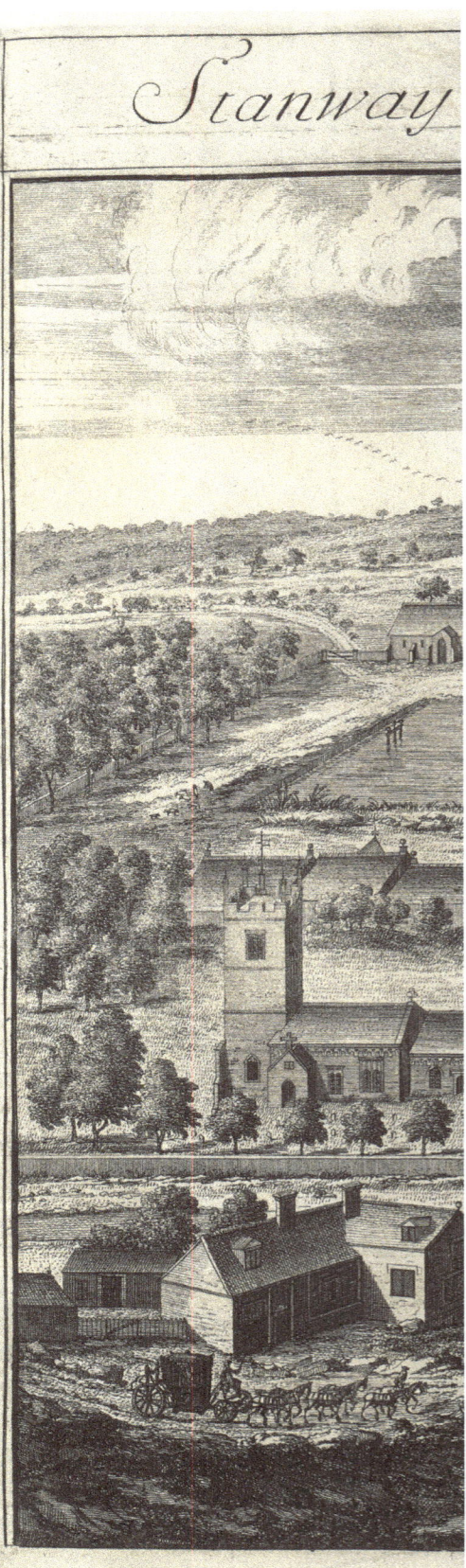

John Tracey or Tracy inherited Stanway aged two in 1682, on the death of his father the Hon. Ferdinando Tracey, third son of John, 3rd Viscount Tracy of nearby Toddington (the subject of a Kip engraving), an estate which the family had owned since before 1057. Stanway had been a Tewkesbury Abbey estate, and the Tracy connection is first documented in 1533, when Richard Tracy, the younger son of William Tracy of Toddington, was granted a lease, subsequently buying the manor after the abbey was dissolved.

John Tracy, named by Atkyns, in 1699 married Anne, daughter of Sir Robert Atkyns of Sapperton, KB, and until 1709 lived in his father-in-law's house at Swell Bowl, the subject of another of the engravings Johannes Kip made for Sir Robert Atkyns the younger's book, *The Ancient and Present State of Glostershire*. It is therefore to be presumed that John and Anne took a personal interest in the engraving Kip made of Stanway in 1708-09 for Anne's brother, and were able to limit Kip's artistic licence.

The south front of the house, facing the viewer, built about 1628, was altered by Francis Smith of Warwick in 1724, when the central door, the mullion-and-transom window to the west of it, and the two windows above on the chamber storey were replaced by large, new-fangled sash windows, giving a charmingly asymetrical effect. (The 1724 arrangement, shown in calotypes about 1850, was undone by 1860, reverting almost to its Kip appearance, but the aperture of the central door was again fitted with a large sash window in 2002).

The steps into the garden from the central door were altered by 1850 to be single-flight and with no stone balustrade; but the Kip arrangement, less the balustrade, was reinstated in 1949. A recent photograph mimics Kip's elevated view (*qv*).

The parapet walk wrapping around the east end of the south range had been abolished by 1748, being covered by a stone gable. In 2001 a passage was cut through this gable, and the parapet walk to the north of it reinstated.

William Taylor in 1748 painted a panoramic view of Stanway from the east. It shows, beyond the south range, a wing of the house, and north of that substantial domestic offices. Kip drew the first wing, but it would appear that he simply left out the range of domestic offices (which were altered in 1860 and pulled down in 1949), merely drawing a small, low building and another, furthest to the north, appearing to be a barn, the kitchen garden being handily close by.

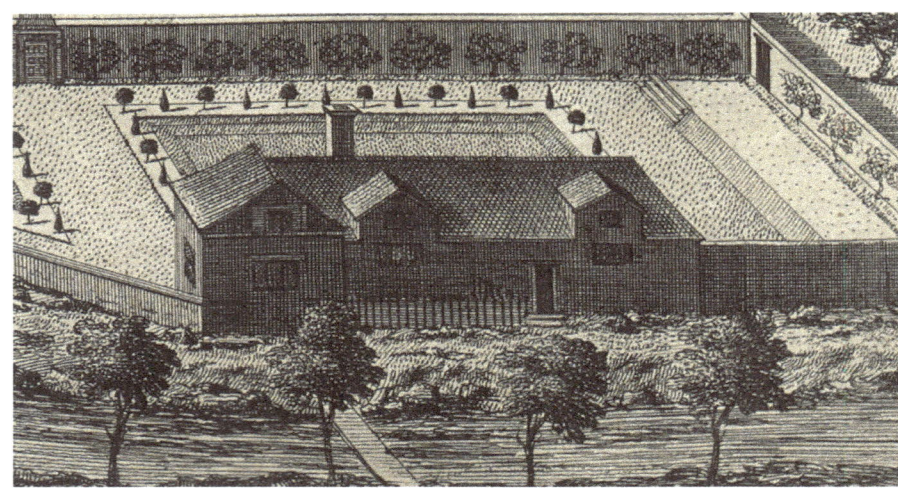

Postcode: Stanway GL54 5**PQ. NGR: SP** 06135 32410. **VCH VI** 223-232.

this and other counties.'

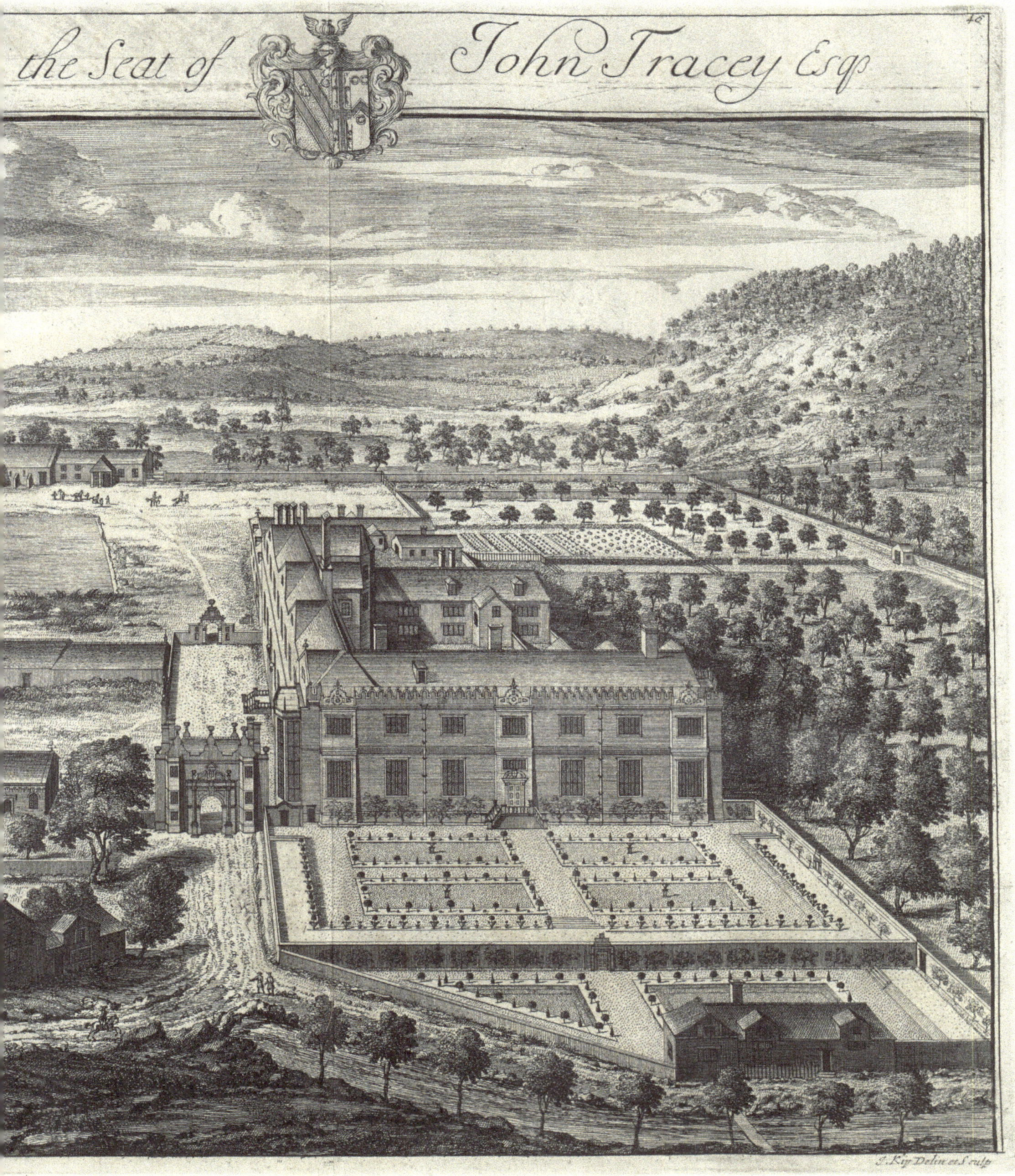

the Seat of   John Tracey Esq.

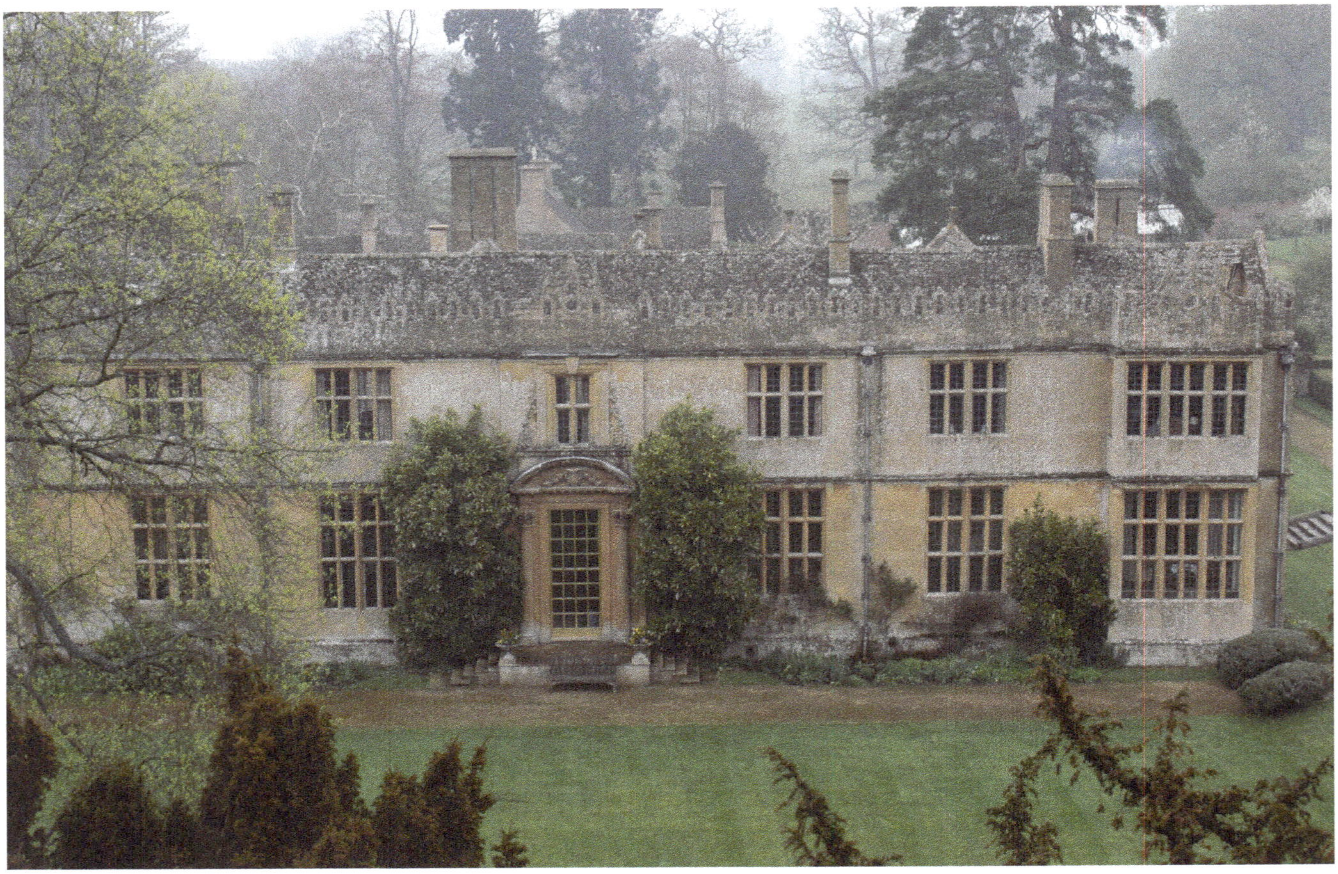

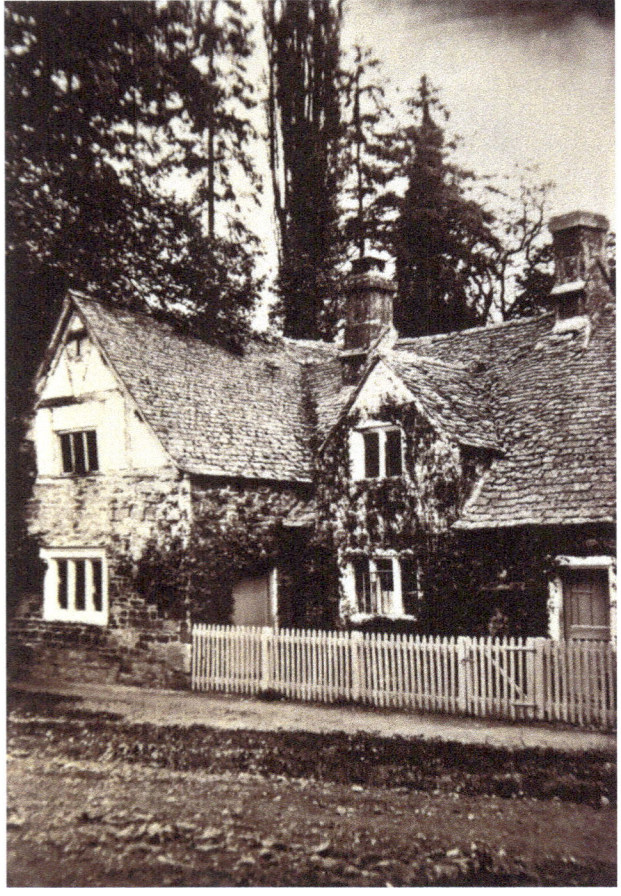

On the further side of the pond is a large barn. It appears similar to the surviving tithe barn behind the church tower, which was built by Tewkesbury Abbey probably in the later fourteeenth century (*qv*) and may have been of similar date. Although in use as a coach house in 1859, it was demolished the following year, together with the adjoining stable.

The parish church is older; a simple nave and chancel were built in the twelfth century, the tower added a century later, and its upper story and pinnacles added in the fifteenth century. Kip observed the carved stones below the eaves. In front is the surviving Old Vicarage, an early seventeenth century house.

The cottage in the right foreground about 1850 (*qv*) - when it closely resembled Kip's image – is described as *Stokes's House* on the 1865 Estate map; it was demolished by 1873 when the continuous extant Estate accounts begin, and is absent from the 1884 Ordnance Survey map. Stokes's House has only one chimney in Kip's engraving (*qv*), but a second had been inserted by the time of the photograph. The stream in front of Stokes's House is narrower than Kip's version, and was culverted in the nineteenth century.

By 1748, the parterres south of the house had been turned into a lawn, although the ghostly outlines of the gravelled paths are revealed during droughts. A bowling green on the east side of the house had replaced the trees drawn by Kip, possibly an orchard; the house is close to rising ground on this side as Kip indicates. The

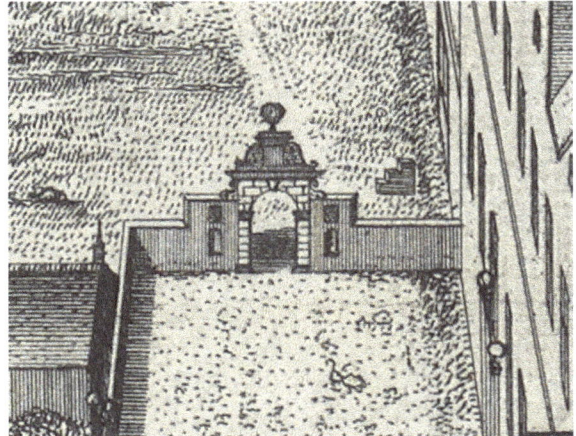

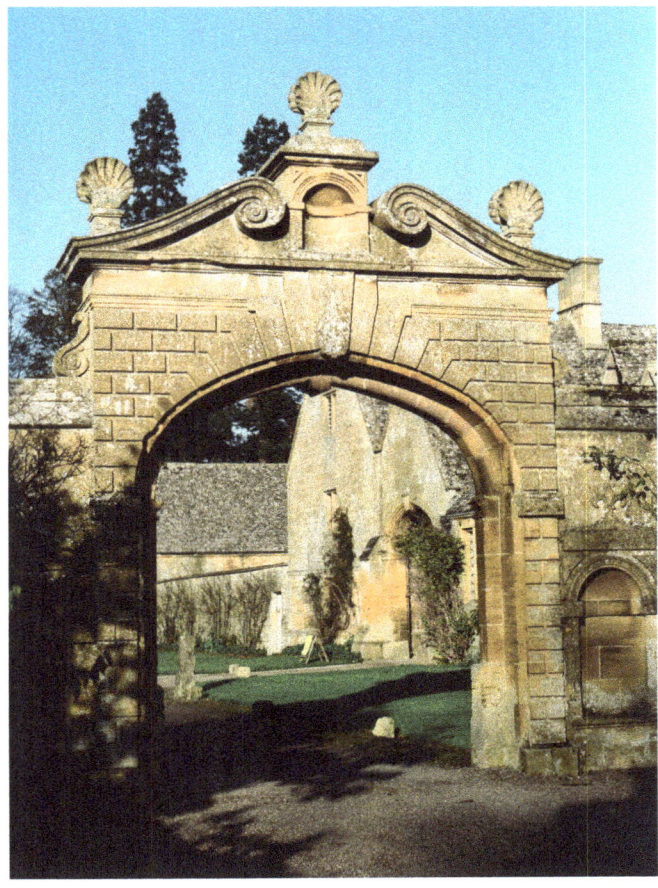

garden wall parallel to the south front, and the wall on its eastern side, had also gone by 1748. Kip drew the now much-photographed south gateway, and also the smaller gateway on the north side of the courtyard, all with an indication of Tracy scallop shells on top, and hints at the gateway to the churchyard (*qv*). The road to Stanton passed through the gateways until it was diverted to the west to go round the church.

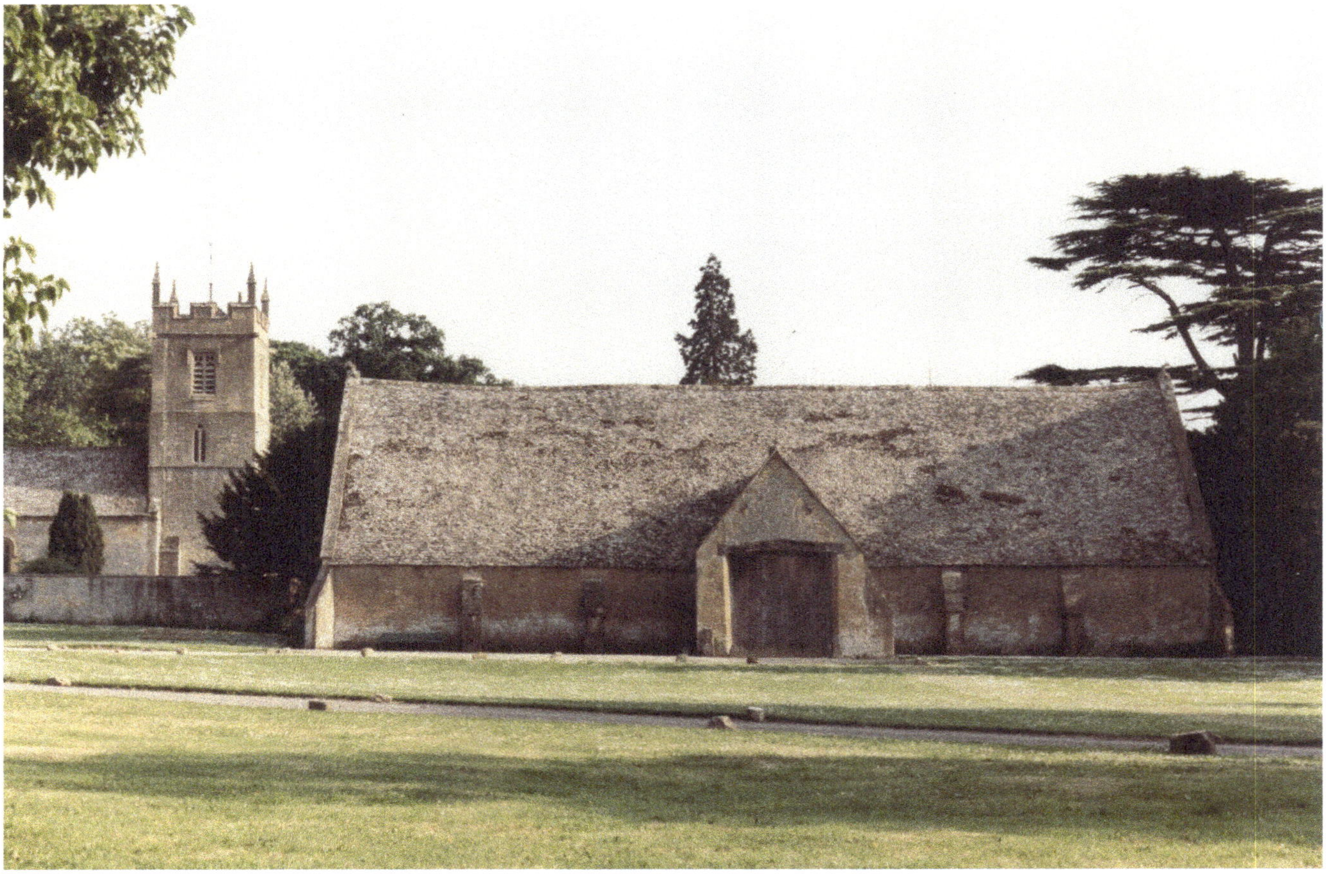

Kip's engraving has seemingly inspired a number of changes, undoing some of the modernisations carried out in the first half of the eighteenth century. Stanway is 'an extemely interesting, unusual and complicated house', and remains much admired.

53 Stoke Gifford the Seat of John Berkeley Esq [Atkyns, Stoke-Giffard, 690-691].

'The manor of Stoke-Giffard was granted to Maurice de Berkeley … near 400 years ago, and has ever since continued in the same family. the Forest of Kingswood, and has a very great estate in this and other places, and serves in the present Parliament as Knight of the Shire.

Kip provided a dramatic presentation of Stoke Park, emphasising the 'high hill' noted by Atkyns, made more imposing by the stone revetment of the long artificial terrace at the head of which the house was built. Behind Kip to the south was a tremendous view.

The house was sixteenth century in origin and sketches of the east front appear on seventeenth-century maps. Though facing a precipitous bank, the entrance-front is this side; Kip shows four regular gables befitting it. The south face is nondescript, its three irregular gables possibly surviving from an earlier building. With such possibilities for drama, the result is anti-climax. Could it have been that the early U-shaped mansion was deliberately turned away from the fast-growing city below, safe in its fastness with its viewing towers?

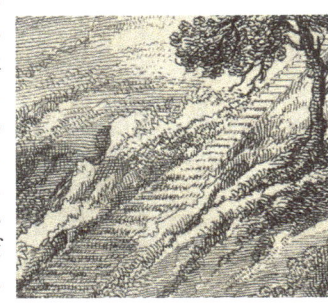

Parallel with the access road, a long, wide flight of steps (*qv*) leads from the south-west corner towards parklands, ponds, and church, while steep tracks lead eastward into woodlands. From the far end of the terrace, two straight double rows of trees march to the head of the bluff past a gabled banqueting house, a walled (possibly kitchen) garden and outbuildings.

A Giffard held this manor in 1086, and Giffords continued there into the fourteenth century. It passed then to Maurice de Berkeley, whose family remained there longer than Atkyns could know. Following Norborne Berkeley's death in 1770, Stoke Park passed to the Somerset family, through Berkeley's sister marrying the Duke of Beaufort. The house today is converted into flats, a staircase being a surviving feature from the house Kip portrayed, as also much of the late sixteenth-century balustrade to rampart and terrace, and some strapwork ornamentation. Extensively remodelled in mid-eighteenth century for Norborne Berkeley, the present Grade II* 'Dower House' (*qv*) does justice to its setting.

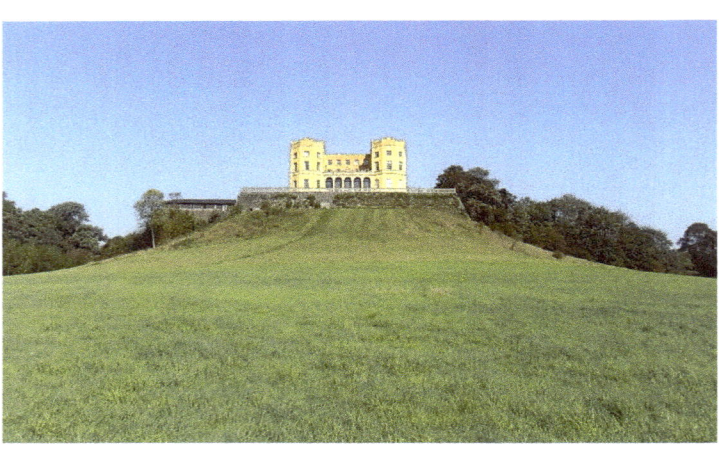

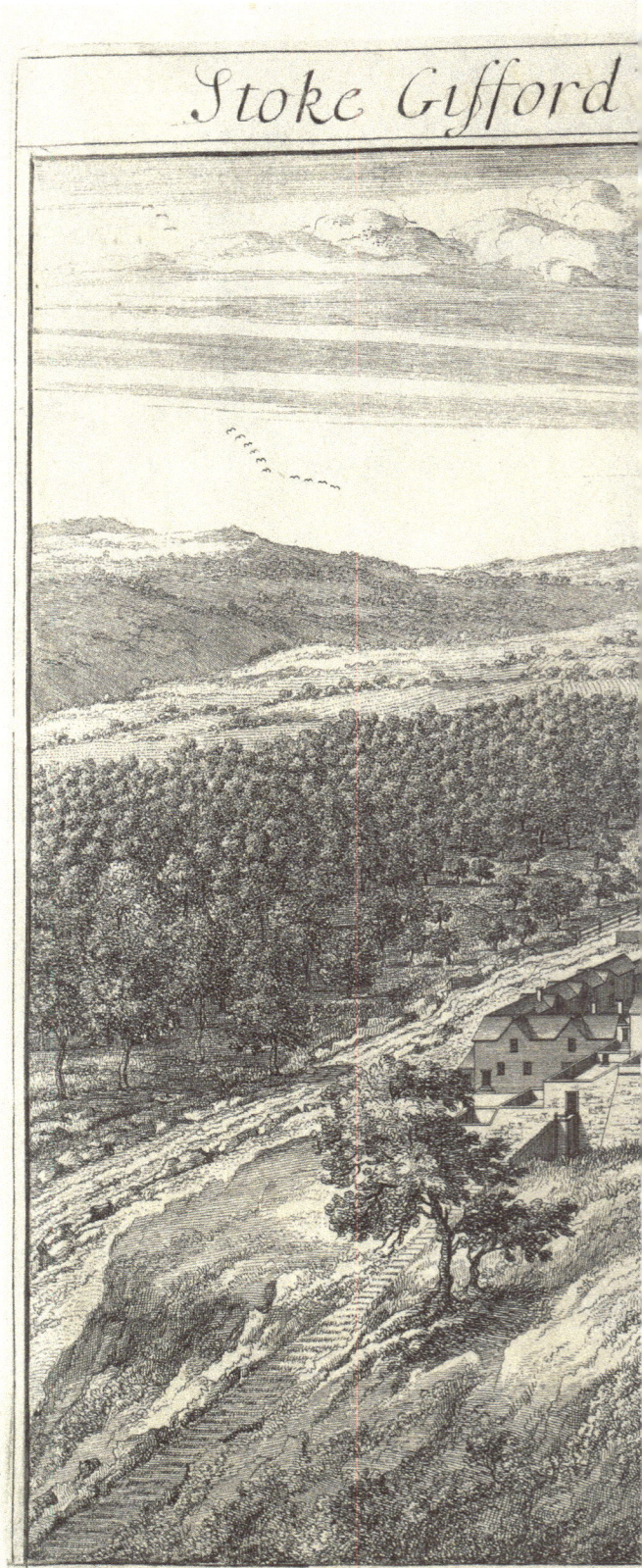

Stoke Gifford

Postcode: Stapleton BS16 1ZS. NGR: ST 62233 77251.

John Berkeley … has a large house and pleasant seat, situated on a high hill, with a great prospect over the City of Bristol, and over

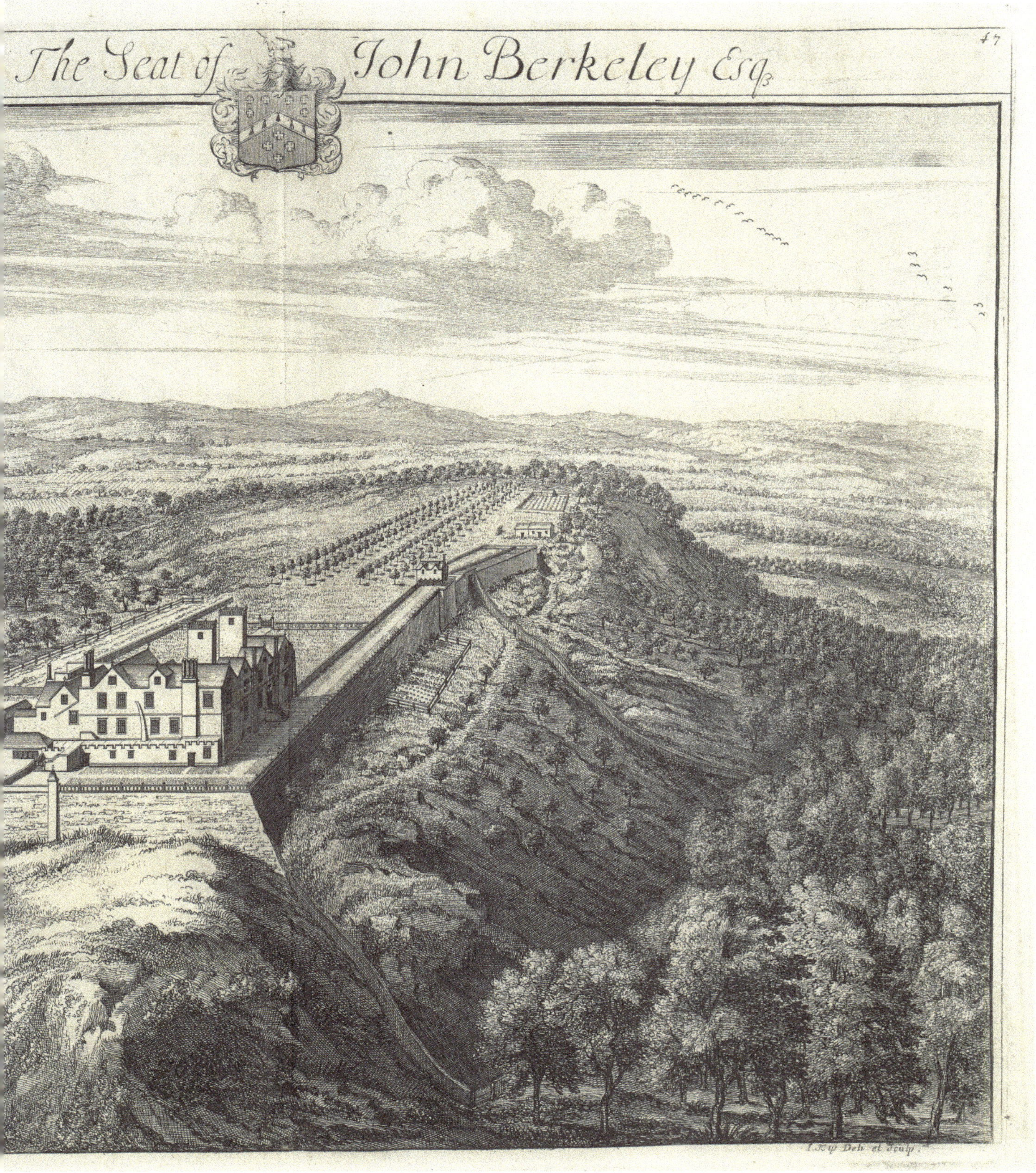

The Seat of John Berkeley Esq;

54 Maugersbury the Seat of Edmund Chamberlain Esq [Atkyns: Stow, 694-695].

John Chamberlain … was eminent for his loyalty, and paid £1246 for composition … [Edmund] is the present lord of the mannor of

Maugersbury village is on the southern slope of the hill on top of which, ½ mile away, is the town of Stow-on-the-Wold, just beyond the reach of Kip's drawing. The hill fort or 'bury', from which Maugersbury is named and in which Stow is sited, is in a corner of Maugersbury township, which nonetheless is in Stow parish. A park existed by 1564, separating village from town. There is no record of deer in the park - Kip shows a shepherd and a flock of sheep in one section

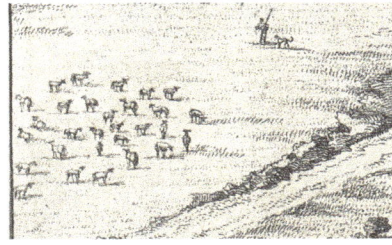

(*qv*). Had he been told that John Chamberlayne lost 100 sheep to the soldiers who were frequently quartered in Maugersbury during the Civil War? ('Chamberlayne' is the modern spelling rather than the form used by Atkyns).

　　Two roads lead from Maugersbury to Stow. One, after winding through the village, joins Park Street at the lower end of the town and probably marked the park boundary. Kip used perspective to increase its apparent length, and drew a long straight line of trees leading towards it which also separated the sheep from the cows. A road passing close to the house, along which a carriage is travelling, also went to Stow, and joined Park Street close to the first and is now a tree-lined track.

　　Maugersbury Manor, Grade II listed and partly seventeenth century, is very recognisable today (*qv*), although the right hand wing has been demolished and 'Diocletian' windows have replaced dormers. It is divided into apartments. As Kip looked eastwards beyond the manor house, he saw a formal garden, walled as today though no longer divided into neat sections; the orchard, reaching to the road to Stow, is now given over to houses. Further away were Oddington hill and Broadwell hill, their steepness a little exaggerated. Behind Kip is a wide view over lower-lying landscape.

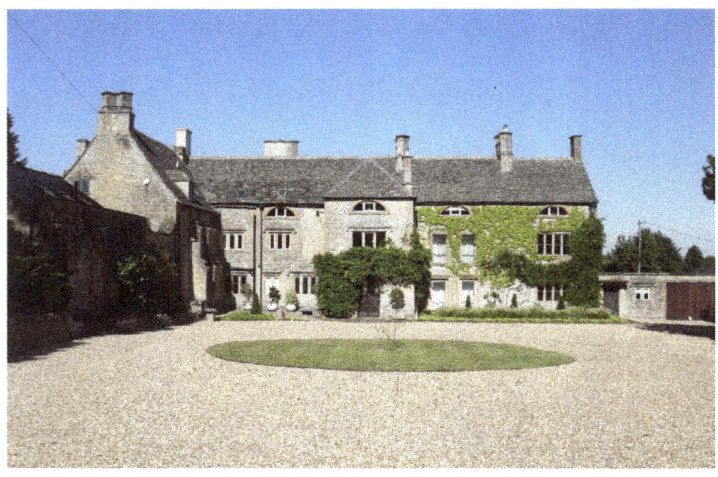

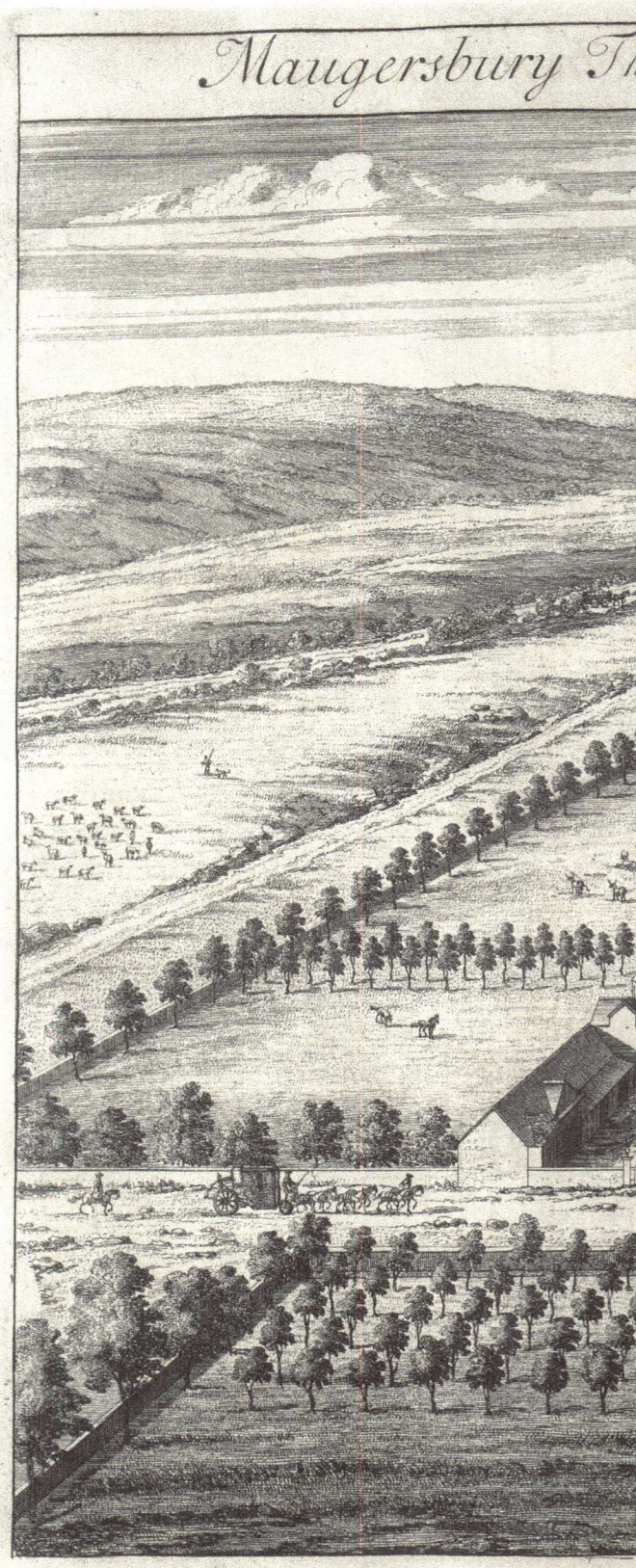

Maugersbury T[...]

Postcode: Cheltenham GL54 1HP. NGR: SP 19741 25180. VCH VI 142-165.

Maugersbury, and has an handsome seat in this place.'

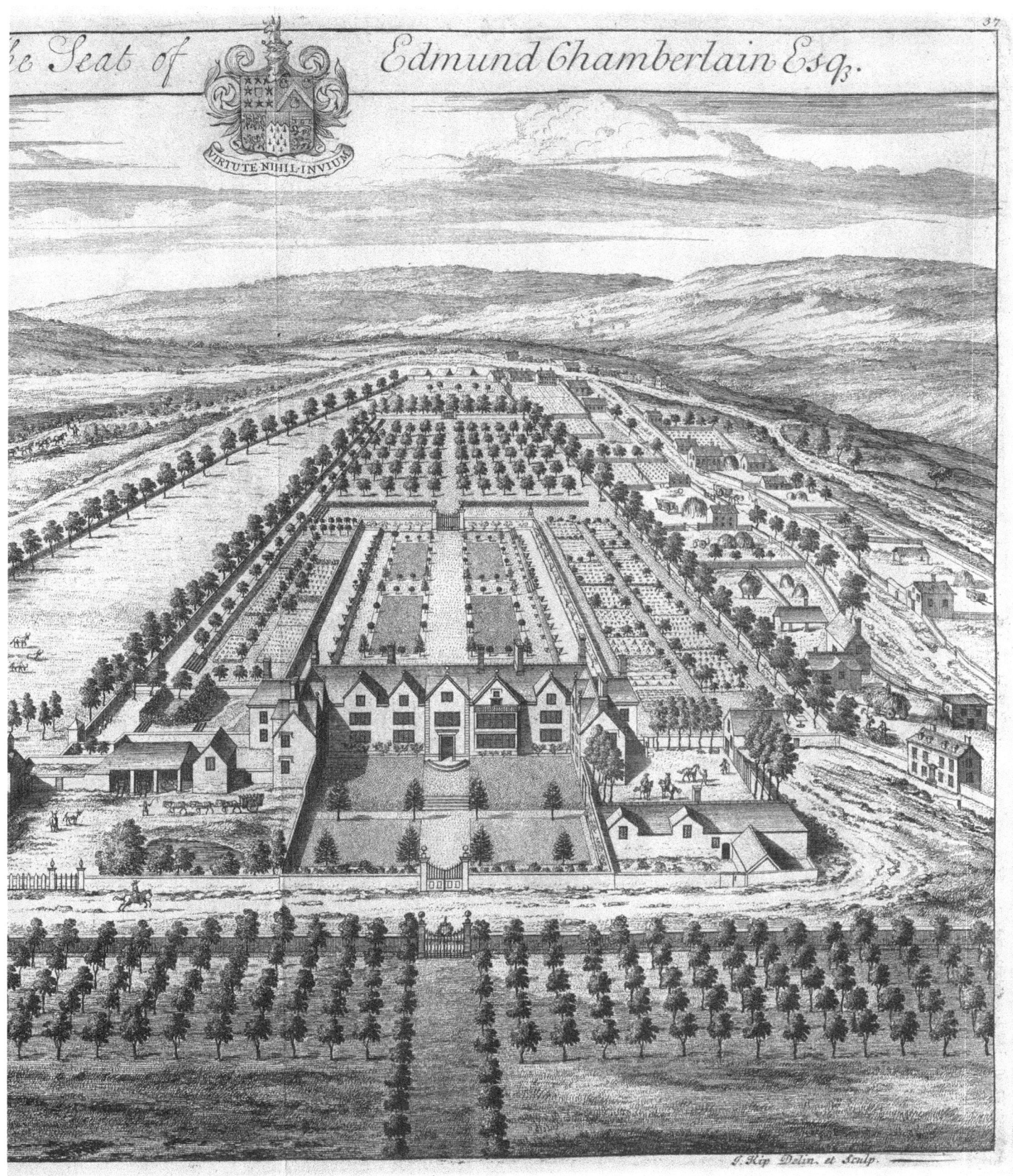

55 **Lupiatt the Seat of Thomas Stephens Esq** [Atkyns: Stroud, Upper-Lypiat, 700-701].

'Thomas Stephens is the present Lord of the Manor of Upper-Lypiat and has a large ancient seat and a great estate in this and other places

Lypiatt was in the large parish of Stroud. Kip's view of Upper Lypiatt is from the north-west and is one of his landscapes in which the central house is a little distanced from the viewer. The road to the top right of the grounds is probably the original road from Bisley to Stroud leading to Round Elm (the new turnpike road was built in 1823). In the far distance to the left are many cottages which will probably be Eastcombe (*qv*).

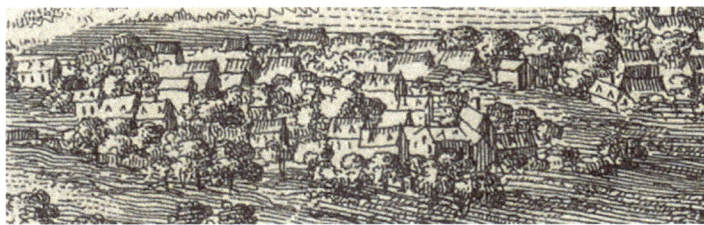

Thomas Stephens bought the manor in 1610, and the family remained there for the next two hundred years. The main house is early sixteenth century, extended about 1700; it remained relatively unaltered from Kip's time until the early nineteenth century, when it was considerably remodelled by the architect Jeffrey Wyatt for Paul Wathen, who had purchased the estate in 1800.

Kip showed a congested site of separate buildings, walled in an irregular fashion. The gatehouse and stables in the foreground were removed by Wyatt, as were the farm buildings to the rear of the main house. A fine thirteenth-century granary and dovecote to the right remain, also the manorial chapel with the bellcote in the front of the house; it was built by one of the last Maunsell owners who held Upper Lypiatt in the fourteenth century; Richard Parsons about 1700 said it was consecrated (*qv*).

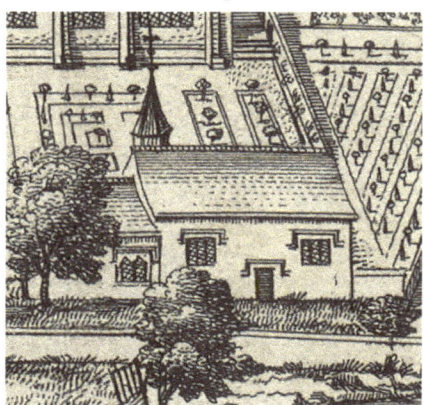

There are no traces of the formal gardens at the rear of the house, which are now lawn and parkland. The long terrace to the left looks over a steep slope down to an ancient park where Kip drew deer; extended by Wyatt, some of the terrace disappeared in a landslide in 1952, as did the lower terrace shown in the engraving as a bowling green.

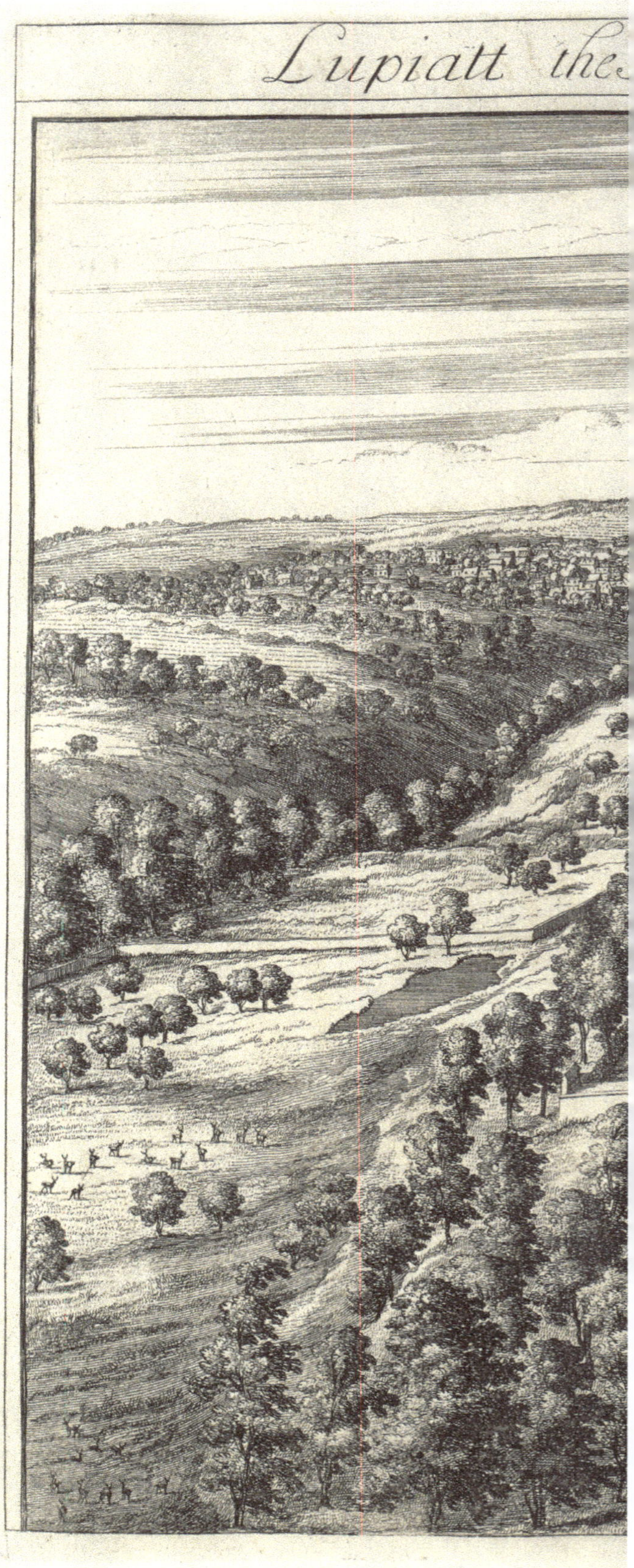

Lupiatt the

Postcode: Stroud GL6 7**LL. NGR: SO** 88945 06010. **VCH XI** 99-145.

There is a handsome chapel near the house which is decently kept in repair.'

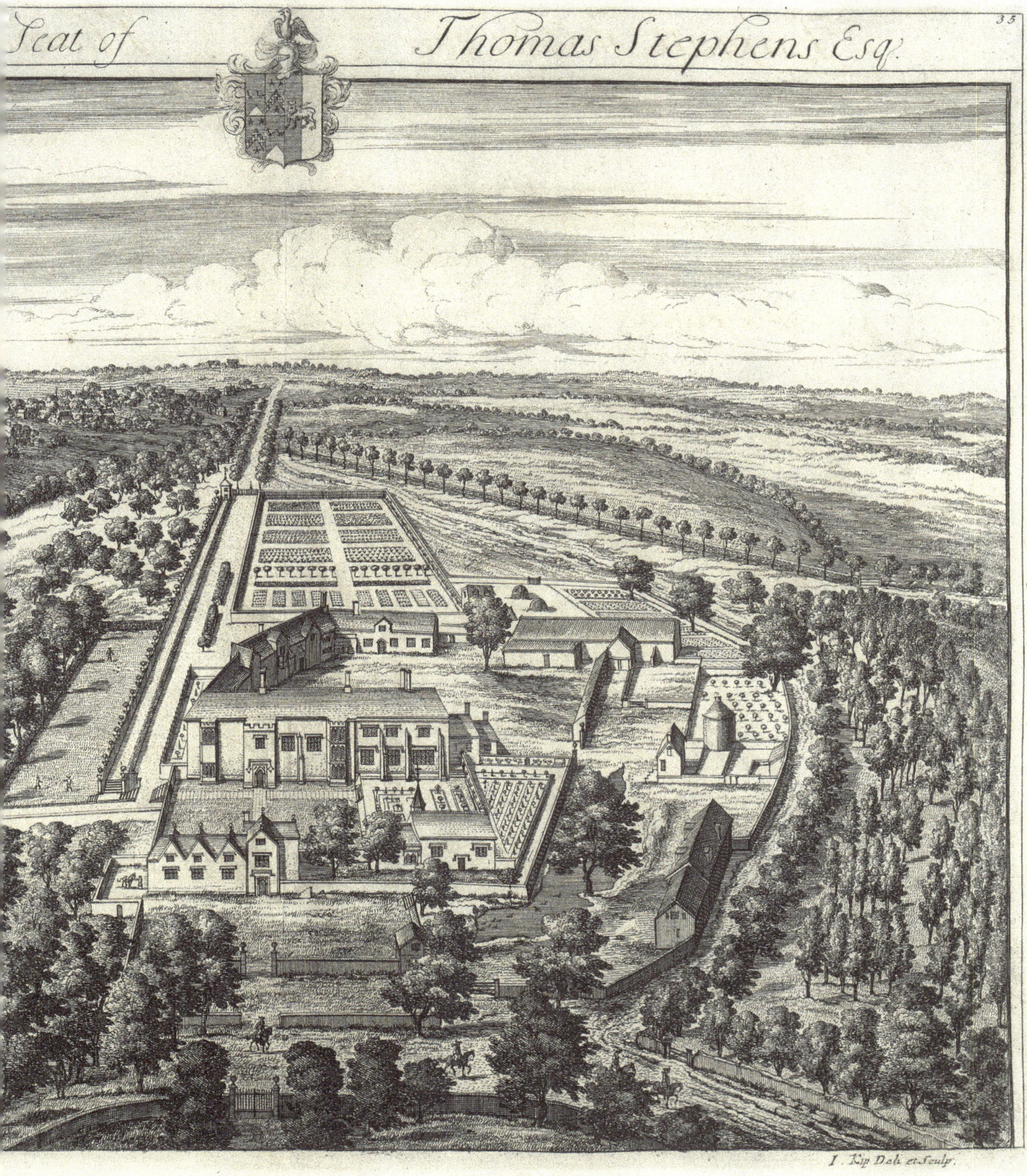

Seat of   Thomas Stephens Esq.

I. Kip Deli et Sculp.

56 Swell the Seat of Sr Robert Atkyns [Atkyns: Swell Lower, 704-705]

'Sir Robert Atkyns of Saperton is the present lord of the mannor, and has a pleasant seat, situated upon the bank of a delightful river,

Sir Robert Atkyns of Saperton is the historian's father and Sir Robert Atkyns junior must have known Lower Swell; the comment on the river is one of the few personal remarks he made relevant to a Kip engraving. The Dikler river was a noted trout stream which Kip hinted at with the two fishermen.

Known as the Bowl or Boulde, the house which Kip drew has been demolished though the present house may incorporate some older fabric. Kip presented the east façade which faced the river and the park, with formal gardens between it and the river. The stable yard is still much as shown by Kip, but the octagonal dovecote has gone though Pigeon House coppice to the north remains.

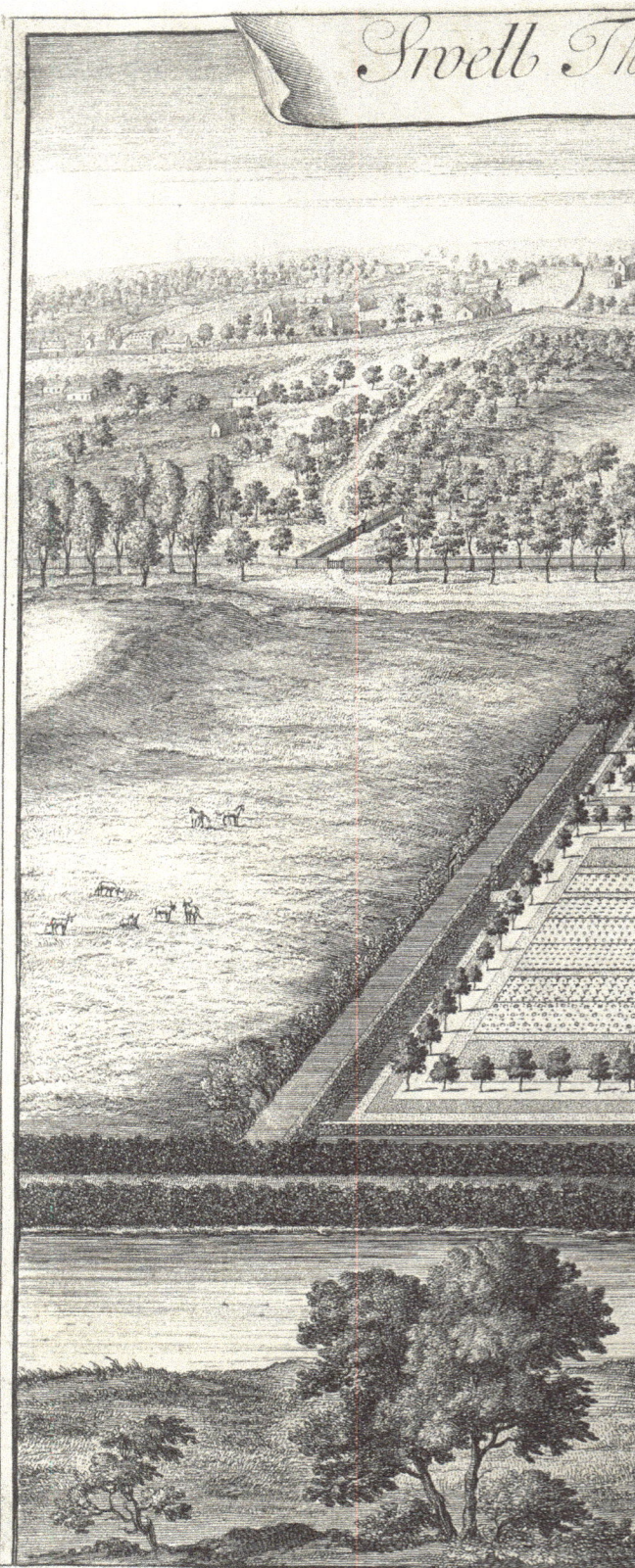

Looking westward, Kip may have exaggerated the size of the orchard and kitchen garden - a walled kitchen garden has since been made further away while the orchard has gone, though in 1999 some old apple trees were left. The ground rises gently to the Lower Swell to Upper Swell road. An older road passing close to the house went to Upper Swell and is now a public footpath (*qv*).

In the distance is Lower Swell church (*qv*), much enlarged by the Victorians. The chancel appears to be detached from the nave. Kip's view confirms Atkyns' comment that 'the church is small, without any isle or steeple'. A holloway can still be seen leading from the churchyard to Lady's Well.

The park occupies ground rising steeply to the Fosse Way and Stow-on-the-Wold. Atkyns did not exaggerate its size, some 400 acres (162 ha) in 1844. It is largely unaltered except for the erection in 1867 of Abbotswood, famous for its gardens.

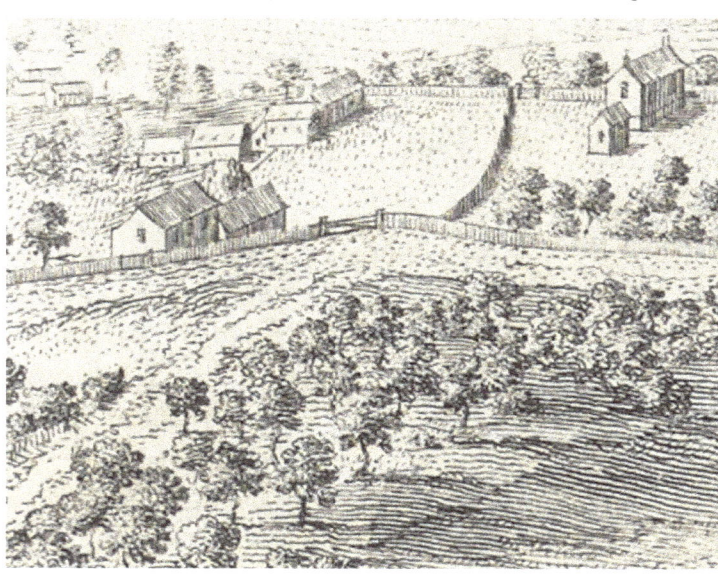

Postcode: Cheltenham GL54 1LE. NGR: SP 17793 25999. VCH VI 165-172.

and a large park of rich ground adjoyning to it.'

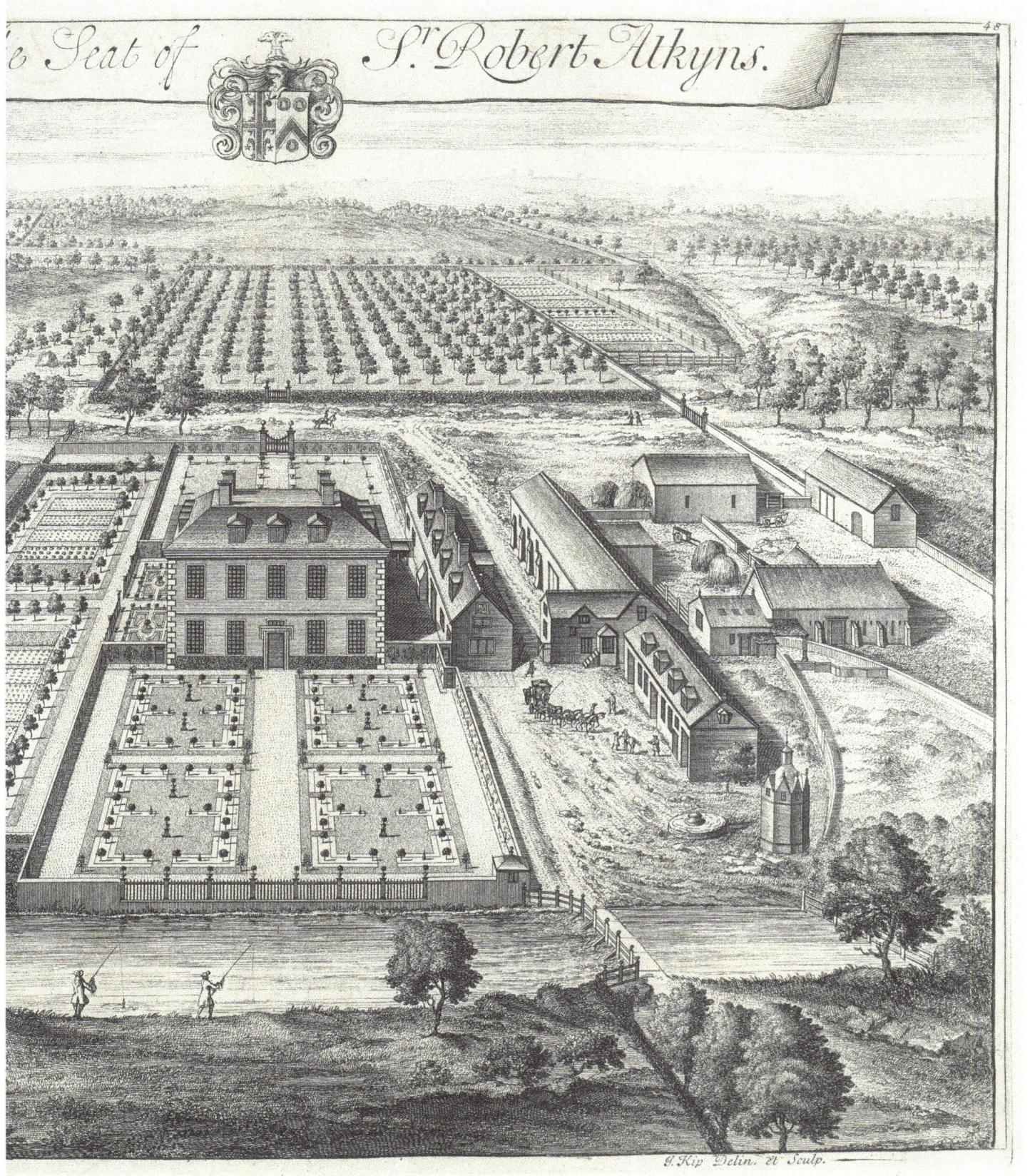

57 **Chepstow Castle belonging to his Grace the Duke of Beauford [Atkyns: Tiddenham,**

'Henry Duke of Beaufort is the present lord of the manor of Tiddenham, and keeps a Court Leet. The parish … is bounded by two great as high a tide as any in the world; it sometimes flows 6o feet.'

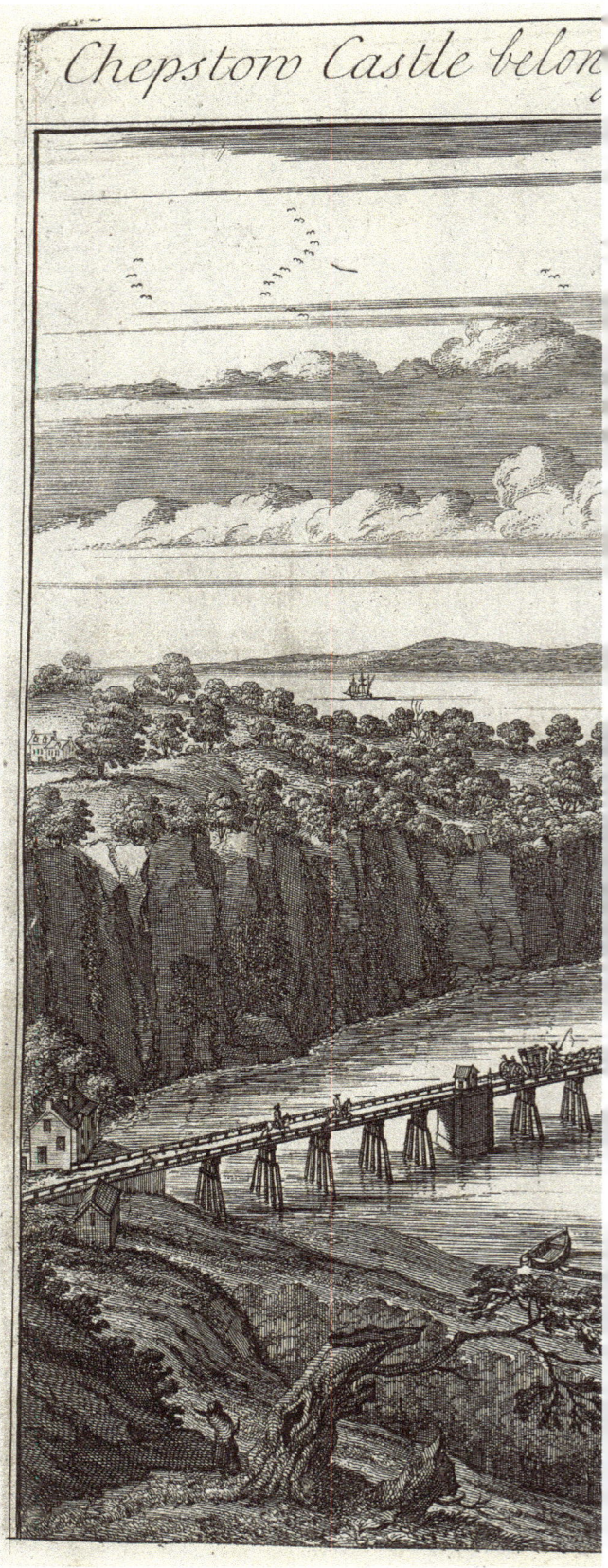

This seems a surprising illustration, as Chepstow Castle was and is in Monmouthshire. The engraving was placed between the pages enumerating the noble holders of the manor of 'Tiddenham' [Tidenham] which the dukes of Beaufort held from the early sixteenth century. Atkyns noted that Badminton was their 'chief seat' in Gloucestershire after the destruction of Raglan castle, but did not mention Chepstow castle. However he was particularly interested in Tidenham and wrote a long account of the manor and its fisheries, and of the families who held it, especially the Mowbrays. As Atkyns himself remarked, an ancestor had been 'an eminent merchant in Chepstow', moving to Gloucestershire in the mid-sixteenth century, and his grandfather owned land in Tidenham.

The river Wye was the main focus of Kip's engraving. He provides a striking image of the river, which is the county boundary. The bends as it flows to the Severn are recognisable if foreshortened. No doubt he enjoyed drawing the widening estuary and the numerous boats on the river. Atkyns noted that tenants of the manor possessed fisheries in the Wye, and moreover 16o acres of land together with a mill in Tidenham were within the Liberties of Chepstow.

Kip was looking approximately from north to south. In the foreground is the bridge between Tidenham and Chepstow, with its many wooden supporting piles; it was just wide enough to accommodate his signature carriage and horses, while the castle is made to look quite distant. The bridge had existed at least from 1228, and was half in Tidenham and half in Chepstow until 1576, when the counties of Gloucester and Monmouth were required by act of parliament to accept responsibility for repairing their halves. Monmouthshire rebuilt their half in 1785, but the Gloucestershire half remained a wooden structure until 1815, when the whole bridge was rebuilt to a design by John Rennie.

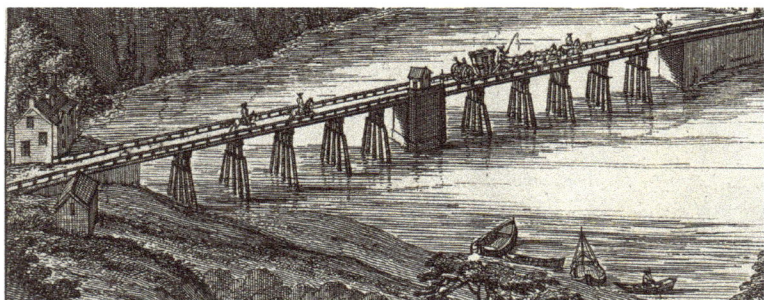

Although both drawn and engraved by Kip, and published in Atkyns' *Ancient and Present State*, this engraving was not included by Joseph Smith in volume 2 of *Nouveau Theatre*.

774-775]. Postcode: Chepstow NP16 **7JQ. NGR: ST** 53993 94250. **VCH X** 50-79.

rivers, the Severn and the Wye … Chepstow bridge is half in this parish, the other half is in Monmouthshire … Under this bridge flows

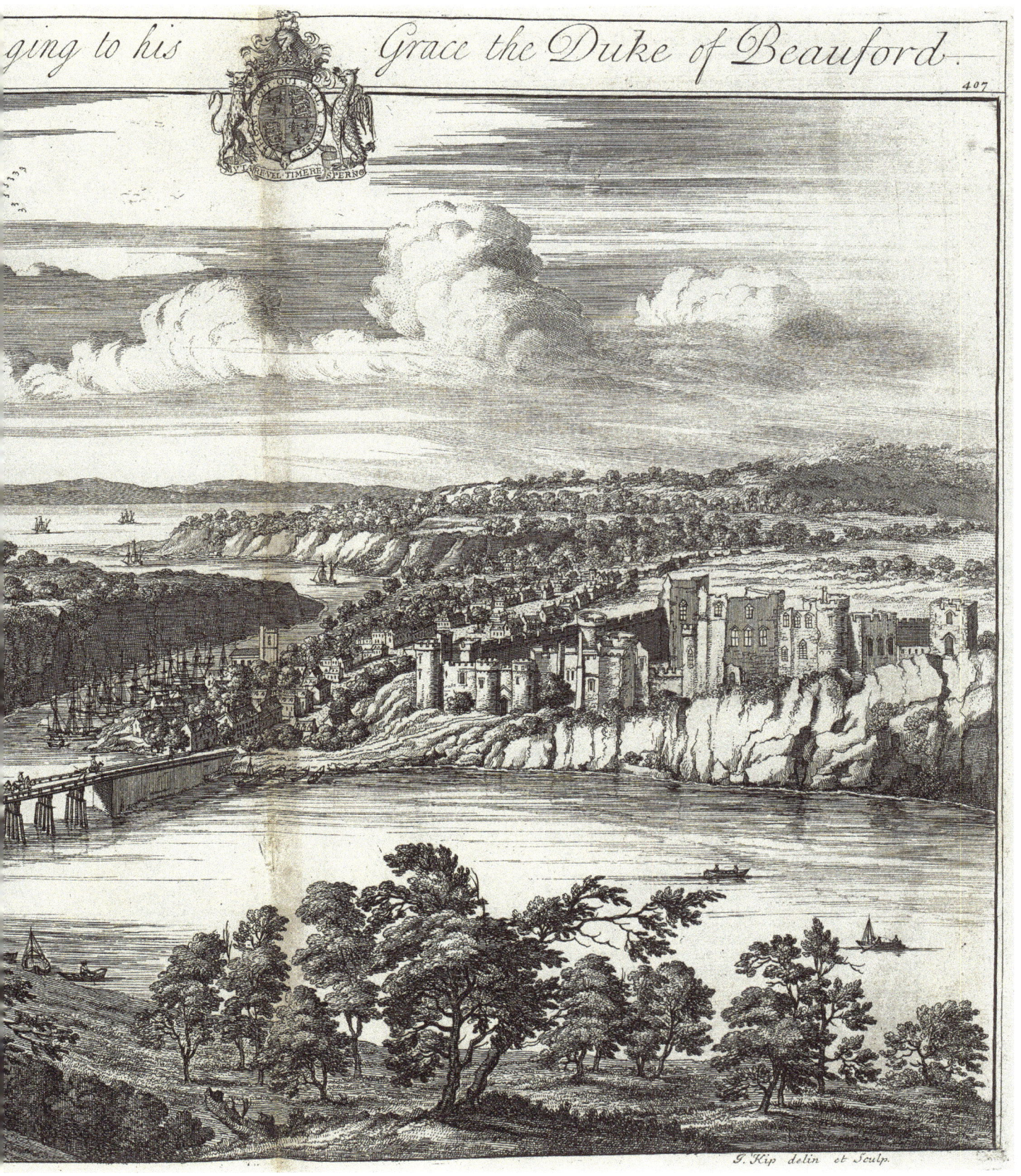

ging to his   *Grace the Duke of Beauford.*

F. Kip delin et Sculp.

58 Toddington The Seat of the Lord Tracy [Atkyns, Todington, 779-782].

'William Lord Tracy is the present Lord of the Mannor of Todington, and has a large house and park in this parish, and a very great

The Tracy family owned Toddington for 950 years, from before 1057 until the early twentieth century. Little remains of the 'large and handsome' house which Rudder said in 1779 was largely unaltered since it was built in the early seventeenth century: only the decorative and crenellated east gate and wall, and the lower part of the south wing, are artfully preserved ruins within the landscaped grounds of the present Toddington Manor (*qv*).

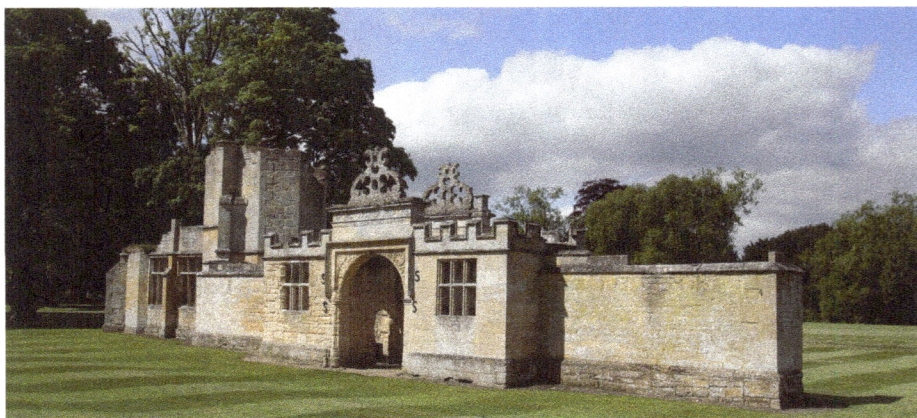

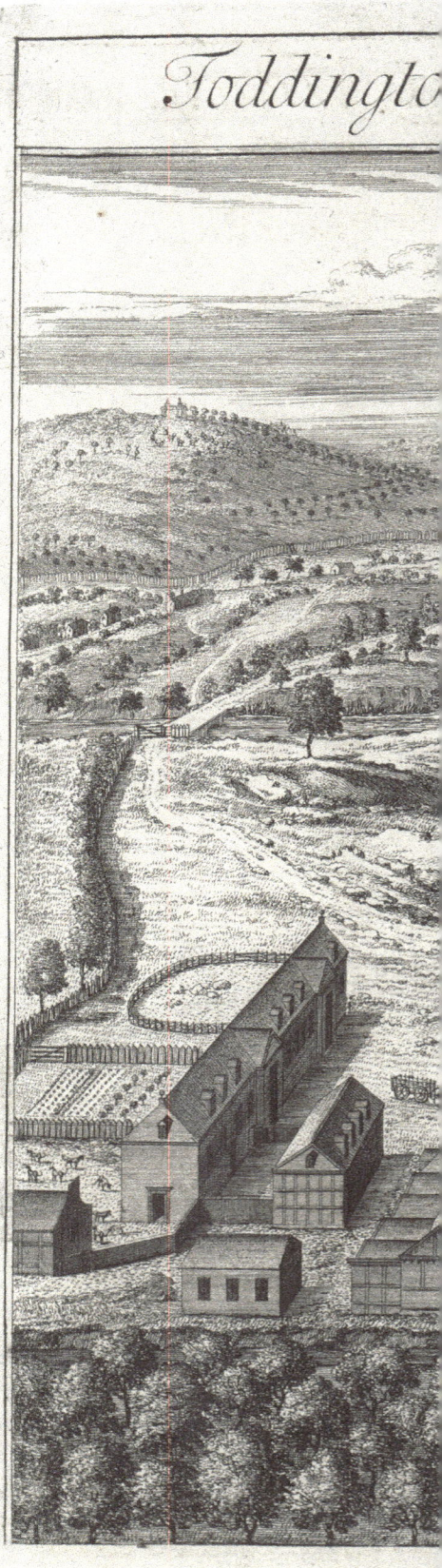

The entrance was through the churchyard, a gateway leading to the garden in a manner reminiscent of Coberley. The wall today follows Kip's line and with the ruin defines the area of the quadrant garden beds. Surprisingly Kip did not include more of the larger garden on the north but did include farm buildings to the south-east.

The house was close to the mill stream, fed from the Isbourne river, which marked the boundary of the garden; Kip drew a large water wheel (*qv*).

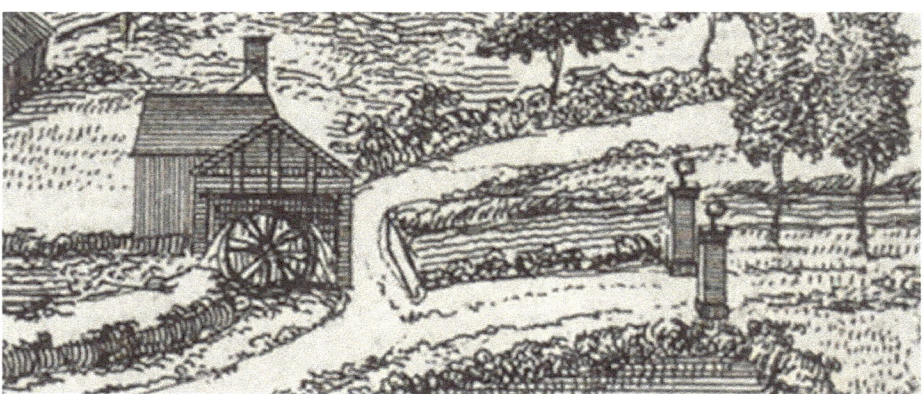

Beyond the river was the park (109 acres [44 ha] in 1847), on a distinctively-shaped hill, on modern maps called The Warren; rabbits may have shared the hill with the deer that Kip drew. Celia Fiennes (1694) noted a 'very good parke', and that the Lodge 'stands so high' that all the park could be seen, and 'the deer running and feeding'. A pale ran along the edge. In the distance Kip indicated Dumbleton Hill, and to the north-east the Cotswold scarp, though distances are foreshortened. Sir Richard Colt Hoare in his *Tour of North Wales* in 1801 observed that the house commanded 'no good qualities in its situation'. Maybe for this reason a new house was built in the 1830s a short distance away; the original gardens were laid to level lawn with occasional mature tree planting. The church has also been rebuilt.

Postcode: Cheltenham GL54 5DN. NGR: SP 03456 33079.

estate in this and other places.'

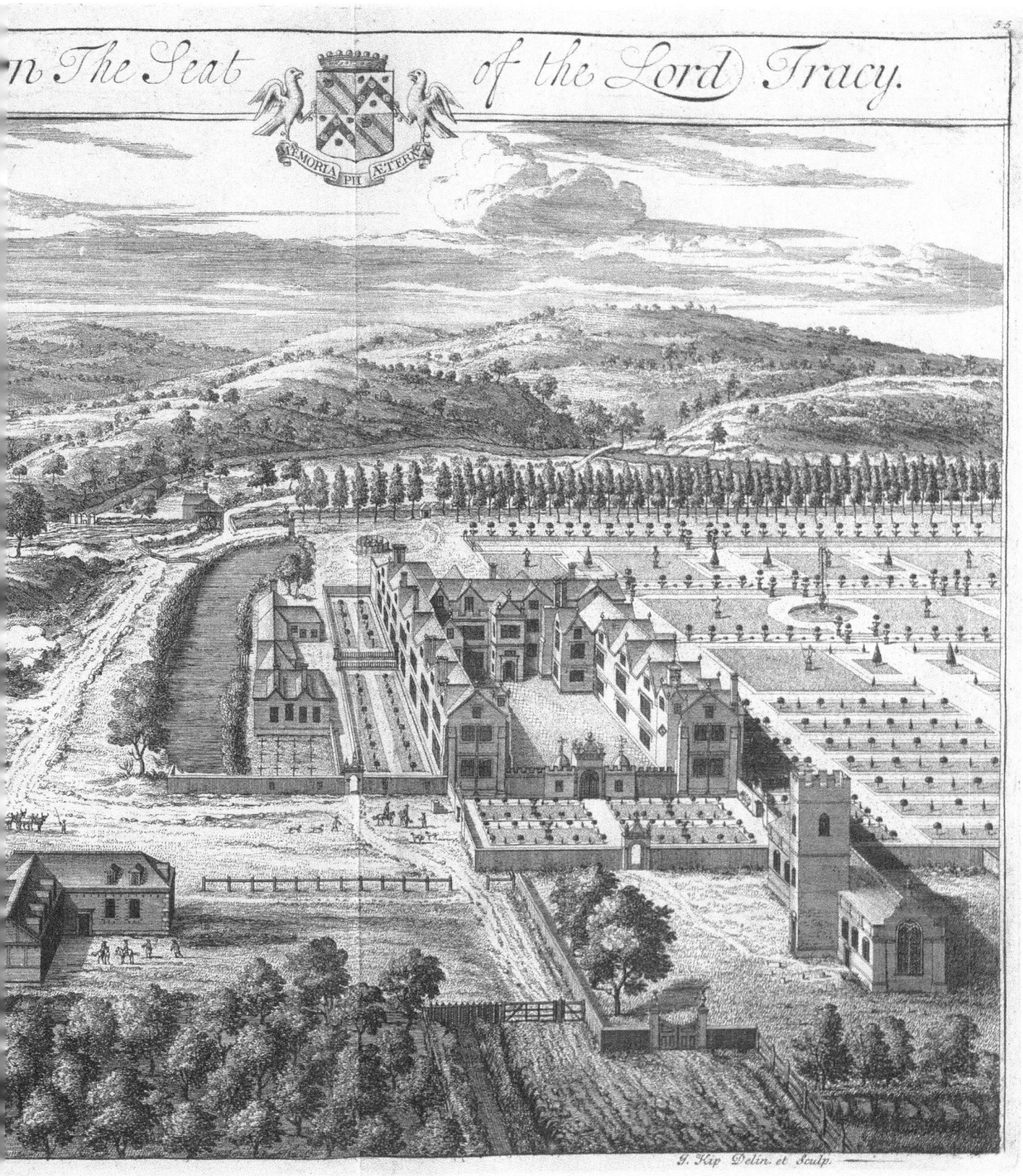

The Seat of the Lord Tracy.

MEMORIA PII ÆTERNA

G. Kip Delin. et Sculp.

59 Tortworth the Seat of Matthew Ducy Morton [Atkyns: Tortworth, 784-785].

'Matthew Ducie Morton … was High Sheriff of Glostershire 1705, and has since served in two parliaments as knight of the shire. He

Kip portrayed a site with much going on architecturally, horticulturally, and topographically. Sir Robert Ducie, Lord Mayor of London, bought Tortworth manor in 1631. Matthew Ducie Moreton, named by Atkyns, inherited Tortworth through his mother; although his family had long-standing interests in Staffordshire, he became active in Gloucestershire and was created 1st Lord Ducie in 1720.

The mainly sixteenth-century manor house consisted of a two-storey entrance block with large gabled attics facing west to a walled court, barns and stables, with Kip's 'signature' coach arriving at a gate, and an almost keep-like three-storey block on lower ground facing east, having Elizabethan-type chimneys. The deer park with a large herd of deer, and the rabbit warren, possibly on rough ground to the right, were medieval, as was the core of the house and the moat which survived on two sides; the canal and the formal walled gardens and walkways are seventeenth century fashions. Next to the moat was the walled kitchen garden.

A map of 1760 shows considerable correspondence with Kip's engraving, even though it has north at the top and Kip has north at the bottom: the moat, the church, the barn and most notably the famous Tortworth chestnut, a solitary tree close to a garden wall. Atkyns commented on it.

It is now fenced round and of enormous size with numerous fallen branches teeming with life and chestnuts. The nuts are said to be good, and the deer park beyond was called 'Nuttree Park' in 1760 (*qv*).

S.S.Teulon in 1849-52 designed a magnificent house, now an hotel, some distance to south-west. The Old Court was gradually abandoned and the gardens reverted to pasture. Two ivy-covered ruins near the church remain. The church was rebuilt 1870-72.

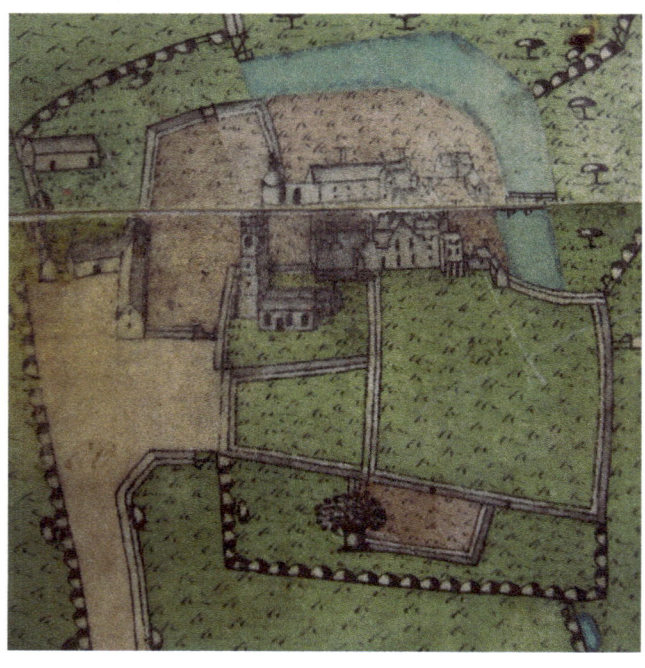

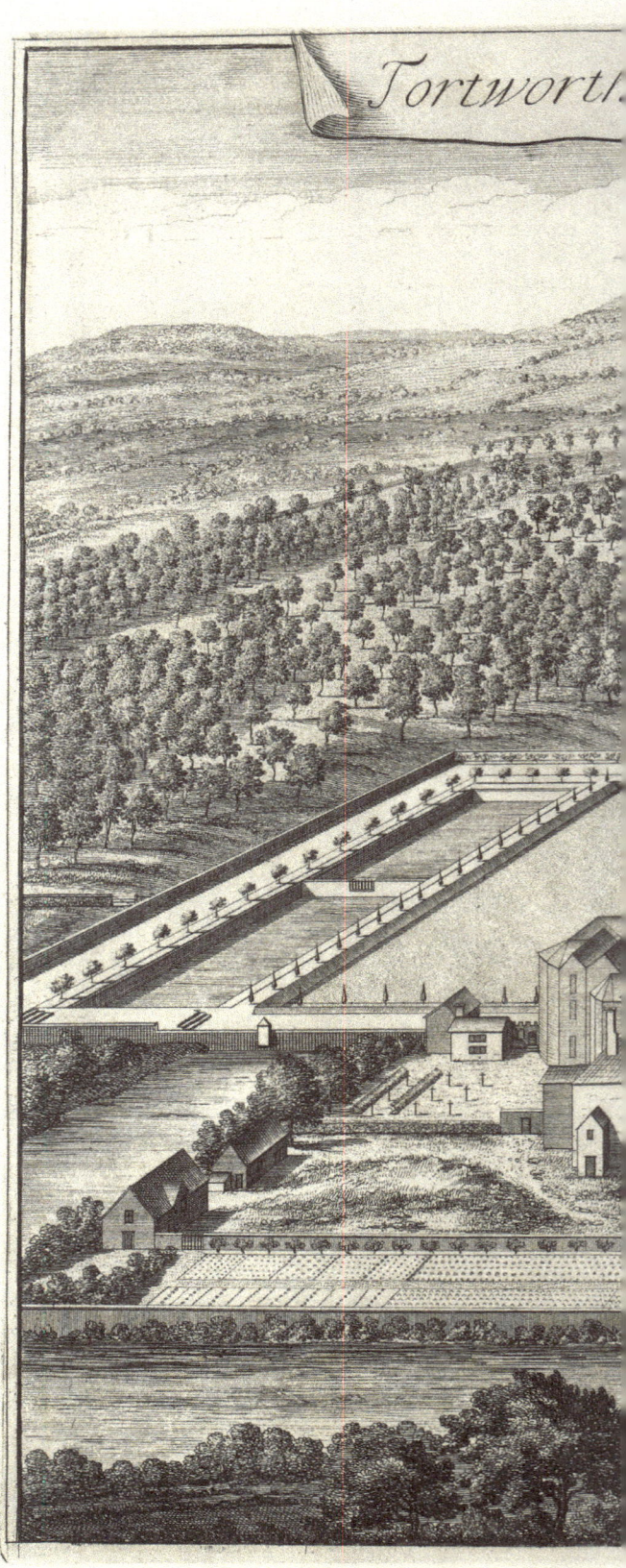

Postcode: Wotton-under-Edge GL12 8HF. NGR: ST 70453 93358.

has a large house near the church, and a very great estate. He has three large parks in this county.'

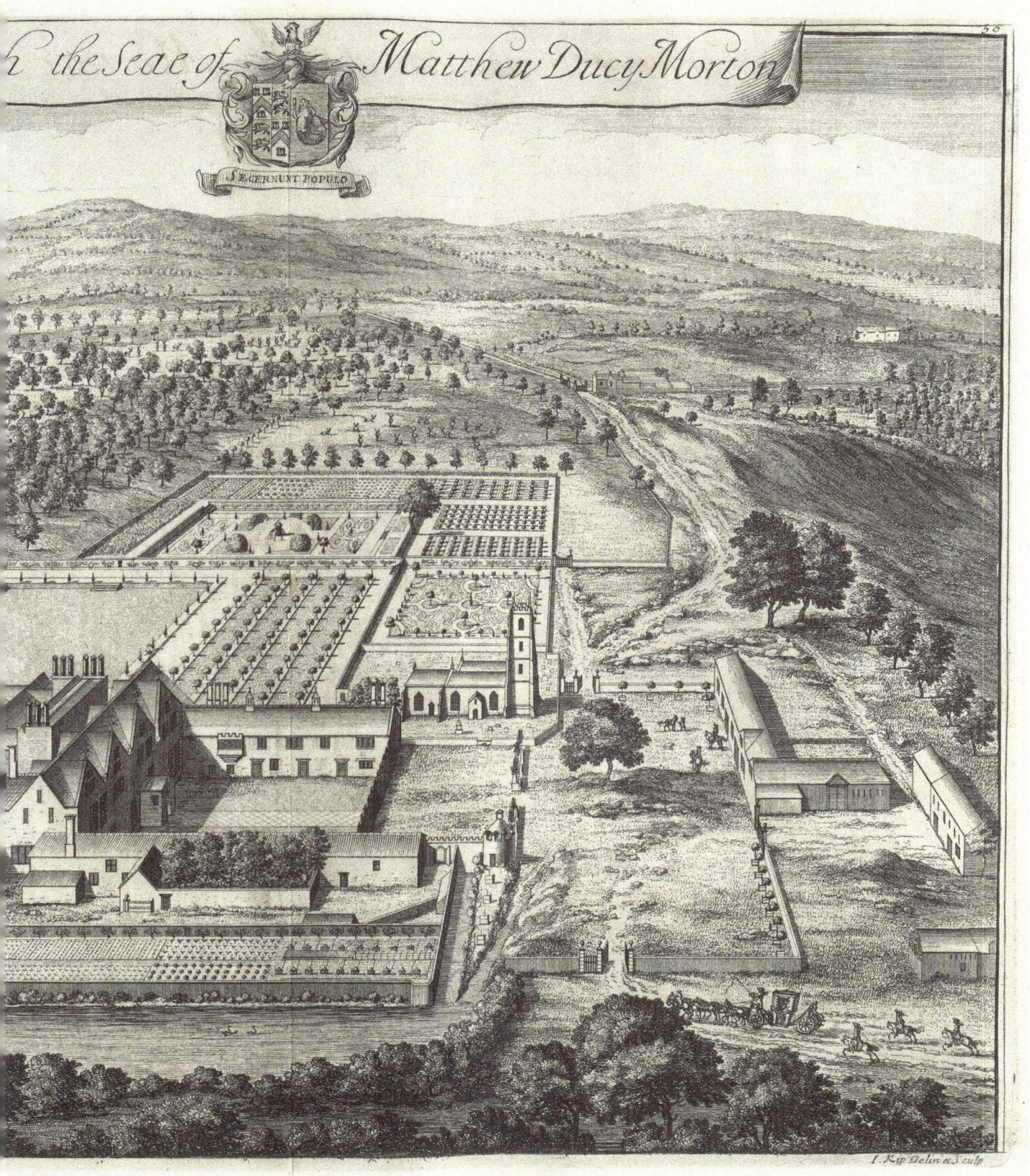

60 Westbury Court, the Seat of Maynard Colchester Esq [Atkyns, Westbury, 798-799].

'Maynard Colchester… has a large house and seat, and a great estate in this and other places.

Westbury Court can claim to be a unique survival (albeit partly by archaeological remains) of a 'Dutch style' water garden. The style became fashionable in late seventeenth-century England; Kip's view from the north-west shows the garden laid out by Maynard Colchester between 1697 and 1705. The inspiration for the water garden may have been nearby Flaxley Abbey, where Catharina Boevey, and prior to his death her husband, both from Dutch families, were creating another garden drawn by Kip which had obvious echoes of the Dutch style. There were links between Catharina and Maynard Colchester: they cooperated in creating a charity school in Westbury, and were fellow founders of the SPCK.

Westbury Court when Kip drew it, with its dominant oriel window on the west side, was basically Elizabethan. It was built by one of the Baynham family who held the estate from the late fifteenth century until 1625. Richard Colchester's grandfather bought the estate in 1641; Maynard Colchester, named by Atkyns, inherited it in 1694. On the south side is a typical Elizabethan knot garden, a bowling green, and a short canal bordered by a well-developed pergola. The stable court was on the north side, with grooms and dunghill. In the background, its perspective accentuated by an avenue,

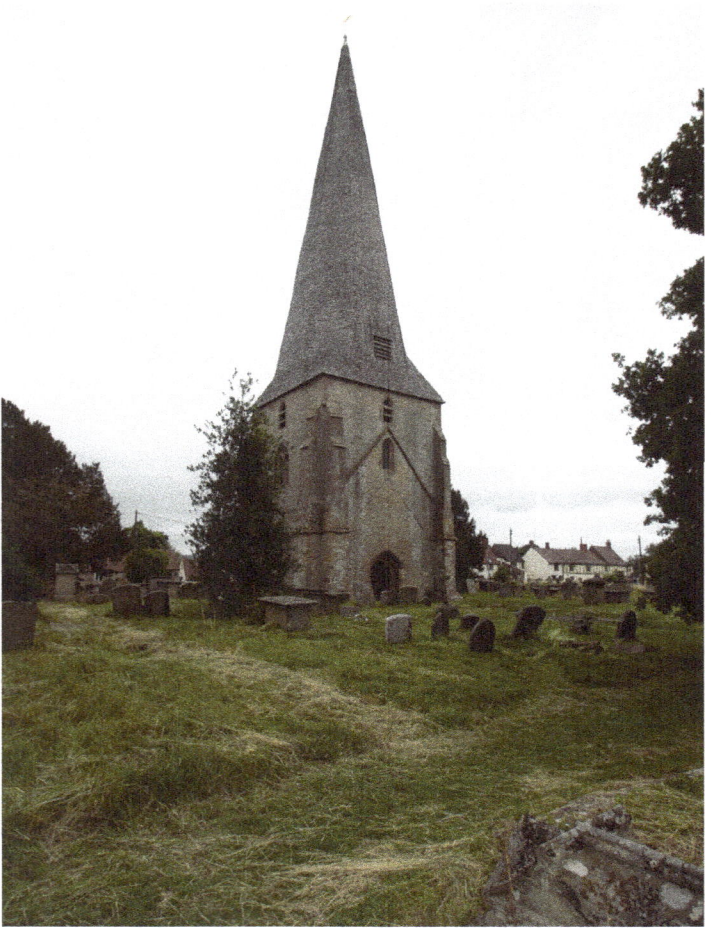

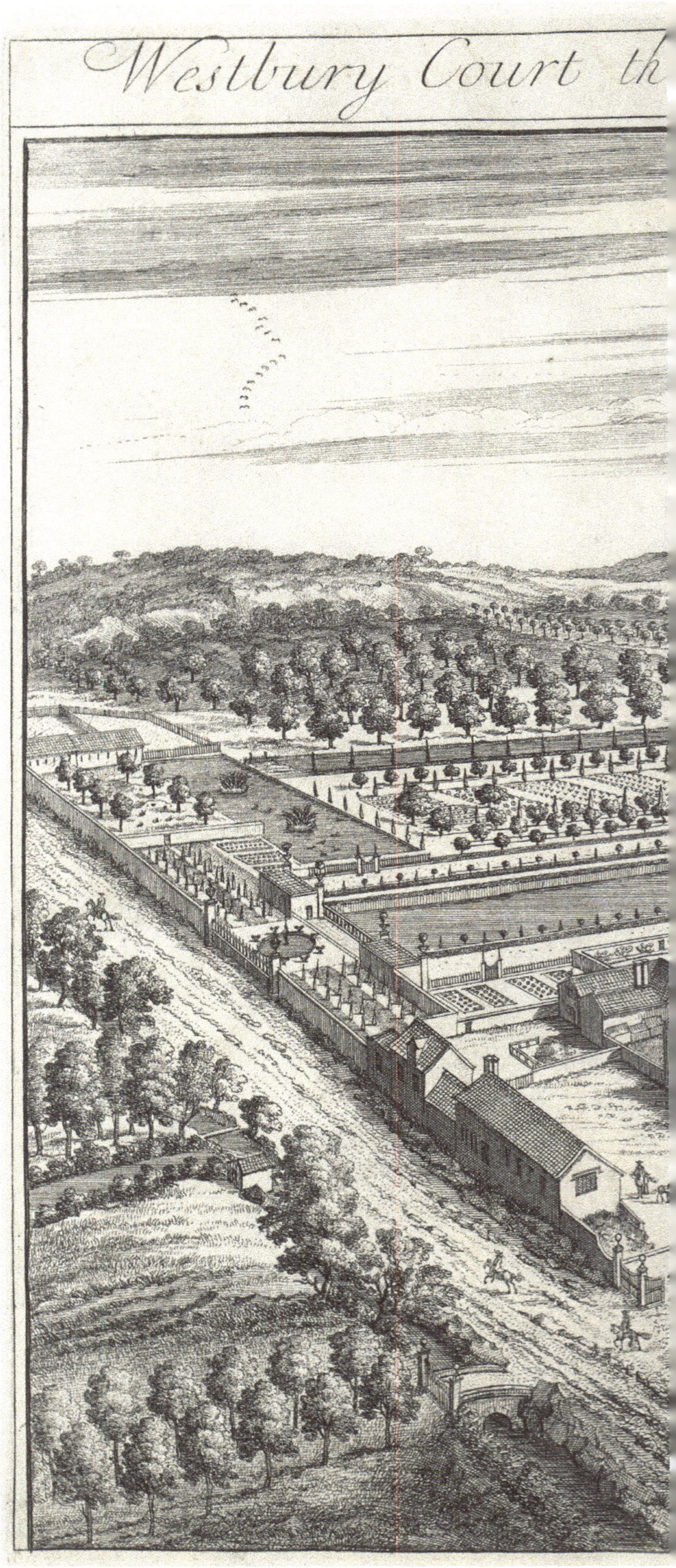

Post Code: Westbury-on-Severn GL14 1**PD. NGR: SO** 71835 13863**. VCH X** 79-102.

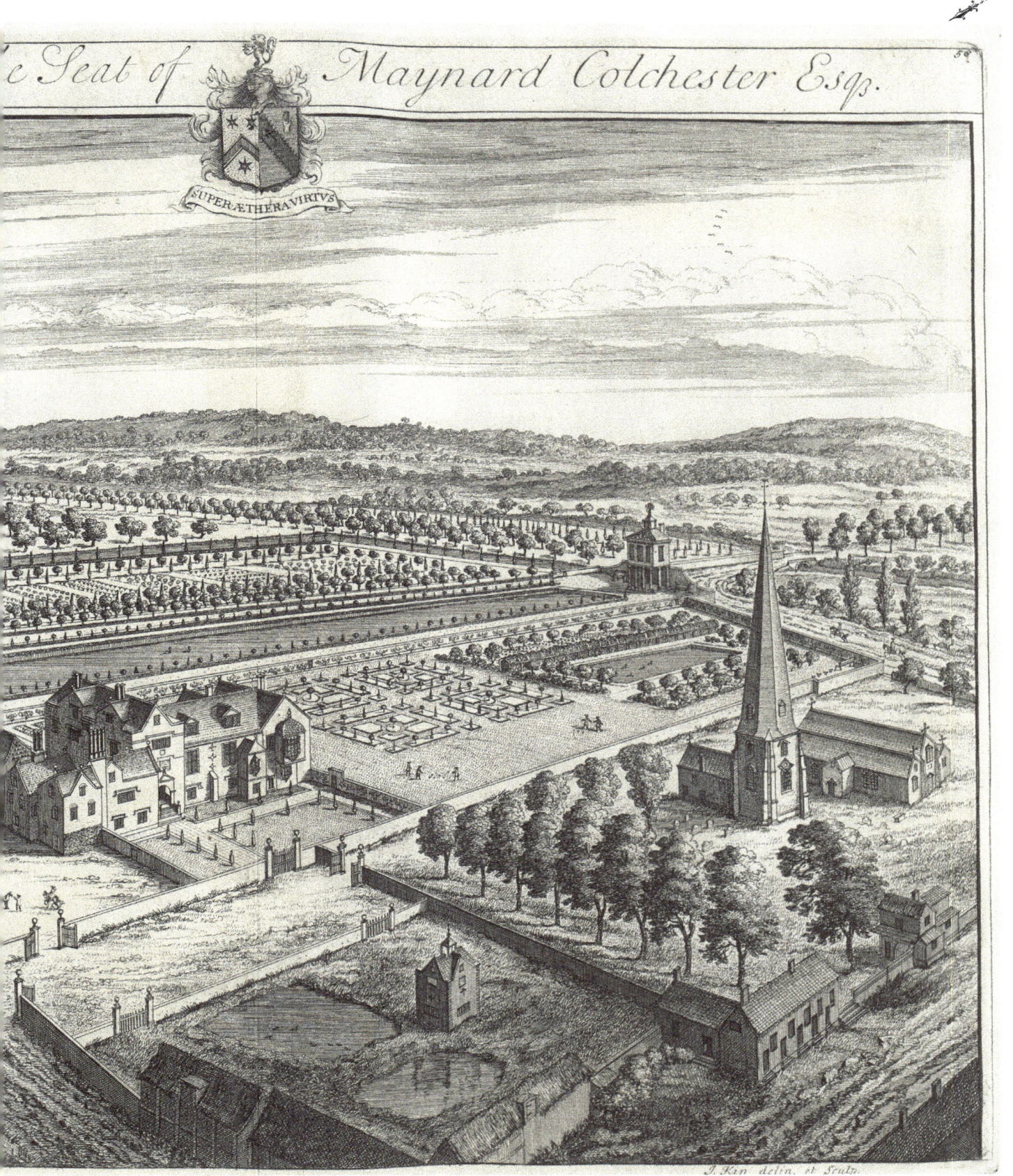

e Seat of Maynard Colchester Esqr.

SUPER ÆTHERA VIRTVS

J. Kip delin. et Sculp.

is a view of distant low hills; unusually Kip has drawn a flight of birds, seagulls perhaps, implying the Severn just out of sight.

The house faced the entrance to the churchyard and Kip gave remarkable prominence to the church and its massive detached tower and tall wooden spire; they provided a counter-balance to the main house, the sacred to the profane perhaps, to a religious man like Colchester. Church and tower remain (*qv*), although in 1862 the latter lost its small attached chapel, at one time used as the charity schoolroom, and the former was refenestrated soon after.

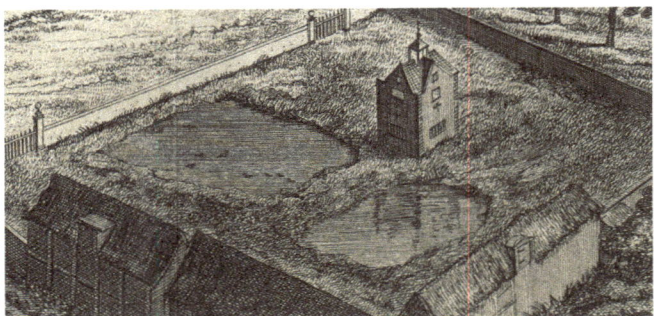

The major new feature was the T-Canal; the cross of the T already existed when Kip recorded the garden. A second *clairvoyée* was created, and he made the small walled garden with its listed summerhouse. The canals are fed by the Westbury Brook, which is on the further side of the road; diverted in 1697, it borders the garden on two sides. The two canals are the distinctive characteristic of the Westbury Court garden.

A map and survey of 1785 (*qv*) confirms the main features. A new house built on the original site between 1743-4, apparently in the Palladian style, is number 1; the elaborate gardens on the south side had become a shrubbery (number 2); the Great Garden and ponds (number 3) covered 4 ½ acres, and there were good oaks in the 5 acre Oxmeadow (number 6), where the first Maynard Colchester had provided an extension to the view from the Tall Pavilion.

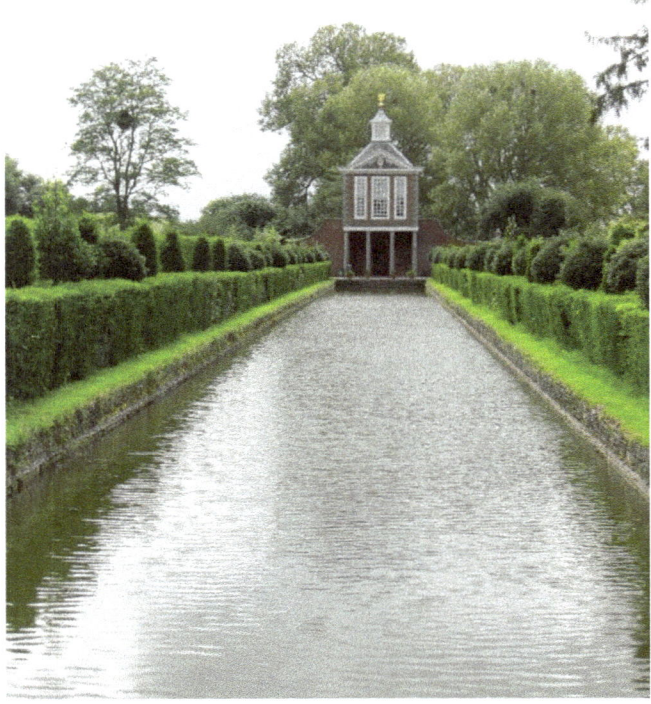

The central feature of the new garden is the Long Canal, with its walks and pyramid yews, hollies and low yew hedges, and the striking Tall Pavilion at its south end, added in 1702-03 (*qv*). A *clairvoyée* of railings in the wall allowed the Long Canal to be seen from the road. Clearly this was a crucial part of the garden for its creator. At the same time, the view outwards from the Tall Pavilion was given interest by planting an avenue in the field opposite.

There are ducks on the canals, perhaps from the duck-ponds in the Culverhay by the dovecote, at the bottom of the scene (*qv*); this ground is now in the churchyard and there is evidence of the ponds in sunken areas. Beyond the Long Canal were vegetable gardens, essential to a self-sufficient country residence.

Maynard Colchester's nephew inherited the estate in 1715, and continued to develop the garden.

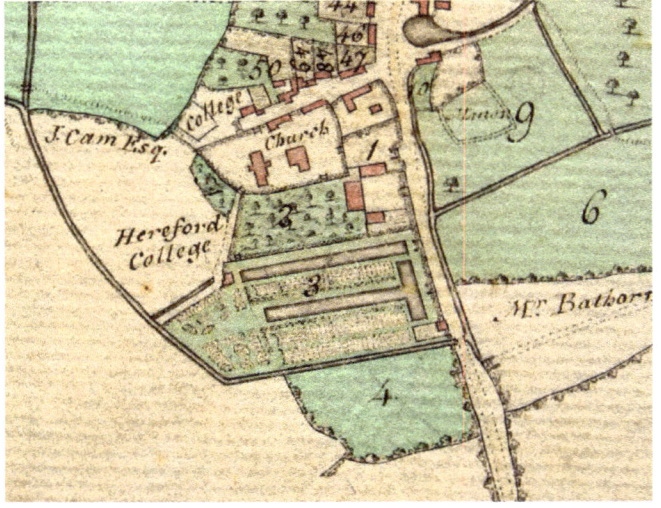

The new house was demolished in 1805, the Colchester family making The Wilderness near Mitcheldean their home. Westbury Court garden was not completely abandoned as it appears some maintenance was done, most likely to keep the canals open. A map made in 1877 shows the canals still clearly defined (*qv*) though surrounded by trees and overgrown shrubs. Some years later the family returned to Westbury, and built a new house in 1895 adjoining the Tall Pavilion.

In the twentieth century the garden became very neglected, and while the structure of the canals

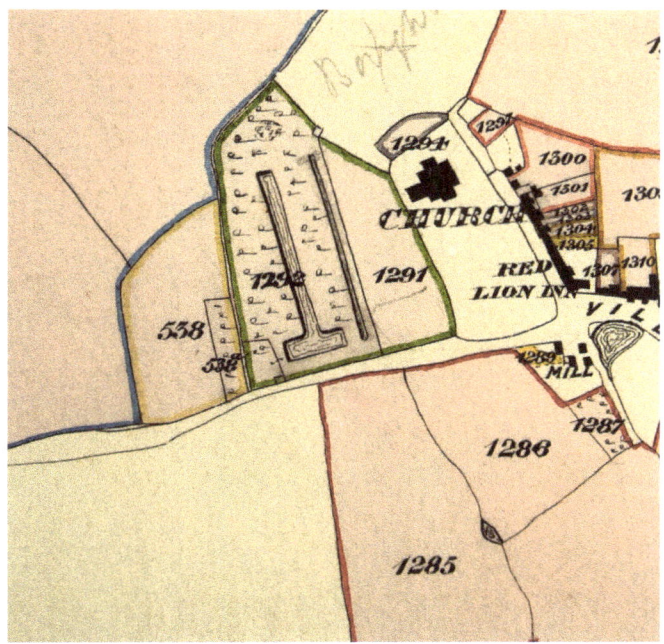

Westbury-on-Trym

Of twelve large houses north and east of Bristol which were drawn by Kip, the two in Westbury-on-Trym: Stoke House and Sneed Park, were nearest to the port and city, which has necessarily governed their development, gradually surrounding them with suburban housing. Westbury-on-Trym civil parish was withdrawn from Gloucestershire and merged with Bristol in 1904, being recognised as a suburb of the city. Nonetheless, notable estates have left marks on the landscape, including important open spaces which are becoming increasingly appreciated.

Westbury-on-Trym was a large ancient parish, 4,600 acres in 1831, bordering on the Severn and Avon. Until the dissolution of the monasteries and other religious foundations, part was controlled by the collegiate foundation in the parish and part by the bishop of Worcester; both parts were confiscated by the Crown. Stoke, its name originally denoting an outlying farmstead, was a tenement of the bishop of Worcester as early as the tenth century. The curving boundary of Stoke House, as engraved by Kip, suggests the bishop of Worcester's early *burh* or manor house site. Sneed was the Bishop's deer park; it is recorded in 1374, and the name, variously written *Sneed, Sneyd or Snead,* described a piece of land which had been separated, in this case from the rest of Stoke Bishop by the Roman road to Sea Mills. Stoke House and Sneed Park were both in the tithing of Stoke Bishop, and both had look out towers to view the Avon and the Severn estuary in or relatively near the house.

remained, although deteriorating, without maintenance they silted up and became choked with vegetation. In 1960 the estate was sold; the house was demolished, and housing for the elderly was built where the Elizabethan house had stood. The garden was handed to the National Trust in 1967. Not only has the Trust restored the canals, but archaeological investigation has established many of the details in Kip's engraving, like the round pond at the head of the Long Canal (*qv*), enabling a more complete recreation of the Dutch garden, which can once more be admired and enjoyed.

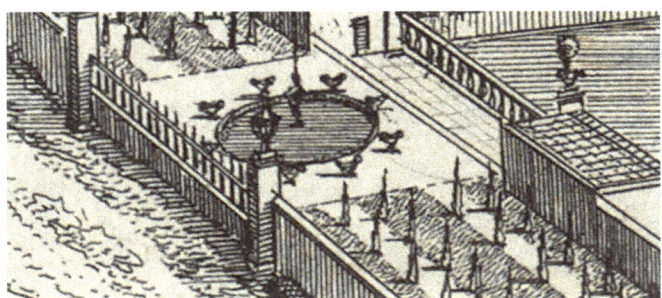

Stoke Bishop

Stoke House is set in undulating semi-wooded parkland. The house pictured by Kip was built for Sir Robert Cann, a Merchant Venturer knighted in 1662, who was Mayor of Bristol in 1662 and 1675, then High Sheriff in 1676, and finally M.P. in 1678. The doorway has a datestone '1669'. The house was occupied by his descendants until 1829.

It is an early centralised double-depth house of three storeys plus attic with three ogee gables suggesting some Dutch influence, behind which were two cupolas which have recently been removed; its east-facing entrance front has an over-detailed full height central porch (*qv*). Internally, the hall still has its original, though restored, newel-framed stair, more typical of the early seventeenth century. Behind the front range Kip drew a crenellated tower above the stairwell, which provided a fashionable viewing platform and still survives. The view of shipping on the Avon and the Severn estuary was important enough for a hillside lookout tower also to

61 **Stoke Bishop the Seat of Sr Thomas Cann** [Atkyns: Westbury [-on-Trym], 804-805].

'Sir Thomas Cann … has an handsome seat and a large estate in this place and in the adjoyning parishes'.

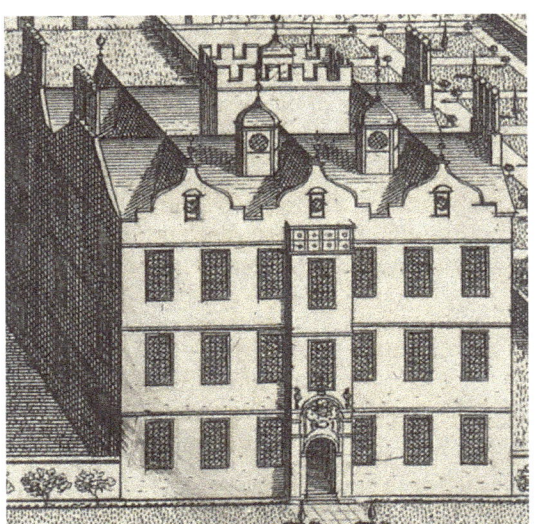

be built (*qv*). Ships were Kip's typical markers of navigable waterways, as coach and horses were of highways.

Extensive gardens with walks are to the south, on rising ground. A gated court separated the house from the highway, and the four-gabled lodge was also seventeenth-century.

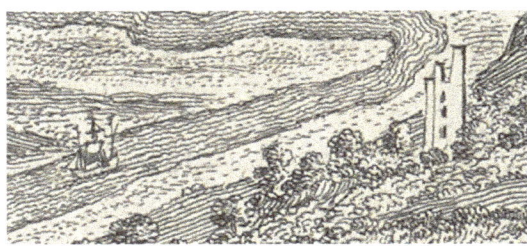

The house was extended in mid-eighteenth century and again in the later nineteenth, when it was refaced and had two-storey bow-fronted wings added, but the seventeenth-century detailing and atmosphere was retained. Currently, the house and its large kitchen wing at the rear, listed Grade II*, and its nine acres of grounds and woodlands, unlisted, are home to an Anglican theological college.

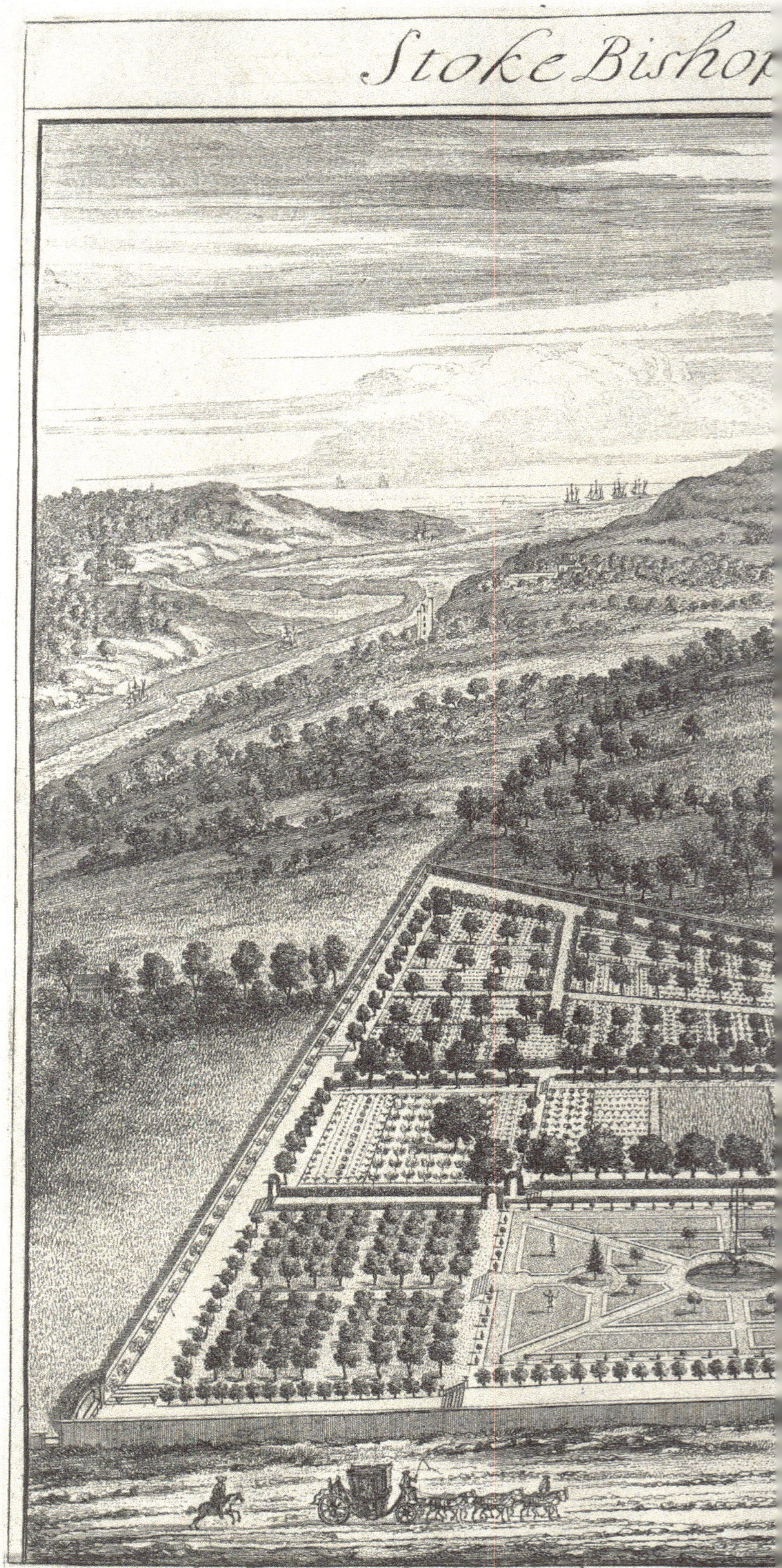

Postcode: Stoke Hill BS9 1**JP. NGR: ST** 56376 75509.

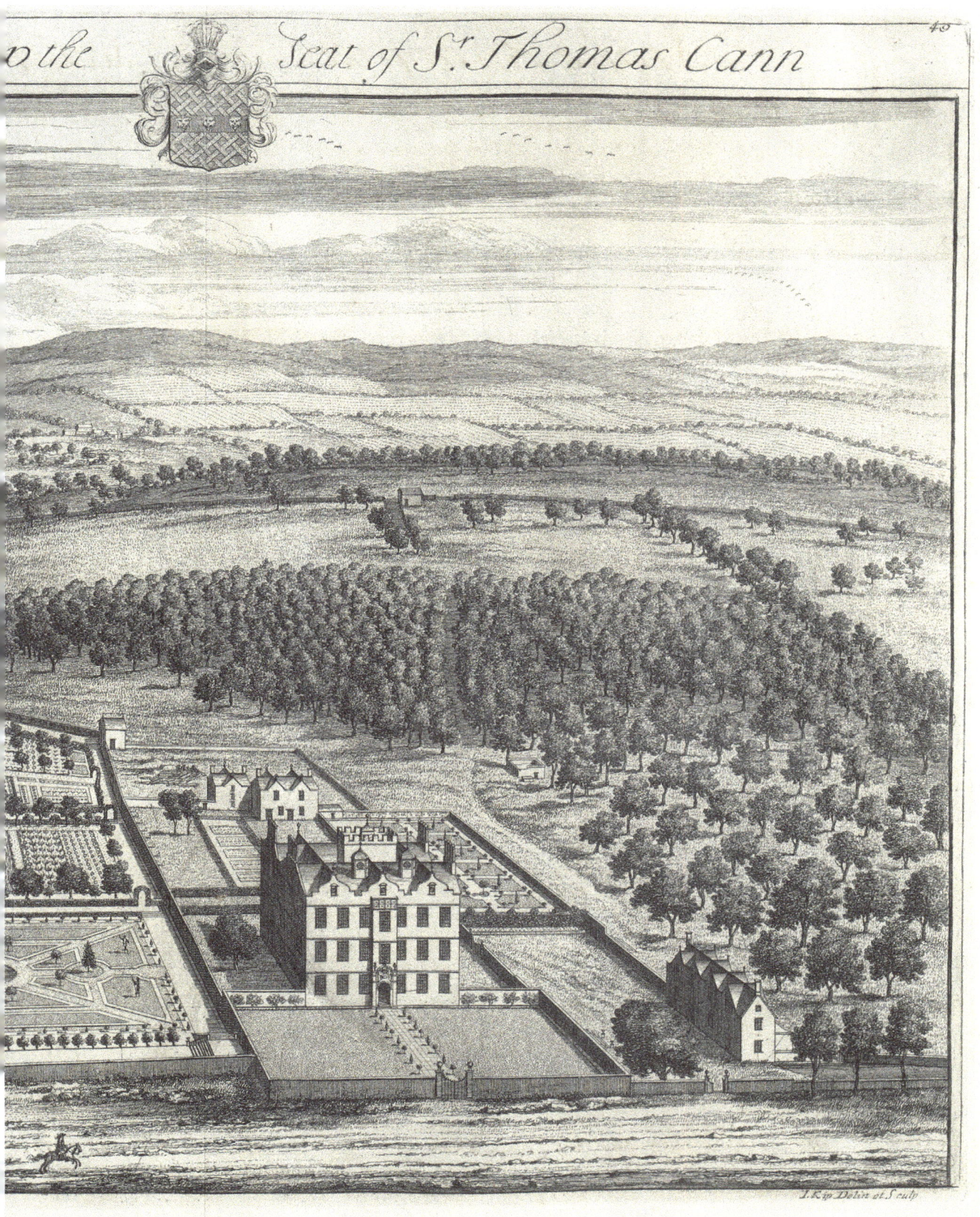

62 Sneed Park the Seat of Joseph Jackson Esq [Atkyns: Westbury [-on-Trym], 804-805].

'Mr Jackson has a good house and a good estate called Snead-Park.

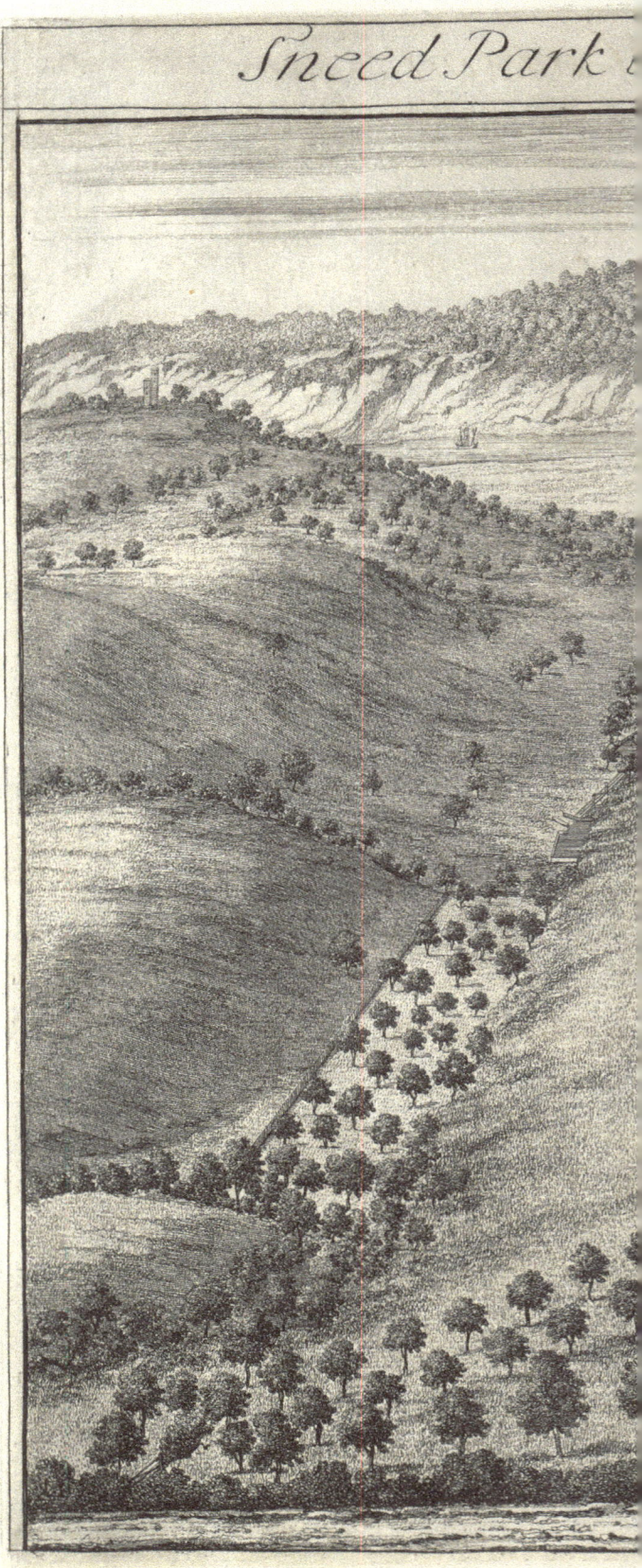

Kip brings out the sweep of the landscape around Sneed Park, the triangular shape of the site following the crest of a low ridge running away to the River Avon and Kingroad busy with shipping. As Samuel Rudder noted, the site was 'remarkable as well for the natural inequality and beautiful variety of the ground as for the striking views it affords.'

Joseph Jackson senior acquired the estate in mid-seventeenth century and his son built the house in 1691; above the entrance was the Jackson coat of arms. Both were Bristol merchants, involved in local politics and the Merchant Venturers. The family owned the house until 1815.

It was a relatively modest L-shaped house, facing north-east, with formal flower gardens and orderly fruit and vegetable plantings on the warmer side of the house. The long terrace which ran south-westwards to the River Avon was very striking, with a look-out tower half-way along. Kip also drew a look-out tower on the highest point above the river (*qv*), built in the late seventeenth century, but now demolished.

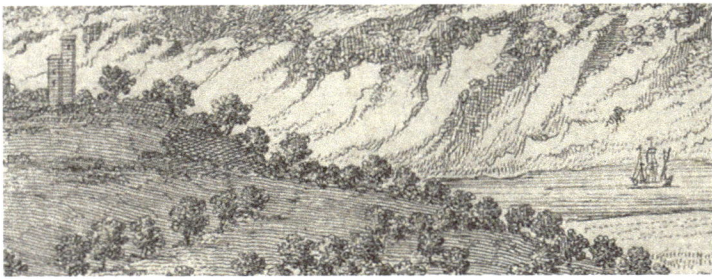

The park wall ran along the south side of the site, and a double row of trees ran down to what may have been fish ponds mentioned by Rudder.

Most of the land was sold for housing after 1853 but the house continued under various owners; an aerial view in 1922 reveals the substantial survival of the garden's structure drawn by Kip (*qv*) and a few yew trees still remain which may date from that time.

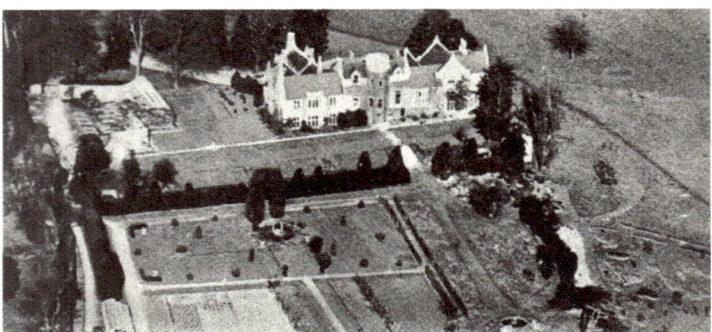

In 1972 the house was demolished after a serious fire. Sixteen acres (6.6 ha) were transferred to Bristol City Council in 1988. The Friends of Old Sneed Park Nature Reserve were constituted in 1995, and it is now officially recognised and open to the public.

Post Code: Glenavon Park BS9 1**RJ. NGR: ST** 55408 75695.

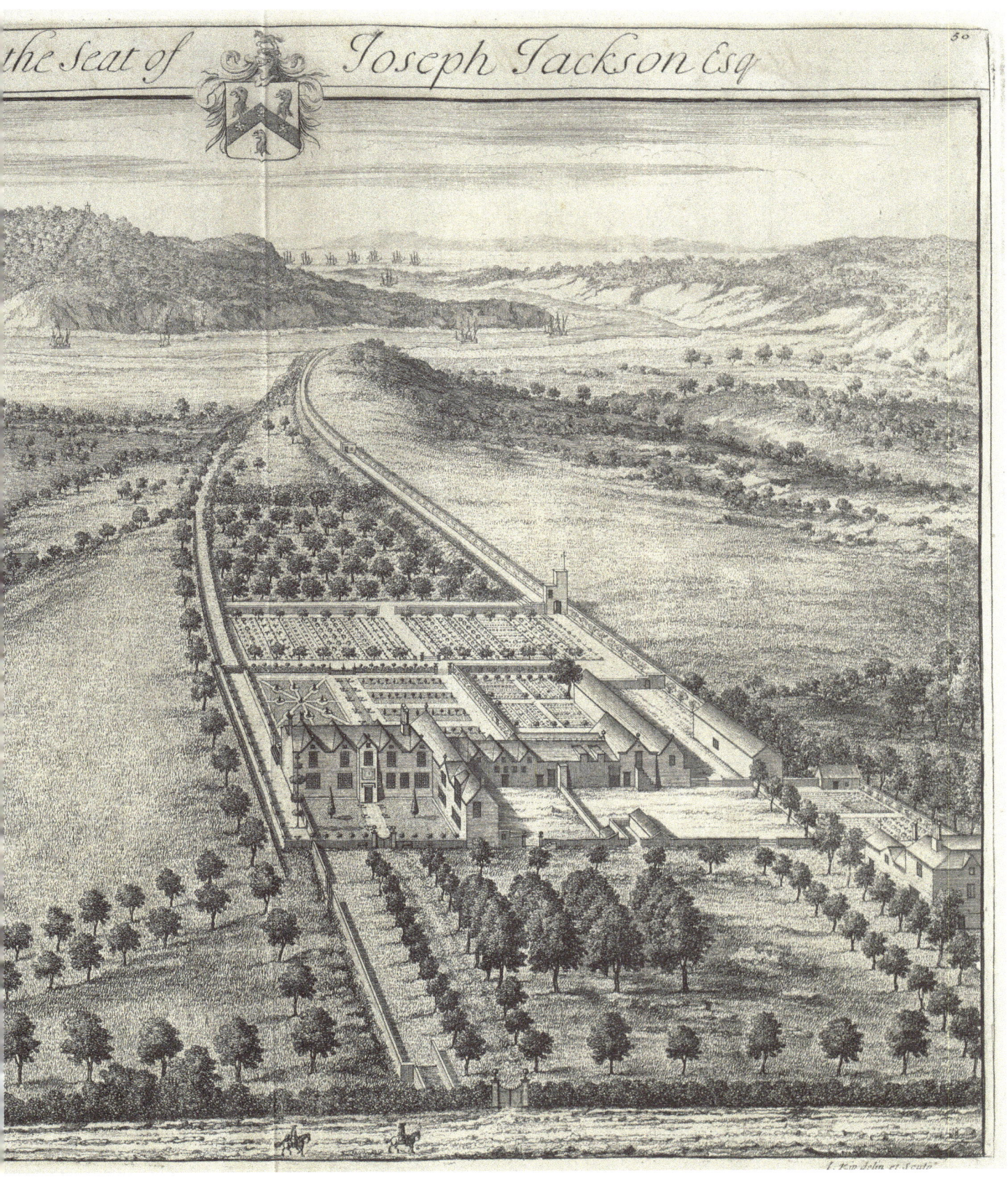

the Seat of Joseph Jackson Esq

63 **Witcombe Park the Seat of Sr Michaell Hickes [Atkyns: Witcomb, 844-845].**

'Sir Michael Hickes … hath an handsome seat and park in this place, and a great estate'.

Lady Elizabeth Hicks acquired Witcombe manor in 1612, and the family owned it for the next two centuries. Her grandson, Sir Michael Hicks, named by Atkyns, built the fashionable south block onto a probably early-seventeenth century six-gabled east range (*qv*). Sir Michael died in 1710. The second house since Kip drew Witcombe has been built in the early twenty-first century in Cotswold stone on the same site.

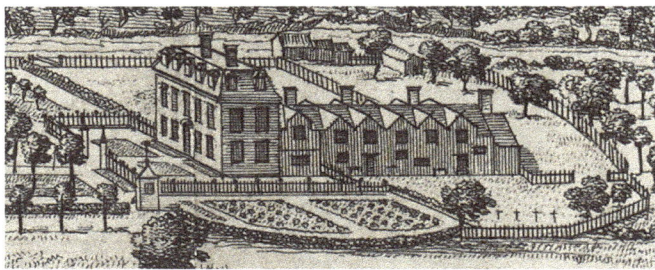

Kip suggests little in the way of a garden had yet been laid out, simply a semi-circle to the east and to the south a courtyard with a gazebo (listed grade II) dated 1697. An avenue had been planted leading from gate piers with large ball and flame finials; a second pair have lost their flames (also listed) and Kip drew two more sets, one at the entrance to the park and one high on the hillside now buried in wood.

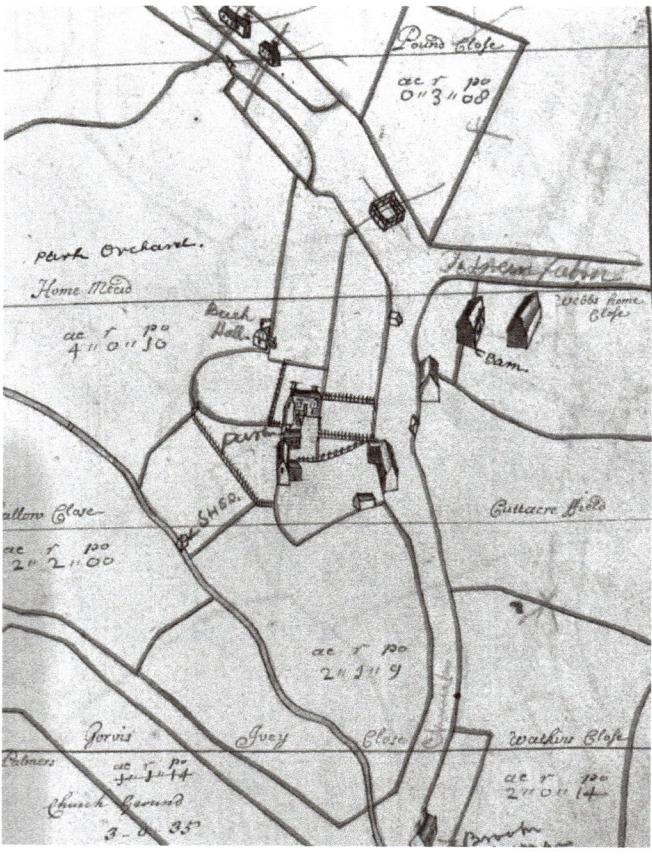

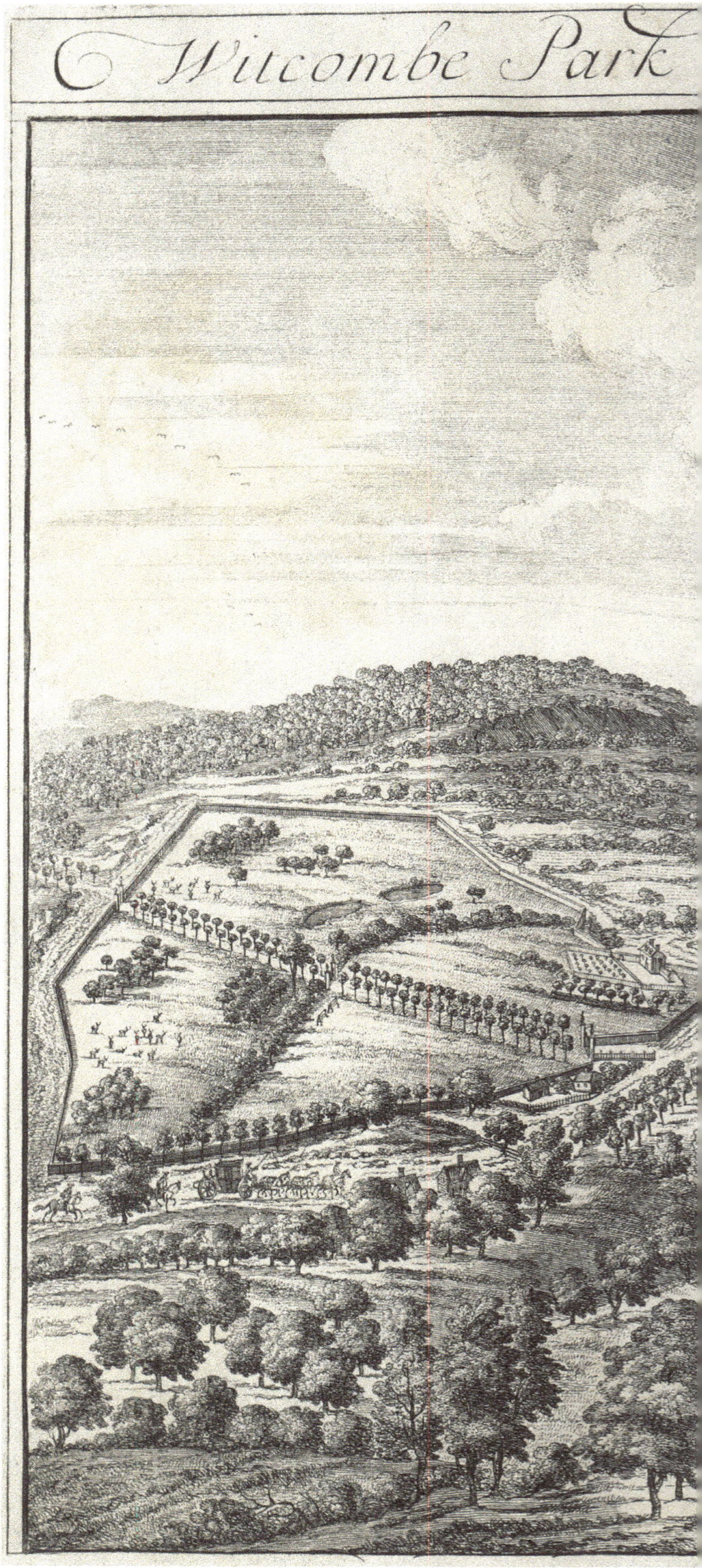

Postcode: Gloucester GL 3 4TT. NGR: ST 91151 14466.

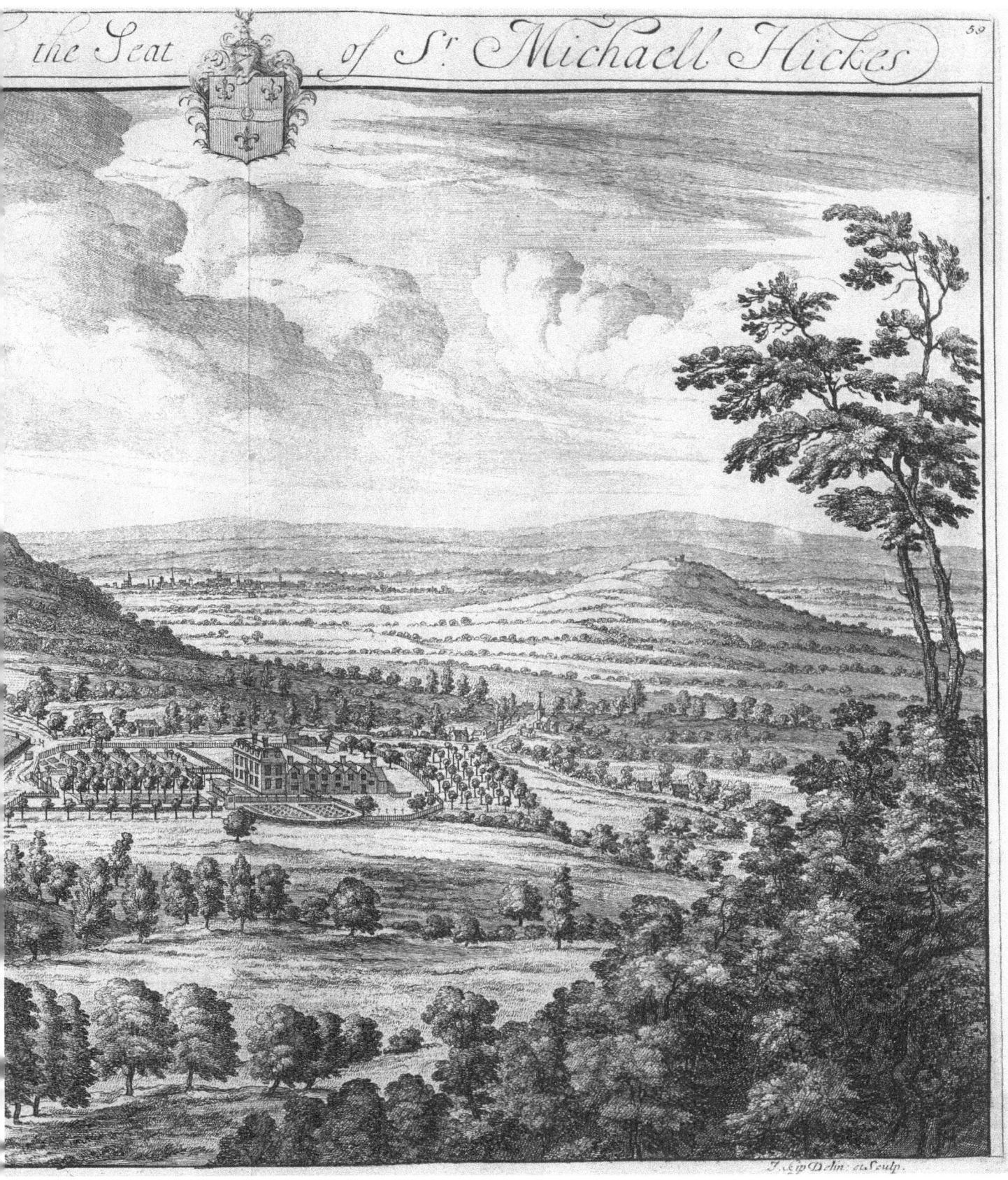

A 'Topographical Description' or map of 1711 (with later pencil annotations) shows a layout of fences and courts round the house matching Kip's drawing (*qv*); the semi-circle of garden is particularly clear. The map is oriented with south at the top; Kip's engraving has west at the top. An interesting confirmation of a small detail is the square pound in the middle of the road; the map shows 'Pound close' behind it, and pencil marks show it was later removed. The barns in the engraving are also marked on the map.

The park, which Kip shows was walled and where he drew deer, was near the summit of the hill, adjoining a wood reaching almost to Birdlip; the map marks the two springs where Kip drew ponds. The avenue leading through the park can be traced today, and the park-keeper's cottage on the west side of the park, dated 1617, still exists. The steep coach road to Birdlip, running by the park wall, was closed before 1837, and in the twentieth century the road leading to the park-keeper's cottage was rerouted so that house and park were not separated. On the road to the village, Kip drew a decorative-shaped tower on Witcombe church (*qv*), since rebuilt in perpendicular style.

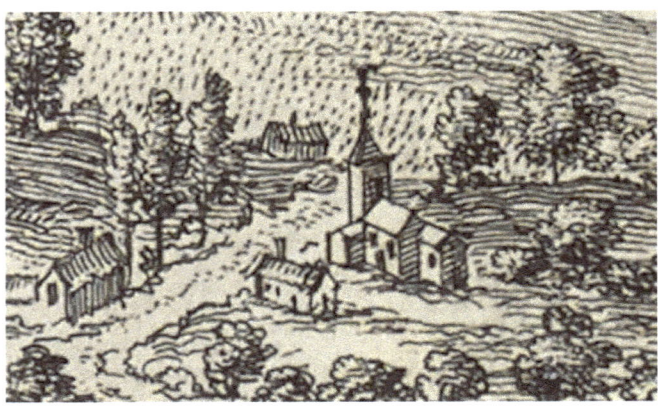

Witcombe, the wide valley or combe, has hills on three sides. To the west is Cooper's hill; a Roman villa was discovered in 1818, the presence of which has completely overshadowed the history of Witcombe Park. Gloucester's spires anad towers can be glimpsed from near the house and to the east Churchdown, with the church on top of Chosen Hill sketched by Kip. Did he know that before the Reformation Witcombe was in the Archbishop of York's barony of Churchdown?

Bradley Court

Bradley manor, owned by the Berkeleys until 1611, came into the ownership of Thomas Dawes in 1692; he died in 1713, living just long enough to see the publication of the Kip view. He possibly constructed the compartmentalised gardens in Kip's engraving: the weather vane on top of the gazebo has his initials and a date 1702.

Bradley Court when Kip engraved the view was already an old-fashioned building. There is a date stone 1559 on the porch, however this may record when the symmetrical polygonal stair towers and porch were added to an earlier house. Several of the houses recorded by Kip had staircase towers, and Bradley Court, like Siston, is one of the houses where they have survived. The house was only one room deep and it retains the layout of a hall house with screens passage; a Georgian block was erected on the parterre to the rear about 1800. Much of the survival of Bradley Court in its original state can be attributed to the fact that in the nineteenth century it was mostly leased, thus avoiding Victorian improvements other than a service wing which has since been demolished. The house is listed II*.

A painting of Bradley Court in 2017 by Jonathan Myles-Lea shows how close to Kip's engraving the house and garden still are. The painting also illustrates the amazingly long reach of the engravings, which after three hundred years are often still found to be relevant to a modern scene. The curtilage of Bradley Court gardens remains the same and the garden today is laid out on the framework of the seventeenth-century footprint. With the field to the right, Bradley Court totals around 9 acres.

The most noticeable difference from Kip's engraving is the south wall in the main entrance forecourt: straight in the Kip engraving with one central gateway, now bowed out with a gate to either side, as seen in Myles-Lea's painting. This change had taken place before 1895, when Elizabeth Hodges published a drawing of the house in *Some ancient English homes* (*qv*).

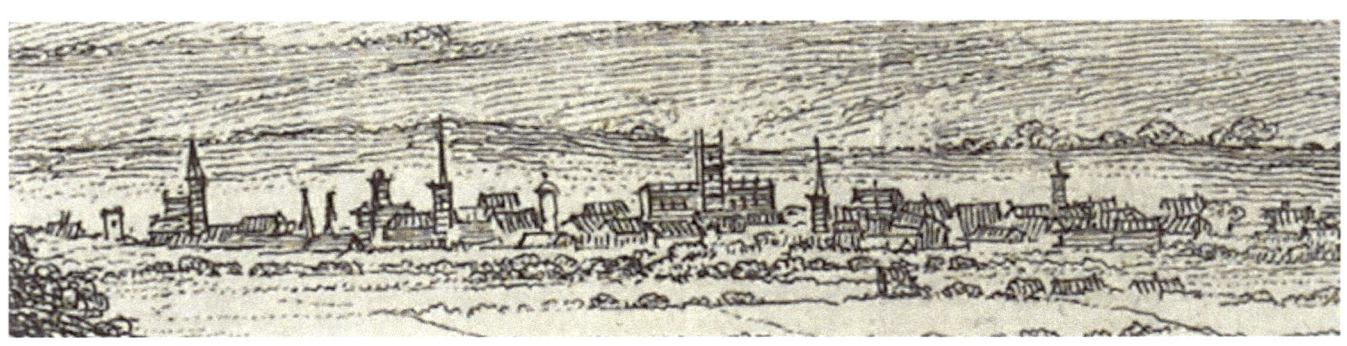

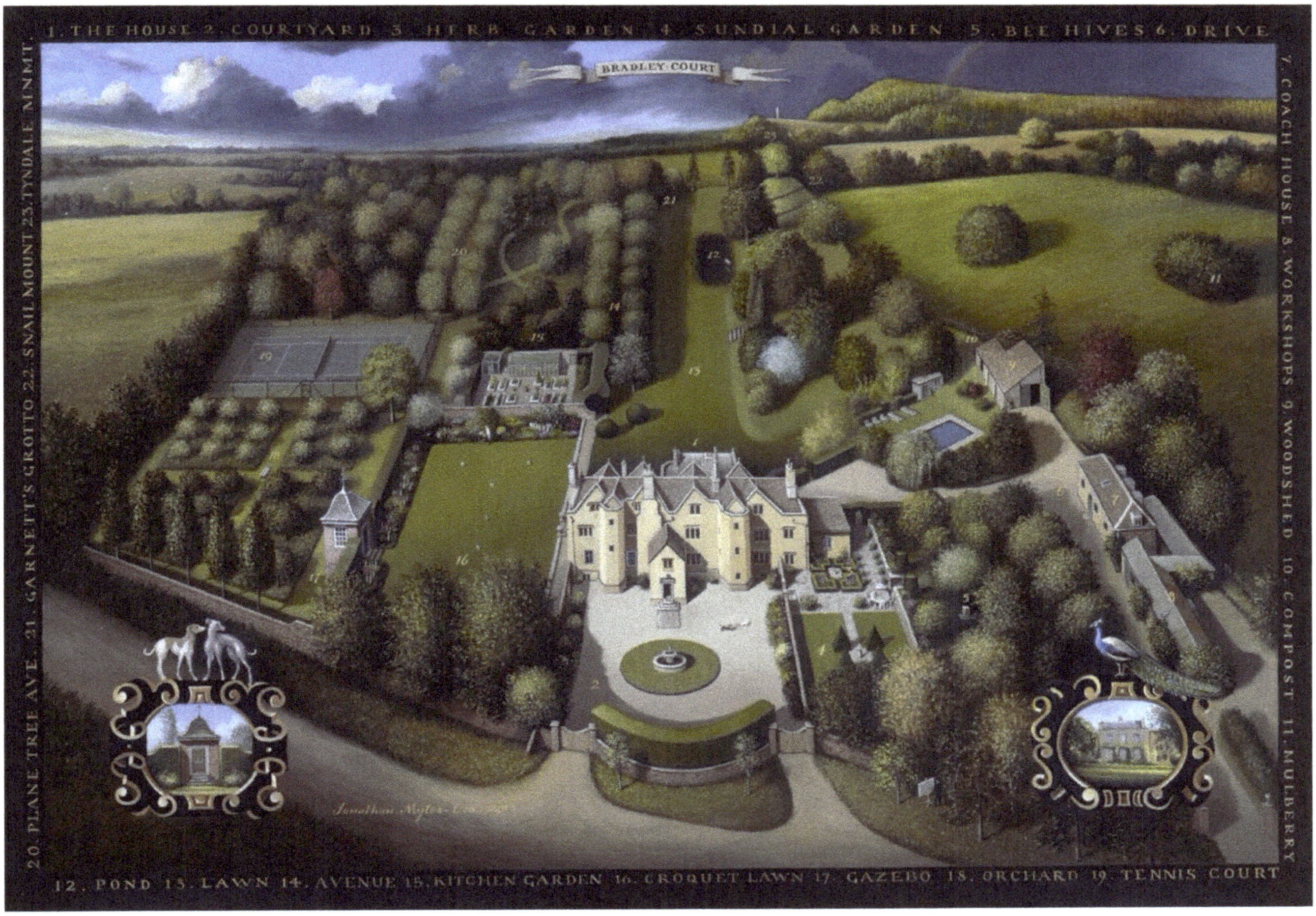

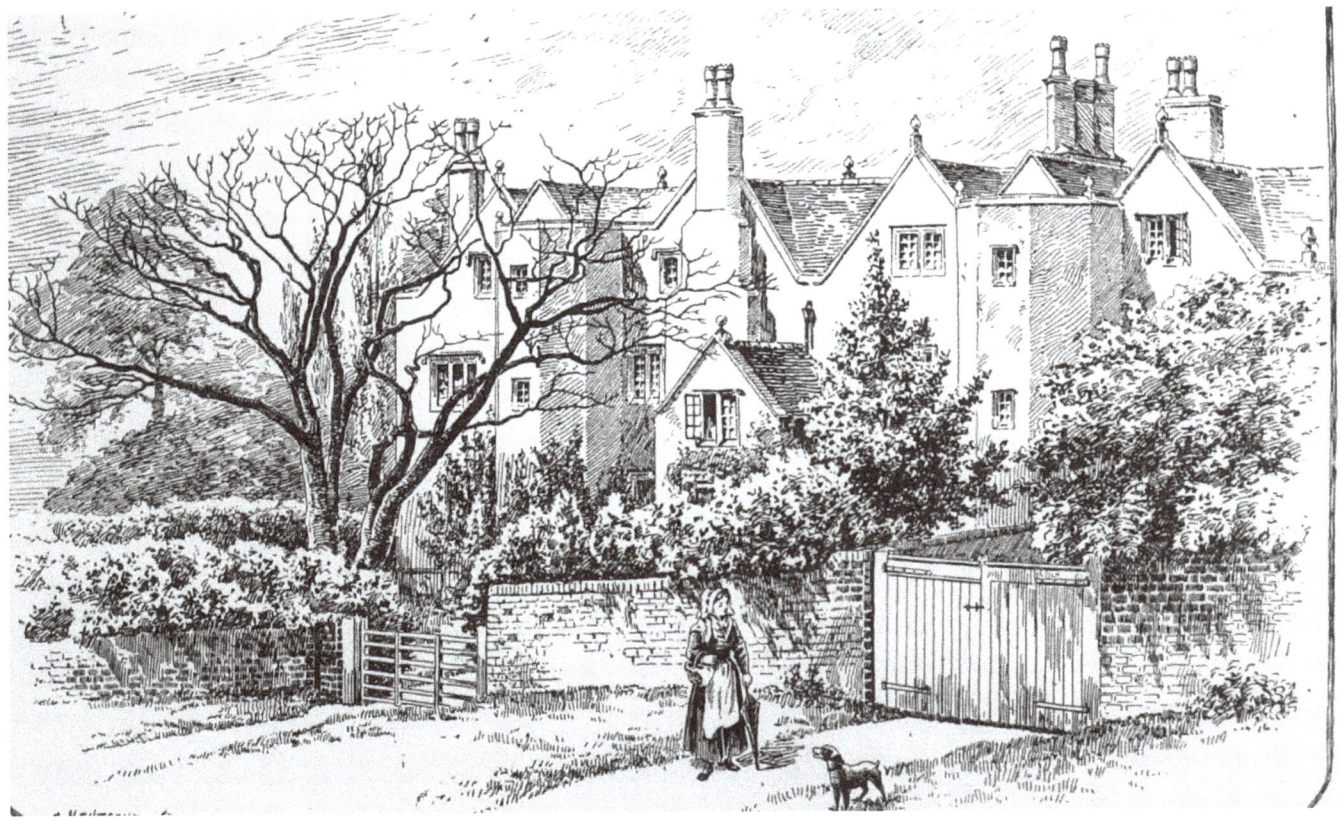

64 Bradley the Seat of Thomas Dawes Esq [Atkyns: Wotton-Underedge, 854-855]

Mr Dawes is the present Owner of the Mannor of Bradley, where he has a large ancient Seat, and a great Estate adjoyning to it

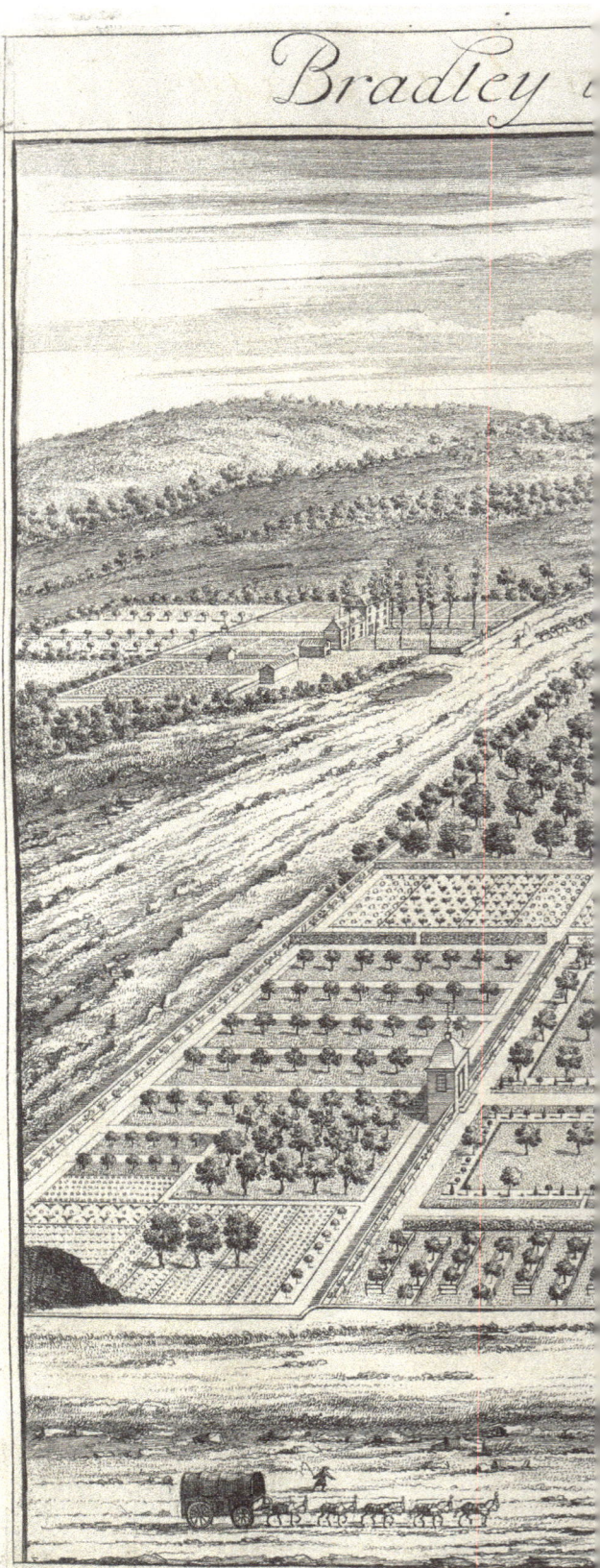

Bradley lies just outside, and west of the ancient wool town of Wotton-under-Edge on the lower slopes of the Cotswold escarpment. To the north is the wooded hill of Nibley Knoll on which the Tyndale monument now stands; it also appears in Kip's engraving of North Nibley. To the north-west a team of horses with a loaded wagon is passing the seventeenth-century Canons Court, a listed building now divided into two (*qv*).

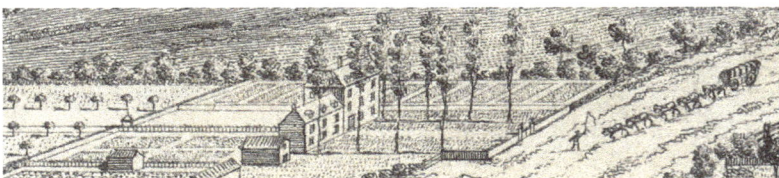

Bradley Court faces north. A large building to the right of the engraving may have been servants' quarter or the home farm, with a kitchen garden behind and wood piles to the north, but has gone. Kip drew what appears to be a pump near the front door (*qv*), evidence of which is a covered-up well in the same location. The ground at the front does fall away though with a less rugged bank and eroded ditch than Kip drew.

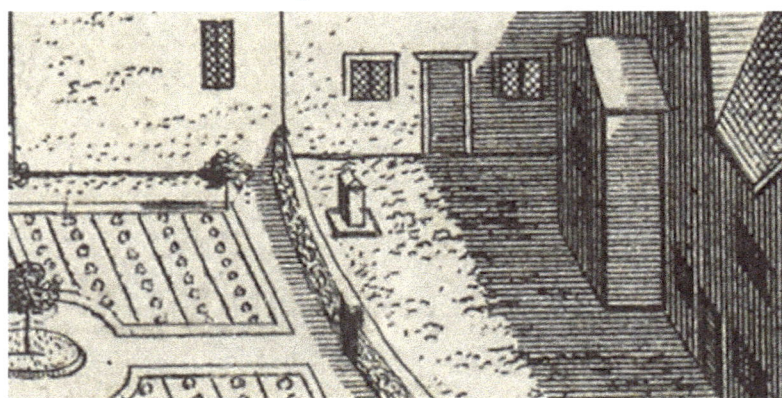

The engraving seems to exaggerate the overall scale of Bradley Court, but small details give a clue to its accuracy. The gazebo's style and position are accurately drawn by Kip. It appears to be one storey from the front, but at the rear has a lower storey due to the site sloping upwards from west to east (*qv*). The formal gardens are terraced with brick walls which may be much earlier.

An ancient yew hedge survives, and a small pond to the right of the avenue; the avenue has recently been replanted. Later additions include the grotto built by Andy Garnett in the 1970 and the snail mount, an addition by the Messels who lived here between 1982 -2014 and were responsible for restoring much of the garden to its present form. These features represent the development but not destruction of this historic garden.

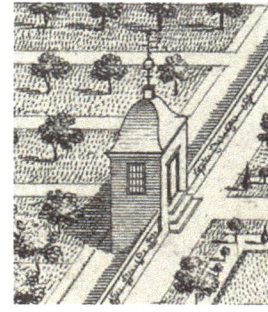

Postcode: Wotton-under-Edge GL12 7PP. NGR: ST 74564 93724.

which he gain'd by his own Industry, and left off his Employment because he knew he had enough.

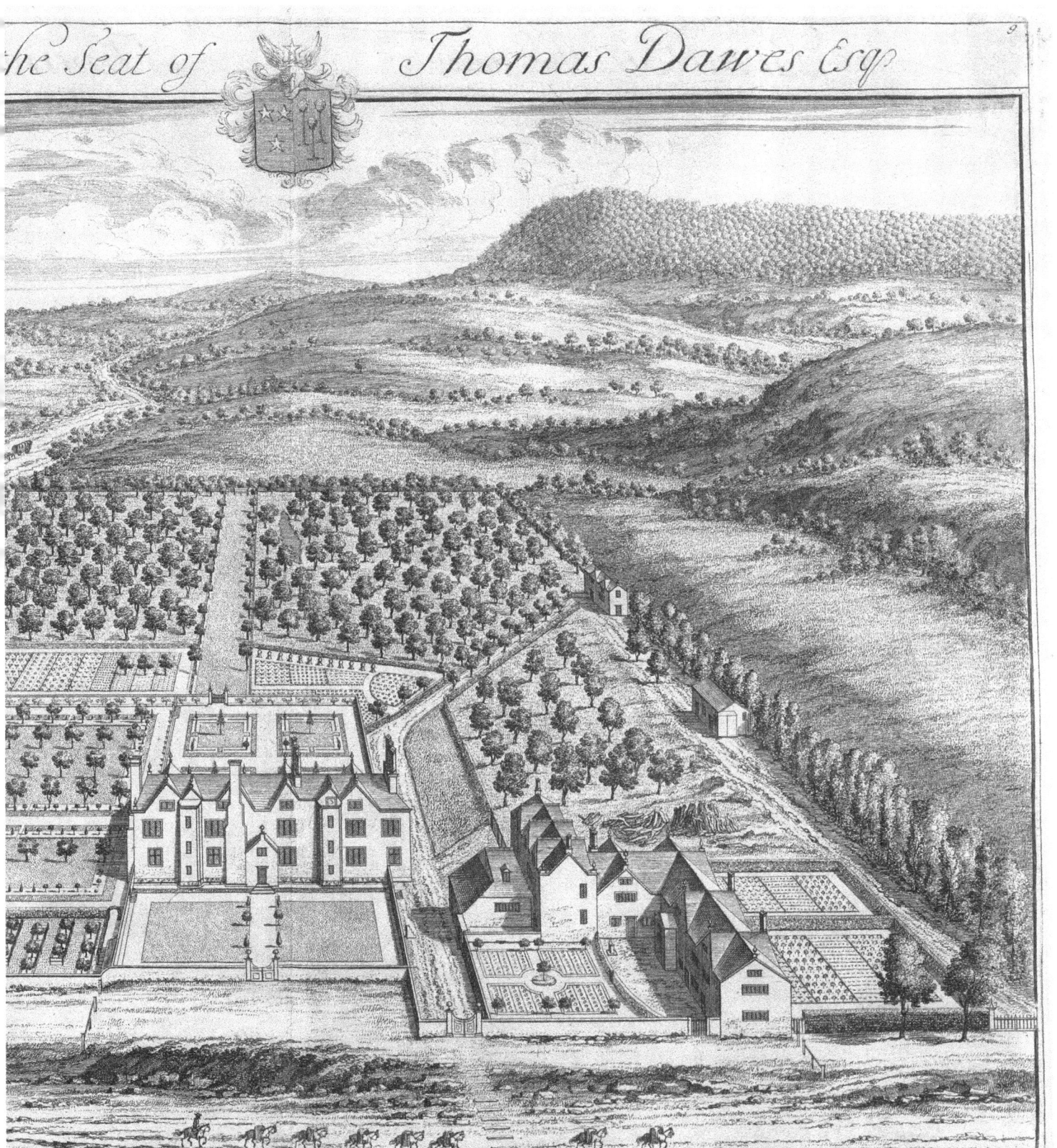

65 Seavenhampton the Seat of Sr Wm Dodwell [Atkyns: 'Seven Hampton, which was

NGR: SP 03310 22518. **VCH IX** 166-187.

Brockhampton is a considerable hamlet in this parish, containing 18 houses … It now belongs to Sir William Dodwell, who ha

As Atkyns engagingly pointed out, Sevenhampton parish, and Kip's engraving, are at the end of the book. This house is now called Brockhampton Park. It is not an ancient manor house. It was built on a field called Ford Hey, bought in 1639 by Paul Pert or Peart, Comptroller of the King's Counting House. Pert's neice, married to Ralph Dodwell of Sandywell Park, inherited the house; their son was the owner in 1712.

Kip's view is looking east, with a suggestion of a cliff face on the hills, where there have been extensive quarries. The main entrance was on the south side, but was re-sited when the road as far as the river Coln was moved further from the house and the garden extended. Beyond the river the road was not altered, and there are houses on the north side where Kip indicated.

By 1712 a formal garden had been laid out, and the Coln canalised; much later a lake was created. The simple bridge drawn by Kip was replaced with a more decorative wooden structure, and the northern avenue through a small park has recently been replanted (*qv*). The garden walls on the north side have been raised, while low walls

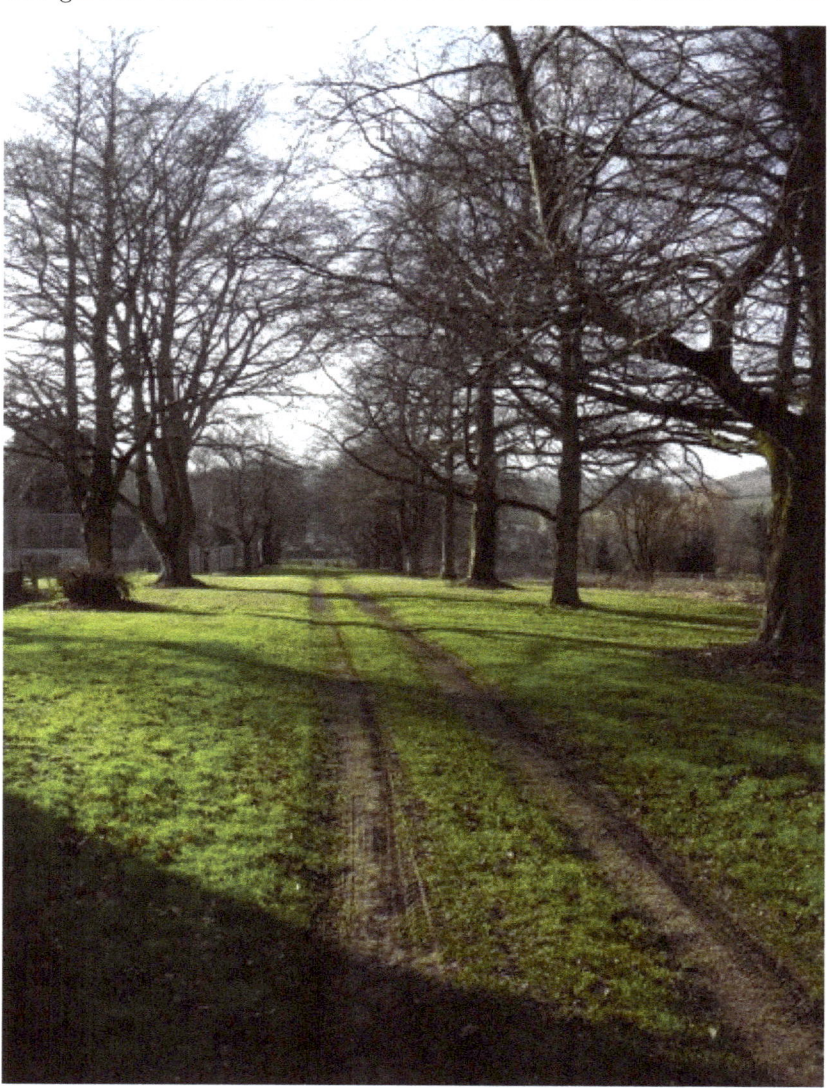

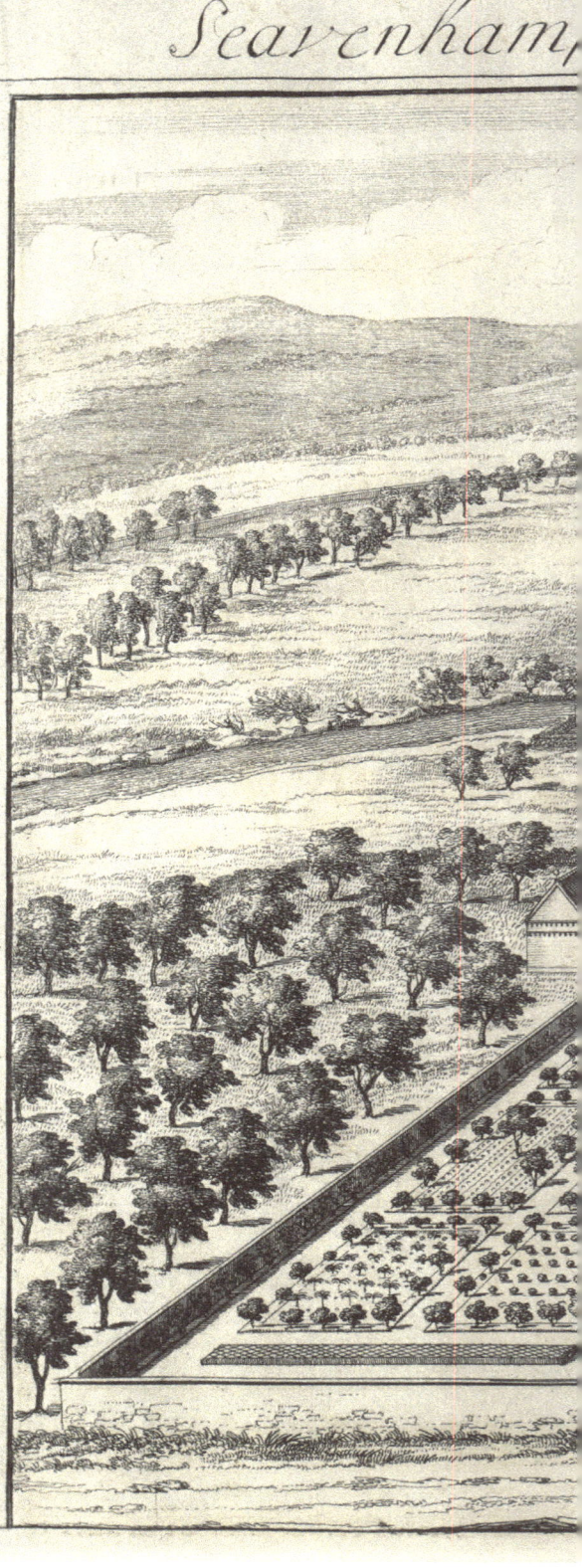

casually omitted in its due order', 858-859] **Postcode: Cheltenham GL54 5SP.**

a large house and a great estate in this and other places.

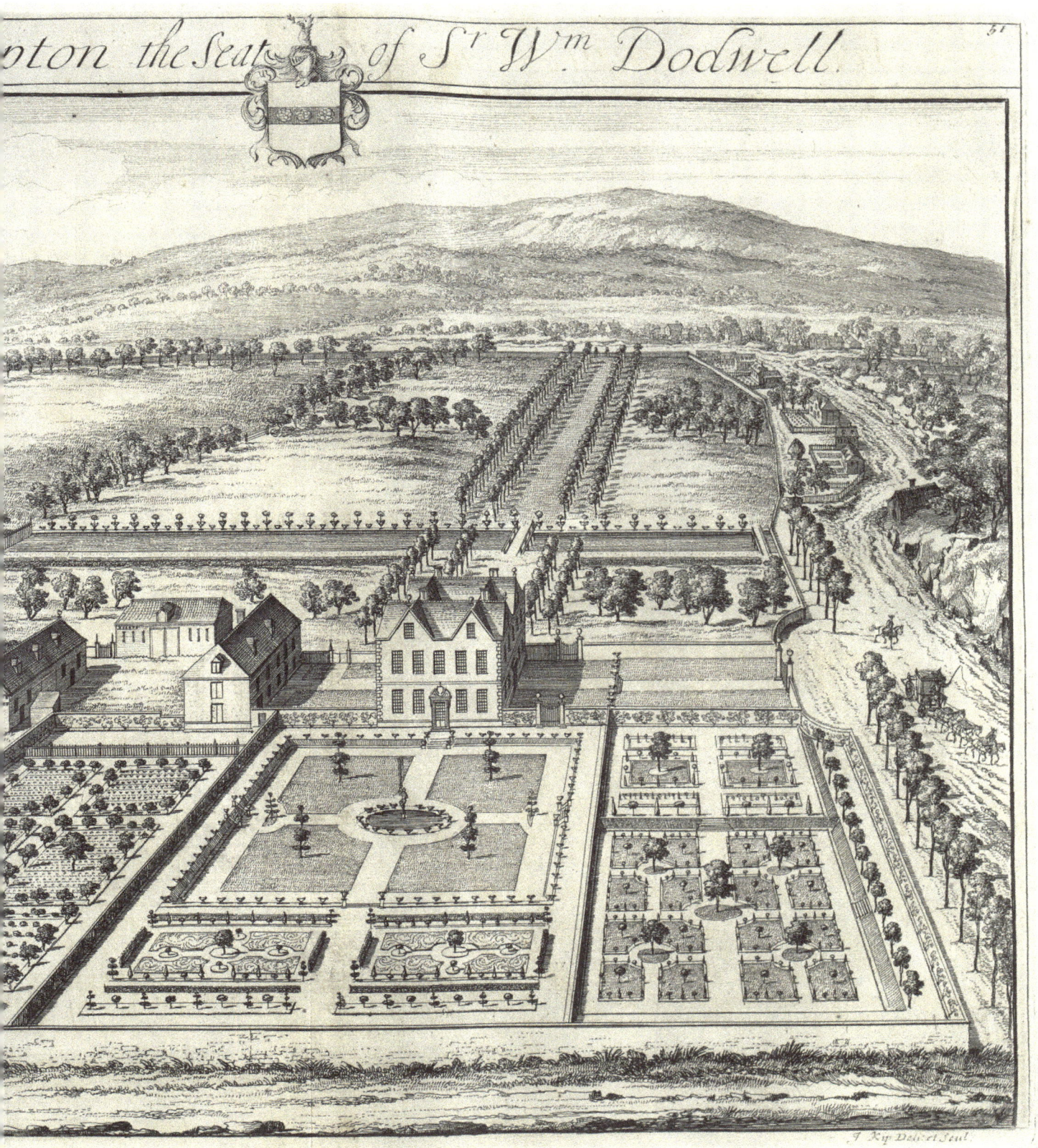

round the central garden remain, although without the fountain and dividing paths (*qv*); this garden is on rising ground, but Kip's steps appear to lead downwards. Brockhampton Court was later doubled in size, and further enlarged in the nineteenth century; the barn, small house and stables to the north have been rebuilt on the same footprint. On the far side of the road to Winchcombe a park stocked with white deer was started a decade or so after Kip's visit; the deer survived into the twentieth century.

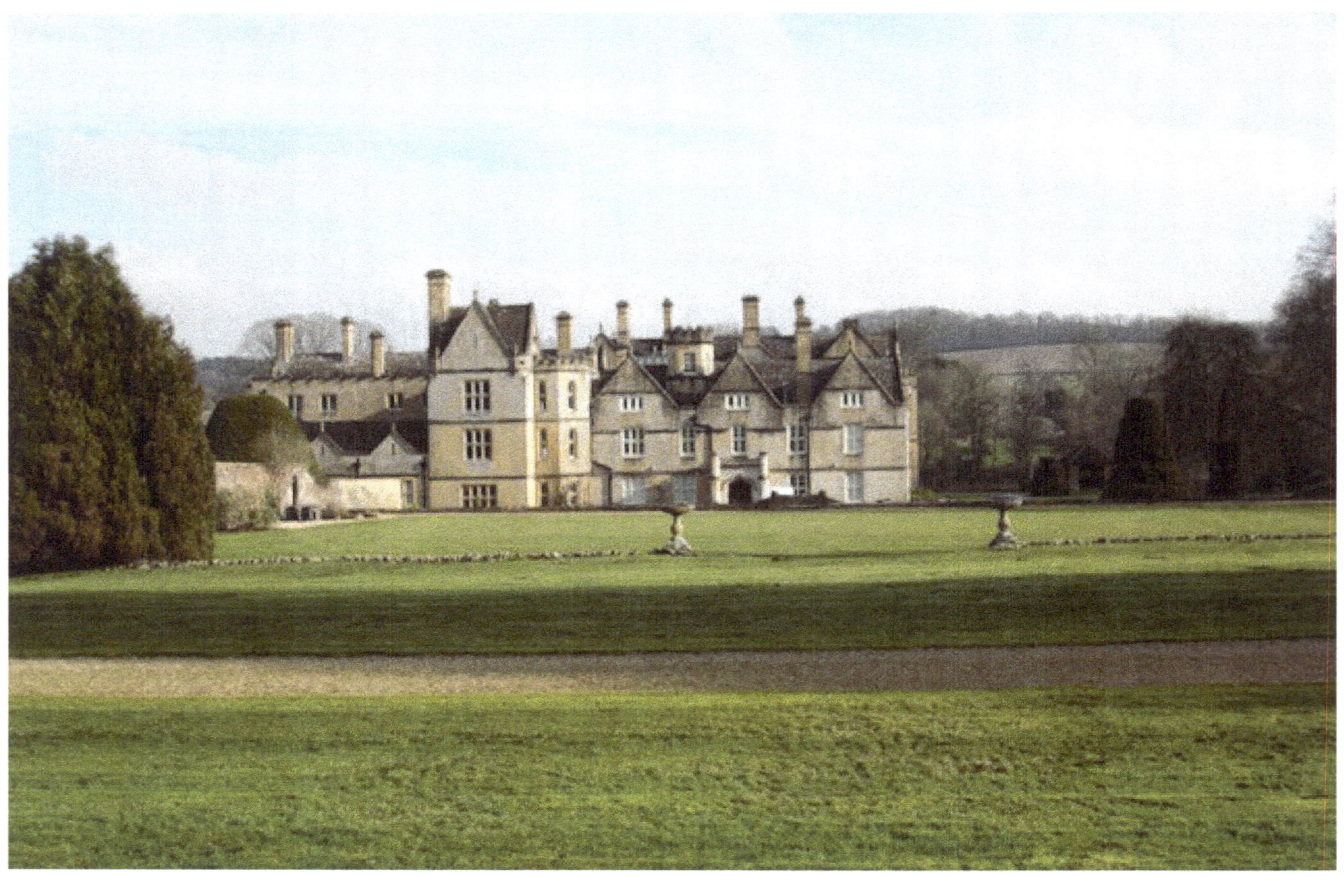

SELECT BIBLIOGRAPHY

The following is a select list of sources, published or available online, of relevance to entries in the gazetteer. (BGAS Bristol & Gloucestershire Archaeological Society)

Sir Robert Atkyns, *The Ancient and Present State of Glostershire* (1712); the reprint (EP Publishing Ltd 1974), with the Introduction by Brian Smith

Ralph Bigland, *Historical, Monumental and Genealogical Collections relative to the county of Gloucester* (reprinted by BGAS, 4 vols, ed. Brian Frith 1989-1995)

(Buildings of England) David Verey & Alan Brooks, *Gloucestershire 1: The Cotswolds* (Yale University Press 2002); *Gloucestershire 2: The Vale and the Forest of Dean* (Yale University Press 2002)

(Buildings of England) Andrew Foyle & Nikolaus Pevsner, *Somerset: North and Bristol* (Yale University Press 2011)

Richard Coates, 'Henbury Awdelett' Notes & Queries, *Transactions BGAS* 133 (2015), 233-35

A W Crawley-Boevey, *The Cartulary and Historical Notes of the Cistercian Abbey of Flaxley oterwise called Dene Abbey in the County of Gloucester* (Exeter 1887)

A W Crawley-Boevey, 'Some recent discoveries at Flaxley Abbey, Glos., and their relation to Mr Middleton's plan made in 1881', *Transactions BGAS* 43 (1921), 57-62

Celia Fiennes, *The Illustrated Joourneys* ed Christopher Morris (1982)

Rupert Goulding, *Dyrham Park and William Blathwayt* (National Trust nd)

Irvine Gray, 'The making of Westbury Court gardens' (Garden History Society Occasional Paper 1, 1969)

Rob Jarman, Frank M Chambers & Julia Webb, 'Landscapes of sweet chestnut (*Castanea sativa*) in Britain – their ancient origins', *Landscape History* 40 (2019) Issue 2

Huw M Jones, *The Illustrations for Garter Bigland's Historical Collections of Gloucestershire* (The Shermershill Press, 2011)

Anthea Jones, 'Johannes Kip (1652-1721) and the Gloucestershire engravings', *The Local Historian* (October 2020), 307-17

R Howes, 'John Smyth the Elder' *Transactions BGAS* 121 (2003), 213-231

Nicholas Kingsley, 'Kip's' Conundrum', *Country Life* (November 15, 1990)

Nicholas Kingsley, *Country Houses of Gloucestershire* vol 1 (1989); vol 2 (Phillimore, 1992); vol 3 with Michael Hill (Phillimore, 2001)

Philip Moss, *Historic Gloucester* (The History Press, reprint 2009)

Timothy Mowl, *Historical Gardens of Gloucestershire* (Tempus Publishing Ltd, 2002)

Nouveau theatre de la Grande Bretagne ou description exacte des palais du roy, et des maisons les plus considerables des seigneurs et des gentilshommes du dit royaume, (Joseph Smith, 1724)

Nicholas Orme & John Cannon, *Westbury-on-Trym: monastery, minster and college* (Bristol Record Society 62, 2010)

Samuel Rudder, *A new history of Gloucestershire* (Cirencester, 1779 reprinted Alan Sutton 1977)

Iona Sinclair ed, *The Pyramid and the Urn The life in letters of a Restoration Squire: William Laawrence of Shurdington 1636-1697* (Alan Sutton 1994)

James Sturmer, *Dyrham Guidebook* (National Trust 1981 printed with corrections 1985)

Victoria History of the County of Gloucester (11 volumes to date) and see websites below

L J U Way, 'The owners of the Great House, Henbury, Gloucestershire', *Transactions BGAS* 33 (1910), 304-37

Theses based on Knyff and Kip's work which discuss some Gloucestershire examples:

Tamsin Victoria Alice Chambers, 'The Arboriculture of West Country Parks and Gardens, 1660-1730' , PhD dissertation University of Bristol (2008)

Hilary A F McKee, 'The bird's-eye views of L Knyff and J Kip, as published in *Britannia Illustrata,* and their use for understanding historic landscapes', PhD dissertation Oxford Brookes University (2004)

Deborah A Wiles, 'For Pleasure and Use: Gardens of the late seventeenth and early eighteenth Centuries as described by Celia Fiennes and drawn by Leonard Knyff and Johannes Kip', MA Garden History, University of Greenwich (2012)

Websites

Bristol & Avon Family History Society https://bafhs.org.uk

Bristol & Gloucestershire Archaeological Society https://www.bgas.org.uk

Historic England https://historicengland.org.uk

Know your place http://www.kypwest.org.uk especially Gloucestershire tithe maps

National Library of Scotland https://maps.nls.uk

Oxford Dictionary of National Biography https://www.oxforddnb.com

Parks&Gardens https://www.parksandgardens.org

VCH Gloucestershire Academy https://www.vchglosacademy.org/vol16.html (Cirencester)

VCH https://www.history.ac.uk/research/victoria-county-history/county-histories-progress/gloucestershire/vch-gloucestershire-publications

ACKNOWLEDGEMENTS

IT HAS BEEN FUN working on the gazetteer of Kip's Gloucestershire engravings, especially because of the co-operative effort by volunteers who have helped with the variety and quantity of information. It is a pleasure to acknowledge the contributions of Michael Beacham, Mary Blumer, Jane Bradney, Gay Chamberlayne, Roger Davies, the Earl of Wemyss and March, Helene Gammack, Jean Gibbons, Piers Horry, Eric Jones, John Loosley, Deborah McCarthy, Philip Moss, Joshua Nash, Sophie Piebenga, Sir George White and Peter Yardley. They have my sincere thanks for their unstinting effort. The editor, as always, has responsibility for errors and misjudgements.

The Kip project originated with Gay Chamberlayne demonstrating the remarkable congruence of a site today with the Kip engraving. She has subsequently supported the project in many ways and with generosity. The Gloucestershire Gardens and Landscape Trust has given valuable support in several ways. I also thank Ros Delany and Avon Gardens Trust for help. Gloucestershire Archives have been important; I am grateful to Andrew Parry who scanned the Kip prints, and to the archivists giving their customary pleasant help despite coping with the covid-19 pandemic. Nicholas Kingsley's three volumes on the *Country Houses of Gloucestershire* have been an important source, and I thank him for his helpful comments and for his Foreword.

One of the pleasures of the project has been travelling to the different sites and exploring the countryside. Owners of 'Kip houses' have been interested and hospitable. My sincere thanks to Christopher Trim, James Whatmore, Wotton House International School, Hatherop Castle School, Ellenborough Park Hotel and Spa, Rendcomb College and Greenway Hotel and Spa.

I am grateful to the people and organisations that have allowed me to use their photographs: Berkeley Castle, Gay Chamberlayne, Roger Davies, Eric Jones, Kings Weston Action Group, Nicholas Kingsley, Jonathan Myles-Lea, Joshua Nash, The National Trust, Christopher Trim, Sir George White, Earl Wemyss, Peter Yardley.

The help of John Chandler of Hobnob Press is gratefully acknowledged. He has offered constructive comments at each stage of the work, and has prepared the maps of Gloucestershire and of Gloucester. This book has asked of the publisher some complicated setting of text and illustrations.

Prepared during the year of covid-19 lockdowns, research on Kip sites has been restricted. But it would be good to think that in the future *Johannes Kip: the Gloucestershire Engravings* will stimulate and encourage readers to explore further, with a Kip engraving in their hands.

Anthea Jones
March 2021

PICTURE CREDITS

The numbers and names in the following list are of the engravings and relevant illustrations are briefly indicated.

Note. GA Gloucestershire Archives; GDR Gloucester Diocesan Records.
Unattributed photographs are the editor's, with owners' permissions gratefully acknowledged.

5   Wick *garden* (James Whatmore)
6   Alderley *map* GDR/T1/3
7   Knole *sale particulars map and picture* George White
8   Over *map* GA D3806/3/10
9   Alveston *map* GA PC 1353; *aerial view* Christopher Trim; *St Helen's church* George White
11   Shurdington *garden* (The Manager, Greenway Hotel and Spa)
13   Barrington, Great *Bigland* GA SR45/49314GS
15   Berkeley *extracts from Account books* GBB_113_118, 134, 140, 146; *Custodian's flat roof* Joshua Nash; *The Chantry*
       Peter Yardley; *aerial view* © Berkeley Castle, courtesy of Eco Mirage
17   Cirencester Abbey *Bigland* GA SR45/49314GS
19   Southam *house* (Reception Manager, Ellenborough Park Hotel)
27   Dyrham *map* GA D2659/16; *east front* 1560623 - ©National Trust Images/James Dobson; *west front* 1390757 -
       ©National Trust Images/John Millar; *accounts* GA D1799/A26
28   Eastington *Bigland* GA SR45/49314GS
29   Wotton *garden* (The Principal, Wotton House International School Gloucester)
30   Fairford *map* GA D674b/P53; *High Street* Eric Jones
32   Minchinhampton *Bigland* GA SR45/49314GS
33   Hardwick Park Court *map* GA D303/P1
34   Hatherop *yew walk* (The Registrar, Hatherop Castle School)
38   Kingsweston *Penpole compass dial* KWAG (David Martin, Kings Weston Action Group)
45   North Nibley *map* GDR/T1/130
46   Rendcomb *avenue* (The Bursar, Rendcomb College)
48   Sherborne *west front* Nicholas Kingsley 1982; *map* GA. D678/1/E4/1A (maps drawn between 1820 and 1862);
       Sherborne brook Roger Davies
50   Shipton Moyne [Estcourt] *map* GA D1571/E1
51   Siston *drawing* Georgina Chester-Master, *Some Gloucestershire Houses* (n.d. [c.1916]) GA B505/28019GS*
52   Stanway *south front & Stokes' house* Earl of Wemyss & March
53   Stoke Gifford *house* Creative Commons Licence
59   Tortworth *map* GA D340a/P3
60   Westbury Court *Long Canal* https://thegardenvisitor.co.uk/contact; *maps* GA D2123/1 & D177 VI/4
62   Sneed *house & grounds* George White
63   Witcombe Park *map* GA D1866/P1
64   Bradley Court *painting* Jonathan Myles-Lea http://www.myles-lea.com; *drawing* by S J Loxton, E. Hodges, *Some
       Ancient English Homes* (1895) GA GAL/E4/8970GS
65   Sevenhampton *avenue* (Gay Chamberlayne)

INDEX

Abbotswood 142
Abingdon abbey 98
Abington, Anthony 70
Abson & Wick [Wick & Abson] 28
Akeman Street 62
Alderley, Alderly (**6**), 15, 16, 30-31, 52
Almondsbury 32-36, 100 *and see* Knole, Over
Alveston (**9**), 16, 37-39
    St Helen's church 16, 37
Ampney Crucis (**10**) 40-41
Amsterdam 9, 10
Ancient and Present State of Glostershire, The 9, 11, 13, 14, 120
    order of prints 9
Andoversford 72
arbour *see* pavilions
Ashton-under-Hill 74
Astrey, Sir Samuel 96
Atkyns, Anne 132
    Sir Robert [Snr] 14, 15, 120-21, 142-43
    Sir Robert [Jnr] 13-14, 15, 16, 120, 132, 142-43
    arrangements with owners 14, 15, 51, 79, 125
    death 9, 15
    monument 120
    relationshhip with Kip 13, 14, 15 *and see The Ancient and Present State of Glostershire*
Aust 98
avenues 12, 15, 28, 36, 40, 44, 57, 66, 72, 74, 92, 96, 100-1, 108, 110, 114, 118, 120, 126, 130, 136, 150, 152, 158, 160, 162, 164
Avon (Bristol) river 15, 32, 96, 100, 101, 153, 154, 156
Awdelett, Audelett 96, 98
    John 98

Badeslade, Thomas 12, 13, 14
Badgeworth 42-43
Badminton [Great] 8, 9, 11 (**no 12**), 12, 13, 14, 15, 16, 25, 44, 144
banqueting house 101, 136 *and see* pavilions
Barker, Samuel 15, 84-85
barns, granary 34, 44, 46, 52, 57, 66, 68, 70, 88, 116, 126, 130, 132, 134, 140, 148, 160, 166
Barnsley, Ernest 120
Barrington, Great (**13**), 14, 44-45
Bath 79
    abbey (St Peter's) 37

Bathurst, Allen (Baron) 16, 54-56
    Lord Allen Bathurst (Earl) 54
Batsford, Battsford (**14**), 15, 16, 46-47
Baynham, Thomas, family 114, 150
Beaufort, Beauford, Duke Henry 68, 144-45
    Duchess of 13
    Somerset family 136
Berkeley (**15**), 9, 14, 15, 16, 48-51, 122
Berkeley family 32, 34, 160
    Charles Earl of Berkeley 48-51
    John 136-37
    Maurice de Berkeley 136
    Norborne 136
Bigland, Ralph 44, 46, 56, 58, 80, 88, 92
bird's-eye views 15
Birdlip 160
Bishop's Cleeve *see* Southam
Bisley 140
Blaise Hill, 'bury', Castle 16, 96, 100
Blanch, John 82
Blathwayt, Anne 76, 101
    William 15, 76-79
Blockley 46
Bonnor, Thomas 56
Bovey, Bouvey Mrs (Catharina) 86-87, 150
    William 86
Bowl, Boulde *see* Swell, Lower
bowling greens 16, 23, 44, 48, 64, 124, 130, 134, 140, 150
Boyd bridge 28
Bradley Court (**64**), 14, 160-63
Bray, Edmond 44-45
Bredon Hill 74
Bret, Henry 72-73
Brimpsfield 112
Bristol 14, 15, 22, 28, 32, 34, 54, 68, 77, 90, 96, 101, 130, 137, 153, 156
    abbey 32
Britannia Illustrata 10-11, 12, 13, 15
British Museum catalogue 10
Broadwell (**16**), 16, 52-53
Broadwell Hill 138
Brockhampton Park *see* Sevenhampton
Bromley Heath 110
Brown, Thomas (Alderman) 20-21, 22, 24
Buck, Samuel & Nathaniel 13
Buildings of England: Gloucestershire [Pevsner] 9, 82, 84
Burford 44, 124, 125
Burghers, Michael 13
Buscot Park (Oxon) 106

canals 16, 44, 50, 64, 74, 86, 90, 108, 148, 150-53, 164
Cann, Sir Robert 153
    Sir Thomas 153
Carlisle cathedral 13
Caroline, Princess of Wales 13
cascade 78, 79
Casey family 64
Castelman, Jonathan 66-67
    Paul 66
Chadwell, William 52
Chamberlayne, Chamberlain, Edmund 138-39
    John 138
    Dr Thomas 52
Chantry, The 51
Charles II 10
Chauncey, Sir Henry 13
Chavenage 80
Chedworth 64
Chelsey College 10
Chelt river 70
Cheltenham 14
Chepstow (**57**), 11, 15, 144-45
Chester-Master, Georgina 130
    R G 54
Chester, Thomas 32-33
    William 32
Chetwood, Knightley dean 12
chimneys 50, 51, 62, 70, 86, 134, 148 *and see* Hearth Tax
Chosen Hill 160
Church Commissioners 68
Churchdown 160
churches, chapel, churchyard 16, 30, 37, 40, 44, 50-51, 66, 68, 72, 74, 79, 80, 84, 86, 88, 92, 94, 98, 100, 101, 104-5, 106, 108, 112, 118, 120, 122-23, 125, 134, 140, 142, 146, 148, 152
Churn, river 57, 118
Cirencester 14, 16, 54-57, 100
    (Bathurst) (**17**), 54-57
    (Master) (**18**), 16, 17, 57-59
Clearwell, Clower-Wall (**44**), 16, 114-15
Cleeve Cloud, Hill 16, 60, 108
Cleve, Cleeve Hill (House) (**42**), 15, 16, 110-11
    Cleve Hill Farm 110
Clower-Wall *see* Clearwell
Coberley (**22**) 66-67, 146
Cocks, Sir Richard 74-75
Codrington, Robert 68-69
    Simon 68
Colchester, Richard 150

Maynard 150-53
Cold Aston 78
Coleshill (Oxon) 84
collieries 110
Coln St Aldwyns 92
Coln, river 70, 72, 84, 164
Comb End (Elkstone) 82
Compton Abdale 64
Conway, Lord [Francis Seymour-Conway] 72
Cooke, William 14
Cooper's Hill 160
Cotswolds, the 15, 51, 60, 106, 146, 162
Coxe, Charles 14
Crippets, the 42
Cromwell, Oliver 14

Daily Courant 13
Daily Journal 9
dating of Gloucestershire prints 12, 14-15, 16
Dawes, Thomas 160
de la Bere, Kinard 60-61
    Richard 60
Dean, Forest 37, 51, 86, 114
deer 16, 34, 36, 40, 44, 51, 64, 70, 72, 78, 84, 90, 112, 114, 118, 122, 128, 130, 138, 140, 146, 148, 153, 160, 166
Denys family 130
Didmarton (**23**), 68-69
Dikler, river 142
Dissolution, Reformation 16, 23, 32, 44, 52, 54, 57, 86, 94, 98, 100, 122, 132, 153, 160
Dodwell, Ralph 164
    Sir William 164-65
dovecotes 44, 46, 52, 64, 80, 88, 125, 140, 142, 152
Dowdeswell 15, 70, 100
    Upper Dowdeswell (**24**), 15, 70-71, 72 *and see* Sandywell
Dowell, John 34-36
Ducie, Sir Robert 148 *and see* Morton, Matthew
Dumbleton (**26**), 14, 74-75
Dumbleton Hill 74, 146
Dutch *see* The Netherlands
Dutton, John 122
    Sir Ralph 14, 15, 122-25
    Thomas 122
Dyrham (**27**), 14, 15, 76-79, 101, 104

Eastington, Easington (**28**), 80-81
Elkstone (Comb End) 82
Ellenborough Hotel 60
Estcourt family 126, 128
    Walter 128-29
Evelyn, John 62, 76

Fairford (**30**), 15, 16, 84-85, 122
Farr, Thomas 96
fields, arable 68, 92, 106
Fiennes, Celia 94, 146
fish ponds 17, 36, 42, 50, 79, 112, 142, 156 *see also* pools, ponds
Flaxley (**31**), 16, 86-87, 150
Fosse Way 52, 142

fountains 74, 76, 79, 90, 166
Foxcote Hill 72
Freeman, Richard 15, 46-47
Freeman-Mitford, A B 46
Frome, brook, river, valley 80, 110, 112, 120
fruit gardens *see* orchards
Fust, Sir Edward 16, 104-5

gallows 25
Garnett, Andy 162
Gatcombe 88
gatehouses, gateways 48, 90, 128, 135, 140
gazebo *see* pavilions
George, William 56
Glevensis 74
Gloucester 90
    abbey 42
    cathedral 9, 11, 12 (**no 4**), 15, 25, 26, 28, 82
    City (**2**), 9, 14, 20-24
    North gate 82
    North Hamlets 82-83
    St Mary de Lode 82
    West Prospect (**3**), 25-27
Gloucestershire 8, 14, 15, 44, 153
Gloucestershire Way 66
Great House (Henbury) 96, 101
Great House (North Nibley) 116
Greenway, The 42
Guise, Sir Christopher 118
    Sir John 118-19
Gumstool brook 58

Hailes, Hales (**35**), 16, 94-95
Haines, Richard 28-29
Hale, Matthew 15, 30-31
    Mrs 30-31
    Sir Matthew Lord Chief Justice 30
Hampton *see* Minchinhampton
Hannington Hill 72
Harcourt, Simon 96-7, 101
Hardwick Park (**33**), 14, 90-91, 128
Haresfield Beacon 90
Harford, J S 96
Harris, John 12-13, 14
Hatherop, Castle (**34**), 14, 16, 62, 92-93
Hauduroy, Samuel 76
Haughton 16
Hazel brook 96, 100
Headda, abbot 70, 72
Hearth Tax 52, 66, 70, 72, 80
Henbury 16, 98-103
    (Sampson) (**36**), 98-102
    (Southwell) (**37**), 102-3 *and see* Kingsweston
Hicks, Sir Michael, Michaell 15, 158-60
Highnam 14, 15
Hill *alias* Hull (**39**), 16, 104-5
Hill, Edward 37-39
Hoare, Sir Richard Colt, *Tour of North Wales* 146
Hodges family 128
    Anthony 52
    Danvers 52-53
    Mrs, Edith 15, 126-27
    John 126

Thomas 15,126-27
Hodges, Elizabeth, *Some ancient English homes* 160-61
Hodges' Barn 126
Hooke, Humphrey 101
Horton, Mary 82
    Thomas 15, 82-83
Horton road 82
houses, demolished 34
houses, survival 16
housing development, modern 15, 16, 34, 36, 54, 110, 153, 156
Howe, John Grobham 14
    Sir Richard 64-65
Hull *alias* Hill *see* Hill
Hurnall, Thomas 76

Ireton, Henry 14, 15, 16, 62-63

Jackson, Joseph snr 156
    Joseph jnr 156-57
Jacob, Christopher surveyor 76, 78
James II & Queen Mary 10

Katherine Lady Berkeley's school 116
Kempsford (**40**) 106-7
Kent, William arbour 110
Kings Weston, Kingsweston (**38**), 15, 76, 96, 100
    Hill 101
Kingroad 156
Kingsley, Nicholas 14, 15
Kip, Johannes draughtsman & engraver 10, 12, 13
    early life 9
    death 9, 13
    influence 76, 104, 132, 135, 153, 162
    reputation 13
    style 10, 15, 16
    ways of indicating terrain 16
    work with John Harris 12-13
    work with Leonard Knyff 10
    and see dating of Gloucestershire prints; Atkyns, Sir Robert, relationship with Kip
kitchen gardens 16, 48, 60, 66, 90, 92, 104, 124, 132, 136, 142, 148, 162
Knole [Park] (**7**), 32-34 *and see* Almondsbury
Knyff, Jacob 10, 13
    Leendert, Leonard 9, 10,13, 14, 16

Lady Maud's Walk 106
lakes 57, 66, 112, 124, 164
Lawrence, Laurence, Dulcibella 42-43
    William 42-43
Leckhampton (**41**), 14, 16, 108-9
Leckhampton Hill 108
Little Compton (**21**) 64-65
Llanthony priory 44
Lodge Park 122 *and see* Sherborne
London, George 62
London Mercury 10
Longleat 106
Lypiatt, Lupiatt (**55**), 14, 16, 140-41
    Lower 14

Lysons, Samuel 94

Malvern hills 51
Mangotsfield
mariner's compass 100, 101
Marshfield 78
Master, Richard 57
    Thomas 57-59
Maugersbury (**54**), 138-39
May Hill 51
melon garden 128
merchants 15, 32, 34, 96, 98, 101, 144,
    153
mills (water & wind) 28, 40, 44, 56, 80,
    86, 92, 96, 101, 118, 144, 146,
    153
Minchinhampton, Hampton (**32**), 16,
    88-89
    Market Hall 88
Miserden (**43**), 14, 16, 112-13
Mitford, John, Lord Redesdale, 46
moats 16, 50, 80, 90, 148
monasteries *see* Dissolution
Monmouthshire 11, 142
Morden, Robert map 8, 9
Morse, George 96
Mortier, David publisher 10, 12
Morton, Matthew Ducy, Ducie 148-49
Myles-Lea, Jonathan 160-61

National Trust 76-79, 101, 125, 150-53
Netherlands, The, Dutch influence 9,
    10, 13, 16, 31, 76, 86, 106, 150,
    153
Netherton 92
Newcastle, Duke of 16
Newland 114
Nibley [North] (**45**), 116-17
Nibley Knoll 116, 162
Norden, John *Surveyor's Dialogue* 15
North, Marianne 30
Northleach 125
Norwood, Revd Thomas 16, 108-9
Nouveau Theatre 11, 12, 13, 25, 144

Oddington Hill 138
Ogilby, John maps 68
Old Church Farm *see* Alveston
Old Sneed Park, Friends of 156
Oldbury-on-the-Hill 68
orchards, fruit gardens 30, 37, 48, 56,
    62, 66, 82, 96, 101, 104, 130,
    134, 138, 142, 156
Ordnance Survey 15, 124, 134
Over (Gloucester) 25
Over [Court] (**7**), 34-36 *and see*
    Almondsbury
    Over Lane 36
owners 14, 16, 51, 79

parapet walk 132 *and see* viewing
    platform etc
park 14, 15, 16, 17 and *passim, and see*
    deer
Parsons, Dr Richard Diocesan chancellor
    92, 140
parterres 16, 44, 52, 86, 94, 101, 110,
    128, 134, 160

pavilions, summer houses, gazebos 46,
    66, 70, 72, 79, 101, 104, 106,
    108, 110, 116, 136, 152, 158,
    160, 162
Penpole headland, Lodge 100, 101
Pert, Peart, Paul 164
pillory 124
Pinbury Park 120
Player, William 110-11
Pleydell, John 40
    Robert 40-41
Plot, Robert 13
pools, ponds 14, 16, 66, 72, 74, 76, 79,
    98, 104, 124, 130, 134, 136, 152,
    160, 162 *see also* fish ponds, lakes
Pound 160
Povey, Thomas 76
Powell, Sir John 25-27
    Mrs Rebecca 56
Powle, Henry 14
print-making techniques 10, 16
Pucklechurch 28

Quenington 92

rabbits 79, 146, 148
Raglan Castle 144
rector, Rectory, vicar, Vicarage 9, 30, 68,
    74, 80, 101, 106, 108, 134
Reformation *see* Dissolution
Rembrandt 10
Rendcomb (**46**), 14, 16, 118-19
Repton, Humphry, Red Book 96
Rich, Edward 70
    Lionel 70-71
Rissingtons 44
roads 16, 60, 68, 90, 94, 124, 135, 140,
    153, 160
Robins, Thomas the elder, painter 94,
    101
Rudder, Samuel 125, 146, 156

Sadleir, Sir Ralph 100
St Helen's church (Alveston) 16, 37
St James's Palace chapel 10
St James's Park 13
St Mary de Lode 82
Sampson, Sansome, John 98-109
    Edward 96, 98
Sandys, William 16, 112-13
Sandywell (**25**), 15, 16, 72-73, 164 *and*
    see Dowdeswell
Sapperton, Saperton (**47**), 14, 15, 16,
    120-21
Sea Mills 153
Sevenhampton, Seavenhampton (**65**),
    164-66
Severn, river 15, 22, 25, 32, 37, 70, 100,
    101, 144, 152, 154
    Severn Vale 104
Sheppard, Shappard, Shepard, Edward
    88
    Phillip 88-89
Shepperdine 104
Sherborne (**48**), 14, 15, 122-25
    Sherborne brook 122, 124-25
Shipton Dovel 126
Shipton Moyne 100, 126-29

(Estcourt) (**50**), 16, 128-29
(Hodges) (**49**), 15, 16, 126-27
Shirehampton 101
Shortwood Hill 130
Shurdington (**11**), 42-43
Siston, Syston (**51**), 16, 101, 130-31, 160
Smallcombe Court 116
Smirke, Robert architect 90
Smith, Francis of Warwick 132
    Joseph publisher 11, 12, 25
Smyth, Edward 116
    George 116-17
    John 116
    Mary 116
Sneed Park (**62**), 14, 15, 16, 156-57 *and*
    see Westbury-on-Trym
Southam [Bishop's Cleeve] (**19**), 15-16,
    60-61
Southam Lane 60
Southwell, Edward 101-103
    Mary 76
    Sir Robert 101
Speed, John 20
staffage, in Kip prints 12
Staffordshire 148
Stanton 135
Stanway (**52**), 132-35
Stephens, Stevens, Edward 80
    Nathaniel 81-81
    Richard 80
    Thomas 140-41
Stoke Bishop (**61**), 153-55 *and see*
    Westbury-on-Trym
Stoke Gifford (**53**), 14, 15, 136-37
    Stoke Park 110, 136
Stokes's house 134
Stopendael, Bastiaen 10
Stow-on-the-Wold 138, 142 *and see*
    Maugersbury
Stow's *Survey of London* 13
Stowell 14, 15
Stratford, Ferdinando maps 36, 37
Strong, Valentine 122
Stroud 140
Strype, John 13
Sue Ryder Hospice 108
summer house *see* pavilions
surveying 15
Swell [Lower] (**56**), 14, 15, 132, 142-43
Swell, Upper 142
Switzer, Stephen, *Ichnographia Rustica* 79
Syston, Siston (**51**), 16, 101, 130-31, 160

Talman, William 78
Tar Barrows 57
Taylor, William painter 132
Taynton (Oxon) 44, 84, 122
Teulon, S S architect 148
Tewkesbury 14,
    Abbey 132, 134
The Ancient and Present State of Glostershire
    9, 11, 13, 14, 120
    order of prints 9
Thoresby, Ralph 13
Throckmorton, Sir Baynham 114
Thynne, Sir Thomas *see* Weymouth,
    Viscount
Tidenham, Tiddenham 144

Tockington 37
Toddington (**58**), 16, 68, 94, 146-47
Tortworth (**59**), 14, 16, 148-49
tower, lookout *see* viewing
Tracy, Tracey, Hon. Ferdinando 132
 John 132-35
 Lord William 94-95, 146-47
 Richard 132
 scallop shells 134
trees, significant 16, 28, 38, 42, 48, 52, 86, 92, 148
 Portuguese laurel 130
Trotman, Samuel, Samuell 130-31
Trye, John 90
 William 90-91
Tunbridge Wells 12
turnpike trusts 16
Tyndale, William, monument 116, 162

Upper Dorvel House 120
Upper Dowdeswell *see* Dowdeswell

Vanbrugh, Sir John 96
Veel, Nicholas 37

viewing platform or tower, lookout tower, watch tower 15, 17, 32, 37, 72, 101, 136, 153, 154, 156 *and see* parapet walk

Warburton, John 13
warren 76, 79, 114, 116, 146, 148
Warren's Court 116
Wathen, Paul 140
Webb, Sir John 92-93
Westbury brook 152
Westbury Court (**60**), 14, 150-53
Westbury-on-Severn 150-53
Westbury-on-Trym 28, 98, 100, 153-57
 and see Sneed, Stoke Bishop
Weymouth, Lord Viscount (Sir Thomas Thynne) 106
Whitcliffe Deer Park 51
White Way 60
Whittington Court 72
Wick, Wyck (**5**), 16, 28-29
Wilderness, The (nr Mitcheldean) 152
William of Orange, William & Mary, William III 10, 14, 76

Williamstrip (**20**), 14, 15, 62-63
Wiltshire 68
Winchcombe 60, 166
 Winchcombe abbey 122
Windrush river 44
Winstone 112
Witcombe Park (**63**), 15, 16, 158-60
Withington 64
Worcester, bishop of 98-9, 153
Worcestershire 46
Wotton Court 82
Wotton House (**29**), 15, 82-83
Wotton-under-Edge 160-63
Wyatt, Jeffrey 140
Wye, river 15, 144
Wyndham, Francis 114-15
Wynter, Sir Edward 28
 Sir George 78
 John 28
 Mary 76

York, Archbishop of 160
Yorke, Philip, earl of Hardwicke 90

www.ingramcontent.com/pod-product-compliance
Lightning Source LLC
Chambersburg PA
CBHW052137170526
45162CB00004B/45